Desegregating Comics

Desegregating Comics

•••••••••••••••••

Debating Blackness in the
Golden Age of American Comics

EDITED BY QIANA WHITTED

Rutgers University Press
New Brunswick, Camden, and Newark, New Jersey
London and Oxford, UK

Rutgers University Press is a department of Rutgers, The State University of New Jersey, one of the leading public research universities in the nation. By publishing worldwide, it furthers the University's mission of dedication to excellence in teaching, scholarship, research, and clinical care.

Library of Congress Cataloging-in-Publication Data
Names: Whitted, Qiana J., 1974– editor.
Title: Desegregating comics : debating blackness in the golden age of American comics / edited by Qiana Whitted.
Description: New Brunswick : Rutgers University Press, [2023] | Includes bibliographical references and index.
Identifiers: LCCN 2022037744 | ISBN 9781978825017 (paperback) | ISBN 9781978825024 (hardback) | ISBN 9781978825031 (epub) | ISBN 9781978825055 (pdf)
Subjects: LCSH: Comic books, strips, etc.—United States—History and criticism. | Comic books, strips, etc.—Social aspects—United States. | Race in comics. | African Americans in comics. | African Americans in popular culture. | African Americans—Race identity—History—20th century. | Racism and the arts—United States. | African American cartoonists—History—20th century.
Classification: LCC PN6725 .D47 2023 | DDC 741.5/352996073--dc23/eng/20230202
LC record available at https://lccn.loc.gov/2022037744

A British Cataloging-in-Publication record for this book is available from the British Library.

This collection copyright © 2023 by Rutgers, The State University of New Jersey
Individual chapters copyright © 2023 in the names of their authors
All rights reserved
No part of this book may be reproduced or utilized in any form or by any means, electronic or mechanical, or by any information storage and retrieval system, without written permission from the publisher. Please contact Rutgers University Press, 106 Somerset Street, New Brunswick, NJ 08901. The only exception to this prohibition is "fair use" as defined by U.S. copyright law.

References to internet websites (URLs) were accurate at the time of writing. Neither the author nor Rutgers University Press is responsible for URLs that may have expired or changed since the manuscript was prepared.

∞ The paper used in this publication meets the requirements of the American National Standard for Information Sciences—Permanence of Paper for Printed Library Materials, ANSI Z39.48-1992.

rutgersuniversitypress.org

For Kenny

Contents

Introduction: "An Apt Cartoon"   1
QIANA WHITTED

Part I   Iconographies of Race and Racism

1   Rose O'Neill and Visual Tropes of Blackness   23
IAN GORDON

2   The Passing Fancies of *Krazy Kat*   39
NICHOLAS SAMMOND

3   "How Else Could I Have Created a Black Boy in That Era?":
Racial Caricature and Will Eisner's Legacy   61
ANDREW J. KUNKA

Part II   Formal Innovation and Aesthetic Range

4   Desegregating Black Art Genealogies: An Invitation   79
REBECCA WANZO

5   Misdirections in Matt Baker's *Phantom Lady*   95
CHRIS GAVALER AND MONALESIA EARLE

6   The Art of Alvin Hollingsworth   121
BLAIR DAVIS

7 "Hello Public!": Jackie Ormes in the Print Culture of the
Pittsburgh Courier   141
ELI BOONIN-VAIL

Part III   Comics Readership and Respectability Politics

8 "Never Any Dirty Ones": Comics Readership among
African American Youth in the Mid-Twentieth Century   163
CAROL L. TILLEY

9 *All-Negro Comics* and Counterhistories of Race in the
Golden Age   181
QIANA WHITTED

10 "This Business of White and Black": Captain Marvel's
Steamboat, the Youthbuilders, and Fawcett's
Roy Campanella, Baseball Hero   207
BRIAN CREMINS

11 Al Hollingsworth's *Kandy*: Race, Colorism, and Romance
in African American Newspaper Comics   227
MORA J. BEAUCHAMP-BYRD

Part IV   Disrupting Genre, Character, and Convention

12 Diabolical Master of Black Magic: Examining Agency
through Villainy in "The Voodoo Man"   247
PHILLIP LAMARR CUNNINGHAM

13 Love in Color: Fawcett's Revolutionary *Negro Romance*   261
JACQUE NODELL

14 An Afrofuturist Legacy: Neil Knight and Black
Speculative Capital   281
JULIAN C. CHAMBLISS

15 "For They Were There!": Dell Comics' *Lobo* and the
Black Cowboy in American Comic Books   297
MIKE LEMON

Acknowledgments   319
Bibliography   321
Notes on Contributors   343
Index   349

Desegregating Comics

Introduction

● ● ● ● ● ● ● ● ● ● ● ●

"An Apt Cartoon"

QIANA WHITTED

The Colored American, a national newspaper based in Washington, DC, announced in the April 20, 1901, issue that a cartoonist had been hired to create "each week an original cartoon, illustrating some feature of the race prejudice which exists in this country."[1] The decision was followed by enthusiastic praise from Black newspaper editors across the United States, and a few months later, *The Colored American* reprinted a notice from an Arkansas paper calling for a "cartoon syndicate." The piece urged the Black press to use its collective resources to commission editorial comics that would help to shape opinions among its readers and counter the misrepresentations of African American life that circulated in popular media. Under the headline "The Power of Cartoons," the editor observed, "Cartoons in journalism are far more powerful than many of our journalists seem to think. We wish the Negro press of the country could form a cartoon syndicate and thus be easily able for all Negro papers to furnish an apt cartoon once or twice a month— or once a week—on live questions. These cartoons would serve as eye opener not only to the race, but they would attract the reading public in spite of prejudice and set the whole American people to thinking more deeply than *Puck* or *Judge* or *Truth*."[2]

A conversation was being brokered in *The Colored American* about how comics and cartoon art communicated through image and text and who should be authorized to take the reins of such a distinct visual rhetoric where race was concerned. The dominant narrative, prompted in this instance by the illustrated satire of white-owned magazines such as *Puck*, would be summed up in another April 1901 piece written by the cartoonist Frederick Burr Opper titled "Caricature Country and Its Inhabitants." In Opper's essay for *The Independent*, the creator of the *Happy Hooligan* comic strip detailed a raucous terrain that was populated with well-known character types. He began by describing gullible farmers, blundering old men, and squabbling spouses alongside policemen that "batter and club from morning till night" and babies that "all cry with their mouths open to enormous widths."[3] Attributes of Chinese, Italian, Hebrew, Irish, German, and "Colored" inhabitants followed, establishing nonwhite racial and ethnic difference as one of the clearest coordinates in a shared cultural imaginary—the same climate in which *The Colored American* would announce its own cartoon feature two weeks later."[4]

Opper's essay is an important reminder that the crude exaggerations and distortions of racial caricature that may make us wince today were an exceedingly common mode of entertainment and social currency that was foundational to the early years of the comics form. The writer Jeet Heer has devoted a significant measure of his critical work on comics to contextualizing taxonomies like Opper's within the popular attitudes and power dynamics of late-nineteenth- and early-twentieth-century society. Heer explains, "It is not just that cartoonists lived in a racist time, but also that the affinity of comics for caricature meant that the early comic strips took the existing racism of society and gave it vicious and virulent visual life. Form and content came together in an especially unfortunate way." He reminds us that with each decade, "Jewish-American and Irish-American groups were becoming increasingly vocal in criticizing ethnic stereotypes that targeted them," leading to declining numbers of these representations in comics.[5] It would take much longer for the concerns of African Americans to be heard by people in positions of authority. The roots of blackface minstrelsy ran deep in all forms of popular culture and shaped the ways that people of African descent were dehumanized in comics well into the twentieth century, hemmed in by the entrenched white supremacy of Caricature Country.

Yet when confronted by what the cultural studies scholar Rebecca Wanzo refers to as "racist visual imperialism," African American voices have also used comics to demand something different.[6] In the decades following the announcement in *The Colored American*, newspapers that served African Americans in cities such as Chicago, Pittsburgh, New York, Baltimore, and Tulsa would continue to hire their own cartoonists to produce original work. During the Great Depression and World War II, fledgling comic book production shops that employed artists from immigrant communities were occasionally willing to hire Black artists, including Elmer C. Stoner and Matt Baker.[7] The period also saw the formation of the Black-owned Continental Features Syndicate, operated by Lajoyeaux H. Stanton to distribute comic strips by cartoonists such as Ollie Harrington.[8] Still, in describing the powerful role that comic art could play, the charge issued by the Black press at the turn of the century emphasized more than retaining creative talent. Comics were valued as a platform for larger conversations about the pressing concerns of the day—clarifying, complicating, and reacting to "live questions" that too often reduced the opinions of African Americans to easy punch lines. Comics served as an important way to enter these debates and to complicate the so-called race problem in the public square.

• • •

Desegregating Comics explores race and blackness in comic books, comic strips, and editorial cartoons in the United States from the turn of the twentieth century through the height of the industry's popularity in the 1950s. The historical perception of Black people in comic art has long been tied to caricatures of grinning minstrels, devious witch doctors, and vicious criminals, yet the chapters in this volume reveal a more complex narrative and aesthetic landscape, one that was enriched by the negotiations among comics artists, writers, editors, distributors, and readers over how blackness should be portrayed. Alongside the recycled plots that relied on stereotypes to add humor and suspense, there were comics about sports, crime, romance, science fiction, and adventure that took significant creative and financial risks by developing more inclusive stories. Large mainstream and small-press publishers expressed an interest in multiracial audiences, and on occasion, artists and writers experimented with new ways to portray Black lives in a medium deeply connected to legacies of racist objectification. Studying these experimental arbitrations and aspirations is the primary goal of the chapters in this book.

This collection builds on a growing body of academic scholarship about African American representations in comics and the major role that race plays in the history of media and popular culture.[9] While publications such as *The Blacker the Ink: Constructions of Black Identity in Comics and Sequential Art* (2015) and *Black Comics: Politics of Race and Representation* (2013) address a wide range of texts, much of the academic study in this area has been devoted to comics published in the past fifty years, with an emphasis on superhero comics and historical graphic novels. Few linger very long on how race operated in the industry's pioneering decades beyond the most egregious stereotypes. As a result, the writer and cartoonist Charles Johnson is not alone in the "revulsion" and "profound sadness" that he expresses in his introduction to Fredrik Strömberg's 2003 book *Black Images in the Comics*, a compilation of cartoons featuring Black characters around the world from the 1840s through the 1940s. Johnson condemns the myopic vision of the overworked caricatures that are referenced in Strömberg's collection and notes, "We should remember that the pictures we are looking at, these Ur-images of blacks, are a testament to the failure of the imagination (and often of empathy, too), and tell us nothing about black people but *every*thing about what white audiences approved and felt comfortable with in pop culture until the 1950s."[10] Readers could easily come away from historical retrospectives such as these with the presumption that, outside of a handful of newspaper strips, African Americans had little meaningful impact on what appeared on the pages of comics during the first half of the twentieth century or that it was only the interests of white readers that mattered to comics publishers.

Nevertheless, the deliberate and consequential debates over blackness in comics started early in the medium's development. In focusing on the "Golden Age," the title of this volume adopts a widely used periodization model, first established by comic book collectors, that divides the growth of comics into ages, including Platinum, Golden, Atomic, Silver, Bronze, and Modern, with later variations such as the Dark Age and the Renaissance. The Golden Age of comics is commonly defined as launching before World War II with the advent of superhero comic books in 1938 and covers the industry's most prosperous and celebrated years until the mid-1950s, when changing trends in popular media and the implementation of the Comics Magazine Association of America's Comics Code Authority in 1954 led to a noticeable decline in publishing and sales.[11] Looking back, however, the sense of nostalgia that buffers traditional understandings of the Golden Age's successes often diminishes the obstacles that African Americans encountered in the industry and downplays the persistence of racism that was manifest in some of the era's most cherished titles. In short, the halcyon vision of a Golden Age in American comics is also subject to debate. A few chapters in the book demonstrate that ongoing questions about racial representation surfaced early during the Platinum Age (1897–1938), when comic strips printed in newspapers and other periodicals dominated the industry. And as the final chapter on *Lobo* suggests, these concerns persisted into the Silver Age resurgence (1956–1970) and beyond.

Archives reveal that there is still much to learn about what comics have to say about race and how the images, characters, and plots were received within specific contexts over time. Two recent collections, by Tim Jackson and Ken Quattro, provide a sense of the breadth of African American representation and talent throughout comics history. Jackson's *Pioneering Cartoonists of Color* (2016) offers descriptive summaries from decades of comic strips and comic books, starting with one of the first Black newspapers to include illustrations, *The Black Republican and Office Holders Journal* in 1865. Quattro's *Invisible Men: Black Artists of the Golden Age of Comics* (2020) focuses on male creators and gathers interviews, newspaper clippings, and pages of original art along with narrative biographies. These volumes join magazines such as *Hogan's Alley* and websites such as the Digital Comic Museum and the *Stripper's Guide* blog in making rare materials accessible to the public.[12]

While these publications offer valuable resources for exploring racial representation, the *absence* of Black people in comics is instructive as well. In Leonard Rifas's research on comic books about the Korean War, for instance, he notes a 1944 study by the communications and behavioral science scholars Bernard Berelson and Patricia Salter titled "Comics Books and Anti-Minority Prejudice." Their research included an interview with "one of the leaders in the comic book publication field," who commented on the decision to completely avoid the depiction of Black characters rather than risk controversy that could affect circulation. Among Berelson and Salter's conclusions were that "the villains must not be members of minority groups (1) because they 'had some trouble' in this connection and (2) because they could expect trouble from representatives of the groups affected. The rule now seems to be, according to this respondent, that Negroes never appear in a comic book (1) because it is difficult to draw them without stressing characteristic Negro features and (2) because it would be difficult to place them in any but comic roles."[13] These observations raise a host of questions, not only about the nature of the "trouble" that publishers had been receiving but also about the long-term repercussions of such awareness on the stories and the images that made it to print, whether Black people were visibly present or not.[14] How have comics been affected over time by a seemingly inextricable relationship between race and the broad visual and verbal typecasting associated with the roles that heroes and villains are allowed to play? We can learn a great deal from the industry leaders whose output was driven by the kind of cost-benefit analysis that Berelson and Salter describe during the 1940s. And ironically enough, as racial politics in the United States intensified during the civil rights movement, mainstream comics would become even more cautious, with publishers taking a Comics Code–approved approach that avoided difficult conversations about race altogether.[15] That is all the more reason why this book recognizes comics writers, artists, and editors who found ways to contend with the realities of race and blackness, not as a source of trouble but as an opportunity for artistic innovation, a risk worth taking.

Given that the earliest and most prolific decades of the comics industry in the United States also correspond with the Jim Crow era, understanding how comics took part in the debates over blackness also means raising questions about access, ideology, and the politics of interracial contact, both in the panels and in the production of the comics. This period was marked by the advent of Black Codes, laws enacted after the Civil War to restrict the rights and behaviors of African Americans mostly in the South. These practices were expanded after Reconstruction to codify white supremacy across the country by disenfranchising Black voters and sanctioning acts of vigilante terrorism such as lynching to maintain social control. By the time the United States confronted the Great Depression and World War II, the racial divide had become enmeshed in the everyday routines of life, where restricted access to housing, transportation, medical care, and leisure was the norm. Not surprisingly, then, each stage in the process of creating, distributing, and purchasing comics was impacted to some degree by the laws and customs of racial segregation. Some of these moments are already widely known in the history of comics in this country: the turn-of-the-century cartoonist who chose to conceal his mixed-race background and "pass" for white in order to pitch his talents to newspaper editors; the African American publisher who debuted the first issue of a new comic book only to have wholesalers refuse to sell him the newsprint for a second; the Comics Code administrator who demanded that the image of a Black astronaut's face be removed to meet industry-approved regulations.[16]

Despite setbacks, Black creators continued to grow in number. Rather than abandon the medium altogether, these enthusiasts found ways to adapt the form's storytelling conventions and expand the capacity of comics to show and tell. Robert C. Harvey describes how King Features Syndicate discreetly kept photos of E. Simms Campbell out of its promotional material so that the editors of the 140 newspapers that carried his comic strip *Cuties* would not know that he was African American.[17] Art shops were another avenue for Black artists to enter the industry starting in the late 1930s, as Ken Quattro explains in *Invisible Men*. The anonymity of the assembly-line-style production in studios owned by Jerry Iger, Bernard Baily, L. B. Cole, and others meant that the work of Black artists could be contracted by comic book editors who refused to hire them directly. This "buffer" probably contributed to the reason why Elmer C. Stoner was one of the first African Americans to join Harry "A" Chesler's comic shop in 1939, and as Quattro notes, "subsequent comic book Black artists, virtually without exception, worked through comic shops at some point in their careers."[18] In turn, Black artists were among the many uncredited Golden Age pencilers, letterers, inkers, and colorists who created comic books.

The struggle to negotiate the era's racial restrictions also made its way into the comics themselves. The *Chicago Defender* staff artist Garrett Whyte created a satirical comic strip called *Mr. Jim Crow* that was published in the newspaper's national edition from 1946 to 1951 to capture what he called the "ineptitude" of segregation.[19] The strip's title character was a white politician from the South with the beak of a crow, whose insistence on the strict divide between the races led to absurd ends. Adorned in a suit with a pompadour haircut and a plantation string tie, his overbearing demeanor and southern drawl was reminiscent of the fictional Senator Beauregard Claghorn from *The Fred Allen Show*.[20] One installment follows Mr. Jim Crow as he gives away free sheets and pillow slips to men and children of different sizes and boasts in the final panel about the "best way" to use the linens, while behind him a parade of Ku Klux Klansmen walks by.[21] In the strip's later years, Whyte invited readers to "win $5.00 cash" by sending in accounts of their "own personal experience or observation, showing the amusing side of segregation or discrimination." Subsequent comics noted the names of the weekly winners whose real-life encounters were dramatized in the strip. A California reader supplied the details of an August 27, 1949, strip about Mr. Jim Crow's visit to a ranch (where he makes a point to note his dislike for black cattle). He demands that the African American ranch hand roll him a cigarette but stops him from finishing the job, saying, "Cullud boy—Ah do mah own lickin.'" The ranch hand's retort—"And Jim Crow—I do my own kicking!"—appears in the final panel above a silhouette of the Black man's fist and boot lifting the shocked Crow into the air (figure I.1).[22]

FIGURE I.1 *Mr. Jim Crow*, by Garrett Whyte, *Chicago Defender*, August 27, 1949.

Whyte leverages the satire in *Mr. Jim Crow* against the invocation of actual events and readers whose experiences with racism are the subject of the strip. Fact meets fiction in the bizarre caricature of a man-sized crow who talks and squawks about the convoluted means through which the separation of races must be maintained. Since Mr. Jim Crow is not the only white man in the comic, Whyte's visual depiction of the bird's daily encounters with human beings creates a cognitive dissonance that brings unspoken anti-Black attitudes to the surface. Mr. Jim Crow gets the last laugh in most of the stories, but for his visit to the California ranch, Whyte uses the final panel to stage an additional ending with the kind of punch line that most African Americans would not have been able to execute in 1949 without serious consequences. The "cullud boy" kicks back and provides a cathartic reward for the comic strip's weekly winner and all those who have experienced a similar humiliation. Perhaps then, as the historian Stephen A. Berrey argues, the routines of segregation were not always so fixed. He notes, "If routines suggested predictability, they could also be revised. To put it another way, on a daily basis, Jim Crow and the meanings of whiteness and blackness were ever in the process of being made, unmade, and remade in the racial interactions between blacks and whites."[23] The *Chicago Defender* comic provided a space not only to critique larger power structures but also to creatively resist and "revise" the seemingly small racial interactions that readers faced every day.

• • •

Another important aspect that contributes to the narrow perception of race in Golden Age comics is the controversy surrounding the medium's role in promoting juvenile delinquency. The mid-twentieth-century dispute over the effects of comics reading on children ran parallel to the growing political and legal battle to end racial segregation—that is, until a mental health clinic in Harlem began to make the case that the two conflicts were entwined. Dr. Fredric Wertham was a Jewish American social psychiatrist from Germany who, along with a small but dedicated team of volunteer clinicians, operated a free psychiatric clinic in the basement of St. Philip's Protestant Episcopal Church in Harlem from 1946 to 1958. The Lafargue Mental Hygiene Clinic opened its doors for two evenings a week "for the treatment of all kinds of nervous and mental disorders and behavior difficulties of adults and children."[24] During a time when such psychiatric services were often targeted to the needs of white people and elite, wealthy patients, the Lafargue Clinic was distinguished by the fact that it treated everyone without referrals, "regardless of a patient's race or ability to pay."[25] The medical historian Dennis Doyle notes that the clinic also stood apart through an antiracist therapeutic approach that emphasized the cumulative impact of everyday social circumstances and hardships on the lives of Harlem residents, rather than relying on "older racialist assumptions that the African American psyche was innately different and inferior."[26]

Wertham's expertise was in forensic psychiatry and child psychopathology. His experience as chief psychiatrist at Queens General Hospital, as well as previously at Bellevue Hospital in New York and Johns Hopkins's Phipps Clinic in Maryland, led him to be particularly disturbed by the racial discrimination that African Americans faced in the mental health system. He was joined in this concern by Richard Wright, Ralph Ellison, and other prominent African American progressives in Harlem. With their support, Wertham recruited an interracial group of psychiatrists and partnered with a bishop whose church was actively involved with addressing the social needs of the local community for what was considered a radical idea in psychiatric care.

In the early 1950s, the Lafargue Clinic attracted even more attention when Wertham provided clinical testimony in *Gebhart v. Belton*, one of the five cases that would be considered before the Supreme Court as part of *Brown v. Board of Education* and the only case that had succeeded in declaring public school segregation unlawful at the state level before the federal appeal. A month after the U.S. Supreme Court handed down its landmark decision in the *Brown* case in May 1954, Wertham published an opinion piece in the *Nation* praising the court for its courage in using the law as an instrument of social change. He also hoped that the judicial victory would embolden U.S. citizens and their representatives to act against what he believed were the increasingly insidious dangers that awaited children *outside* the classroom in comic books: "More race hatred has been instilled in American children through comic books in the past ten years than in the preceding hundred years. As Constance Curtis writes in her Harlem Diary: 'From the time they can hold a book and look at a picture—long before they can read—the children are learning the most vicious stereotypes of the white superman and the dark degenerate.' If race prejudice is outlawed in children's school hours, should not its instigation be outlawed in their time of leisure?"[27]

The study of comic books for which Wertham is most well-known today began at Harlem's Lafargue Clinic as part of his examination into the causes of youth behavioral problems. Intake forms routinely asked children what they were reading, and counseling sessions made observations about how the young people related the stories to their daily lives. By 1954, the time of the publication of Wertham's infamous polemic *Seduction of the Innocent: The Influence of Comic Books on Today's Youth*, the Lafargue Clinic proudly boasted of its role in bringing yet another "public health problem" to the attention of the nation.[28] Wertham occasionally applied the rhetoric that he and his staff used to discuss the impact of racism to strengthen his claims about the long-term impact of comics. For instance, a clinician at Lafargue drafted a letter to the *Pittsburgh Courier* in May 1953 noting, "The fact that many Negroes in the U.S. have attended or are attending segregated schools without apparent harmful influences is no argument. By the same token *many children are exposed to the polio virus* and escape crippling injury. This fact, however, does not prevent the mobilization of every available scientific resource to conquer the disease."[29] In *Seduction of the Innocent*, Wertham writes, "It is true that many children read comic books and few become delinquent. But that proves nothing. Innumerable poor people never commit a crime and yet poverty is one of the causes of crime. Many children are exposed to the polio virus; few come down with the disease. Is that supposed to prove that the polio virus is innocuous and the children at fault?"[30]

This connection would have been most evident to the clinic's supporters, who received a succession of holiday cards and brochures that shifted from photographs of children to images of Wertham scouring the pages of comic books.[31] Letters requesting funding for Lafargue noted both the Delaware segregation case and the anticomics study as the two notable achievements of the clinic. Once articles by and about Wertham began appearing in *Collier's*, *Ladies' Home Journal*, and *Time*, the Lafargue Clinic became inundated with speaking requests from librarians, parent-teacher associations, and civic and religious organizations from New York, New Jersey, Connecticut, and Rhode Island. If Wertham could not answer their requests himself, he sent his colleague Dr. Hilde Mosse or another clinician to give a standard lecture. Suggested speaking fees were $25, but in many instances, Wertham and Mosse requested that donations be given to the Lafargue Clinic in lieu of any fees.[32] In other words, the fight against comics directly helped to fund the free clinic's operations.

Along with Wertham's warnings against explicit depictions of violence and sexuality in comics, the psychiatrist expressed concerns about how American readers were affected by racial stereotypes. As with his piece in the *Nation*, he often took note of superhero and jungle comics that associated virtue and heroism with white characters who battled dark-skinned villains.[33] Yet in the national profiles that took up Wertham's crusade, the published features tended to steer away from this problematic racial imagery or its impact on Black urban youth. The illustrations and photographs that accompanied the articles in *Reader's Digest*, the *American Home*, and other magazines during this period clearly demonstrate who was most at risk: white, middle-class American children. In the written text of the *Collier's* piece from 1948, the children's racial identities are not made explicit (though they could be inferred from the Lafargue Clinic's location). Instead, the subjects are differentiated by socioeconomic class and intellectual ability.[34] Multiple clients from the Harlem clinic are quoted in the piece, including the opening anecdote from an eleven-year-old boy in which he pretends to be "the crook" who ties up the actress played by his sister.[35] On the pages, however, all the professional models reenacting the scenes are well-dressed white suburban children (figure I.2). Their menacing expressions perform the dangers hidden from view and reinforce the conclusions drawn by the *Collier's* writer that "not even the so-called upper classes are immune" from the "extreme and abnormal avidity" of comics reading.[36]

Comic book reading is portrayed in these articles as a deviant and harmful activity that first ensnares the poor, uneducated, and unsupervised urban

FIGURE I.2 Photograph by Martin Harris for Judith Crist's "Horror in the Nursery," *Collier's*, March 27, 1948.

youth whose circumstances have made them deeply susceptible to the power of the comic's suggestions. But the real "horror in the nursery" was not the reading habits of Black adolescents in Harlem; it was the fears among some white parents that their children would be next. After a meeting in Meriden, Connecticut, a librarian told Dr. Mosse about one particularly rebellious comic book fan from a strict, upstanding family of five children. Of the boy's behavior after reading comics, the librarian said, "He is like from another race."[37] To what end do these perceptions serve? White comic book readers are perceived as impressionable consumers who nevertheless have a number of choices available to them when it comes to their reading material and leisure activity—they simply need the right guidance to help them make good decisions. Underprivileged Black youth are positioned as easy prey for the predatory comic book; they lack the resources to fend off the midcentury boom of cheap sensational fare. To be clear, Wertham's study generally fails to account for discerning young readers of any race, as scholars such as Christopher Pizzino and Carol L. Tilley have demonstrated.[38] Yet the psychiatrist's insistence on framing Black children as acutely vulnerable and "passive in their encounter with a cultural pathogen," to borrow Pizzino's phrasing, has significant repercussions for the way Wertham's research about comics reading was received among parents, legislators, and comic book publishers.[39]

• • •

Our critical understanding of this period changes, however, when we acknowledge that Black readers were not as defenseless as Wertham claimed. Many came to the five-and-dime spinner racks and sidewalk newsstands with their own set of reading practices and cultural decoding skills. At the close of my 2019 book *EC Comics: Race, Shock, and Social Protest*, I place the company's approach to visual narratives of race and social justice within the context of such a newsstand, one of many in the United States during the first half of the twentieth century that would have been packed with ten-cent comic books. An urban vendor that was "willing to stock an issue of *Negro Romance,* or a sports comic with Jackie Robinson on the cover," I wrote, "would have also sold imperial titles like *Jungle Comics* that vilified people of color and newspapers featuring the final appearances of Ebony White's buffoonish antics in *The Spirit*."[40] How did consumers during the Jim Crow era make meaning out of the competing codes of strength, justice, and power that these comics offered? And how do the dynamics of identification and participation play out in a medium that asks Black readers to invest in fantastic feats of imagination, some of which marginalize and denigrate their very existence?

Stuart Hall's concept of "negotiated" decoding practices can inform this broader speculation about the ways that marginalized readers bring "a mixture of adaptive and oppositional elements" to bear on their appraisal of the words and pictures in comics.[41] Hall describes reading strategies that concede certain elements of the status quo while pushing back against racist and sexist assumptions that are relayed through components of the character and plot. Consider, then, the resistant readers prior to the 1960s who, rather than rejecting a comic altogether, enacted a multitude of story-world adjustments and "situated logics" with each turn of the page, until they found an interpretive path in which their reading could be rewarded. As Hall writes of this negotiated process, "it acknowledges the legitimacy of the hegemonic definitions to make the grand significations (abstract), while, at a more restricted, situational (situated) level, it makes its own ground rules—it operates with exceptions to the rule."[42]

Resistant readers who went a step further can be found among the group of multiracial junior high school students from New York called the Youthbuilders. They visited Fawcett's executive editor Will Lieberson in 1945 to make the case against Captain Marvel's buffoonish sidekick, Steamboat. As Brian Cremins notes in chapter 10 in this volume, the group concluded by holding up an image of the character and declaring, "This is not the Negro race, but your one-and-a-half million readers will think it so."[43] In another example, Heer's research uncovered an exchange between an editor at King Features Syndicate and the cartoonist Roy Crane over the appearance of Black characters in two installments of the adventure comic strip *Buz Sawyer*. The editor cautioned Crane against including such images: "Experience has shown us that we have to be awfully careful about any comics in which Negroes appear." The editor continued, "The Association for the Advancement of Colored People protests every time they see anything which they consider ridicules the Negro no matter how faintly."[44] In 1947, a "group of black schoolchildren" wrote to the Dell Comics editor Oskar Lebeck about the racist caricature of a young Black boy from *The New Funnies* called Li'l Eightball, which was based on a Universal Studios cartoon. Soon after the complaints and added pressure from the Cultural Division of the National Negro Congress, Lebeck discontinued the character.[45] Rather than accept the hegemonic readings encoded in these problematic representations, Black readers petitioned for changes and insisted that their enjoyment of titles such as *Captain Marvel*, *Buz Sawyer*, and *The New Funnies* should not come at the cost of their dignity. Undeterred by the customs of Caricature Country, they called into question the naming power of the industry and the role of all its creative professionals in shaping attitudes about blackness. Of course, not every comic featuring a racist character generated letter-writing campaigns and visits from civil rights organizations (or resulted in the hiring of more Black cartoonists). Without these examples, though, our picture of U.S. comics history is incomplete.

As a result, the chapters in *Desegregating Comics* focus on comics from the first half of the twentieth century, with most contributions targeting the apex of productivity during the 1930s–1950s. This volume is broader in scope than my monograph on EC Comics and demonstrates that while the social justice comics (called the "preachies") that Bill Gaines published during the Atomic Age were exceptional, the company was not alone in its efforts. Most of the fifteen chapters are arranged chronologically, yet the scholarship abounds with rhizomatic connections between the comics under investigation, their historically situated logics, and the interpretive frameworks used to analyze them. Part 1, on iconographies of race and racism, introduces the disputes over caricature and the adaptation of blackface minstrelsy in comics as one of the collection's recurring concerns. Contributors model different ways to grapple with the historical significance of racist imagery and the limits of symptomatic readings across the larger body of work produced by Rose O'Neill, George Herriman, and Will Eisner. Part 2, on formal innovation and aesthetic range, contextualizes the artistic choices of African American comics creators such as Matt Baker, Alvin Hollingsworth, Jackie Ormes, and Romare Bearden. Scholars place the debates within Black culture over "art vs. propaganda" in conjunction with questions about the low cultural status of comics relative to fine art and, in the case of Ormes, investigative journalism. The chapters also highlight elements of craft—the use of line and texture, disruptive layouts, and elements of misdirection—that exemplify the stylistic range of the cartoonists throughout the book.

Part 3, on comics readership and respectability politics, focuses on readers who purchased and shared comics, while also analyzing how these visual narratives influenced public opinion, particularly among Black audiences. Chapters recall the DC boys who put down their bikes to read comics in Gordon Parks's 1942 photographs, the group of teenagers that visited Fawcett's New York office, and the comic books left behind on Emmett Till's bed in Mississippi. An analysis of the single issue of Orrin C. Evans's *All-Negro Comics* is used to illustrate what was at stake for an independent African American comic book publisher who wanted to provide an alternative reading experience for Black youth. A closer look at Hollingsworth's comic strip *Kandy* reveals how colorism and class conflict within Black communities informed the gendered visual dynamics of the romance-adventure serial. Part 4 scrutinizes key disruptions in genre comics and explores how different storytelling conventions influence the way blackness is conveyed on the page. The trajectory of Neil Knight in the *Courier* from military pilot to space adventurer expanded the Afrofuturist possibilities of comics, while the depiction of Black couples in *Negro Romance* encouraged Fawcett to make small but meaningful changes to its romance formula. Other chapters address how the tropes of jungle adventure and cowboy Westerns, in which

FIGURE I.3 *Girl with Comic Book in Store* (1947). (Photo by Charles "Teenie" Harris / Carnegie Museum of Art via Getty Images)

racial hierarchies are already deeply embedded, become even more complicated when Black characters take on primary roles.

The cover of this book features an extraordinary photograph by Charles "Teenie" Harris of a young unnamed African American girl sitting in front of a wall of comic books in April 1947 (figure I.3). A dog stretches comfortably across her lap as she reads a copy of *Mickey Mouse and the Submarine Pirates* #141. To her left and right are pulp detective tales, romance stories, and newspapers, while behind her rise shelves and shelves of comic books: *Wonder Comics, Zoot, Superman, Real Life Comics, Raggedy Ann and Andy, Picture Stories from American History*, and more. Harris, who worked as the first staff photographer for the *Pittsburgh Courier* before opening his own studio, took this picture of the young girl inside a confectionary store owned by his oldest brother, George Harris.[46] The shop was located in the heart of Pittsburgh's predominantly Black "Hill District" on Wylie Avenue, and the picture, taken during the business district's most prosperous years after World War II, reflected a larger attempt on the part of Harris to spotlight more cheerful, optimistic moments that called attention to "a side of black life not usually portrayed in the white media."[47]

As with so many spaces during the segregation era, the Wylie Avenue confectionary store was part of a society partitioned in ways that sought to deny the full humanity and citizenship rights of African Americans. Yet what Harris manages to capture is a moment of respite from Jim Crow, an interior space encapsulated by an astonishing abundance of reading pleasures. The photograph invites us to view this bounty of stacked and overlapping comic books as much more than a Golden Age of productivity and profit. The newsstand also functions as a saddle-stitched interzone in the popular representation of race; its shelves showcase the rounds of marketing gambits and creative breakthroughs, clashing ideologies and attitudes, and insurgent readerships that distinguish the debates over blackness in early comics. Research from the 1940s and 1950s indicates that Black girls and boys in the United States were avid comic book consumers, but all too often, the interests of these readers are underestimated.[48] The joys and concerns about the comics that they encountered tend to be set apart, even in critical studies of the period. *Desegregating Comics* relocates their curiosity to the center of the Golden Age newsstand and uses moments like the one captured in Harris's photograph as a frame of reference for considering how such a transformational period in our nation's social and political development also proved to be so pivotal for the history of comics.

Notes

1 "Announcement No. 2," 8; "Cartoon Feature," 10. Special thanks to Maryanne Rhett for bringing these sources in *The Colored American* to my attention. For more on the publisher of *The Colored American*, Edward Elder Cooper, read T. Jackson, *Pioneering Cartoonists of Color*, 13–15.
2 "Power of Cartoons," 3.
3 Opper, "Caricature Country and Its Inhabitants," 780.
4 Opper, 778.
5 Heer, "Comics Chronicles."
6 Wanzo, *Content of Our Caricature*, 22.
7 Carpenter, introduction to *Invisible Men*, 8.
8 T. Jackson, *Pioneering Cartoonists of Color*, 36.
9 These important contributions include Wanzo, *Content of Our Caricature*; Austin and Hamilton, *All New, All Different?*; Santos, *Graphic Memories of the Civil Rights Movement*; Whaley, *Black Women in Sequence*; S. Howard, *Encyclopedia of Black Comics*; Gateward and Jennings, *Blacker the Ink*; Howard and Jackson, *Black Comics*; Costello and Whitted, *Comics and the U.S. South*; Adilifu Nama, *Superblack*; Aldama, *Multicultural Comics*; Foster, *Looking for a Face like Mine*; Jeffrey Brown, *Black Superheroes, Milestone Comics, and Their Fans*. For biographical studies of

milestone figures, read Tisserand, *Krazy*; Inge, *Dark Laughter*; Goldstein, *Jackie Ormes*; Strömberg, *Black Images in the Comics*.

10   C. Johnson, foreword to *Black Images in the Comics*, 13.
11   For additional background on the ages of comics, read Coville, "History of Comic Books"; Morrison, *Supergods*; Burgas, "What Should We Call This Age of Comics?"; Ayres, "When Were Superheroes Grim and Gritty?"; Adair, "We Are Not in a 'Golden Age' of Comics."
12   Jackson, *Pioneering Cartoonists of Color*; Quattro, *Invisible Men*. *Hogan's Alley: The Magazine of the Cartoon Arts*, edited by Tom Heintjes, has been publishing since 1994. The *Stripper's Guide* blog was started in 2005 and is edited by Allan Holtz with contributors Alex Jay and Jeffrey Lindenblatt: http://strippersguide.blogspot.com. The Digital Comic Museum hosts free public-domain Golden Age comics: https://digitalcomicmuseum.com. Another important contribution is Christopher J. Hayton and David L. Albright's in-depth essay on race in war comics during the civil rights era, which begins with a substantial overview of African American representation in comics from the 1940s and 1950s. Hayton and Albright, "Military Vanguard for Desegregation."
13   Bernard Berelson and Patricia Salter, "Writer's War Board Study: Comic Books and Anti-Minority Prejudice," December 28, 1944, quoted in Rifas, *Korean War Comic Books*, 113.
14   Adilifu Nama, in his analysis of race and science fiction cinema, also notes the importance of the "structured absence and token presence" of Black people in cultural representations in which racial codes and signifiers are used to relay deeper ideological conflicts (10). Nama, *Black Space*, 10–41.
15   Jeet Heer also references a "larger ethnic cleansing of the comics" that occurred in the wake of the civil rights movement, pushing many of these conversations underground. Heer, afterword to *Black Comics*, 255–256.
16   Tisserand, *Krazy*, 67–81; T. Jackson, *Pioneering Cartoonists of Color*, 80–81; Whitted, *EC Comics*, 104–108.
17   Harvey, *Insider Histories of Cartooning*, 97.
18   Quattro, *Invisible Men*, 36
19   "Bluford Library Archives: Garrett Whyte '39."
20   Holtz, "Obscurities of the Day."
21   Whyte, "Comic 4," 23.
22   Whyte, "Comic 3," 23.
23   Berrey, *Jim Crow Routine*, 4.
24   Lafargue Clinic Records, Box 1, Bolder 15, Manuscripts, Archives, and Rare Books Division, New York Public Library, Schomburg Center for Research in Black Culture, New York, NY.
25   Doyle, "Fine New Child," 174.
26   Doyle, "Where the Need Is Greatest," 748.
27   Wertham, "Nine Men Speak to You," 499.
28   Wertham, 499.
29   Charles Collins to the *Pittsburgh Courier*, May 1953, in research files for *Seduction of the Innocent*, Fredric Wertham Papers, Box 111, Folder 7, Manuscript Division, Library on Congress, Washington, DC (emphasis in the original).
30   Wertham, *Seduction of the Innocent*, 245.
31   Assortment of Lafargue Clinic holiday cards, Lafargue Clinic Records, Box 1, Folder 15.

32. For speaking invitations to Wertham and Mosse, read Lafargue Clinic Records, Box 1, Folders 4–5.
33. Read also Mendes, *Under the Strain of Color*, 122.
34. Crist, "Horror in the Nursery," 96.
35. For more on Wertham's observations about Black youth and the pathologizing of comic book reading, read Carol L. Tilley's chapter 8 in this volume.
36. Crist, "Horror in the Nursery," 97.
37. Hilde L. Mosse, notes from "Comic Book Committee" meeting in Meriden, Conn., Lafargue Clinic Records, Box 1, Folder 10.
38. Pizzino, "Doctor versus the Dagger"; Tilley, "Seducing the Innocent."
39. Pizzino, "Doctor versus the Dagger," 639.
40. Whitted, *EC Comics*, 135.
41. Hall, "Encoding, Decoding," 486.
42. Hall, 486.
43. In addition to Cremins's chapter 10 in this volume, read also Cremins, *Captain Marvel and the Art of Nostalgia*.
44. Heer, afterword to *Black Comics*, 255.
45. Markstein, "Li'l Eightball."
46. Glasco, "American Life," 11.
47. Glasco, 14.
48. Witty and Moore, "Interest in Reading the Comics among Negro Children," 306–307.

Part I

Iconographies of Race and Racism

●●●●●●●●●●●●●

1

Rose O'Neill and Visual Tropes of Blackness

●●●●●●●●●●●●●●

IAN GORDON

In 2020, the centennial year of the ratification of the Nineteenth Amendment to the U.S. Constitution, which granted women the right to vote, the Norman Rockwell Museum in Stockbridge, Massachusetts, celebrated the artist Rose O'Neill's contribution to the suffrage campaign. Laurie Norton Moffatt, the director of the museum, equated O'Neill's work with Congressman John Lewis's "lifelong work on voting rights."[1] O'Neill lent her Kewpie characters, which had achieved widespread popularity as licensed dolls, to the suffrage campaign at the height of their fame, and they appeared in numerous cartoons and other forms advocating for the vote for women. Regarding O'Neill's action as akin to the moral gravitas of John Lewis is not unique to Moffatt. In a 2018 *Smithsonian Magazine* article celebrating O'Neill's life, the author Adina Solomon characterized the Kewpies as "cute characters with a message, often mocking elitist middle-class reformers, supporting racial equality and advocating for the poor."[2]

Rose O'Neill is an underappreciated figure in American life.[3] Beyond her contributions to the suffrage campaign, she gained renown as the creator of the Kewpies, first as a comic for the *Ladies' Home Journal* in 1909 and then as a licensed doll that generated over $35 million in royalties for her in 2022 terms.[4] The Kewpies were effectively an early form of transmedia, and although the popularity of the dolls has faded, a Japanese brand of Kewpie mayonnaise licensed in the 1920s still exists and since 2010 has targeted expansion in Southeast Asia and the Middle East with a halal version.[5] As a full-time artist for the illustrated humor journal *Puck*, O'Neill published over six hundred cartoons between 1897 and 1905.[6] She was a woman determined to march to her own beat and by age thirty-three had discarded two useless husbands.[7] As a crusader for racial equality, though, O'Neill's record is a little thin and seems to rely on an episode of the Kewpies and some underanalyzed early work in *Puck*.[8] An examination of O'Neill's depiction of African Americans provides a clearer look at this oft-overlooked period of her career that has been eclipsed by her success with the Kewpies. More importantly, O'Neill's cartoons show that humor journals like *Puck* gave visual form and wide circulation to racist stereotypes of African Americans. In an era when the last vestiges of radical reconstruction were being swept away by, among other things, the Supreme Court decision in *Plessy v. Ferguson*, handed down a year before O'Neill joined *Puck*, such images helped underpin the structural racism of Jim Crow.[9] Glenda R. Carpio has pointed to the long life of such stereotypes, as notions of African American men as lazy and irresponsible could readily be dusted off as moral failings of individuals, for example, when the 1960s civil rights movement helped dismantle some of the racist structural aspects of American life. The "deadbeat dad" of the 1980s and 1990s was simply a newly coded lazy African American man.[10] Analyzing O'Neill's cartoons helps in understanding the visual dimensions of the stereotype, its context, and the uses to which it was put. I bring her use of the trope of the lazy African American man into sharp focus to show the way cartoons worked discursively to create such stereotypical tropes.

O'Neill's "The Kewpies and the Little Browns" from *Woman's Home Companion* in July 1912 is a story of thoughtless, instinctive racism. The full-page comic consists of four panels and eleven stanzas of poetry. It tells the story of two African American boys who play with three white children until the latter's mother, Mrs. McBride, stops the activity with cruel words. The despair of the two boys is quickly overcome by the arrival of Kewpies, who whisk them away "far, far from town," and they frolic by the sea. The cartoon fit a sentimental view of childhood often expressed in O'Neill's work (the Kewpies after all are a romanticized version of childhood innocence) and in the late nineteenth and early twentieth-century United States more generally. Young African American children were particularly sentimentalized in racial terms as pickaninnies, most central as the advertising figures the Gold Dust Twins, and this extended to a general infantilization of African Americans as a whole.[11] The way O'Neill constructed her narrative has the African American boys, literally the Brown boys Sam and Jasper, grateful to spend time with "playmates they had admired so." And when the white mother breaks up the gathering, "her only fault was family pride," and O'Neill stresses that she has had a hard day. Of course, this is all the conceit of O'Neill's narrative, and it sets up the intervention of the Kewpies that is the whole purpose of the comic. O'Neill addresses racism by separating the parties, provides excuses for the behavior, and offers no admonishment to Mrs. McBride. It is instructive that the solution is to magically remove the Browns from the scene and transport them "far, far" away. Even without reading this comic as an allegory of separate but equal or for repatriation of African Americans to Africa, O'Neill's deployment of race in a comic drew on a discourse that figured the existence of African Americans as an issue to be solved and an opportunity for humor through visual typographies and stock jokes.[12] Indeed, in 1912, when O'Neill transformed her Kewpies into their most famous forms, the at one point ubiquitous Kewpie Dolls, she marketed a Black version as a Hot'n'Tot—a play on the racist terminology most infamously used in the display of Sara Baartman, who was labeled as the "Hottentot Venus."[13] The 1912 comic and the 1915 doll, then, were an outgrowth of O'Neill's earlier work and her frequent deployment of racist stereotypes of African Americans when she worked as a cartoonist for *Puck*.

O'Neill was one of the first, or perhaps the first, published American woman cartoonist and worked full-time on the otherwise all-male staff of the illustrated humor magazine *Puck* from 1897 to 1905.[14] Her comic "The Old Subscriber Calls" from *Truth*, September 19, 1896, is often held as the first comic strip by a woman and presaged her illustrated narrative work that in form is somewhat separate from the gag cartoons she produced for *Puck*. In her work for *Puck*, O'Neill created a range of cartoons working familiar veins of humor, and these included a significant number of cartoons featuring African Americans.

Shelly Armitage argues in her *Kewpies and Beyond* that O'Neill's work in this area redirected the gag away from the usual object—denigrating Black life and experience—and called into question the prejudices of the middle-class reader. For Armitage, O'Neill's career at *Puck* involved her using "the conventions of 'male' humor to explore the female as underdog."[15] In one example Armitage provides, "Quieted Him" from the October 14, 1903, issue of *Puck*, an African American couple engage in banter about a new coffee grinder the wife has bought that does not work. The wife equates the grinder with the husband. The joke so obviously relies on the racist stereotype of the lazy, unreliable African American man that Armitage spends a paragraph or so contextualizing the image as apparently undercutting that typography.[16] Armitage argues that O'Neill's cartoons of African Americans always subverted prevailing images of African Americans through an "illustrative rather than caricaturing style," and although she used expected conventions in text and formula, her carefully drawn cartoons "expressing individualized characters, settings, and cultural concerns" directed the humor "outward toward the viewer, subverting through redirected comedy the erroneous and bigoted stereotypic concepts."[17] Armitage's unpacking of the cartoons for her academic readers suggests that she was not sure her view of O'Neill's intentions would find ready acceptance. To be sure, to my eye, the visual tropes and the typographies used overrode any subtlety that may have been intended by O'Neill. Or more bluntly, the joke only worked because of the trope.

Indeed, O'Neill created a series of cartoons supporting women's suffrage, and in this case, Armitage's reading privileges O'Neill's treatment of women over that of African American men. O'Neill's cartoon of October 14, 1903, may have supported women's rights, but it did so in such an abstract fashion and at the expense of African Americans that reading it as such requires major acts of interpretation and faith. Any use of the visual tropes associated with the extensive range of stereotypes of African Americans (indeed whites created stereotypes for almost all facets of African American life to undercut any concept of shared humanity) have a slim chance of rising above their racist conception. O'Neill's use of these forms of representation had none of the nuances, as Rebecca Wanzo has so wonderfully shown, that African American cartoonists have brought to their use of such imagery.[18] From my reading of a range of O'Neill's work, it seems doubtful that she had the purpose in mind that Armitage attributes to her. In my reading of her cartoons from *Puck*, it seems more likely that along with her male contemporaries, she saw little wrong in deploying such stereotypes to generate the racial discourse that passed for humor.

It is a common defense of racism that we should not judge the past by anachronistic standards and see artists and others by the light of their contemporaries. On the one hand, this is a morally ambiguous notion because it posits that we cannot demand morality or righteousness of anyone if it is absent in the majority of others, but on the other, with regard to what is shaping particular tropes, it suggests that work must be contextualized in some sort of discursive framework to be sufficiently understood. In this manner, Armitage wanted to place O'Neill's work not in a framework of racial cartoons but within a context of feminisms and shaping the right to suffrage. In analyzing O'Neill's cartoons that used African American figures, rather than seeing them as part of a broad set of her cartoons that pushed for votes for women using various forms of representation, a discourse of suffrage that just happened to have racist overtones, I show that they were racist cartoons and part of the overall racist discourse on display in *Puck*. These cartoons are racist because of their depictions on several registers. O'Neill used caricature in her visualization of African Americans, and these visual representations replicated the exaggerations of minstrelsy's blackface and loud attire. On another level, the use of a fake Black patois connoted a simplicity of character. This use of imagery and language combined to represent the sort of typographies found in minstrelsy, the bumpkins Tambo and Bones, the dandy Zip Coon, and so on.[19] Furthermore, O'Neill's cartoons fit a general racist discourse of *Puck*, whose numerous cartoonists, including the infamous E. W. Kemble, Frederick Burr Opper, and Frank Nankivell, produced a steady stream of similar cartoons. Minstrelsy, cartoons, and other early mass-media forms like sheet music turned these representations into the all-too-familiar racial stereotypes, and O'Neill's work, whether consciously or not, helped embed these in American consciousness.[20]

Two cartoons of O'Neill's for *Puck*, among her first to use typographies of African Americans, show the importance of analyzing the totality of the cartoon in the manner I have suggested. O'Neill's December 28, 1898, cartoon under the heading "Local Color" showed a caricatured African American woman doing the laundry with her two children next to her. An African American man from the doorstep says, "Doan' be skeered ob me, chillum! I ain't the bogey man!" One of the children, "Little Lucretia," replies with a knowing look and to a delighted expression on her mother's face, "We knows you ain't. De bogey man am a white man" (figure 1.1). The bogey man is commonly understood as a mythic masculine figure used to scare children into behaving well. O'Neill's racialization of this figure as white, from the mouth of an African American child, suggests that to her mind, there was a gag in African Americans' fear of white folks and the way this was used to scare children. A sympathetic reading of the cartoon would be that O'Neill thought that African Americans were rightly teaching their children to be

FIGURE 1.1   Rose O'Neill, "Local Color," *Puck*, December 28, 1898.

careful around white people, a nineteenth-century version of "the talk" or Ta-Nehisi Coates's book *Between the World and Me*. But with no shift in sentiment, and for another reason entirely, O'Neill could have been reminding her audience that African Americans had a racial consciousness that figured white people as a threat. This latter understanding is lent credence by *Puck*'s white readership and the way typographies of African Americans were employed by its cartoonist to replicate and disseminate stereotypical views of African Americans.

A second of O'Neill's early African American cartoons, one for the cover of the April 11, 1900, issue of *Puck*, might on first appearance seem to be an argument for her support of African American civil rights (figure 1.2). Certainly, it shows that O'Neill opposed lynching. The caption to the image reads,

IN GEORGIA.
PETE.— Am dis much bettah dan de ole slav'ry days, Uncle Tom?
UNCLE TOM.— I dunno, zac'ly. In dem times we wuz too valy'ble to be lynched!

The image shows a family drawn in stereotypical style, with a mother holding a child and shielding her eyes with her hand to look at a distance. Pete, a young man or teen, who poses the question, is pictured pointing with his thumb in the same direction as the mother looks. The uncle to whom he addresses the question is kneeling and has an angry, frustrated look as he holds back, or comforts, a young girl with a shocked expression. If one follows the gaze and the thumb to the upper left of the cartoon, there are four figures, presumably white, walking away, and two, perhaps three of these are clearly armed with rifles. Looking briefly at the image, which strongly foregrounds the African American figures, and quickly moving to the caption, as a reader familiar with the conventions of reading cartoons would, one might have just missed the significance of the figures in the top left.[21] But all the

FIGURE 1.2 Rose O'Neill, "In Georgia," *Puck*, April 11, 1900.

visual elements point to this being a group of white men taking an African American away to be lynched and a powerless, shocked, enraged, but unable-to-intervene family pondering their situation. O'Neill's "In Georgia" heading referenced the one-a-month lynching in that state between 1890 and 1900.[22] The cartoon is strong stuff. But the gag, and there is a gag, is that slavery offered better protection than freedom. Such a judgment fit the sort of racist discourse that slavery was better than freedom for African Americans because it protected them from the vicissitudes of the market and among other things, as in this case, mob violence. Daina Ramey Berry has shown just how contemptuous this argument about value is in that the monetary value placed on slaves in a process of commodification devalued their existence as humans.[23] Reading this cartoon in the context of O'Neill's other work, then, is important. As laudable as being anti-lynching might have been (although what sort of a person is pro-lynching?), the imagery used, the gag about value, and the language in which it is expressed do not lend themselves to seeing O'Neill as challenging the dominant discourse of race in the United States. In short, O'Neill was not subverting, but rather circulating, tropes, as were her fellow cartoonists at *Puck*.

There are at least two instances that show a clear link between an O'Neill cartoon that used racial typographies and the work of another artist, and this helps us see the immediate social conditions under which O'Neill created her cartoons. This comparison shows that rather than subverting conventions, she was willfully and joyfully engaging in them and taking delight as a professional cartoonist in matching her male contemporaries. A John Harmon Cassel cartoon published in *Puck*, April 17, 1901, deployed racial stereotypes. Under the heading "A Provisional Fiancée," Cassel depicted a well-dressed African American man, Mr. Johnson, on bended knee proclaiming to a woman on a chaise lounge, "I adoah you, Miss Phoebe! Only name de day!" to which she replies, "How will de day you strike a stiddy job suit?" O'Neill's cartoon in *Puck* the following week, April 24, 1901, worked with this worn path of racist humor. Her cartoon "His Limited Provisioning Capacity" suggested that Miss Smallwage could not marry Mr. N Ervate because all he was good for was providing chickens, which carried an implication that the well-dressed African American man holding a banjo in the cartoon was a chicken thief. These two cartoons that work the same trope suggest too an interplay between the different cartoonists working for *Puck*. That the lazy African American gag at the core of both cartoons also revolved around workings of the word "provision" raises the possibility that the cartoonists were in dialogue with each other. If they did not bounce ideas off each other directly, then they at least found inspiration in others' cartoons and perhaps a desire to top their humor. The larger racist trope at play here was the shiftless and sexually profligate African American man, and a May 15, 1901, Louis Dalrymple piece in *Puck* expressed this broadly. His cartoon has one African American woman ask another why she married a homely man, and the reply is because he would stay at home rather than "kite aroun.'" Dalrymple, who was to die five years later from syphilis-induced paresis and was no doubt quite adept at kiting around himself, was not so much depicting the moral superiority of women in this cartoon but rather, like O'Neill, working a trope.[24]

A second instance of O'Neill responding to another artist's cartoon saw her borrow a theme from the Australian-born artist Frank Nankivell. Although it was only around 1907 that Nankivell and O'Neill had studios opposite each other in the same building on South Washington Square, the two shared similarities in style, particularly in Nankivell's color work for *Puck*; and it seems that Nankivell followed O'Neill's work, so the respect may have been mutual.[25] Nankivell's cartoon of May 15, 1901, showed a woman Christian proselytizer in Chinatown addressing a Chinese man in a mandarin jacket. The missionaries in China, she informs him, "are helping your poor countrymen to save their souls." To which he replies, "May be! Only thing poor countrymen have left!" The following week, O'Neill took the missionary gag premise and transformed it into a rather standard joke at the expense of the Black church and ministers. In her May 22, 1901, cartoon, a Sunday-school teacher asks her students why "we send mish'naries to preach to de heathen in foreign lans?" An older, raucous-looking boy answers, "Wal, mah dad says dey does it jes fo' a 'scuse fo' takin' up collections." O'Neill included an African American figure offering an "oh my" and breaking the fourth wall, gazing directly at the reader, which added a dimension of minstrelsy to the cartoon. Nankivell's cartoon at least hinted at the carving up of China by European powers in which the missionaries played a part, perhaps informed by his own complex relationship as a self-conscious white citizen of the British Empire who had lived in Japan.[26] O'Neill's cartoon lacked any broader engagement and suggested that African American churches and missionaries were only in it for the money. Clearly O'Neill's use of race in this cartoon is not linked to pointing out the need for women's suffrage and the inequalities between men and women.

To understand the dimensions of O'Neill's work, it is helpful to examine the types and styles of cartoons she created. I have focused on 1901 for this study partially because of some limitations to my initial research.[27] For 1901, I located ninety-eight cartoons by O'Neill. Of these, twenty-seven cartoons revolved around gendered gags—belles and their beaus—and the like, eight were on race/ethnicity (African Americans, Irish, Jews), and seven worked themes of race and gender together. Of the latter, four of these took the Irish as subjects, with stereotypical subjects like Norah the maid and Pat the policeman. Her cartoons featuring Jews had the sole gag, if it can be called that, that Jews are only interested in money. For instance, her July 17, 1901, cartoon had a daughter playing the piano while a father reading the paper comments to her. Their exchange appeared under the heading, "An Attraction":

> ISAACS. — If I had der time I mighd look into dot Chreestian Zience
> MISS ISAACS. (astounded). — Vof tor?
> ISAACS. — Vell, dere seems to be some moneysh in it.

O'Neill's cartoons of African Americans, then, did not exist in a void, and the context of her other race/ethnic-based cartoons suggests that she simply employed all the available typographies with little or no intention to subvert norms. Examining these O'Neill cartoons allows a closer examination of her use of race in cartoons that dealt with gender relations and some clarity on whether she deployed racist tropes more in support of women's rights or simply as a gag mechanism. In addition to the aforementioned April 24 cartoon, two others focused on African Americans and gender. A November 24 cartoon showed two African American women contemplating Sam Black's lack of luck. The gag was that even a rabbit's foot would not help a man who would not take a job. On the surface, the cartoon could have easily made the same joke about a white man, but of course, the gag lay in the notion of the shiftless African American man, with the added measure of superstition about a rabbit's foot bringing luck. In this mix, then, O'Neill's imagery in her "Carnegiesque" cartoon of June 19 is surprising. Jim Jackson relates to Mose Mossbanker that "Ole man Johnson" would give him his daughter's hand in marriage if he promised "to maintain her afterwards." Mose replies that anyone would think "he was giving away a free public library." But while the visual imagery in this cartoon is a rarity in lacking stereotyped depictions of African American men, their names and the dialogue carry the freight of racism. The notion of "Ole man Johnson" engaging in a philanthropic venture along the lines of the Carnegie Foundation's donation of public libraries lampoons those who are acting above their station. The exchange perhaps calls more attention to this aspect than to a set of gender relations in which a father gave his daughter to a man.

One way to contextualize O'Neill's race cartoons and to ascertain whether her use of racist tropes was in the service of women's rights or simply what they seem on a first take—the use of a tired stereotype of lazy African American men—is to review her cartoons that focused on gender. Some of O'Neill's twenty-one gender-themed cartoons from 1901 that did not feature African Americans addressed issues of the worthiness or unworthiness of men, but much more by implication than in the direct fashion that her use of racial stereotypes allowed. For instance, "The Fiancés," a February 27 cartoon, captioned an illustration of a well-to-do couple on a chaise lounge with,

SHE. — What did Papa say when you asked him, Bertie?
BERTIE. — He said, "This is so sudden."

The caption implies that the young woman's father thinks Bertie not worthy of his daughter, and so he is playing for time to prevent a marriage. While O'Neill's cartoon mocks a man and perhaps even a type—young men looking for a likely marriage prospect, another familiar-enough trope in *Puck* cartoons—it employs none of the visual caricature or the faux patois that featured in O'Neill's race cartoons. It's a refined jibe at male attitudes and expectations.

In another O'Neill cartoon, one from May 29, another couple on a chaise lounge have the following exchange:

HE (fervently). — You are the only girl I have ever loved
SHE. — Ah! What lots of fun you have ahead of you!

O'Neill's target is the naïve and somewhat foppish young man, but in a cartoon that takes aim at the social behavior of the well-to-do class or the well-enough-to-do, the force of the joke relies on the sharpness of the young woman's words. O'Neill worked the not-quite-appropriate fiancé theme in cartoons on July 24, August 21, September 18, October 2, and November 27. Alongside this crop, O'Neill produced cartoons about spinsters (August 28), children replicating adult gender relations (July 7 and September 4), and the care given at Christmas by a woman to purchase something her husband would not want so that it could be returned in exchange for something she desired (December 25).

O'Neill's 1901 output, then, suggests that when it came to gender, she was more interested in the humor to be had about variegated class positions and aspirations, and a range of other gags, than with an inherent disparity between genders demonstrated in lazy attitudes by males. Moreover, she almost exclusively employed the lazy-male gag when using imagery of African Americans, which suggests that her intent in using such imagery was much more focused on racialized notions than on gender disparity. A September 1, 1901, cartoon shows that even when O'Neill was dealing with African American gender relations, her focus was most often on the racist gag to be had, in this case about perceived food preferences. A young woman asks of her male companion,

> Miss Black (archly). — I s'pose you doan' like coquettes
> Mr. Johnson. — Oh, yes, 'deed I do! 'Specially chicking coquettes!

Nonetheless, racial imagery was a relatively small part of O'Neill's work. Of the eight O'Neill cartoons that used racial tropes for the humor, these were split almost evenly with three for African Americans, two apiece for Irish and Jews, and one that featured white people talking about Uncle Tom. For the eight cartoons that dealt with both race and gender, four focused on the Irish and four on African Americans. In 1901, then, only about 7 percent of O'Neill's work employed imagery of African Americans.

The year 1901 is representative for O'Neill's *Puck* cartoons. In her first two full years working for *Puck*, 1898 and 1899, O'Neill produced 73 and 77 cartoons, respectively. In 1900, her most published year, she had 129 appear. Thereafter, her published output was 98 in 1901, 93 in 1902, 77 in 1903, and then dropping off to 50 in 1904 and only 28 in 1905. In 1900, over 16 percent of her cartoons featured African Americans, but such works accounted for only between 6 and 10 percent of her published work between 1901 and 1905. The African American cartoons published in 1900 and between 1902 and 1905 were mostly similar in tone and scope to those from 1901. O'Neill used a familiar set of tropes: the hen/egg-stealing African American male (January 14, 1903), stereotypical eating habits (December 5, 1900), having African Americans address each other using the n-word (November 28, 1900; and May 14, 1902), policy playing (August 22, 1900), superstition (November 28, 1900), the minister and Black Church interested more in raising money than saving souls (February 14, 1900; December 16, 1903; and June 1, 1904), and the lazy African American man (April 25, 1900; June 6, 1900; October 31, 1900; August 6, 1902; March 30, 1904; and June 1, 1904). In the lazy-man cartoon from 1902, a wife is worried at her husband exhausting himself sitting up to three in the morning determining the best horses to wager on at the next day's races, which of course means he has no real employment. In the first from 1904, O'Neill has an African American man collecting laundry, for his wife to do, from a white woman. In answer to her question on whether he wrings the clothing for his wife, Mr. Jackson replies that his wife finds half the pleasure of washing is in using the patent wringer. In the second from 1904, an African American woman tells her beau that he is the laziest human she has set eyes on. He replies, "Ah, quit yo' flattehin', honey: — I'se li'ble teh git de big head an' nebeh be any use." Although not a bastion of her work, when O'Neill drew cartoons using African Americans as the object of her humor, the lazy man was somewhat of a mainstay.

Given O'Neill's experiences with men, and her husbands in particular—the first stole her money to fund a rakish life, and the second used the financial security she provided to quit his job and write novels—it may be that she expanded her understanding of lazy men beyond the racist trope applied to African Americans and started to see it as a more general feature of gendered relations. In any case, on two occasions, O'Neill did come close to using a gag of lazy white men as a form of gendered criticism. In a December 18, 1901, cartoon of children in a classroom, published shortly after O'Neill's first divorce, she employed the following dialogue:

> TEACHER. — Suppose an irresistible force should meet an immovable body, what would happen?
> LITTLE GIRL. — Please, sir, Ma says I mustn't talk about our family affairs.

The joke, and the implied criticism, here is not as obvious as when O'Neill used racist tropes, since it requires an act of interpretation to understand that the immovable object must be the husband and father because it is the child's mother who insists on family matters not being made public.

In one of O'Neill's last cartoons as a staff artist for *Puck*, on October 18, 1905, she depicted two men, one conservative in dress and appearance and the other "artistic," with a bush of hair, in an art gallery. The exchange went,

> THE TRUE ARTIST. — Ah. the heedless folly of those who say that genius is but a capacity for work.
> THE LOYAL FRIEND. — Cheer up, old chap! No one will ever say that yours is that sort of genius.

The foppish nature of the artistic figure, the reverence that the solidly middle-class older couple in the background are giving to the art on the gallery walls, and the admiring sideways glance, directed at the artist, of the couple's twenty-something daughter speak to a set of gender relations in which "genius" men exploit their talent, real or imagined, at the expense of women, often as in O'Neill's case, younger women. This supposition, if true, might add to an understanding of O'Neill's support for the women's suffrage campaign, but it may also well reflect a growing dissatisfaction with her second husband, whom she divorced in 1907. If O'Neill had this capacity for reflection and was able to move beyond a racialized viewpoint, that would nonetheless not change the force and the impact of her cartoons depicting lazy African American men.

An overview of O'Neill's cartoon work suggests that she did not have a particular penchant for racial tropes but deployed them just as much as other professional cartoonists of the era. She was no better, if no worse, than her contemporaries on this matter. To single out O'Neill for attention when examining racist tropes might seem harsh since many of the other cartoonists at *Puck*, and indeed in the other humor magazines and emerging funnies sections of newspapers, were equally adept at such racial imagery. But few of these had the range and reach of O'Neill. Her career might not have received the attention she deserves, but she was, as Richard Graham and Colin Beineke have argued, easily the equal of Richard Outcault, whose Yellow Kid and Buster Brown have brought him much attention as the key progenitor of the American comic strip.[28] O'Neill was not simply a great woman cartoonist; she was one of the finest and most important cartoonists of her day. Not only does her work thus deserve more attention, but O'Neill also requires fuller examination and analysis as an artist who shaped the form of cartoons and comics in the United States. And in such an examination, it is important to pay attention to the full dimension of her work, and indeed the full dimension of the form, and acknowledge its implication and imbrication with the shaping and dissemination of racist tropes.

Notes

1   Norman Rockwell Museum, "Rose O'Neill."
2   Solomon, "Prolific Illustrator behind Kewpies."
3   Only one scholarly book is devoted to O'Neill: Shelley Armitage, *Kewpies and Beyond: The World of Rose O'Neill*. Trina Robbins discusses some of O'Neill's work in *Pretty in Ink: North American Women Cartoonists, 1896–2013*, and there is a short popular illustrated biography by Linda Brewster, *Rose O'Neill: The Girl Who Loved to Draw*.
4   Solomon, "Prolific Illustrator."

5   Gordon, "Rose O'Neill's Kewpies and Early Transmedia Practices," 79.
6   Armitage (*Kewpies and Beyond*, 76) estimated five hundred or so. My count is from reviewing all issues of *Puck* in these years.
7   O'Neill and Formanek-Brunell, *Story of Rose O'Neill*, 88.
8   Armitage, *Kewpies and Beyond*, 73–86.
9   *Plessy v. Ferguson*, 163 U.S. 537 (1896).
10 Carpio, *Laughing Fit to Kill*, 3–4.
11 Strasser, *Satisfaction Guaranteed*, 8–9; Mehaffy, "Advertising Race/Raceing Advertising"; Saguisag, *Incorrigibles and Innocents*.
12 Armitage discusses this comic (*Kewpies and Beyond*, 122–123), but her description of it is inaccurate. She suggests, for instance, that the comic includes a Black Kewpie. It does not.
13 Theriault, *With Kewpish Love*, 57; Qureshi, "Displaying Sara Baartman."
14 Useful works on *Puck* include West, *Satire on Stone*; Kahn et al., *What Fools These Mortals Be!*
15 Armitage, *Kewpies and Beyond*, 10.
16 Armitage, 83.
17 Armitage, 82, 86.
18 Wanzo, *Content of Our Caricature*.
19 For accounts of minstrelsy, see Toll, *Blacking Up*; Boskin, *Sambo*; Lott, *Love and Theft*; and Bogle, *Toms, Coons, Mulattoes, Mammies, Bucks*.
20 Just how familiar? Nicholas Sammond shows that animated characters such as Mickey Mouse are not simply drawn from minstrelsy but are indeed minstrelsy. See Sammond, *Birth of an Industry*. See also chapter 2 of this volume, by Sammond.
21 Laubrock, Hohenstein, Kümmerer, "Attention to Comics"; and Kirtley et al., "Reading Words and Images."
22 Tolnay and Beck, "Lynching."
23 Berry, *Price for Their Pound of Flesh*, 27–28.
24 "Obituary: Louis Dalrymple," *New-York Tribune*, December 29, 1905.
25 Frank A. Nankivell, "A Bowl of Rice and Other Grains," 239, cited in Stewart, "Contextualizing Nankivell."
26 Stewart, "Frank A. Nankivell's Japan: From Means to Marker," 51–72.
27 In 2020 and 2021, because of the global pandemic, I was unfortunately limited to the issues of *Puck* available online through the Hathi Trust in researching this chapter. The years 1897–1900 and a good part of 1902–1905 were unavailable. Fortunately, most of 1901 was available. In early 2022, I discovered the PDF versions of the microfilmed *Puck* that archive.org put online in August 2021. Consequently, I was able to examine a total of 627 of O'Neill's cartoons from 1897 to 1905, up from an initial 190.
28 Graham and Beineke, "In Love with Magic and Monsters."

2

The Passing Fancies of *Krazy Kat*

●●●●●●●●●●●●●

NICHOLAS SAMMOND

> What it means to be a Negro in this country is that you represent, you are the receptacle of and the vehicle of, all the pain, disaster, sorrow which white Americans think they can escape. This is what is really meant by "keeping the Negro in his place."
>
> **JAMES BALDWIN**, "The White Problem" (1968)

Baldwin's is a real description of a fantastic relation.[1] This is an essay about animation and cartoons. It is also about the misspoken, the misheard, and the misinterpreted in and through the Black/white binary in the United States. It is about the tensions between identification and appropriation, empathy and complicity, celebration and co-optation, community and nation. You know, small things. More to the point, this essay closely reads different iterations of George Herriman's *Krazy Kat*, by Herriman himself and by a succession of animation producers, comparing how they relate to and interpret the racial formations that circulated around and through Herriman's life and work.[2]

Unlike much other recent work that has examined Herriman's cartoons through the lens of his blackness and his denial of the same, I am not interested in engaging in a symptomatic reading of either the man or the Kat. Rather, I want to question that move to the symptomatic, the need to impose order and meaning on the man and his work—an impulse that is of a piece with the practices of racial taxonomy. Indeed, one can find in Herriman a usefully distorting mirror to the Black/white binary—in his early history, his passing as white, and in his expressions of fantastic alterity in *Krazy Kat*. Rather than name the effect of his passing on his most famous and durable creation or read that creation for clues as to how he understood that act of passing—with the goal of assigning a clear and stable meaning to either—I choose to maintain the indeterminacy that describes Herriman's racial history, which finds its articulation in the denizens of Coconino County, as a means of meditating on the weight placed on the binary in the name of faith, clarity, honesty, and other related virtues. Like Gayle Wald, I am concerned with "how passing narratives produce the sense of an ending or narrative resolution in the context of the contradictions that the subject-who-passes must inevitably confront in appropriating that stability on which the fluidity of 'race' depends."[3]

At the same time, a reading of Herriman's passing in relation to the (racialized) imaginary of *Krazy Kat* cannot help but confront the very real and substantial effects of the binary on the lives of Black people in the United States. As Rebecca Wanzo, the most astute and nuanced reader of Herriman and *Krazy Kat* to date, has asked about the social and visual discourses within which Herriman and other Black artists of the twentieth century worked, "what happens if we understand some African American producers, and specifically black cartoonists, as crafting a complex, aesthetic reaction to visual attacks on black citizenship through participation in a tradition of racist caricature?"[4] In some instances, as in the revolutionary propaganda of the Black Panther Emory Douglas, that reaction has involved the subtle reappropriation and revision of racist caricature; in others, such as in the work of Charles White, it involved countering those caricatures with images of pride and uplift.[5] Herriman, in his own life and on the page, inflected racist caricatures through the visual and verbal idioms of blackface minstrelsy. Whether he did so to facilitate his passing or as a means of critiquing the racial binary is the stuff of symptomatic reading—of a compulsive need for clarity. But Herriman eschewed narrow legibility, and in that spirit this essay favors instead the uncertainty that comes from and with allowing for more than the binary of yes or no, Black or white.[6]

It is now well accepted that George Herriman was born Black (or, more specifically, "colored") and died white. Yet I am not so much interested in rooting out secret clues to Herriman's identity in his comics and cartoons as I am in reflecting on how the abusive and loving relationship between Krazy Kat—whose gender and race were mutable—and the object of her ardent affection, Ignatz Mouse, might serve as a useful metaphor for a life lived in passing—"metaphor" itself connoting an oscillating passage between two signifiers.

I hope to find in Coconino County a psychic landscape of racial formation and a celebration of semiotic uncertainty—especially the joyful uncertainty of language—as a quiet rebellion against the normative and the binary. In doing so, I am treading on the ground of speculative history, to create what Saidiya Hartman has described as "a fugitive text of the wayward . . . marked by the errantry it describes," reading Krazy Kat as Herriman's attempt to imagine "life reconstructed along radically different lines."[7] What I will find, however, are the inevitable limitations that flow from substituting one indexical gesture for another, as if the act of pointing were not always a bit of legerdemain, of misdirection. What is significant and important about *Krazy Kat* in this instance is its balance between the orderly and predictable—the brick, the head, the love, over and over—and the chaotic and unpredictable—the language, the landscape.

To begin, I'd like to engage in a brief historical reflection on the term that some people might have used to describe Herriman in his prime, had they known he was Black: "mulatto." A meditation on this term, Oscar Micheaux's 1920 film *The Symbol of the Unconquered: The Story of the Ku Klux Klan*, was a rejoinder to D. W. Griffith's noxious 1915 offering *The Birth of a Nation*. In what remains of *Symbol*, Micheaux converts Griffith's fantasy of the Klan as noble defenders of white virtue by making them into a scruffy band of thieves, con men, and vagabonds determined to steal land and wealth from honest Black folk. Yet the two films do have one thing in common: a villain who is called a mulatto. (In Micheaux's case, an intertitle calls him an "odious mulatto.") For Griffith, mixing white and Black blood produced the insane corruption of the villain Silas Lynch and his co-conspirator Lydia Brown, while Micheaux's Driscoll, who passes as white, is tortured and corrupted by internalized racism. In Griffith's interpretation of the insidious logic of the one-drop rule, somehow the admixture of two races necessarily amplifies the worst innate qualities of both. In Micheaux's rejoinder, the choice to pass as white necessitates the internalization of racial hierarchy, which is maddening. Yet either way, the tragic figure of the passing mulatto, so well established as a stereotype by the early twentieth century, inevitably signaled derangement by racial formation. As Susan Gubar puts it, "Encased inside a hostile white culture, most passers are displayed feeling cut off from a nurturing black world. Making themselves white (though born black), they become 'tragic mulattoes,' suffering psychological and cultural splitting that reduces them to self-destructive liminality. Since whiteness ends up bringing them nothing but ontological insecurity, they ultimately experience their racechange as a kind of life-in-death."[8]

By all accounts (especially the recent meticulously detailed biography by Michael Tisserand), Herriman quite enjoyed his life and experienced no outward signs of derangement from passing as white. (He did die at the young age of sixty-three, from cirrhosis of the liver, ostensibly unrelated to alcohol.) Tisserand informs us that George Herriman III was born in New Orleans in 1880. His parents, George and Mabel, were Creoles and were registered in the census as "colored," a shorthand category between Black and white in New Orleans's detailed racial hierarchy. Elizabeth Fussell describes the city's complex and changing racial taxonomy in the nineteenth century in diasporic terms, noting that after the 1809 revolution in Haiti, "the Saint Domingue refugees included French colonists, free Creoles of color, and ex-slaves, many of whom were returned to bondage after setting foot on American shores. . . . Their arrival consolidated the tripartite racial order. The 1810 census records the city's population as about one-third white, one-third free people of color, and one-third African slaves, who constituted the bottom of the labor market and the socioeconomic ladder."[9] Thus, chattel slavery and a thriving middle class—both white and of color—coexisted in New Orleans until the collapse of Reconstruction. Herriman would have been about twelve years old when the "octoroon" Homer Plessy boarded a whites-only railway car in New Orleans, setting in motion a legal case that cared little for the finer details of New Orleans racial taxonomy and that enshrined in law for the next half century the principle of "separate but equal" and codified and justified Jim Crow.[10]

That ruling was handed down in 1896, ten years before Herriman began working for William Randolph Hearst. Herriman got his start with Joseph Pulitzer and after a few years moved to the Hearst organization, for which he worked for the rest of his life. His early work for Hearst often involved illustrating the newspapers' sports pages. He specialized in boxing, so of course he drew cartoons that covered the glorious and notorious career of Jack Johnson, including his easy defeat of the "Great White Hope," Jim Jeffries, in 1910. As Jeet Heer points out in his fine introduction to *Krazy & Ignatz* (2005), "Herriman's early work reflected the larger trend in both cartooning and American racial politics. . . . During the heyday of Jim Crow, white cartoonists almost invariably portrayed African Americans as dim-witted, thick lipped, and childlike."[11]

That racist caricature circulated in and through blackface minstrelsy, a performance form on the wane but still quite popular in the early twentieth century. Krazy Kat, a creature unmoored by/in gender, participated in the blackface masquerade that was early twentieth-century comics and animation, yet in a register quite distinct from, say, his fellow feline Felix. Krazy embodied minstrelsy's tensions and contradictions, embodying a morphing derangement of the distinct racial formations she inhabited during her long career. Her shifts in register are not merely a symptom of Herriman's displaced anxiety around passing, nor a simple representation of his lifelong act. Rather, I choose to see in Krazy's morphing personae, and in Herriman's self-representation alongside her, a pas de deux, a vaudevillian two-act of anxiety and desire—performed not only by Herriman but by everyone who interacted with the two of them—by all of us. That bittersweet modality was best represented by the Black blackface minstrelsy practiced by artists such as Bert Williams or Miller and Lyles, who deftly deformed vicious stereotypes such that their meaning was destabilized, decoded, and parodied for their cruel inanity.

That artistry was not evident, though, in how Herriman depicted Johnson and the Canadian boxer Sam Langford. He drew them as minstrels, but with no hint of implicit critique. At the onset of his career, he seemed quite willing to participate in the more brutal registers of racial caricature. As Tisserand recounts in detail, over the course of several chapters, Herriman spent nearly ten years trying to break into the daily and weekly newspaper comics sections with one strip after another, each of which lasted from a few weeks to a few months before being canceled. His first continuing character was Musical Mose (1902), a Black musician/minstrel who tries to pass and is beaten for it at the end of every strip. While it would be tempting to see Herriman in Mose, Wanzo cautions against reading the character as a stand-in for the cartoonist:

But how could one *not* interpret the black artist, accepted and entertaining until discovered, beaten and brutalized for the sin of passing, as evocative of the risks in Herriman's life . . . ? What, then, would we make of the traditional racist caricature of Mose's phenotype if he is Herriman's double? Is it a representation of how he might be seen? Is Mose an example . . . of an idea of blackness far from how Herriman identified himself? Is Mose a kind of abject black subject he would never be? Reading Herriman as "black" could thus result in an antiracist reading, or it could mean that we have even more reason to imagine a self-hating assimilationist ideology captured in these few frames.[12]

In the meantime, Herriman continued his sports cartooning, both in Los Angeles and in New York, and in 1907 he illustrated the program for a minstrel show put on by his employer, the *Los Angeles Examiner*.[13] (Herriman also blacked up himself in 1910, for a benefit minstrel show.) Krazy Kat or her ancestor appeared first in 1909 in another short-lived comic called *Mary's Home from College* (1909); he turned up again later that year in another early Herriman effort, *Gooseberry Sprig* (1909–1910). During 1911, Krazy appeared occasionally at the bottom of a strip first called *The Family Upstairs* and then *The Dingbat Family* (1910–1916), then she finally got her own strip. In August of that year, Ignatz heaved his first brick at Krazy. Yet it was only in 1913 that *Krazy Kat* became Herriman's main product and in 1916 that Hearst began producing animated *Krazy Kat* film shorts.

To properly approach the complex operations of race that circulate in and through Krazy Kat, a distinction must be made between how Herriman portrayed her on the page and how white animators translated her for the screen. This involves parsing several distinct moments in the production, circulation, and reception of the Krazy Kat franchise. The first moment runs from the beginning of the strip in 1913 until 1916, when the Kat began appearing in animated cartoons. The second moment runs from 1916 to 1925, when cartoons based on the strip were produced by Hearst-Vitagraph and Hearst's International Film Service, then by John and Margaret Bray, then by Margaret Winkler and Charles Mintz. The third runs from 1926 to 1944, when animator Bill Nolan put out Krazy Kat cartoons for Winkler and Mintz (1925–1939); it also comprises Hearst's move to color in the Sunday newspaper strips in 1935 and ends with Herriman's untimely death in 1944. This division is important for understanding the difference between Herriman's shifting and subtle uses of blackface minstrelsy on the page, which were quite distinct from the conventions and tropes of blackface in American animation, which were committed to maintaining the racial binary through the violent regulation of the animated minstrel on the big screen.[14]

The life of Krazy Kat, then, begins in 1913, when the strip started its daily run in William Randolph Hearst's *New York Evening Journal*. What had begun as a sidebar gag of a mouse beaning a cat with a stone became in short order the complex interspecies community residing in the arid, dusty landscape of Coconino County, both a fantastic imaginary home and a county in Arizona wherein resides America's greatest metaphor, the Grand Canyon. The canyon itself never makes an appearance in the strip yet is present, perhaps, in its not infrequent gags about echoes. And, although the central motif in *Krazy Kat* is a compulsive and repetitive act of violence—that brick to the head—the general tenor of interaction between the denizens of Coconino County is one of warm camaraderie, tinged with philosophical speculation on the nature of life, both human and otherwise.

Indeed, even if most critical readings of the strip focus on the physical relationship between cat and mouse, what sets the comic apart from most of its contemporaries is the sheer amount of conversation that fills almost every installment. And that conversation is far from pedestrian. As has been noted elsewhere, Herriman's Catholic-school education in New Orleans had steeped him in the classics, and the strip abounds with references to Shakespeare, Plato, Darwin, and Cervantes.[15] Yet more than simply dropping references to great literature, the words spoken in Coconino County are themselves playful, polysemous, and allusive. In this, they echo the complex play with language that marked the nineteenth-century minstrel show, both in the patter between the Interlocutor and Tambo and Bones and in its stump speech, a parody of politicking as it was practiced before radio and television.

There is a signal difference between the arc of that blackface stage performance and the magic that Herriman wrought in Coconino County. Stage minstrels of the nineteenth and twentieth centuries were invariably fantastically black and equally invariably enacted a white fantasy of blackness, a vigorous reinscription of the color line in every performance. Herriman's genius was that he imagined the minstrel's deformation of language, and the rethinking of human relations imagined through that distortion, as still a minstrel act—but one that transited across racial lines. It did not *transcend* race ... there is no doing that ... rather, it bound the denizens of Coconino County in an ongoing rendition of the performance of a delightfully corrupted white fantasy of racial superiority. It wasn't just the characters who could easily be coded as Black who were the minstrels; *everyone* was. We don't know the motivation behind that choice, which perhaps explains critical readings of *Krazy Kat* that remain centered around Herriman's race, identity, and identification. However, delving into what sort of minstrelsy his characters performed, and how it did or did not relate to dominant forms of blackface in the late nineteenth and early twentieth centuries, may produce a compelling speculative reading of *Krazy Kat* as racialized critique.

Blackface minstrelsy is undoubtedly a racial insult, or really the amalgamation of many racial insults into an evening's entertainment, at the great expense of Black people—and, after the Civil War, also of Indigenous people and of any immigrants deemed less than white. But blackface is not singular, either in its history or in its form. The individual performers who claimed to have originated blackface minstrelsy in the 1830s, such as T. D. Rice or G. W. Dixon, often appeared solo—like their blackface descendants on the twentieth-century vaudeville stage—or as part of larger burlesques. By the 1850s–1870s and the heyday of blackface impresarios such as George Christy or Dan Emmett, minstrelsy had grown into an elaborate extravaganza, its centerpiece performances the stump speech, the banter of Tambo and Bones, and the large-cast olio. In the twentieth century, it would find its way onto the screen in movies and cartoons, on radio and on "race records," while lasting on the vaudeville stage into the 1930s. Yet blackface was not the province of white performers alone, and a full accounting of blackface—which never discounts its virulent aggression toward Black people—also requires acknowledging the great Black practitioners of the form and the many singularly important vernacular styles and genres they generated as they bent it to their will, alloying the pain, disgust, and offense of blackface with their own experiences and interpretations. Artists such as Bert Williams and George and Aida Overton Walker used this insult to their advantage, creating immensely popular extravaganzas such as *In Dahomey* (1903), *Abyssinia* (1906), and *Bandanaland* (1907), whose subtle parody of blackface, and of racist caricature more broadly, hinged on double entendre and allusion and which popularized songs such as "Nobody" (1905) and dances such as the Cakewalk (which parodied whites dancing at parties and had been performed during "prize walks," command performances of slaves dancing for the families of their "masters"). Modern tap dance has its origins in the Juba dance and Jump Jim Crow of the nineteenth-century minstrel stage, and the rapid-fire patter and confused misdirection of vaudeville comedians such as Burns and Allen or Abbott and Costello traces back to Tambo and

Bones, as do the great practitioners of indefinite talk such as Miller and Lyles or Scatman Crothers.[16]

One example of this sort of wordplay is the routine "Free Translations," dated December 1850, which offers a lampoon of the nineteenth-century bourgeois notion of "small Latin and less Greek" as markers of a cultivated person:

> A: Well, now, you've been to college two years, I suppos [sic] you can translate Latin some, can't you?
> B: Yes, I can translate anything.
> A: Can you? Well, what does this mean—Poeta nascitur non fit?
> B: Oh! That means, a nasty poet is not fit![17]

(It more properly translates as "a poet is born, not made.") Likewise, a stump speech attributed to J. Martin, delivered in March 1861, makes light of and hints at the tensions of the looming Civil War:

> Look at the patriots ob dis country. Talk 'bout Kossuth and Garibaldi; ain't we got Henry Ward Beecher, Horace Greely, Wendell Phillips, and W. L. Yancey? Talk 'bout Garibaldi consolidatin' Italy. Why dem fellers is goin' to make any quantity of countries out ob dese United States, dem's de fellers dat tinks E Pluribus Unum sounds vulgar, so dey're goin' to changer it to E Unibus Plurium. Dat's what's de matter.... In de year Aunty Dominix, 1776, how was dis country bounded. I'll tell you—it was bounded on de Norf by dat celebrated female Sara-toga.... It was bounded on the de Souf by Gin'ral Jackson and de Cotton Bales. On de East by Moll Pitcher de Salem Witchcraft and de Boston Tea Party. An' on de West by—by—a howlin' wilderness. Now how is it bounded? Its bounded on de Norf by eberytin' dat's good to eat and drink; its bounded on de Souf by Secession; its bounded on de East by New Jersey, Harper's Ferry, and de Great Eastern.... Dat's what's de matter.[18]

(At the time this was performed, all of the men save Beecher were in favor of secession, though of very different political persuasions and beliefs.) In both of these instances, the minstrel's apparent guilelessness, a condition of his ostensible exclusion from polite white society and of his seeming inability to grasp the finer points of language, ideology, social norms, or historical fact, allows him to send up the pretensions of the dominant classes. Yet it also provides a fantastic outsider's view of an emergent history in which he seems an object, rather than a subject. In the white-supremacist imaginary, the blackface minstrel, as stand-in for the chattel slave (or for their northern counterpart, the free but never fully assimilated Black person), embodies the outside: as an object, they are outside the flow of history; paradoxically, their containment on the plantation places them outside free society. They exist on the margins of cognition, speech, and action, which is imagined as a privileged vantage point from which to convert institutional and immediate violence on the Black body into a violence against an oppressive and unquestioning common sense.[19]

None of this is meant to valorize or forgive the racial insult and institutionalized violence of blackface minstrelsy. However, it may provide useful context for Herriman's appearance on the minstrel stage in the early part of his career and perhaps for his love of misdirection, manipulation, and evasion through language. Like many other Black artists in the early twentieth century, he borrowed freely from, and reimagined, white fantasies of Black speech to deform and destabilize language and meaning in Coconino County. That he passed as white while doing so does not detract from this reading of language in *Krazy Kat*; rather, it offers us one avenue for considering the operation of that (suppressed) blackness beyond its visual and iconographic representation on the page or the screen.

For obvious reasons, critiques of blackface minstrelsy have tended to focus on the visuals—grotesque faces, bodies, and costumes. In the case of American animation, silent for its first twenty years, that makes sense. But the tradition of minstrelsy, as much as it was about song and dance, absurd and outsized costumes, and the fantastic deformation of Black bodies, was also about the contortion of the English language. Likewise, there is a profound difference between minstrelsy as it was performed on the stage, in sound recordings, and on the radio and how it appeared in animation: arising in a silent visual medium, the animated minstrel concentrated on physical comedy and later song and dance much more than on *speech*; other blackface minstrels, on the other hand, spoke . . . a lot.

At the center of the whirlwind of words in *Krazy Kat* is, of course, Krazy herself. While quite a few of the other characters in the strip have accents, the cat speaks a peculiar argot that blends words that seem vaguely German or Yiddish with creole slang and idiosyncratic mispronunciations. Regardless, though, of where his voice wanders, Krazy Kat speaks with an innocent enthusiasm for life and an awe and wonder that it has such creatures in it. Of Krazy's word play, Wanzo argues, "Applying a racial identity hermeneutic to this strip, Krazy's interrogation of language reads as an attack on a white and Western logic that orders the world. Their argument is uncommon common sense. Language is a tool used to oppress with categorizations and alleged transparency of meaning. . . . Krazy has a buoyant resistance to violence, rejection, and being misunderstood."[20]

One of many examples of this dense interplay of language and image is a strip from May 1918. A congregation of Coconino County's luminaries troops up an incline toward the Little Green School House on the "Mesa Espiral" (which bears a passing resemblance to Bruegel's rendering of the Tower of Babel; see figure 2.1). There they are to attend a charity gala put on by Joe Stork (elsewhere described by Herriman as a "purveyor of progeny to prince & proletarian").[21] The regulars—Offissa Pupp, Kolin Kelly, and Ignatz Mouse—are joined by dignitaries such as Don Kiyoti and his servant Sancho Pansy (a nod to Cervantes), the Mock Duck (à la Carroll), and Walter Cephas Austridge (Cephas being another name for St. Paul or for a place in Mesopotamia), among others. They have gathered to make a charitable contribution to the adoption of two as-yet-unseen orphans, whom Krazy (late to the party, being too much a plebe to have warranted an invitation) overhears named "North and South." In the next panel, the assembled dignitaries flee, again in single file, as it is revealed that the orphans are skunks—that is, black with a white stripe down the middle. The caption to the final panel, in which Krazy reads a fairy tale to North and South, announces, "And so, Charity, to whom Mammon erects super-temples, finds sanctuary in the heart of the proletariat." In addition to its allusions to Cervantes, the Bible, and *Alice's Adventures in Wonderland*, the strip highlights the quasi-vaudevillian and easygoing interplay of races, cultures, and ethnicities—Irish, Spanish, Mexican, Jewish, Chinese—which also are identified by their status, high and low. North and South are both an admixture of Black and white, equally miscegenated as it were, and they threaten to stink up the joint—striking fear into the hearts of the assembled denizens. Yet Krazy treats them with love and gentle affection in spite of their status as outcasts.

The play with language isn't limited to how the characters speak or describe their world. Some of the shifting signifiers in the strip are the pronouns used to identify Krazy herself. Tisserand offers one classic example: "Kuriosity has led our heroine thus far—but seeing what he sees 'kuriosity' no longer impels her—he is now actuated with a sweltering confusion of benevolence." "Here," Tisserand notes, "Krazy's gender switches no fewer than four times in one sentence."[22] The slipperiness of those indexicals signaled the variable and unstable inflection of the central relationship in *Krazy Kat*. When Krazy was marked as feminine, the love the cat held for the mouse could be read as heterosexual (though cross-species); when both

FIGURE 2.1 Denizens of Coconino County progress in a procession, babbling their way toward the Tower of Babel (aka "La Mesa Espiral").

appeared masculine, it took on a patina of homoeroticism; and in the drift between the two, it hinted at the fluidity of a desire that refused stable definition. On top of that, Ignatz was married and had children, so monogamy was also up for grabs. (This calculus doesn't even take into account Offissa Pup's unrequited love for Krazy.)

Nor were the erotics of that relationship any more straightforward. Remember: the central act that joined Ignatz and Krazy was a brick to the back of the head. And if that weren't enough, that act was misinterpreted every single time: what Ignatz means as an act of violence, Krazy inevitably understands as love's caress. In its compulsive repetition, that gesture could read as sadomasochism.[23] In that Ignatz aims the brick at Krazy's head, it could also be an attempt to convince her that his animus is genuine, to get it through their thick skull. Or it could be the sorry, sad grinding on of domestic violence, the mutual misapprehension of cruelty as loving attention. As an act of repetitive violence always misunderstood as a gesture of love, it is hard not to see the brick as a metaphor for tolerating and rationalizing the violence of white supremacy. Or all of the above. As the artist and filmmaker Arthur Jafa recently put it,

> The cat loves the mouse, the mouse hates the cat.... The dog, Officer Pupp, loves the cat, but the cat can't see him because the cat loves the mouse. And what makes it worse is that the mouse keeps throwing a brick at Krazy Kat's head, which is an act of violence, but the cat sees the violence as an act of love, and so the circle continues. The absurdity of it strikes me as being as good a model of Black love and hate in white society as we've ever seen, a profound and absurd meditation on the thin line between love and hate.[24]

Yet the reading that has most obtained, since Herriman was outed as Black by the sociologist Arthur Asa Berger in 1971, goes beyond this metaphorical take on vexed love in Coconino County. The truism/assumption most often inferred is that the tortured relationship between mouse and cat is an expression of Herriman's anxiety around living and passing in the Black/white binary. Perhaps the most extreme expression of that reading is by Eyal Amirand, in a piece titled "George Herriman's Black Sentence": "The strip returns every day for thirty years to a repetitive plot that is itself about repetition and obsession. Herriman emerges in the strip as one possessed by ideas of an historical and a racial self. He elaborates what amounts to a theory of the necessity of race for narrative, and of narrative for race. There is no narrative without color, for Herriman, because narrative is made of color, of

FIGURE 2.2 Herriman, "Krazy Kat—Dyeing for Attention." In 1931, Krazy Kat's cosmetological race change renders her invisible to their love interest, Ignatz Mouse. (Krazy Kat © 1931 King Features Syndicate, Inc., World Rights Reserved)

figure-and-ground perceptions of color difference."[25] In symptomatic readings of *Krazy Kat*, the slipperiness of gender is overshadowed by instances in which cat and mouse change from black to white, or vice versa, to demonstrate that the strip is deeply concerned with race in Jim Crow America. In one of many gags around passing, Krazy emerges from a beauty parlor as a "blonde," Ignatz ignores them, and Krazy returns to the beauty parlor and becomes a "brunette" to regain the mouse's "affection" (figure 2.2).

In readings such as Amirand's, the symptomatic tendency ends up saying less by saying too much. To say that the strip is concerned with race in every aspect of its being is not only absurdly reductive; by reinscribing the racial binary, such a reading also reinforces common tropes of racial legibility that have been imposed for generations in the Jim Crow United States (and continue to be in the ostensibly post–Jim Crow moment we occupy today). I'd like to suggest that it may be more productive to read *Krazy Kat* as a vernacular expression of the wide range of affects that attended the act/practice of passing in the United States in the early twentieth century. At the end of his otherwise excellent introduction to a collection of *Krazy Kat* strips, Jeet Heer writes, "Despite all the biographical bickering, a few clear statements can be hazarded: George Herriman had African-American ancestors and was aware of this fact. As an adult he adopted different strategies to deal with what his society taught him was an embarrassing ancestry. At times he hid his background and adopted the contempt his white friends had for black people. On the other hand, through his art Herriman tried to grapple with issues of identity and created a playful utopia, where different cultures could meet on equal ground."[26]

While I agree with Heer's description of Coconino County as a "playful utopia," it seems reasonable to point out that what Herriman faced as a man threatened by the one-drop rule was a society in which lynchings were commonplace and were, for many in the white population, a social event from which spectators could walk away with souvenirs that ranged from postcard photographs of the tortured, desecrated bodies of Black people to actual parts of those bodies. Walter White, spokesperson for the NAACP in the 1930s and 1940s, was a light-skinned Black man of roughly the same age as Herriman who had collected pertinent data on forty-one lynchings and eight race riots, including the infamous 1921 riot and Black massacre in Tulsa, Oklahoma. Of that threat, he noted,

> I was a Negro, a human being with an invisible pigmentation which marked me a person to be hunted, hanged, abused, discriminated against, kept in poverty and ignorance, in order that those whose skin was white would have readily at hand a proof of their superiority, a proof patent and inclusive, accessible to the moron and the idiot as well as to the wise man and the genius. No matter how low a white man fell, he could always hold fast to the smug conviction that he was superior to two-thirds of the world's population, for those two thirds were not white.[27]

The 1910s and 1920s, when *Krazy Kat* was in its heyday, were also when most of the statues of the so-called heroes of the Confederacy, which have only recently and finally begun to come down, were erected as a clear designation of public space as white space—Jim Crow set in stone. This was also the historical moment that witnessed the rebirth of the Ku Klux Klan in both the South and the North. To say that in this context Herriman's ancestry was "embarrassing" is a bit of an understatement. And naming that complex racialized ancestry within the Black/white binary also reinscribes his family history as a forced submission to that binary.

In spite of whatever embarrassment Herriman might have felt, the denizens of Coconino County and the gender-bending, racially ambiguous, and semiotically chaotic world they inhabited endured happily on the printed page until the 1940s. The same cannot be said of the second and third versions of the animated *Krazy Kat*, neither of which was long-lived. The years that the cat sashayed on the movie screen describe her gradual shift into a mode of performative and stereotypically reductive blackface more akin to early American animation's inflection of minstrelsy than to the blackface stage spectacles of the late nineteenth and early twentieth centuries. It was a gradual shift rather than an abrupt one because, as others have pointed out, there were already hints of the minstrel in the strip from its inception. Heer claims that "Krazy is not just a cat with black fur but also, in a profound way, an African-American cat. Krazy is revealed to have an uncle named

Tom who lives in [a] cotton (or kotton) patch and sings the blues.... With the introduction of Uncle Tom some features of Krazy look slightly different: we can see for example that his/her banjo is part of the minstrel tradition."[28] It should be noted that Krazy is not African American, even if she is a minstrel. They are a cat. Amirand, in a very long passage that, like Homer's catalogue of ships, counts all the ways that Krazy reads as Black, notes that beyond having an Uncle Tom—who is not Black but an abolitionist fantasy of blackness—the cat also has a relative named Kitty Kottentail, that in one historical fantasy Krazy becomes Kleopatra, and that she at another time refers to herself as a Hottentot. Amirand also tries to make the case that their cousin Katfish is coded as Black, but like her other cousin, Katbird, these figures seem more interesting as indications that catness, or even Krazy Katness, operates across a range of species. One can read this cross-species ambiguity as racial, but it may also read as another example of a shared queerness. As Fiona I. B. Ngô has said of the time, "The mixed-race body evoked the mixed-gender body."[29] Perhaps the inverse is true, that Krazy's mixed-gender body points out of the panel toward Herriman's mixed-race body. Or perhaps not, since indeterminacy may be more useful than a taxonomic fixation.

Yes, Krazy played the banjo and sang the blues. Yet the more substantial way in which *Krazy Kat* invokes stage minstrelsy is through the element with which I began this essay: language—the endless and delightful mangling of the King's English, the blending of other tongues with it. The banter and wordplay in the strip echo the back and forth of Tambo and Bones as they made a fool of the Interlocutor through misdirection and feigned ignorance; they call back to the stump speech, a locus for coded political commentary and a parody of the affectations of the ruling class. It was play with language that was key to the careers of African American blackface minstrels such as Flournoy Miller and Aubrey Lyles or Amon Davis, well into film's sound era, and it was those feats of elocutionary legerdemain that were gradually replaced in the filmic versions of *Krazy Kat* with the slapstick and violent minstrelsy of cartoon blackface. That is, if we accept that Herriman imagined Coconino County as an ongoing minstrel show, then the form that show took, how he seemed to imagine it, and how it related to other forms of performance, both Black and blackface, in the nineteenth and twentieth centuries becomes very important. Noting that "identity indeterminacy can be the site for not just survival but joy," Wanzo suggests a complex and not entirely negative relationship between Herriman passing and the semiotic instability of language in Coconino County.[30] That indeterminacy is the

FIGURE 2.3 The three ages of Krazy Kat on celluloid. From left to right, *Krazy Kat Goes a Wooing* (Hearst, 1916); *The Great Cheese Robbery* (Bray, 1920); *The Minstrel Show* (Columbia, 1932).

exact opposite of the central impulse of animated minstrelsy, which used the reductive force of the racial binary to mobilize violence against (imaginary) Black bodies for the enjoyment of ostensibly white audiences.

Krazy Kat's cinematic life unfolded between 1916 and 1925, when she was animated, first by Hearst-Vitagraph and Hearst's International Film Service (IFS), then by the Brays, then by Margaret Winkler and Charles Mintz. Of all of these, the IFS materials were the truest to the strip, in that they at least featured playful language in speech balloons and Krazy was still crazy for Ignatz. However, they eliminated the strip's complex interplay between characters other than Krazy and Ignatz, and even that relationship gradually declined toward niggling domestic strife and finally into the slapstick violence that was the hallmark of animated minstrelsy.

The Bray years maintain some of the strip's central romantic tension between cat and mouse. But language balloons were largely replaced by intertitles, and the drawing style, particularly when it came to the backgrounds, lost Herriman's signature minimalist technique of creating depth of field by varying character scale in panels largely composed of white space. Increasingly, the backgrounds took on the appearance of vaudeville flats—a look common in cartoons of the early 1920s—and the action devolved even further into barely loving bickering.

The third and final era of the animated *Krazy Kat* began when the animator Bill Nolan took over the cartoon in 1925 and ran to about 1944. Nolan produced the cartoon independently but soon began supplying it to Winkler and Mintz—best known today for stealing Disney's Oswald the Lucky Rabbit, which spurred Disney to create Mickey Mouse. The Winkler/Mintz period, first with Paramount, then with Columbia, was terrible: in the early Winkler years, Krazy became a hybrid of Felix the Cat (complete with magical tail) and Tom from Tom and Jerry, with Ignatz as Jerry, and they fought like Itchy and Scratchy. Nor did they physically look like the cat and mouse of Coconino County: Ignatz resembled Disney's mice in *Alice*

Rattled by Rats (1925) and its Mickey Mouse remake, *When the Cat's Away* (1929). Leonard Maltin quotes the animator Harry Love, who claimed that the *Krazy Kat* animators at this time would watch Disney cartoons to "see what [they] could steal in ideas and everything."[31]

Eventually, in the early sound era, after Mintz moved the cartoon to Columbia, the animators Manny Gould and Ben Harrison took over the franchise. Krazy became rounder and softer, and their gender, which had tilted further toward male under Nolan, was firmly settled as masculine. There are a couple of exceptions in this period, such as *Prosperity Blues* and *Hollywood Goes Krazy*, both from 1932; but even in those, any gender ambiguity involved only what Maltin refers to as a "falsetto voice," and Krazy is paired not with Ignatz but with a girlfriend, a feline version of Minnie Mouse. In short, on-screen Krazy became male and straight.[32]

In these early sound-era cartoons, race remained coded as binary and was represented through minstrelsy, but as song and dance, not as wordplay. The intro music for each *Krazy Kat* episode's title card was Gus Kahn's 1922 "Toot Toot Tootsie Goodbye," which the blackface minstrel Al Jolson had made famous in the Broadway musical *Bombo* (1922) and brought to the screen in *The Jazz Singer* (1927). Beyond that obvious nod to the blackface stage, though, this final cartoon Krazy was firmly in the animated minstrel mode of Felix, Mickey, and Bosko. Nowhere was this truer than in *The Minstrel Show* (1932), in which, as in Disney's *Mickey's Mellerdrammer* (1933), the already implicitly minstrel characters doubled down by blacking up and performing a scaled-down version of a minstrel show's olio. In short, then, while in print Krazy Kat was part of a minstrel show created by a Black man passing as white, the cartoons delivered blackface created by white men for imagined white audiences.

Here it is important to differentiate, as Harvey Young reminds us in *Embodying Black Experience*, between the minstrel's fantastic black body and the real lives and bodies of African Americans, then and now. That fantastic body, Young notes, is "mapped across or internalized within black people" and becomes a justification for the myriad forms of objectification that run the gamut from the erotic to the homicidal.[33] Passing, then, is ineluctably linked to that fantastic black body—one version of which is the minstrel—as an effort to dissolve the link between lived experience and the violent passions that fuel racist caricature.

What remains unknown is how Herriman understood that violence—hence, the symptomatic readings. Yet, as Adrian Piper has noted about the psychic weight of passing in her own family and about the ethics of calling them out, "a person who desires personal and social advantage and acceptance within the white community so much that she is willing to repudiate her family, past, history, and her personal connections within the African American community in order to get them is someone who is already in so much pain that it's just not possible to do something that you know is going to cause her any more."[34] Having been born into one racial taxonomy and, post-*Plessy*, being designated as Black in the formalized binary of Jim Crow, Herriman chose to be white and to draw minstrels—that much we can say—rather than risk falling victim to the stereotypes they represented and the violence of which they were a part (that much we speculate).

Whether Herriman's avatar or not, Krazy Kat did not become a minstrel only when she was turned into a cartoon by white animators. As more than a few people have argued, Wanzo and Tisserand perhaps most recently, Krazy seemed a minstrel from the get-go and certainly not the first that George Herriman had drawn . . . or performed, for that matter. It is the change in the inflection of that minstrelsy that is important here and perhaps its relationship to Herriman's decision to pass as white. What changed was the evacuation—first in the silent era and even when sound was added to the cartoons—of the complex and playful language of the strip, which had some of its roots in blackface minstrelsy. Krazy was a minstrel who was too quickly deprived of their voice. And not only she was silenced; everyone in Coconino County was made speechless in the cartoons, and in that silencing, what was truly radical about Herriman's *Krazy Kat* strip was also stifled.

Here I want to ask, what happens when we consider every single character in Coconino County a minstrel? That is, if we can speculate on the meaning of Herriman's choice to pass and on how it inflects our reading of Krazy, should we not also speculate on the whole of that work, not just its more blatant caricatures? The genius of George Herriman was that he created, in cheap ink on flimsy newsprint on a weekly basis, an ongoing debate about the nature and the practice of human existence, performed by a collection of minstrels, rendered as anthropomorphic animals, and representing in good vaudevillian fashion through their accents a wide range of ethnicities and nationalities. This reading of *Krazy Kat* sees Herriman making an implicit argument that the whole damn "American experiment" was (and is?) a minstrel show, a massive phantasm on the scale of the Grand Canyon, in which we each encounter the contingent nature of our existence, the practice of being in the world with others, as performances of race, of gender, of speciation. It is messy. It sometimes confuses violence for love and love for

FIGURE 2.4 Blackface legend Bert Williams in his rooster costume from the theatrical revue the *Ziegfeld Follies* in 1910. (Photo by White Studio © Billy Rose Theatre Division, The New York Public Library for the Performing Arts)

violence. It is most legible when performed as blackface—and that is part of the point—but is truly *everywhere*.

Blackface arose as a facet of a white-supremacist society and is a comic inflection of the viciousness of racism. Yet to end with that description is to ignore the many ways that the inflection may bend in the service of criticism and commentary. Bert Williams dressed as a crow is a minstrel performance that was degrading to him and to African Americans (figure 2.4). At the same time, because he was a very gifted performer whose work critiqued the form he occupied, it may also stand as an early example of Afro-Surrealism, inflected simultaneously as commentary *and* as minstrelsy, submission and parodic resistance. Williams and his partners, George and Aida Overton Walker, mounted lavish productions around a minstrel fantasy which could be read one way by white audiences and another way by audiences of color. Within a racist art form were the means of critiquing it, of undermining the very taxonomy and rhetoric of racial domination.

George Herriman died in 1944 at the young age of sixty-three. He passed from this world as a white man. When scholars and biographers point first to Herriman's blackness and then immediately to *Krazy Kat*, they risk asking a too-small question, on the order of, "Where can we see evidence of Herriman's blackness in his cartoons?" The drop of blood becomes the drop of ink. What that sort of question so underestimates is that the lens is not the binary, not whether Herriman *was* or *was not* Black. No, what is far more important is the liminality of his passing, the yes-and and neither-nor and their relationship to the ambivalence and indeterminacy that permeates Coconino County. The cartoon remains a fantastic realm of relationality, of the potential instability of meaning and of identity. That more expansive question (yet no less indexical for it) is not only about Herriman's relationship to passing, his fantasies of being both and neither, but also about our desire to read that relationship into submission, to reimpose the one-drop rule on him through his work.

Tisserand is not alone in his need to read *Krazy Kat* symptomatically, to ferret out, in 550 pages, clues that George is Krazy is a Black man covertly commenting on the American Black/white binary. Heer does it. Amirand does it. And quite frankly so am I, right now. I have shifted the terms by trying to prove that Herriman, instead of signaling his blackness, was coyly pointing not only to his race but *also* to his take on early twentieth-century racial formations. I have invoked the trope of passing as if that reading were no less an invitation to the symptomatic, my efforts no less indexical. Like any good scholar, I stand at a distance and critically read not only *Krazy Kat* but Tisserand, Amirand, and Heer for what they tell us about the will to pass and the interdiction against speaking of it in any but the most pejorative terms, as at best a slow-motion tragedy and at worst a betrayal. I have tried to argue that, like many critics, I have an insight into this material that demonstrates something other than my complicity, as if the negation of that complicity were solely mine to achieve. It is as if we were all engaged in a game of hide-and-seek with Herriman's ghost—or more apropos, a game of cat-and-mouse, in which love, hate, and desire are muddled in the stew of racial formation. As Krazy put it, "And so they lived heppy evva efta-wids."

Notes

1. This essay is deeply indebted to Michael Gillespie's *Film Blackness*, especially the chapter "Smiling Faces: *Chameleon Street* and Black Performativity."
2. An earlier version of this essay appeared in the blog *animationstudies 2.0*. Sammond, "Three Lives of Krazy Kat." In keeping with Krazy Kat's fluid gender identity in Herriman's comic strip, the pronouns used to refer to the character in this chapter alternate between she, he, and they.
3. Wald, *Crossing the Line*, 6–7.
4. Wanzo, *Content of Our Caricature*, 22
5. Wanzo, 48.
6. For an earlier speculative take on trying to read the relationship between Herriman's racialization and Krazy Kat's performance of race, see Gordon, *Comic Strips and Consumer Culture*, 75–79.
7. Hartman, *Wayward Lives, Beautiful Experiments*, xiv, 197.
8. Gubar, *Racechanges*, 104.
9. Fussell, "Constructing New Orleans," 848.
10. In January 2022, 125 years after *Plessy v. Ferguson*, Louisiana Governor John Bel Edwards pardoned Homer Plessy. Justice moves at a deliberate and leisurely pace.
11. Heer, "Kolors of Krazy," 10.
12. Wanzo, *Content of Our Caricature*, 34.
13. Tisserand, *Krazy*, 152–172, 189–200.
14. See Sammond, *Birth of an Industry*.
15. Tisserand, *Krazy*, 48–52, 163, 185–186.
16. The poet Paul Laurence Dunbar wrote the book for several of these musicals. See, for instance, D. Brooks, *Bodies in Dissent*; Jayna Brown, *Babylon Girls*; Chude-Sokei, *Last "Darky"*; Knight, *Disintegrating the Musical*.
17. From the journal of George Christy, Special Collections Research Center, University of Chicago. The aphorism is not clearly attributed but is usually credited to the English poet John Clare, who may have meant to paraphrase Aristotle. Lewis Carroll inverted the phrase in his poem "Poeta Fit Non Nascitur."
18. From the journal of George Christy. Henry Ward Beecher was the brother of Harriet Beecher Stowe, author of *Uncle Tom's Cabin* (1852).
19. For a discussion of politics and speech in minstrelsy, see Lott, *Love and Theft*; or Toll, "Social Commentary in Late-Nineteenth-Century White Minstrelsy."
20. Wanzo, *Content of Our Caricature*, 44.
21. Herriman, *Krazy Kat*, June 27, 1936, 91.
22. Tisserand, *Krazy*, 311–312.
23. See Deleuze, *Masochism*, esp. chapter 2.
24. Quoted in Tomkins, "Arthur Jafa's Radical Alienation."
25. Amirand, "George Herriman's Black Sentence," 58.
26. Heer, "Kolors of Krazy," 14.
27. Gubar, *Racechanges*, 14–15. See also Gaines, *Black for a Day*, 27.
28. Heer, "Kolors of Krazy," 12.
29. Ngô, *Imperial Blues*, 209n101.
30. Wanzo, *Content of Our Caricature*, 44.
31. Maltin, *Of Mice and Magic*, 206–207.
32. Maltin, 206–207.
33. H. Young, *Embodying Black Experience*, 7.
34. Piper, "Passing for White, Passing for Black," 246.

3

"How Else Could I Have Created a Black Boy in That Era?"

• • • • • • • • • • • • • •

Racial Caricature and Will Eisner's Legacy

ANDREW J. KUNKA

Ebony White—the Black, caricatured sidekick to Will Eisner's crimefighting hero, the Spirit—debuted in the series's first Sunday section from June 2, 1940, though he is not identified by name. Instead, he is an anonymous cab driver appearing in just one panel. He shows up again, still unnamed, in the second story, but only in the third story is he actually identified by name, when the Spirit comments, "Every time I call a cab, you turn up! Are you the only cabby in town?"[1] From this point on, the Spirit hires Ebony to be his personal cab driver, and soon after, Ebony is identified as the Spirit's "valet."

So Ebony, with his big saucer eyes, giant red clown lips, and minstrel speech, is a fixture of the series from the very start, serving as valet, sidekick, and comic relief. These characteristics align Ebony with the "coon" figure, one of the Black stereotypes that Donald Bogle identifies in Hollywood film. According to Bogle, the primary role for the coon was comic relief, "presenting the Negro as amusement object and black buffoon," often appearing as the "pickaninny" subtype and played in film by Black children. Bogle further identifies the coon as "the most blatantly degrading of all black stereotypes."[2]

Eisner ended the *Spirit* section in 1952, when he shifted his creative focus almost exclusively to *P.S.* magazine, an instructional periodical that he produced for the U.S. Army, and to publishing other educational comics through his company, American Visuals. But fans of the strip retained a nostalgic fondness for it, leading Eisner to pursue reprint opportunities later. Harvey Comics released a two-issue reprint series in 1966.[3] In 1973, Eisner began a long professional relationship with Denis Kitchen, whose Kitchen Sink Press published two more issues of *Spirit* reprints, along with some additional new Spirit stories. These two issues proved successful enough that Eisner took the property to Warren Publishing, which was known for producing black-and-white horror and science fiction comics like *Creepy*, *Eerie*, and *Vampirella* in a magazine-sized format that circumvented the restrictions of the Comics Code. Warren published sixteen issues of *The Spirit* magazine and one special between 1974 and 1976, at which point Kitchen Sink took over for an additional twenty-five issues.[4] In 1983, Kitchen Sink switched the reprint series to a standard comic book format that ran for eighty-seven issues until 1992. The goal of this series was to reprint the postwar Spirit stories in color and in chronological order; however, the color printing proved cost-prohibitive, and the series switched to black and white from the twelfth issue on. DC Comics picked up the Spirit license in 2000 and over the next nine years released *Will Eisner's "The Spirit" Archives*, a twenty-six-volume hardcover series containing every *Spirit* section plus additional material.

Though Eisner produced little new Spirit material after 1952, later license holders (Kitchen Sink, DC, and, most recently, Dynamite) published new Spirit comics by various creators. These new stories showed creators wrestling with Eisner's legacy in an attempt to modernize the series. In Darwyn Cooke's *Spirit* series for DC, he kept Ebony White as a young, cab-driving sidekick to the Spirit, but he removed the egregious caricature elements and drew Ebony in the same register as the other characters in the series. Other Spirit creators followed suit. For DC's 2010 *First Wave* series, the writer Brian Azzarello and the artist Rags Morales made Ebony a female sidekick, while the various miniseries published by Dynamite had Ebony as a professional private detective and later successor to the Spirit. Therefore, although Spirit stories have gone in and out of print since their debut in 1940, the series remains relatively vital today. And with it, readers and creators have wrestled with the representation of Ebony White over those eighty years.

Will Eisner died in 2005, at the age of eighty-seven, having seen his early work on *The Spirit* celebrated as groundbreaking comics that expanded the formal possibilities of the medium and influenced generations of creators. Eisner reveled in his role as a comics pioneer, often citing how he had always seen comics as an art form that could break free of the stigma that it was juvenile and subliterate.[5] However, he also experienced strong criticism over the creation of Ebony White and the racism inherent in the character's portrayal. Eisner's responses to this criticism evolved over time but invariably took a defensive posture, with claims that such images were so commonplace in popular culture of the time that he had no real choice in how a young African American boy would be depicted. As he asked in a 1978 cat yronwode interview, "I realize that Ebony was a stereotype because I drew him in caricature—but how else could I have created a black boy in that era, at that time?"[6] Certainly, Eisner was not alone in creating such a racist caricature; in fact, as Rebecca Wanzo notes about the use of racist caricatures in Thomas Nast's political cartoons, "Racist caricature was . . . not a side note to US cartooning's emergence. It was central to it."[7] Therefore, Ebony White is just one part of a long tradition. However, such defenses stand in curious contrast to Eisner's claim to an important historical role as an innovator and experimenter in the comics form: on the one hand, he actively pushes against many comics traditions and conventions; on the other hand, he stands helpless in the face of another. Eisner is defensive because the accusations of racism taint his legacy as an innovator. The comics writer Brian Michael Bendis encapsulates this dichotomy in his foreword for Eisner's *Fagin the Jew*: How could Eisner have created such a racist caricature when "everything about Will and his writing had been progressive and sometimes substantially ahead of its time"?[8] Why are these two roles—comics innovator and retrograde racial caricaturist—seen as incompatible?

Eisner expresses exasperation with questions about Ebony in the 1978 interview, yet he would have thirty-seven more years of interviews in which the topic comes up. Similar answers would be repeated often over those years: he would claim an equal number of complaints and praise from fans; he would cite the popularity of similar racial caricatures at the time, especially *Amos 'n' Andy*; he would explain that comedy often involves stereotyping and laughing at others' foibles, including their informal speech patterns; he would argue that Ebony was a well-rounded, complex character created with tremendous affection, and that set him apart from other racial caricatures that were created to be demeaning; and he would explain that after World War II, the series became much more progressive, with Ebony being phased out in favor of more realistic African American characters, including a detective named Lt. Grey. Others have picked up on Eisner's explanations and accepted them uncritically. For example, in *Black Images in the Comics*, Fredrik Strömberg writes,

> [Ebony] began his career as a traditional Black supporting character and, with his balloon lips and Southern drawl, represented a very conscious use of classical stereotype.... Ebony gradually developed into more than just a humble sidekick, however. A change is especially visible when Eisner returned to the series after his service in World War II; Ebony received a more pronounced and equal role, and new Black characters were introduced to the strip. Among them were detective Lt. Grey, who was drawn in a more realistic way and spoke grammatically correct English, without any trace of Southern dialect.[9]

N. C. Christopher Couch is critical of Ebony's caricatured appearance, but he also cites the same talking points in defense of the character:

> Ebony's appearance and speech patterns were based on the depiction and dialect used by black entertainers in films and by white performers in blackface on the vaudeville stage, but his personality and accomplishments were never those of the demeaning characters who were so often used for comic relief. Ebony was a full and intelligent partner in assisting the Spirit in solving crimes. After the war, Eisner felt even more strongly that African-American characters should not be stereotyped, and Ebony soon gained an even fuller range of professions. ... Eisner also introduced other African-American characters to the feature, characters who had no accents and were professionals, like Lt. Oren Grey, who collaborated with the Spirit on several cases.[10]

Such explanations have become fixed in the history of Eisner's career; however, they are all problematic and, in some cases, do not hold up to close scrutiny and evidence from the comics. Of particular note here, though, is a distinction that Eisner also makes: a distinction between caricatures that are created with some hateful or degrading intent and characters that are created with care and compassion. In this distinction, image attains less importance than authorial intent. This character/caricature distinction pops up frequently in the discourse on Ebony White, especially as a point of contention with readers and fans of *The Spirit* and Eisner in general.

In a 1968 interview with John Benson, Eisner offers what will become a fairly standard answer to questions about Ebony. He explains that "somewhere around 1949," he received two letters on the same day: one a complaint about Ebony from a former school friend who was "shocked and dismayed" at the character, the other from the editor of a Black newspaper in Baltimore "congratulating [him] on the courage ... in showing a character like that." Neither of these letters, however, survives.[11]

Some surviving letters from the early 1940s do indicate that Eisner probably received such mixed messages of support and criticism. In a letter dated October 17, 1941, Eisner responds to praise about Ebony from Charles Fisher, an editor at the *Philadelphia Record*, by thanking the editor in the character's voice: "Golly, dis heah Mist' Fisher sho' done write us a keen article - - - - considerin' the awful po' subject he had to work wif." Late that same month, Eisner received a letter from the office manager at the Register and Tribune Syndicate, which handled the *Spirit* sections: "We had a letter from a youngster in New Jersey saying that he and a group of his friends had formed a club called 'The Ebony's.'"[12] The young man, whose race is unidentified, requests a drawing of Ebony for the club. Then, in mid-November 1941, Eisner had a meeting with Chuck Lounsbury, a newspaper editor who was responding to complaints about Ebony in the *Spirit* daily strip that was running at the time. Lounsbury "established boundaries [and] advised caution on the handling of Ebony."[13] Later letters from that month indicate Lounsbury was satisfied with changes Eisner made to the strip.[14]

Eisner claimed, in a 1965 interview in the *New York Sunday Herald Tribune Magazine* with Marilyn Mercer, that Ebony never received criticism from Black organizations.[15] However, other comics publishers did receive complaints about their racial caricatures, some coming from organizations that specifically targeted comics. For example, in 1945, Fawcett editor William Lieberson dropped Steamboat, a coon stereotype similar to Ebony, from the Captain Marvel comics due to a specific request from an organization named the Youthbuilders. In 1947, Dell Comics dropped Walter Lantz's Li'l Eight Ball feature from *New Funnies* after receiving protests from a group of Black schoolchildren and by the Cultural Division of the National Negro Congress, which also targeted similar characters from other publishers.[16] Therefore, it would seem unlikely that a comic like *The Spirit*, with distribution in over twenty newspapers that amounted to over five million copies per week, did not see similar protests.

When Eisner was drafted in 1942, he turned over *The Spirit* strip to ghostwriters and artists. The artists Lou Fine and Jack Cole are among the most commonly credited during this period, along with the writers Manly Wade Wellman and William Woolfolk. cat yronwode cites Wellman's southern, genteel upbringing as a reason for the lack of sensitivity about Ebony's appearance at this time: "Wellman . . . having been raised in the South with black servants, tended to cast Ebony into the then-traditional 'black' role. His use of the Ebony-scared-of-ghosts motif, for instance, was pure stereotyping."[17] Eisner also later claimed that Lou Fine's depiction of Ebony was problematic, according to Bob Andelman: "Eisner complained about the way Fine drew Ebony, giving him a large ass that wasn't there before. Eisner felt it crossed the line of even acceptable stereotyping for the day."[18] It is curious that the size of Ebony's rear end is the limit that Eisner establishes for offensive racial stereotypes while so many other characteristics get to pass.

Eisner returned from military service late in 1945 and soon went back to work on *The Spirit*. He frequently explained that his experience in the war, seeing the segregation and unfair treatment of African American soldiers, caused him to rethink Ebony White's role in the strip, especially after seeing that his ghostwriters and artists had ramped up the stereotypical depiction of the character. In the February 10, 1946, section, titled "As Ever Orange," Ebony romances a young woman, named "As Ever," for Valentine's Day. Ebony faces competition from a rival suitor, Fraternization H. Shack, captain in the Army Air Corps. "As Ever" rejects Ebony because "he sounds like a Civil War minstrel man." Heartbroken, Ebony decides "to go to school t' git ejakated so's [he] c'n speak wif a No'thern drawl!" (figure 3.1).[19] Ebony then leaves for school, only to be quickly replaced in the following story by the Spirit's new Eskimo sidekick, Blubber. Ebony returns to the series twice while away at school, but in both cases, he tellingly does not speak due to laryngitis. The May 12, 1946, strip—three months after Ebony left for school—features a homecoming party for Ebony, and Blubber returns to his own home in the Arctic, never to be seen again. However, Ebony's dialect and appearance do not seem to be significantly changed here.

Many who write on Eisner cite this particular story as a turning point for Ebony. Robert Greenberger claims that when Ebony returns from school, Eisner, at the very least, adjusts his speech patterns and dialect. Greenberger also writes, "Eisner finally sent the youth off to school in 1946, and Ebony was rarely seen again until years later."[20] However, Ebony remains a regular

FIGURE 3.1 Will Eisner, "As Ever Orange," from the February 10, 1946, *Spirit* section. (Copyright the Will Eisner Estate)

character in the series until the September 18, 1949, story, "Lurid Love," at which point he becomes replaced by the Spirit's new sidekick, Sammy. He then disappears without any explanation until the June 24, 1951, section, "School Is Out," a story focused entirely on Ebony and his friends that was written by Jules Feiffer and drawn by Andre Le Blanc, probably without much input from Eisner at all. From this point on, Ebony stays in the series until it ends in 1952. Therefore, claims that Ebony substantially changes or rarely appears following "As Ever Orange" do not match the facts of the series.

When *The Spirit* briefly returned in 1973 in a short-lived reprint series from Kitchen Sink, Eisner contributed four new, one-page stories to the first issue. Each of these stories seems to be addressing some criticism of the old Spirit stories, like liberal accusations that the Spirit's violence against criminals was authoritarian. One strip features the return of Ebony White, and it uses a strawman to offer complaints about Ebony (figure 3.2). Here, a Black reporter interviews Ebony, accusing the character of "Uncle Tomism" for taking on a secondary, subservient role as the Spirit's partner instead of a stronger, central, leading role that would better serve the cause of raising "black identity." The interview is interrupted by the Spirit, who asks Ebony about the status of an investigation into a drug pusher who has been dealing at local schools. Ebony explains how he single-handedly gathered evidence against the pusher and then captured him. After the explanation, Ebony turns to the reporter and asks him to "repeat the question," while the reporter looks away sheepishly.

The purpose of this strip, then, is to offer proof that Ebony does not warrant the criticism he has received on racial grounds because he is, in fact, a resourceful, independent character who is capable of fighting crime on his own. However, this argument deflects some of the primary problems with the character as a racial caricature, especially his appearance and voice. In fact, for this strip, Eisner has toned down Ebony's dialect considerably from the character's past appearances, leaving out common expressions like "Yassuh, Mist' Spirit," a clear sign of subservience that would actually support the reporter's argument. It also belies the fact that, in most of Ebony's appearances from the *Spirit* section, he is used as comic relief. In addition, the drug dealer that Ebony captures to demonstrate his positive social impact is a criminal type that would not have appeared in the original series, and so this scene presents Ebony in a role that he never had previously.

The one-page comic also makes an argument that Eisner and others would return to in defense of Ebony: that "character" transcends "caricature." In this "character versus caricature" dichotomy, proponents of character prioritize the way a character is written over the way that they are drawn. The character's personality, ethics, and actions should be the primary basis of judgment, whereas the character's image is tied directly to the historical period and culture from which they are created. Late in Eisner's career, he makes this distinction in his introduction to the 2003 graphic novel *Fagin the Jew*, which is an attack on antisemitic stereotypes in literature as filtered through Charles Dickens's character from *Oliver Twist*. Eisner stops short of self-condemnation for the apparent hypocrisy by distinguishing between "'good' stereotype" and "'bad' stereotype." He argues that, in the creation of Ebony White, "intention was the key." Ebony was created with good intentions, relying on "gentle humor that gave warmth" to his stories and on "accepted stereotypical caricatures" like *Amos 'n' Andy*, Stepin Fetchit, and

FIGURE 3.2 Will Eisner, *The Spirit* #1 (January 1973), published by Kitchen Sink Press. (Copyright the Will Eisner Estate)

Rochester. Nonetheless, Eisner does acknowledge, "Since stereotype is an essential tool in the language of graphic storytelling, it is incumbent on cartoonists to recognize its impact on social judgment."[21] The necessity of stereotypes in comic art harks back to an oft-cited point that Eisner espoused in his instructional text *Graphic Storytelling and Visual Narrative*: "Comic book art deals with recognizable reproductions of human conduct. Its drawings are mirror reflection, and depend on the reader's stored memory of experience to visualize an idea or process quickly. This makes necessary the simplification of images into repeatable symbols. Ergo, stereotypes."[22]

Though the first Kitchen Sink reprints only lasted two issues, they were successful enough to show that there was an audience at the time for *The Spirit*. Eisner then made a deal with Warren Publishing to produce magazine-sized, black-and-white reprints for newsstand distribution. In the letter pages of the *Spirit* magazine, however, the debate over Ebony White returned in earnest starting in the fourth issue, with a letter from William Williams, who wrote, "The basis for my complaint is the character Ebony in THE SPIRIT series. I find him *offensive*. His appearance and speech, even in reprint, *cannot* be condoned. . . . I, as a black man, who manage to speak and write English to a fair degree and who does not look like a monkey, must explain this book to my children. And if that is the case, I challenge the appearance of that character in the book as *bigotry*." The editorial response follows many of the typical patterns: Ebony is a product of his time, the character was created with affection and dignity, humor often depends on stereotype, and so on. The response also points out that stereotypes are prevalent in contemporary culture: "True, Ebony is a stereotype and a parody. But no more so than Archie Bunker is of middle-class America, or Desi Arnaz of the Cuban immigrant."[23] Williams returned in the letters page of the following issue, arguing that such a comparison was "a *farce*."[24] Other letters began appearing in support of Ebony and Eisner, including one by an African American reader from Los Angeles named Jim Brown, who says he finds Ebony inoffensive.[25] The controversy continued to stir in subsequent issues, dominating the letters page. The future comics writer Mike W. Barr states that Eisner gave, "for the first time, a Black character a major role in an adventure strip" and that "*Ebony* has always been an individual of great warmth, humanity and courage," comparable to other great literary sidekicks.[26] Warren responded to the controversy by publishing a special "All Ebony Issue" in issue 7, complete with a new cover by Eisner depicting a weeping Ebony rescuing a wounded Spirit.

The stories reprinted in the "All Ebony Issue" paint a narrow picture of the character and are ostensibly meant to support the claims that Ebony is a well-rounded, independent, industrious character. Several of these stories involve Ebony taking on various occupations: private detective ("The Big Sneeze"), bill collector ("Cheap Is Cheap"), veterinarian ("Young Dr.

Ebony"), and explorer ("The Explorer"). Defenders of Ebony's character often cite these occupations as evidence that Ebony was a trailblazing figure, taking on jobs that were otherwise closed to African Americans at the time. However, this trait is the very source of the humor in these stories—the inversion of expectations represented by an uneducated Black youth who could think that he was a doctor, private detective, or Arctic explorer. Ebony does not demonstrate a breaking down of racial barriers; instead, he demonstrates the credibility of those barriers by showing how humorously inept and misguided he is. In "Young Dr. Ebony" (May 29, 1949), a send-up of popular hospital melodramas like the *Young Dr. Kildare* series, Ebony decides to leave crimefighting for a life in the medical profession. The job he gets, though, is as a janitor at a veterinary hospital. "The Explorer" (January 16, 1949) has Ebony once again giving up on crimefighting and heading to the North Pole. While Ebony thinks that he has arrived in the Arctic, he has not left Central City, and what he thinks is the "North Pole" is actually a telephone pole. Again, the humor in the story lies in Ebony's gross misunderstanding and abject failure at these professions, rather than Ebony relying on intelligence and ingenuity to support the Spirit's crimefighting.

Issue 8 includes a long letter from Charles S. Cascone of Orange, New Jersey: "As a black man I cannot *help* but be offended by Ebony. And as a political activist, the sting is all the worse. But Ebony was a product of the times, and that is that." He goes on to argue that Ebony's offensiveness should not be grounds for ending the series, but that does not validate the defenses of the character: "But for God's sake, please stop trying to justify this racist *caricature*."[27] The controversy seems to stop by issue 10.

The defenses of Ebony, including Eisner's own, create an interesting and troubling paradox: an individual creator like Eisner may be hailed as an innovative genius for the characters he creates while being powerless against the zeitgeist for the images that he uses. If he was not innovative in the creation of Ebony, he would have to be innovative in a similar but perhaps better way—hence Eisner's frequent recourse to his creation of Lt. Oren Grey, a well-spoken, nicely dressed Black detective who originally appeared in the first installment of the two-part "Hoagy the Yogi" story (March 16, 1947) and came back almost a year later in "The Return of Roger" (February 29, 1948). As Eisner said in 1986, "It was 1947, the war was over, and people were becoming conscious of what is now called civil rights. I had strong feelings about the matter myself, so I introduced Lt. Grey. As far as I know, he was the first black man in popular fiction who spoke without a Southern drawl, didn't act like Stepin Fetchit, and was a man accepted in the community."[28]

This is incorrect on several levels. For one, Grey would not even be the first character of this kind in comics, let alone all of popular fiction. In comics, there are many examples that fit Eisner's description, coming from both white and Black creators. Balbo, The Boy Magician, whose series ran in Fawcett's *Master Comics* from 1942 to 1944 (most likely created by Bert Christman), partnered with a Black sidekick named John Smith, who resisted all of the Black sidekick stereotypes of the era. Around the same time that Grey appeared in 1947, *All-Negro Comics* was featuring the private detective Ace Harlem.[29] Extending into pulp adventure fiction, in the Street & Smith series *The Avenger*, the hero, Richard Benson, partners with the African American couple Josh and Rosabel Newton, who appear regularly in the series starting in 1939. Josh and Rosabel notably only turn on the stereotypical dialect when going undercover, and it allows them to become invisible to the white criminals they pursue. The same is true for Jericho Druke, a Black member of the Shadow's team of crimefighters in that pulp series. Such claims to Grey's uniqueness present a narrow view and general ignorance of the comics and popular fiction from this period.

In Eisner's commentary on "The Return of Roger," he extends his discussion of Grey's impact on the series: "I guess I was beginning to develop a greater social consciousness, if you will. Grey allowed me to deal with the black community as it should be dealt with. To have a realistic black police officer in 1948 was, as far as I was concerned at the time, something that might be novel. I don't know of anyone who was dealing with that in comics at the time."[30] This narrows the novelty of Grey a bit, from all of popular fiction to just comics, though even that still was not the case. Eisner also says that he considered making Grey a regular partner for the Spirit, but that did not work out in the end. He mentions that the story drew positive responses from readers: "I remember getting some fan mail on this story, commenting favorably. But what do you do with a letter that comes in and says 'It's about time you decided to treat black characters like human beings'? I'd say, 'Well, it *is* about time,' and move on."[31]

The impact of Lt. Grey's appearance in *The Spirit* gets inflated as a counterexample to Ebony and a sign of progress in the series as a whole. Even though Couch claims that Grey "collaborated with the Spirit on several cases," he appears in only two Sunday sections. In "Hoagy," Grey (who is in six panels total) does not team up with the Spirit but instead searches for the missing Ebony while the Spirit separately investigates the death of Skinny Flint. Meanwhile, Ebony is working with Fabulous Frank, a "zip coon" stereotype who serves as Flint's butler. As Jeet Heer points out, the contrast between Grey and Ebony makes Ebony's otherness even more striking: Grey "serves to highlight by comparison that Ebony is a visual alien and a purely comic character. Perhaps the problem was that Grey was too true to his name. He was a gray, colorless character, whereas Ebony was bursting with color, in more ways than one."[32] Therefore, the claims that this story represents a breakthrough in nonstereotyped Black characters is exaggerated. Grey plays a more central role in "The Return of Roger," in which he investigates a missing dog that has ended up in Ebony's possession. He does, however, team up with the Spirit to solve a separate blackmail case.

In addition, some significant revisionism has to occur to argue that Lt. Grey marks a more enlightened and progressive turning point in Eisner's race consciousness. Lt. Grey's first appearance precedes the creation of another recurring character, one that does not get much attention in discussions of Eisner's work. The story "Be Bop" from April 20, 1947, features the overweight jazz trombonist Tailgate Smear and also introduces the tiny piano player and master of the Dozens Teebo, who conveniently fits into Ebony's pocket. Eisner himself found "Be Bop" indefensible. He confessed, "No one in his right mind today [1986] . . . would attempt a story like this, would attempt a characterization of blacks in this fashion. Today it seems very demeaning."[33] Eisner goes on, then, to justify the story in terms of its historical context, once again taking up the defense that it was the context, and not he, that was responsible. Teebo returns, still fitting in Ebony's pocket, a couple of months later in "Circus of Crime" (June 1, 1947).

In the "character versus caricature" debate, caricature is acceptable if the reader can detect some "love" or affection for the character on the part of the creator, but if the character is created out of hate, then the image exacerbates that feeling. This is the argument that Eisner uses to justify the difference between the sort of caricature in his own work and the antisemitic ones he criticizes in *Fagin the Jew*. Though he still defended his creation on those grounds late in his career, his views on the matter were softening. In a 2003 interview, Andrew D. Arnold presses the issue by asking, "The idea of fleshing out another author's character is interesting. I'm wondering how you would feel if somebody wrote a biography of Ebony White?" Eisner responds, "I would deserve that. As a matter of fact that probably would be a very worthwhile idea. I think more, if I were somebody else and were to undertake that, I would probably do something about his psychology. He lives with the Spirit, his engagement was solely tied up with the Spirit and

I would probably touch on the slave mentality that he probably had."[34] This final statement alone contradicts the 1973 comic's claim for Ebony's independence—a sign that Eisner's view of Ebony progressed in some way.

As Charles Johnson notes in his foreword to Strömberg's *Black Images in Comics,* early twentieth-century images of Black characters like Ebony White demonstrate the limitations of white creators' "imagination" and "empathy": they "tell us nothing about black people but *every*thing about what white audiences approved and felt comfortable with in pop culture until the 1950s."[35] Though Ebony disappears along with the Spirit in 1952, just around the time that Johnson cites as the point at which the civil rights movement changed popular acceptance of such caricatures, the response to Ebony's return in reprints from the 1970s on and later assessments of Eisner's career show white audiences continuing to approve and defend such images. This demonstrates just how hard it is to disentangle such problematic images from beloved comics series and creators. Ebony represents the limitations of imagination and empathy for both readers and a creator who could not envision any other options for a Black character in the late 1940s (despite examples of such options being numerous) or who try to defend a racist caricature on the grounds that the image should weigh less in the assessment than the more abstract and subjective qualities of his character and the creator's intent.

Occasionally, the *Spirit* section included a strip that offered instructions on "How to Draw Ebony," inviting readers to participate by drawing their own racial caricature in their own hand, to become accomplices in the choices that Eisner made in depicting the character.[36] Readers had a choice to test their own talents at racial caricature or reject the invitation. Readers are also faced with a choice when confronting Will Eisner's *Spirit* comics today. The final question is, How should Ebony White factor into Will Eisner's legacy? Foremost, the character's racist portrayal is undeniable and indefensible. Racism is not measured on a balance sheet, where the creation of a little-used character like Lt. Grey wipes the slate clean or where the heroic qualities of Ebony's character somehow counterbalance the caricature and stereotypes. As such, acknowledging and identifying this stain is an important and necessary component of Eisner's legacy as a comics creator, whose work remains in print and widely available for readers' assessment, more than eighty years after its creation.

Notes

1. *Will Eisner's "The Spirit" Archives*, vol. 1, 37. Many references to specific Spirit stories come from reprints in *Will Eisner's "The Spirit" Archives* collections published by DC Comics. It is important to acknowledge that these reprints are not always identical to the original published newspaper supplements. For example, they are often recolored or otherwise silently "touched-up" in the production process. Eisner also made changes like redrawing panels for some of the reprints. There has yet to be a thorough documentation of the changes that Eisner made to these strips over the years.
2. Bogle, *Toms, Coons, Mulattoes, Mammies, and Bucks*, 8–9.
3. It is worth noting that Ebony does not appear in any of the Spirit stories reprinted by Harvey.
4. For more on Eisner's business relationships with Kitchen and Warren, see Andelman, *Will Eisner, a Spirited Life*, 183–202; and Schumacher, *Will Eisner*, 165–186.
5. This refrain runs through most interviews with Eisner, as can be seen in those collected in Eisner and Inge, *Will Eisner*.
6. yronwode, "Will Eisner Interview," 76.
7. Wanzo, *Content of Our Caricature*, 7.
8. Bendis, foreword to *Fagin the Jew*, 1.
9. Strömberg, *Black Images in the Comics*, 87.
10. Couch, "Human Spirit," 25.
11. Benson, "Having Something to Say," 19. I searched through the Will Eisner Collection at The Ohio State University's Billy Ireland Cartoon Library and Museum on several occasions looking for these specific letters and could not find them. I would like to thank the staff at the Billy Ireland for their invaluable assistance during my research visits, including Lucy Shelton Caswell, Jenny Robb, Caitlin McGurk, and Susan Liberator.
12. Harriet B. Wetrich to Will Eisner, n.d., Will Eisner Collection, Billy Ireland Cartoon Library & Museum, Ohio State University, Columbus, OH.
13. Will Eisner to Henry Martin, November 12, 1941, Will Eisner Collection.
14. The letter recounting this meeting does not identify specific complaints about Ebony in the daily comic strip. At that point, in mid-November 1941, the daily strip had been running for only a month, and the few Ebony appearances do not seem much different from what we can see in the Sunday sections. However, in a February 1942 Ebony-centric sequence, Ebony branches out on his own to take on the masked identity of "Super-Ebony" and ends up serving as the U.S. aide to King Hamhock III of the Nockney Islands, previously known as the Cannibal Islands. The king has been fighting a rebellion to return the islands to their cannibal roots. The story ends abruptly after only eleven days. The Spirit daily comic strips are reprinted in *Will Eisner's "The Spirit" Archives*, vol. 25.
15. Mercer, "Only Real Middle-Class Crimefighter."
16. Brian Cremins details the Youthbuilders' successful efforts with Steamboat (*Captain Marvel and the Art of Nostalgia*, 98–123). Michael Barrier documents editor Oskar Lebeck's decision about Li'l Eight Ball (*Funnybooks*, 237). Jeet Heer offers the additional example of how, in 1943, the cartoonist Roy Crane and King Features Syndicate received pushback from readers for Black caricatures in the *Buz Sawyer* comic strip ("Comics Chronicles").
17. yronwode, "Central City Zeitgeist."
18. Andelman, *Will Eisner, a Spirited Life*, 82.

19 The February 10, 1946, *Spirit* section is reprinted in *Will Eisner's "The Spirit" Archives*, vol. 12, 51.
20 Greenberger, *Will Eisner*, 61.
21 Eisner, *Fagin the Jew*, 3–4.
22 Eisner, *Graphic Storytelling and Visual Narrative*, 11.
23 W. Williams, "Letter to the Editor" and editorial response, *Spirit* #4, 5.
24 W. Williams, "Letter to the Editor," *Spirit* #5, 5.
25 Jim Brown, "Letter to the Editor," 5.
26 Barr, "Letter to the Editor," 5.
27 Cascone, "Letter to the Editor," 5.
28 Schreiner, "Stage Settings," *Spirit* #15, inside back cover.
29 See also the numerous comic strips created by African American cartoonists discussed in other chapters of this collection.
30 Schreiner, "Stage Settings," *Spirit* #28, inside front cover.
31 Schreiner, 16.
32 Heer, "Comics Chronicles."
33 Schreiner, "Stage Settings," *Spirit* #17, inside front cover.
34 Arnold, "Never Too Late."
35 C. Johnson, foreword to *Black Images in Comics*, 13.
36 The "How to Draw Ebony" strip was used as a filler for *Spirit* sections that were distributed at the larger, tabloid size, as was the case with the *Philadelphia Record*. *Spirit* sections were normally standard comic book size for the era. The larger-format inserts required additional artwork and material to fill otherwise-blank space. The "How to Draw Ebony" strip was reprinted on page 125 of *Will Eisner's "The Spirit" Archives*, vol. 14. Thanks to Denis Kitchen for providing information on the different formats for *Spirit* sections.

Part II

**Formal Innovation
and Aesthetic Range**

● ● ● ● ● ● ● ● ● ● ● ● ●

Desegregating Black Art Genealogies

● ● ● ● ● ● ● ● ● ● ● ● ● ●

An Invitation

REBECCA WANZO

In 1926, W.E.B. Du Bois published "Criteria of Negro Art," in *The Crisis*, in which he claimed, "All Art is propaganda and ever must be, despite the wailing of the purists. I stand in utter shamelessness and say that whatever art I have for writing has been used always for propaganda for gaining the right of black folk to love and enjoy. I do not care a damn for any art that is not used for propaganda. But I do care when propaganda is confined to one side while the other is stripped and silent."[1] Du Bois's investment in art was about both showing the aesthetic capabilities of Black artists and countering white propaganda about Black people circulated through racist caricature. Alain Locke's "Art or Propaganda?" was a response to Du Bois, in which he argued that propaganda's "besetting sin" is monotony and that it "perpetuates the position of group inferiority even in crying out against it."[2] Many scholars have explored this conflict by questioning not only what places the "Black" in Black art but the criteria we use to define art at all. "It's not art" is often used either to dismiss creative works or as a disclaimer when expressing enjoyment of them and thus results in genealogies that not only devalue some creators but risk overlooking connections that can help us understand art traditions. The problem of drawing firm distinctions between propaganda and art is placed in stark relief when we consider a set of Black artists who were shaped by the Harlem arts community in the 1920s and 1930s and created editorial cartoons, a creative practice often not described as having the aesthetic value of art that graces the walls of galleries and museums.

A number of African Americans best known as painters and muralists also were cartoonists early in their career. These artists include Charles Alston (1907–1977), who produced a number of cartoons for the Office of War Information during World War II. His cousin by marriage, Romare Bearden (1911–1988), would become one of the most prolific and well-known African American artists of the twentieth century and drew editorial cartoons for the *Baltimore Afro-American*. Charles White (1918–1979) was also part of this New York Black art circle, crafting political cartoons for leftist publications. He became one of the most prominent social realist artists in the middle of the twentieth century. Robert S. Pious (1909–1983) was never as celebrated as these peers and may be best known for a painting of Joe Louis and a poster for the American Negro Exposition in Chicago in 1940. However, his editorial cartooning may be some of his most interesting work.

Critics tend to treat the cartoons of White, Bearden, and Alston as part of a commercial phase and separate from their other work. Bearden himself thought that cartooning would "hurt" his painting, suggesting that editorial cartooning was something that needed to be abandoned if he were to become a better artist.[3] And White agreed with critics who devalued his satirical and propagandistic work as a career "misstep."[4] Excluding these artists' cartoons in retrospectives or rigorous discussions of phases of their art careers obscures art genealogies and perpetuates a line between cartooning or comics and "art" not only in discussions of their work but also in discussions of art history. I thus wish to rescue cartoons not only from critics who devalue these works but also from the devaluation practiced by some of the artists themselves.

This essay is thus a supplement but also a response to Bart Beaty's *Comics versus Art*, which challenges a tendency in North American comics to treat close reading and other kinds of methodologies derived from literary studies as the primary approaches to comics and cartoon art. Beaty explores various reasons that critics such as Thierry Groensteen have given for the artistic devaluation of comics—such as the belief that comics and cartoon art are infantile and the association with caricature as "one of the most degraded branches of the visual arts."[5] However, if we apply what I have termed an "identity hermeneutic" not only to reading these artworks but to the split between comics and art, a focus on the Black comics tradition places a new lens on the divide.[6] While caricature has been derided (even though artists such as Honoré Daumier and William Hogarth are treated as important artists), the dismissals of caricature take on a different resonance with the Black art tradition, given the ways in which racist caricature has specifically been used against Black people. Moreover, the splits between "high art" and commercial artwork—which is the phrase I use to designate work for hire, such as editorial cartoons, illustrations, and comic books—can be interpreted differently when propaganda becomes part of debate.

The claim that art is not Black if it is not political or understood transparently as about protest or uplift has its roots in the disagreement between Du Bois and Locke and also can be seen in what is known as the "Hurston-Wright" debate, the Black Arts Movement, and conversations about "post-Black" art.[7] We can see aesthetic connections between various kinds of Black cultural productions when we let go of such categorizations. For example, finding the "Black" in abstraction has sometimes been an issue because of a belief in the importance of realism and representational aesthetics in Black art projects. But a few artists who began as cartoonists turned to abstraction, and there is arguably a sensibility that links the editorial cartoon—the most indexical of art forms—and abstraction. Phillip Brian Harper's description of abstract art offers a generative starting place to think about bridges between such seemingly separate aesthetic practices. He writes that abstract art "emphasizes its own distance from reality by calling attention to its constructed or artificial character—even if it also enacts real-world reference—rather than striving to dissemble that constructedness in the service of the maximum verisimilitude so highly prized within the realist framework."[8] While he goes on to say that abstraction disrupts "the easy correspondence between itself and its evident referent," something editorial cartoons do not do, his other arguments about the work of abstraction can apply to cartooning and should prompt a consideration of the aesthetic connections between both modes of art production.[9]

Just as scholars of African American art and visual culture often give short shrift to cartooning, scholars of Black comics often ignore editorial cartooning. This division is about a field-specific emphasis on making the case for sequential art as a separate medium, which ignores the single-panel works considered important in the history of comics.[10] Cartoonists may do editorial cartoons, comic strips, advertisements, illustrations, and "high art," and critics and artists often treat the segmented labor as common to the art gig economy and do not necessarily draw linkages between very different work. This essay, however, is an invitation to push against artistic silos that limit the frameworks through which we interpret Black liberatory aesthetic practice, which I have described elsewhere as "a response to imperialist aesthetics that construct notions of not only alterity and the beautiful, but ideal political subjects."[11] I invite scholars to connect artists' editorial cartoons to later work and also to broader aesthetic sensibilities that have informed African American art production in order to expand understandings of Black art history and threads that connect various traditions.

One of the questions that emerges in drawing links between commercial work and the more respected phases of artists' careers is the question of influence. Black aesthetics are shaped by wide-ranging artists of various nationalities and schools. Romare Bearden is illustrative of this point. The range of his influences can be traced through various phases of his career as a cartoonist, as an abstract expressionist, and in the work for which he was arguably best known, his collages.

Bearden was critical of the suggestion that what we should characterize as African American art is an adherence to African traditions, given the ways in which the diaspora and hybridity shaped African American experience.[12] Knowing the diversity of the Black experience and aesthetic practices, Bearden took issue with much of what was supported as "Negro Art" but believed in doing political work that spoke to the Black experience. He also believed that depicting African Americans was compatible with representing "universal" human experience.[13] What might link various modes of his aesthetic production is the fact that he very much appreciated that "Impressionists, the Post-Impressionists, the Cubists, the Futurists, and hosts of other movements" were "commendable in the fact that they substituted for mere photographic realism a search for inner truths."[14] Cartoon aesthetics are criticized for exaggeration and a distance from realism, and at the same time, figurative realism was disfavored by many critics in the twentieth century. Thus, we can see that two characteristics common in editorial cartoon work of the time might also carry through various kinds of work Bearden might do in his career: representational practices that gesture to the universal and an embrace of nonrealist aesthetics.

Bearden's early training in political art was shaped by his work with George Grosz at the Art Students League in New York in the early 1930s. Grosz was an artist who "considered himself a propagandist of the social revolution."[15] Grosz would later say that he understood "caricature as a minor form of art," which might have also influenced Bearden's belief that cartooning might interfere with his painting.[16] Even if it is a genre that he abandoned, Amy Kirschke makes a connection between Bearden's cartoons and later work, arguing that he had "a visual vocabulary of political protest" that he borrowed "from European traditions that were vital to the development of his persona as a political artist, and indeed were the foundation of his later politically charged paintings and collages."[17] Kirschke claims that his "cartooning figures followed some of the stock political figures and slogans of other anti-fascist artists of the mid-1930s."[18] Robert O'Meally sees Bearden's work as a cartoonist as both beneficial and detrimental to his art practice, arguing that "at best Bearden's mature paintings retained the power of the expedient lines of the cartoon figure and scene" and that "elsewhere, truth be told, this quick work could devolve into quick simplicity at its worst."[19] The criticism here—stock figures, quick simplicity, and the more complementary attribution of expediency—point to a skill set in cartooning that also can have value in various other "fine" art forms.

Let us take a 1937 New Year's editorial cartoon about the unemployed. Here we see the kind of aesthetic style that Kirschke is referencing: a male figure with nondescript features in shadow, in the front, as the faint outline of a line of other male figures fade into the distance behind him, the words "the unemployed" overlaying where their bodies would be. This sort of representative worker would frequently be the subject of cartoons, propaganda, and social realist art. The first wave of social realist art—not to be confused with Russian *socialist* realism—refers to various forms of art production that merged between the twentieth-century world wars and focuses on the concerns of the working class and hegemony. Well-known visual artists of the period include the Mexican muralist Diego Rivera, the German printmaker Käthe Kollwitz, and an African American artist also associated with the Mexican school, Elizabeth Catlett. These historical boundaries are porous, with nineteenth-century European realism being an influence and various other artists producing social realist work or neorealist work in later decades. The linking of race and class oppression and a transnational solidarity shaped Black social realist work in first half of the twentieth century.[20]

The influence of this work is clear in the link between race and class oppression in the Bearden cartoon. The general transnational worker was often depicted as white, but there was diversity in the social visual imaginary. And African Americans are miner's canaries in a politics of disposability in labor in the United States. While socialist art often represented cross-racial solidarity, the racial ambiguity produced by the Black and white "stock" characters of European protest art placed in Black publications position African Americans in a universalist worker frame.

Bearden's consistent practice of depicting Black people without features or with very simplified features clearly references a kind of representative blackness. But if he admired some of the revered European artists for their representation of universal themes, we might see the simplified features and form as also part of that tradition—one that imagines Black people as representative not only of blackness but also of working-class experience. Another example of this aesthetic is the cartoon "Still on the Outside," which was printed on March 7, 1936, in the *Baltimore Afro-American*. It depicts the almost ghostly shaded figures of men in hats standing over a building with smoke stacks, and it is the smoke from the stacks that shapes their bodies. On the roof of the building, Bearden places the words "American industry." Written over their barely visible bodies is "colored labor." While this imagery explicitly references the Black worker, this is also the visual vocabulary of universalist social realist representations of labor.

Bearden's cartoon work should be placed in a genealogy of not only his own work but also other art traditions in order to foreground the ways in which Black comics art should be an important part of the history of social realism. As Stacy I. Morgan explains in his discussion of the legacy of *The New Masses*, the leftist publication was a space where artists could combine the "didactic communicative aims of political cartooning" and "high art" traditions, and the "visual language" it provided was a major influence on political cartoonists and social realist artists.[21] It is thus "hardly coincidental" that African American artists like "Charles Alston and Hale Woodruff did substantial work in cartooning early in their respective careers."[22] Nor is it coincidental that Bearden did so.

Other works of Bearden depicted African American subjects victimized by monstrous white supremacy. He often accomplished this through scale, drawing the African American citizen as very small and the state as large. Examples include a 1937 cartoon depicting a large white hand and leg filling the right side of the frame, with a Black man tethered to a rope in the hand. The man is in a prison uniform and burdened by a ball and chain. A sign says, "To Arkansas Forced Labor Camps," and the caption above the frame reads, "Lincoln Freed the Slaves in 1863?"[23] Disproportionate scale was often used to depict the hegemonic force of racism. On September 12, 1932, Bearden published a cartoon, "Caught in the Tentacles Again," that depicts a large squid lying over a city that has a man enclosed in one of its arms. "Angelo Herdon" is written above the figure, so we know him to be the African American labor organizer who was arrested for attempting interracial labor organizing.[24] This representation of white-supremacist violence as a monstrosity shares an aesthetic link with many of the editorial cartoons of Robert S. Pious, who often used horror iconography to depict racism.

Bearden worked as a cartoonist for a short period of time, but as an artist known for practicing different aesthetic styles over the course of his long career, can we see someone sometimes called "America's finest black painter" as still being influenced by his cartoonist roots in later work?[25] Later in his career, Bearden said he was definitively not creating "protest images" with his famous collages.[26] He is more focused in using color and shape to show the vibrancy and joy of everyday Black life. Perhaps the various stages of Bearden's career illustrate the ways in which the cartooning of protest gives way to the possibilities of life beyond the protest that also is part of the everyday. Each phase is a part of the Black quotidian, giving a full range of Black experiences.

While Bearden would be best known for collage and figuration that deemphasized or crafted impressionistic facial features in his collages, Charles White would draw from socialist aesthetic traditions that emphasized the Black face. White moved from murals to powerful black-and-white lithographs and charcoal drawing to color in his art practice later in his career, but the Black visage was constantly a prominent feature in his work. White would earn a full scholarship to the Art Institute of Chicago in 1937 and, like many Black creatives in the period, would work for the Works Progress Administration. He would eventually end up in New York and become part of the vibrant Black arts scene, which had some significant overlap with the leftist communities. He contributed work to the Marxist publications *The Daily Worker* and *Masses and Mainstream* in the late 1940s and early '50s.

Like some other Marxists, White saw the art arbiters' high valuation of abstraction in the midcentury art world as a move away from working-class interests in support of the ruling class.[27] His review of a book collecting the works of the painter Edward Biberman's work gives a clear sense of his philosophical approach to art production. In "Humanist Art," he praises Biberman for his "clarity of form" despite the "obscurity and anti-Humanism" that "prevail in so much of American art."[28] He also believes Biberman's treatment of African Americans is, for the most part, instructive for other progressive artists: "What challenges and inspires the artist is not so much the recording of various physical types but rather the revealing of inner traits and particular elements which point up the specific national character of the oppressed Negro people.... The Negro has to be portrayed not only as a symbolic figure related to other national groups, or in terms of class identification, but also in his *particular* social, cultural, and political role."[29] White's review reveals his commitments: an investment in humanism and rejection of abstraction, a preference for works that depict subjects as individuals as opposed to representative types, and subject matter that shows everyday life of the working class. The rejection of "types" might be surprising, as that was common in social realist art of the period. It was particularly common in cartooning, and perhaps that is why some of the works in which the stylization may suggest an archetype might be viewed by critics as his weakest. Erica Moiah James argues that his works for Marxist publications in the 1940s and '50s "lack the aesthetic and ideological power of his earlier compositions," and other critics and White himself would agree that "satire and printed political propaganda [was] ill-suited to his artistic enterprise and characterized much of the imagery he produced in the '50s as a misstep in his career."[30]

Works such as "The Return of the Soldier" (1946) would presumably fit in this category of weaker art. It could easily function as an editorial cartoon in a newspaper. Topical, the charcoal drawing is a commentary on the treatment of Black soldiers returning from World War II. Three soldiers are at the feet of a policeman, one on his knees choking, one on his back, and the other kneeling and possibly trying to block the arm holding a gun on them. The Black faces are stylized and slightly different from each other but not totally distinct. A hooded Klansman stands behind the cop with one hand on his shoulder. This has the triangulated structure of the editorial cartoon.[31] Two points of view are represented in the cartoon, and while racist cartoons often make fun of violence toward Black people, the title of the cartoon also directs the sympathetic gaze. "The Return of the Soldier," without the racial designation, directs the interpretation toward disparity.

It is not hard to find examples of how this image resonates in other Black press publications. The work is also reminiscent of Thomas Nast's "This Is a White Man's Government" (1868), which depicts an African American under the feet of three white men supporting the Democratic platform: the founder of the Klan, Nathan Bedford Forrest; a rich white capitalist holding a stack of money; and one of Nast's ape-like caricatures of an Irish man. The shape of the hat on the ground suggests that the African American man was a Union soldier and is a veteran. In his right hand, he is clutching a flagpole with the U.S. flag, which is also crumpled and beneath the white men's feet.

I am not suggesting that White was clearly influenced by Nast but that recognizing the structural similarities leads us to see that White's editorial aesthetic has forerunners. Classification also helps us see the frequent atemporality of the editorial cartoon depicting antiblackness. Editorial cartoons are very much of the moment, but sometimes the cartoons could possess an atemporality in depicting the nonprogressive thrust of history. Despite the clear historical markers—particularly in Nast's cartoon—white supremacy is still doing the same work decades later.

A cartoon by White from the *Congress View* (1946) is also a commentary on treatment of African American veterans (figure 4.1). On February 4, 1946, a police officer killed two African American veterans and wounded a third. They were all brothers. The community rose up to protest, and the state violently crushed their resistance. In Columbia, Tennessee, later that month, a shopkeeper failed to fix a radio that an African American woman, Gladys Stephenson, had brought to the shop to repair. They had an argument, and as the woman and her son James (a veteran) were leaving the shop, the white shopkeeper decided that he did not like how James looked at him

FIGURE 4.1 Charles White, *Congress View* 3, no. 12 (National Negro Congress, 1946), Charles W. White Papers, 1933–1987, bulk 1960s–1970s, Smithsonian Archives of American Art.

and hit him in the back of the head with his fist. The two men fought, with Gladys attempting to assist her son. The Stephensons were arrested, and this was the initiating spark to African American citizens taking up arms to defend themselves against white mob violence and police who claimed that they were there to protect them. It was the first major "race riot" after World War II, after which African American veterans demonstrated their increased willingness to defend themselves against white-supremacist aggression.[32]

In White's cartoon, an African American soldier is the largest figure. Around his neck is a noose that that has been cut, and the KKK figure conspiring with a police officer in the foreground possesses the rest of the rope. Cut chains are on the soldier's wrists, and there is a lighted torch in his right hand, as the smaller bodies of people fighting in "Freeport" and "Columbia" are in the lower-right corner of the image. The soldier's tortured face and open mouth are calling out something we cannot hear. The light from the torch also blends with the smoke and fire of the ruins that frame the intertwined, struggling, bodies. The soldier's body almost seems as if it is being pulled apart from all these forces—the chain of slavery and a history of discrimination holding him back, the threat of contemporary racist violence around his neck, as he forcefully attempts to light the way to a better future.

The aliveness of this image is delivered through White's skilled figuration. White focuses on the Black visage throughout his career, but this kind of stylized pathos is not a characteristic of his later creations. Figuration and composition do a different kind of work than treatments of blackness that are often characterized as "dignified." If part of what we understand White as doing, as some discussions of his work have noted, is eschewing stereotypes in his "dignified" representations, the affective excesses of his earlier work should not be seen as any less real. Moreover, he lends his talents to chronicling—as with some of his murals—the visceral violence of his present.

Art historians often trace the changes in figuration over an artist's career and have done so with both Bearden and White. Their work as cartoonists should be seen as an important part of aesthetic genealogies, illustrating the different outcomes that "quick simplicity" or varied approaches to humanism might have on interpretations of Black bodies. Charles Alston moved the most toward abstraction of all of these artists. He gradually began transitioning from his mural and more realistic figuration in the 1950s but would move back and forth because "some things evoked feelings of abstraction, while others were figural."[33] Alston was hired to produce propaganda by the Office of War Information, placing work that supported the war in the Black press. Harry Amana argues that all of Alston's "cartoons" in this period can be placed in varied categories: "War Heroes," tributes to the Black press, celebrations of Black Nations, images about "Integration/National acceptance" of African Americans, "Black History," news about racial progress, representations of ship dedications named after African Americans, and nationalist representations encouraging contributions to the war effort.[34]

These categorizations highlight the complexity of the line between cartoons and illustration. People sometimes wrongly argue that all editorial cartoons are humorous or satirical, when many editorial cartoons simply offer a commentary or point of view. It is not uncommon for some editorial cartoons to focus more on pathos than irony. In the Black press, the editorial cartoon often offered a point of view merely through the positive representation of African Americans—that itself was an editorial commentary, contrasted with the representations that were seen in the white press. I am not sure all of Alston's work for the Office of War Information can properly be called cartoons, but placing these images in conversation with other cartoons as well as with his other works can help us rethink genealogies that scholars deploy to categorize these works.

Alston's illustrations/cartoons celebrating prominent African Americans have a format similar to many biographical single-frame illustrations/cartoons in the period. The *Pittsburgh Courier* cartoonist Sam Milai, for example, had many cartoons with the same format. The largest image is a portrait of the person, surrounded by texts and smaller images that depict moments in the person's life and accomplishments. Multiple moments represented in single frames were frequently published in newspapers and periodicals in the nineteenth and twentieth centuries, and we still often see this format in comics today. Single panels depicting multiple moments might be understood as an example of sequential art. Alston's treatments of the figures and scenes are also similar to some of the depictions in his murals, which could invite us to think about the relationship between murals and the comics medium. Insisting on definitive categorization of these kind of images as either a cartoon or illustration might be a pedantic exercise and less useful than applying a hermeneutic that recognizes connections in the absence of definitive categorization.

The work of Alston, as someone explicitly hired to produce propaganda, does suggest a division between this state-sponsored work and work speaking more to his artistic vision. His drawings encouraging the war effort as well as racist caricatures of the Japanese may seem to have less value for preservation and analysis than other artwork. But his editorial point of view may still speak to certain Black aesthetic genealogies, particularly the varied ways in which artists depicted U.S. racism. While Alston's work lacked, as Amana notes, the biting critique of U.S. racism present in Jay Jackson's World War II cartoons for the *Chicago Defender*, we still see commentary on racism. Take, for example, "Right between the Eyes," which comments on race discrimination in pay (figure 4.2). Alston seems to be using the story of David and Goliath, in showing a small man using a slingshot to take down a large man with "WAGE DIFFERENTIALS BASED ON RACE" written on his back. Goliath was a Philistine, which is used here as shorthand for someone who has no appreciation of culture and the arts, but there is nothing about the story that suggests he should be depicted as a caveman or Neanderthal, as he appears to be here. Goliath had a well-equipped army, and David had little; but in Alston's drawing, Goliath is barely clothed, hairy, and possessing only a club. Alston is thus slipping in a critique of the United States by treating this perspective as prehistoric, and moreover, he is critiquing racism without the presence of the Black body.

The varied ways that artists depicted white supremacy (and thus, often, the United States) as a monstrosity deserve their own focused attention in the history of cartoon art. And perhaps no artist was better at that than Robert Savion Pious. Pious was born in Mississippi and studied at the Art Institute in Chicago, but like many Black artists, he made his way to New York. He is probably best known in the history of Black visual culture for his poster for the American Negro Exposition in 1940. The poster design competition resulted in nearly one hundred entries, and Pious's won the prize.[35] The image is of a Black man and Black woman with nude torsos, arms raised, and recently cut shackles. The rose shadow of Abraham Lincoln's face is in the background. Pious did pencil work for a number of horror, science fiction, and adventure comics, such as *Adventures into the Unknown* (1949, 1950), *The Beyond* (1952), and *Chilling Tales of Horror* (1971). These comics do not suggest that he was much more than an artist for hire (as opposed to a collaborative cocreator), and we do not see many signs of racial allegory in those works. But the fact that he consistently brought these themes to his editorial cartoons can help us think about his contribution to a Black horror or speculative imagination.

In the twenty-first century, Black horror has gained a greater attention, particularly in the wake of Jordan Peele's *Get Out* (2017), which made much of white racism as part of the quotidian horror of Black life. Scholars such as Robin Means Coleman and Kinitra D. Brooks have traced long genealogies of horror that involve Black people or are crafted by Black creators.[36] In the comics context, Qiana Whitted has traced EC comics' treatment of

Desegregating Black Art Genealogies • 91

FIGURE 4.2 Charles Alston, "Right between the Eyes," 1943. (Office for Emergency Management, Office of War Information, Domestic Operations Branch, News Bureau, 6/13/1942–9/15/1945, Series: Artworks and Mockups for Cartoons Promoting the War Effort and Original Sketches by Charles Alston, ca. 1942–ca. 1945, Record Group 208: Records of the Office of War Information, 1926–1951, National Archives)

racial and ethnic minorities who were "mainly victims of wrongdoing in segregated neighborhoods, graveyards, military platoons, and even in outer space."[37] Moreover, the ethical logic of these EC comics often depicted those who were committing acts of violence being punished. With this backdrop of the horror imagination in comics, we might see the horror allegories in some of Pious's editorial cartoons as examples of a Black speculative imaginary influenced by his work with horror comics but given full rein in his editorial cartoons.

When Pious treats "America" as the monster, it suggests that the state itself is villainous at the core. The atemporality of editorial cartoons is clear with his work, as a number of his cartoons were reprinted on multiple dates and have general themes. For example, a cartoon that ran on June 10, 1953, could run at any time. A drooling, bald Nosferatu that also seems to have blood or some other fluid seeping from its arms hovers over two groups of standing people, the clawed hands dividing them. "AMERICA" is written at the bottom of the frame, and the caption beneath the cartoon reads, "Segregation: An Evil that Breeds Misunderstanding." This same cartoon runs again on November 26, 1958, with a different caption: "Dividing Us When Unity Is Needed Most" (figure 4.3). Nosferatu appears again in a cartoon that ran on October 4, 1962. While this cartoon, too, could have had relevance at various points in the civil rights movement, it was probably addressing a specific incident. Nosferatu is seen slightly cowering from a large sword in the foreground. The words "Discrimination in Institutions of Learning" appears on his robe, while "Justice" and "Supreme Court" are written on the sword. The caption reads, "Only by Enforcing Court Decision Can Monster Be Removed." While there had been various efforts at desegregation in the previous decade following the *Brown v. Board of Education* decision in 1954, schools had been slow to desegregate. But on October 1, 1962, James Meredith began school on University of Mississippi's campus. This followed whites rioting on the campus on September 30, in which three hundred people were injured and two people were killed. Pious's cartoon thus clearly seems to be created in reference to the desegregation of the University of Mississippi and white people's violent response.

Pious often used scale in his works, and the scale emphasized monsters crushing vulnerable Black men. Given the long-standing treatment of Black men as monsters preying on white people—particularly Black women—this reversal in editorial cartoons flipped the logic of horror in the U.S. imagination. Bearden, Alston, and White invite drawing connections to art traditions that preceded them as well as their contemporary moments, while Pious's work deserves to be placed in conversation with twenty-first-century discussions of Black horror aesthetics across media.

This essay is not an exhaustive attempt to explore the relationship between African American artists in the twentieth century and cartoon art. It is merely an invitation to consider integrating editorial cartoons into a genealogy of African American art history and Black comics scholarship. We should try to find, preserve, and curate the cartoons of Black artists for study. We can also bring artists who are better known as cartoonists, such as Ollie Harrington, more substantively into a history of African American art. Integration of these artists and works can help us understand different

FIGURE 4.3 Robert. S. Pious, "America," *Atlanta Daily World*, November 26, 1958.

practices as artists refine their liberatory aesthetics. It can help us think through different approaches to humanism, realism, and speculative aesthetics across media. It is not uncommon to see preliminary sketches of artists preserved and displayed in museums, but original cartoon art typically holds less currency. There is a difference between categorizing original work as primary documents and art, affecting methodological approaches as well as hermeneutics. These archives have value for comics scholars, art historians, historians, and anyone interested in African American visual culture.

Notes

1 Du Bois, "Criteria for Negro Art," 296.
2 Locke, "Art or Propaganda?," 260.

3   Ghent, "Interview with Romare Bearden," 55.
4   James, "Charles White's *J'Accuse*," 17.
5   Beaty, *Comics versus Art*, Kindle loc. 259.
6   Wanzo, *Content of Our Caricature*, 4.
7   The Hurston-Wright debate refers to arguments attributed to the writers Zora Neale Hurston and Richard Wright about the ways that African American life should be portrayed in the arts, with Hurston emphasizing folk culture and vernacular expression within Black communities and Wright drawing on more social realist methods to highlight the sustained impact of white supremacist terror in America. The Black Arts Movement (BAM) of the 1960s and 1970s would continue to explore similar questions of authenticity in the artistic representation of Black liberation politics and pan-African identity. And during the late twentieth century, "post-Black" artists and writers further complicated these debates by engaging racial themes that were less tied to recuperative and respectability politics.
8   Harper, *Abstractionist Aesthetics*, 2.
9   Harper, 2.
10 Beaty, *Comics versus Art*, Kindle loc. 665–667.
11 Wanzo, *Content of Our Caricature*, 71.
12 Murrell, "African Influence in Modern Art."
13 See Bearden, "Negro Artist and Modern Art"; Bearden, "Negro Artist's Dilemma."
14 Bearden, "Negro Artist and Modern Art," 87.
15 Kirschke, "Romare Bearden," 146–147.
16 Kirschke, 148.
17 Kirschke, 156.
18 Kirschke, 151.
19 O'Meally, "Pressing on Life," 3.
20 Morgan, *Rethinking Social Realism*, 2.
21 Morgan, 112.
22 Morgan, 112.
23 Bearden, "Lincoln Freed the Slaves in 1863?," 4
24 Bearden, "Caught in the Tentacles Again"; Charles Martin, "Communists and Blacks."
25 Tomkins, "Putting Something over Something Else," 53.
26 Tomkins, 53.
27 Murphy, "Charles White," 285.
28 C. White, "Humanist Art," 59.
29 C. White, 60.
30 James, "Charles White's *J'Accuse*," 17.
31 Wanzo, *Content of Our Caricature*, 20–21.
32 For a full account of these events, see O'Brien, *Color of Law*.
33 Wardlaw, *Charles Alston*, vii.
34 Amana, "Art of Propaganda," 88.
35 A. Green, *Selling the Race*, 25.
36 See Means Coleman, *Horror Noire*; and K. Brooks *Searching for Sycorax*.
37 Whitted, *EC Comics*, 43.

5

Misdirections in Matt Baker's *Phantom Lady*

●●●●●●●●●●●●●

CHRIS GAVALER AND
MONALESIA EARLE

Matt Baker, the most successful Black artist in midcentury U.S. comics, amassed over six hundred credits in roughly 150 titles between 1944 and his death in 1959 at the age of thirty-eight.[1] Born in 1921, he started his art career at the age of twenty-three, contributing backgrounds to *Sheena, Queen of the Jungle* at Iger Studio, and *Phantom Lady* was his last project before moving to freelancing in 1948. Because of the notoriety of *Phantom Lady*, it is also his best-known work. The anticomics psychiatrist Fredric Wertham included Baker's *Phantom Lady* #17 cover in his *Seduction of the Innocent* with the caption, "Sexual stimulation by combining 'headlights' with a sadist's dream of tying up a woman."[2] An enlargement hung in the 1954 Senate Subcommittee Hearings into Juvenile Delinquency that led to the creation of the Comics Code, but Baker goes unmentioned in the transcripts presumably because none of the senators knew that a Black man drew the image.

Baker's "visible invisibility" was an inescapable reality of his time. He would have been aware of the almost routine lynching of Black men across the United States but particularly in the South. The killing of Black men happened under white supremacy, what Charles W. Mills describes as the "unnamed political system that has made the modern world what it is today."[3] This chilling assertion has played out repeatedly, and oftentimes blatantly, in the political, judicial, educational, and social arenas of the United States. Therefore, one of the reasons the Senate subcommittee may have been unaware of Baker's race, or even unconcerned about his existence, is because white supremacy turned on what Mills terms the "Racial Contract," one "explicitly predicated on a politics of the body which is related to the body politic through restrictions on which bodies are 'politic.'"[4] This results in bodies that are "impolitic" and "whose owners are judged incapable of *forming* or fully *entering into* a body politic."[5] Yet the irony of Baker's exclusion from the larger discursive frame was perhaps inadvertently underscored by Alberto Becattini when he noted that, since Baker was a penciller of backgrounds for other studio staffers, Baker's "earliest efforts [were] hidden within somebody else's artwork."[6] This is important in understanding how Baker, through his work in predominantly white male spaces, performed misdirection in his pseudonymous work for others.

Trinh T. Minh-Ha has argued that the marginalized are compelled to "fight for a space where identity is fearlessly constructed across difference."[7] Black people labored under the strictures of a "postcolonial visual regime" that was operationalized in what Sarah Haley, in her article on the enforced servitude of Black women in Georgia's prison system, describes as the "domestic carceral sphere."[8] Black bodies were tamed, neutered, and rendered powerless through threats of prison or death. It is, then, little wonder that Baker and other minorities in the 1940s and 1950s kept their own counsel. A fellow artist recalled that Baker "would go off on his own" during lunch breaks, "acutely aware of the perceived chasm that separated him."[9] Another recalled that Baker "never looked for trouble," "never even mentioned the word 'black' or whatever," and "never got involved in that racial type thing."[10] Baker's half brother recalled that away from work, neither he nor Baker looked at things in the context of race, as long as others treated them right. Yet he also acknowledged that when he and Baker were alone, they "definitely talked about it then."[11]

A central question we seek to unravel in this chapter is whether Baker's understanding of his marginality as a Black man, in what was at the time a country that gazed on Black bodies with hostile intent, was inserted into his work as an implicit counternarrative to the ever-present threat of violence that Black people faced. Phillip Crawford's description of Saidiya Hartman's writings on "critical fabulation" has relevance to an unquestionable existential crisis of the Black underclass then and now; he writes, "I embrace fabulation and speculation in order to disclose neglected pasts and propose alternative futures. In doing so I marvel with, through, and as the raced, gendered, and variously othered supra-human who hovers without cape or mask, a floating signifier tied down by the double-bind of difference."[12] Crawford's remarks have a corollary in misdirection, in the agency that has historically been denied to the oppressed yet forcefully contested through Black artistic expression. As a signifier that turns here on Stuart Hall's argument that "race can be linked to other signifiers in a representation," misdirection is also "relational and . . . constantly subject to redefinition in different cultures, different moments."[13] As we explain later in this chapter, misdirection functions as a series of performative feints: as a "signifying strategy defined by the contexts through which it seeks to effect perceptual shifts."[14] Indeed, in the context of centuries-long oppression through which blackness sought to effect perceptual shifts as a survival strategy, Black masculinity writ large became a well-rehearsed performance of misdirection, of transgression.

In Baker's panels, the floating signifier is laid down so impishly in the lines and angles of his work, and indeed in the female form, that for all intents and purposes, one could argue that the "servicing" of the white male gaze was in fact controlled by Baker's invisible hand at work in the white space of the comics pages, in the white space of the United States' national consciousness, and in the regulated white space of the unspoiled female body. In this way, Baker's invisible transgression "has its entire space in the line it crosses."[15] By virtue of his race and the fraught times in which he lived, Baker's lines (and the crossing thereof) were probably operationalized through an oppositional yet historically fractured gaze. Moreover, since he was also presumed to be gay, Baker's depiction of white female bodies in BDSM-suggestive poses for straight, white, preadolescent boys in an industry dominated by straight, white men troubles multiple midcentury racial and sexual expectations. Those misdirections are further complicated by Baker's relationship to the layout norms that structure their content. His idiosyncratic approach to viewing paths may be his most significant contribution to comics and also his most salient self-expression in an industry and culture doubly biased against his race and his presumed sexual orientation.[16]

Each of the eleven issues of the *Phantom Lady* run (#13–#23) includes two or three title-character episodes ranging from seven to twelve pages.

Roughly a third of the layouts break standard Z-paths, requiring viewers to navigate right to left within pages otherwise dominated by left-to-right viewing and to leap over panels in order to follow content-implied paths. While these techniques are not unique to Baker, he employs them to an atypical degree. It is suggestive that a Black comics artist who disrupts norms just by existing is also disruptive at a deeper visual level. While it is impossible to prove that his layouts are a product of, and potentially a protest against, his racial relationship to the midcentury comics industry, this chapter establishes a compelling correlation. Moreover, even if Baker was not explicitly creating images and layouts situated *at* the margins, by virtue of his race and the assumptions about his sexual orientation, he was certainly drawing *from* the margins. What Baker demonstrated through his drawings was not just a deterministically inscribed awareness of his secondary status in the United States (hence drawing *at* the margins) but most certainly a deliberate *decentering* of the white gaze on his Black body by drawing *from* the margins—that is, drawing empowerment from his marginal status.

Misdirectional Viewing

According to Joseph Witek, "high baroque" layout style was "widely used in the comic books of the 1940s" and included "wavy or jagged lines for panel borders, circular, triangular, or other unusually shaped panels . . . and extensive use of figures which appear to emerge from within the panels onto the physical page."[17] Baker appears to be prototypical. Kaitlin Pederson and Neil Cohn studied the layouts of forty superhero comics from the 1940s to 2014, finding "an average of 6.5 panels per page in the 1940s."[18] Essentially all of Baker's pages vary between six and seven panels.

While following these norms, Baker's *Phantom Lady* pages are unconventional with regard to what Scott McCloud terms "flow," how "the arrangement of panels on a page or screen, and the arrangement of elements within a panel," guides "readers between and within panels" by "directing the eye through reader expectations and content."[19] Neil Cohn identifies contemporary "reading path" conventions according to frame and gutter positions, deriving a flow chart of viewing preferences:

1 "Go to the left corner."
2 "If no top left panel, go to either the highest and/or leftmost panel."
3 "Follow the outer border."

4 "Follow the inner border."
5 "Move to the right."
6 "Move straight down."
7 "If nothing is to the right, go to the far left and down."
8 "Go to the panel that has not been read yet."[20]

According to McCloud, such navigating should be "a simple, intuitive process," one that will "be transparent to the reader" so that "the reading flow can continue uninterrupted."[21] He therefore warns prospective artists to avoid "inherently confusing arrangements," including ones "obscured by too many 'fourth wall' breaks," because they produce "just enough split-second confusion to yank readers out of the world of the story."[22] Witek expresses the same aesthetic preference, critiquing "high baroque" techniques when "the reading process of the story is subordinated to an immediate visual effect," because "readers who are trying to figure out the proper way to read the page are readers who are not immersed in the story."[23]

While McCloud and Witek are correct that many of Baker's atypical viewing paths probably slow flow and reduce story-world immersion, they are incorrect that flow and immersion are necessarily priority goals. Comics that follow Cohn's directives are common but not universal, and, as Charles Hatfield notes, "there is always the possibility that different protocols will be invoked, different elements stressed."[24] Baker provides a major example.

Layout, John Bateman, Francisco Veloso, and Yan Ling Lau correctly observe, "is one of the most salient features of graphic novels and comics," yet "methods for engaging systematically with the analysis of page design in comics and graphic novels are still in their infancy."[25] Comics scholarship offers two primary terms for categorizing viewing paths. Z-paths are row based, and N-paths are column based. Both assume that contiguous panels are viewed consecutively as determined by their placement in approximately straight horizontal or vertical paths and that when a path segment ends, typically at the physical border of a page, viewers skip to the beginning of the next row or column. Such skips are termed "saccades" in vision science, and they typically create a backward, page-wide, diagonal leap over a lower horizontal gutter dividing the next row (or over a vertical gutter dividing the next column). Forward viewing movements within segments (either rows or columns) typically involve no leaps because images are contiguous and parallel. Given these norms, categorizing Baker's atypical viewing paths requires additional terms. We introduce five here and expand on each in subsequent subsections.

1. Mixed path: a layout that includes both rows and columns
2. Parallel saccade: a backward but nondiagonal leap over a middle image that has not yet been viewed to reach the beginning of a next row or column
3. Segment leap: a forward leap over a previously viewed image to reach the next conceptually linear but physically noncontiguous image within the same row or column
4. Reversed path: a path that moves from a right image to the next contiguous left image
5. Misdirecting appendage: a portion of an image drawn as though extending beyond its frame and into another panel that is not next in the viewing path

Baker regularly employs all five strategies.

Mixed Paths

Mixed paths typically feature a pair of subcolumns (which do not extend the full length of the page) with one or more rows above, below, or both.[26] Mixed paths are relatively common, and Cohn's directives account for them, with the underlying assumption that viewers will always choose a Z-path over an N-path. Twenty-seven *Phantom Lady* pages feature mixed paths. They are Baker's most common Z-path misdirection. In most cases, he draws a tall panel along the top left corner margins with a multipanel subcolumn to its right, producing a brief N-path segment before the next row reestablishes a Z-path.

The pattern is apparent in the first four diagrams in figure 5.1.[27] The first provides a prototype for Baker's mixed-path approach. The tall left-corner panel and the shorter right-corner second panel require an upward-moving saccade, followed by a downward movement from the second to the third panel, both of which define N-path viewing. The subrow of panels 3 and 4, followed by the full row of panels 5 and 6 restore a Z-path. The second diagram repeats the pattern with the variations of an unframed fourth panel and a circular sixth. The third diagram varies the layout by dividing the top right panel with a curved gutter and the last two panels with a diagonal gutter. The fourth diagram features an additional panel, creating two subrows parallel to the opening panel. Baker also occasionally draws a tall panel at the bottom-left-corner margin, breaking the Z-path of the preceding row.

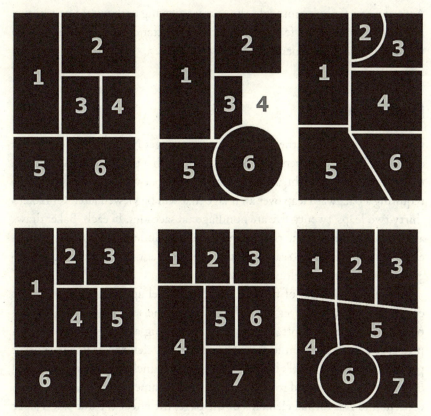

FIGURE 5.1 Mixed paths

The remaining two diagrams illustrate this mixed-row variation. The fifth begins with a three-panel row, followed by a tall fourth panel that produces an N-path saccade to the fifth. The pattern is the same for the sixth diagram, except the penultimate panel is circular and begins a lower subrow rather than ending a higher subrow.

Because mixed paths require switching between row-based and column-based viewing, they sometimes present navigational challenges. In each of the preceding examples, a viewer could interpret the page as following an N-path by following the top-left-corner panel to the bottom left corner immediately below it. Cohn's directives would prevent this in most cases, prioritizing outer borders over inner borders. When the vertical right edges of left-margin panels do not align, aligned horizontal edges instead direct attention across the row rather than down the would-be column. Some of Baker's mixed paths violate this assumption. In the third diagram, the gutter between panels 1 and 5 is higher than the gutter between panels 4 and 6.

According to Cohn's protocols, the correct viewing path would be 1, 5, 2, 3, 4, 6. The sixth diagram features a juncture of gutter corners, producing two viable paths, the one ordered as shown and 1, 4, 2, 3, 5, 7.

Parallel Saccades

Columns appearing on the left side of a page trigger N-paths with minimum confusion because viewers are not presented with a path choice. When columns appear on the right, a viewer must choose between contiguous panels, requiring a backward leap over an image that will be viewed later. Of Baker's thirty-two leaps, twenty-five are nondiagonal saccades. In each, Baker draws a tall panel bordering the right margin that concludes a row of shorter panels, requiring viewers to scan over unviewed content to reach the right margin and begin a new multipanel row.

In the first diagram of figure 5.2, the tall panel appears in the top-right corner, causing a leap over the fifth panel.[28] In the second diagram, the tall panel appears in the bottom-right corner, causing a leap over the seventh panel. The third diagram features the additional element of image content protruding from a panel's broken frame into a panel that must be scanned over to begin the second row. Since panels and frames are themselves drawn content and not formal elements of the page, the effect is paradoxical since the protruding content only appears to protrude but is enclosed by the circular gutter surrounding the fifth panel.

Parallel saccades violate Cohn's protocol, "If nothing is to the right, go to the far left and down," because the required movement is to the far left but

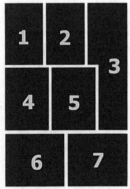
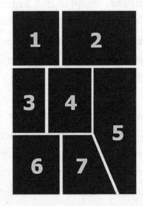
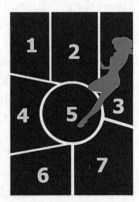

FIGURE 5.2 Parallel saccades

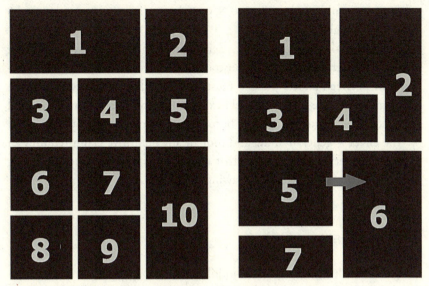

FIGURE 5.3 Mills's mixed path and Kirby's parallel saccade

not down and typically up. If the directives were imposed, the first diagram might be viewed as a mixed path, either 1, 2, 4, 5, 3, 6, 7 or 1, 4, 2, 5, 3, 6, 7, depending on how a viewer navigates the first nonaligned vertical gutter juncture. Alternatively, the page might produce an N-path, ending in a partial third column: 1, 4, 6, 2, 5, 7, 3. The second diagram allows for three similar possibilities. All are wrong because they do not reflect the actual viewing paths of Baker's original pages. The third diagram is more ambiguous, due to its diagonal gutters, circular center panel, and frame-breaking content. While we are not certain what path Cohn's directives might produce, it is not Baker's actual path because a parallel saccade is never an option.

Other 1940s artists avoid parallel saccades by creating mixed paths. The first diagram in figure 5.3 is derived from a pattern that Tarpé Mills repeats three times during her 1941–1944 run of *Miss Fury* Sunday comics (December 27, 1942; February 21, 1943; and August 22, 1943). The larger newspaper page allows for more panels than a standard comic book page can accommodate, and Mills works with a grid of square panels, doubling the first in the first row for the title and doubling the final panel by merging it with the panel directly above it. While the layout resembles Baker's from the second diagram in figure 5.2, Mills's viewing path treats the right edge of panel 7 as a right margin and panels 6 through 10 as a pair of subcolumns, the first with two subrows. If Mills instead followed Baker's viewing path, the bottom half of the page would produce 6, 7, 10, 8, 9, with the distance between 10 and 8 requiring a parallel saccade.

The second diagram in figure 5.3 derives from page 3 of Jack Kirby's *Black Bolt* #10 (March 1941) and demonstrates a parallel saccade when the viewing path between panels 3 and 4 must skip over the yet unviewed panel 5. The parallel saccade is due to panel 2 extending below the bottom horizontal gutter of panel 1 and sharing the bottom horizontal gutter of panels 3 and 4. The effect is generally rare, and though any definitive claim requires an exhaustive overview, we suspect that other artists were routinely avoiding saccades by the time Baker was drawing *Phantom Lady*.

Segment Leaps

Leaps occur within rows when a middle panel from a higher row (or frame-breaking content extending from that panel) protrudes into a lower row. Baker's remaining seven leaps require viewers to skim over significant image content protruding from a previously viewed row.

The first three diagrams in figure 5.4 show the second panel of a first row dividing the first two panels of a second row.[29] Except for differences in panel shapes, the first and second diagrams produce the same path, but in the third, the protruding content is not contained within a panel but is instead combined with the top-right panel. The last three diagrams demonstrate similar effects lower on the pages. The fourth diagram echoes the second, but the fifth and sixth produce more complications due to irregular panel shapes and nonparallel gutters.

Segment leaps violate Cohn's directives, because following either an inner or outer panel border to either the right or straight down does not reach the next panel in Baker's viewing path. In each case, viewers would default to N-paths in the top three diagrams, moving from panel 1 to panel 4 in the first, from panel 1 to panel 4 in the second, and from panel 1 to panel 3 in the third, as well as from panel 3 to panel 6 in the bottom three diagrams. If viewers attempted to maintain a Z-path, they would remain at panel 6 in the bottom three diagrams and at panel 4 in the second. The leaps in the first and third diagrams are less extreme because a small portion of the next panel is contiguous in the bottom corners.

The third diagram presents a more fundamental challenge to Cohn's directives because the frame-breaking figure undermines the notion that panels are the determining units of viewing paths. Because roughly three-

Misdirections in Matt Baker's *Phantom Lady* • 105

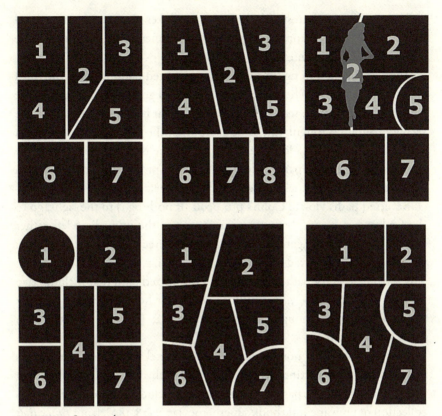

FIGURE 5.4 Segment leaps

quarters of the figure is outside the implied panel borders, it is diegetically linked to the content of the second panel but is a visually free-standing unit that also serves the function of a gutter dividing panels 3 and 4. Alternatively, the figure could be categorized itself as a panel—though one with no surrounding gutter and one that is diegetically integrated into another panel, features that challenge the meaning of the term "panel."

Reversed Paths

Reversed paths violate left-to-right viewing. Reversed paths and segment leaps are similar because both proceed nondiagonally from a right panel. They differ according to the number of panels in the row. If there are three, the path requires a segment leap. If two, no leap is possible because no image divides the left panel from the originating right panel, and so a right-to-left path reversal occurs automatically. Sixteen of Baker's layouts feature a panel juxtaposition that requires a right-to-left movement within an otherwise left-to-right Z-path context.

The first diagram in figure 5.5 features a reversed path between the third and fourth panels, which share a lower horizontal gutter.[30] Baker repeats the layout elsewhere in the series four times, making it his most prominent. The second diagram is roughly the same except that the third panel is circular, a variant he employs an additional three times. The third diagram places the norm-breaking fourth panel below the top row, producing a reversed path into the bottom-left panel instead of the middle-left panel.

Reversed paths violate Cohn's protocol, "If nothing is to the right, go to the far left and down," because movement is to the immediate left rather than the far left. Navigated according to the directives, the first diagram would begin with a mixed row in the panel order 1, 2, 4, 3. The third diagram would begin as an N-path before shifting to a mixed path that includes two subrows: 1, 5, 2, 3, 4, 6, 7. It is difficult to predict how the second diagram would be navigated, though either 1, 4, 2, 3 or 1, 2, 4, 3 are more likely than Baker's actual path.

Reversed paths are not unique to Baker. Witek observes "Jack Kirby's early habit of constructing layouts which end at the bottom left rather than the bottom right of the page."[31] Greg Sadowski includes three examples in his collection of prewar comic book superheroes (177, 178, 180), from *Black Bolt* #10 (March 1941) and diagrammed in figure 5.6. In each, the arrangement of the top half of the page varies (including the parallel saccade discussed earlier), but the lower half is identical, with a discursive arrow directing the viewing path from panel 5 to panel 6, leaving the reversed path from panel

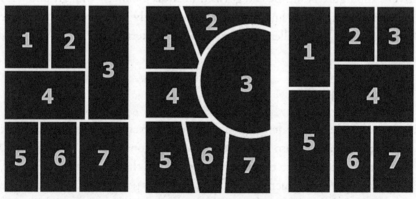

FIGURE 5.5 Reversed paths

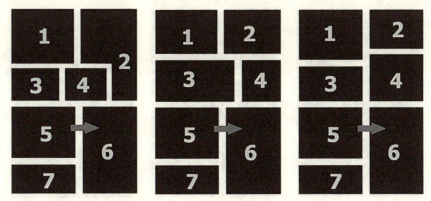

FIGURE 5.6 Kirby's reversed paths

6 to panel 7 implicit. The arrangement is relatively rare. Pederson and Cohn note for their study, "Leftward and up-left directions were excluded from analyses because of too few data points."[32] This may be partly due to the relative smallness of their data set, which included only five comic books from the 1940s, when reversed paths would be most likely to appear. Kirby's later 1960s layouts avoid and probably eliminate reversed paths.

Misdirecting Appendages

A broken-frame panel is an image with a portion drawn to appear as though protruding over its drawn frame. The seemingly protruding portion may be termed an "appendage" and the overall image an "appended panel." Baker's appendages are almost always also diegetic appendages—literally legs. While appendages can direct viewing along intended paths, Baker's misdirecting appendages, as floating signifiers of female disembodiment, work against intended panel order with arrangements that probably produce delay and possible confusion as a viewer evaluates path options. These misdirections are not a kind of viewing path but instead present momentary obstacles or detours to correct viewing order.

Baker's pages feature twenty-four misdirecting appendages, including the second and third diagrams in figure 5.7.[33] The first establishes the general principle, with a rectangular panel extending into a lower row, directing attention to a panel outside of viewing order. The second and third diagrams have image content extending beyond panel borders into a lower nonsequential panel. Baker routinely breaks borders, but we classify only those

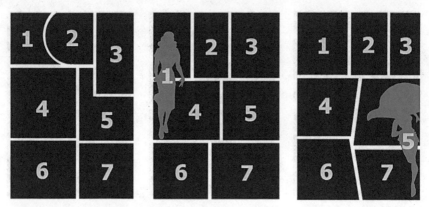

FIGURE 5.7 Misdirecting appendages

with prominent extensions (the majority of a leg but not, for example, a foot alone) as misdirecting appendages. The frame-breaking figure in the second diagram extends from the waist down, and the figure in the third extends from the hips down.

If the figures were viewed as path indicators, the second diagram's panel order would move from panel 1 to panel 4, and the third diagram's panel order would move from panel 5 to panel 7. The first diagram would move from panel 3 to panel 5. Each would then lead to either a reversed path (for the first and third diagrams) or no clear path (for the second). If followed, the misdirecting images would violate Baker's intended path. By including them, Baker thwarts effortless viewing flow.

Misdirecting appendages would violate Cohn's directives if they correctly indicated paths that varied from each page's underlying Z-path. Still, even when correctly ignored, appendages produce challenges. For the first diagram, Cohn's seventh instruction, "If nothing is to the right, go to the far left and down," is problematic since a viewer would first need to follow panel 3's left horizontal gutter up before being able to continue left and down. The extended figures in the second and third diagrams undermine panel conventions entirely since their borders are embedded into other panels with no gutter edges to follow. If a viewer followed the edges of the figures instead, viewing paths would dip almost to the bottom edge of lower rows before angling back up. According to Witek's description of this "high baroque" technique, "the panel becomes only a notional 'container' of the action."[34] If so, then panels are not the fundamental units of a comics page generally because their borders do not necessarily frame content or determine viewing paths.

Baker's misdirecting appendages, usually the Phantom Lady's legs, appear in the bottom halves of panels, disrupting reading in two senses. Viewers may pause over the appended image instead of proceeding with the separate task of reading the content of nearby word containers, and viewers may also momentarily lose the progression of the image order. The leg acting as an abstract signifier decorporalized, a truly floating signifier, can be rearranged and collaged within a mental representation or within the boundaries of an art product; this hairless leg forms the perfect partial object or signifier, as its genderless status and minimalist form allow it to act in a multiplicity of ways in the construction of the imaginary.[35] Baker's layouts combine form and function by highlighting his equally disruptive content. If the array and predominance of his phantom legs "verge on the narratively incoherent," as Witek might suggest, that incoherence serves the nonnarrative but primary function of the baroque design.[36]

Combined Misdirections

Baker combines strategies, as demonstrated in figure 5.8.[37] The first diagram features both a mixed path and a reversed path in the lower portion of the page. Tall panel 4 requires an upward saccade to panel 5, and panel 6 requires a right-to-left movement to panel 7. The second diagram repeats the pattern but in the upper portion of the page and with nonrectangular panel shapes. The third diagram combines three strategies: a segment leap from panel 2 to panel 3; a mixed path with the paired subcolumns of panels 3, 4, and 5; and a concluding reversed path from panel 6 to panel 7 (which especially requires

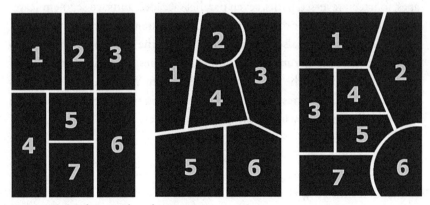

FIGURE 5.8 Misdirectional combinations

story content to determine). Each combination violates Cohn's directives. The lower portion of the first diagram would instead be read as subcolumns: 4, 5, 6, 7. The second diagram is ambiguous but may produce the same pattern: 1, 2, 4, 3. The third is also ambiguous, perhaps suggesting 1, 3, 4, 5, 2, 7, 6. None of these are Baker's actual viewing paths.

Not counting mixed paths, the 243 pages of *Phantom Lady* include seventy-two misdirections, which is over a third of the series. This is atypical of even Witek's high baroque style. While an exhaustive analysis of 1940s layouts is beyond the scope of this chapter, we offer preliminary comparisons.

Joe Shuster's viewing paths for the first 165 pages of Superman adventures from *Action Comics* #1 (June 1938) to #13 (June 1939) include four mixed paths (64, 66, 67, 68), all from #5, an issue probably created from panels rearranged from earlier drafts intended for newspaper formats.[38] Of the 183 *Superman* Sunday comics pages published from 1939 to 1943, only one includes a mixed row, and it is contained within a subdivided panel.[39] Shuster uses none of Baker's misdirectional techniques. Bob Kane's paths for the first 173 pages of Batman adventures from *Detective Comics* #27 (May 1939) to *Batman* #1 (Spring 1940) include four misdirecting appendages in which a rectangular panel extends significantly below its row's lower horizontal gutter (64, 68, 160, 174) and one parallel saccade (162) but no mixed paths, reversed paths, or segment leaps.[40] The collection *Marvel Firsts: WWII Superheroes* includes forty-three stories published from 1939 to 1943 with 416 layouts by approximately thirty different artists.[41] While Z-paths dominate, forty pages feature mixed paths. If Shuster, Kane, and the *Marvel Firsts* layouts are combined, roughly one-twentieth include misdirections. If that reflects a 1940s norm, Baker is well outside it. Of Baker's misdirectional arrangements, the collection includes twenty potential misdirecting appendages, fourteen reversed paths, seven parallel saccades, and two segment leaps, for a total of forty-three disruptions, or roughly one-tenth of the pages.

Misdirections may also provide insight into the questioned authorship of the *Phantom Lady* run. Becattini includes issues 14–20 in Baker's list of career credits but not the final three issues, and Jim Vadeboncoeur questions Baker's participation in issues 18–20.[42] Combining the five techniques, each issue includes the following number of occurrences:

#13 (August 1947): 7
#14 (October 1947): 6
#15 (December 1947): 8
#16 (February 1948): 14

#17 (April 1948): 14
#18 (June 1948): 10
#19 (August 1948): 9
#20 (October 1948): 10
#21 (December 1948): 5
#22 (February 1949): 6
#23 (April 1949): 5

Judging by layouts, Baker appears to have the clearest presence in the five middle issues, 16–20. This contradicts both Becattini's claim that Baker penciled most of the early issues and Vadeboncoeur's claim that Baker was absent for issues 18–20.

Layouts may also reveal authorship of the additional nine "Phantom Lady" stories that appeared in Fox's *All Top Comics*. The installments are shorter, usually seven pages rather than ten, and published in alternating months. Becattini and Vadeboncoeur attribute most to "Baker and/or Iger Shop," meaning Baker's contributions may have been total, partial, or non-existent.[43] Tallying the five types of Z-path misdirections is more suggestive:

#9 (January 1948): 2
#10 (March 1948): 2
#11 (May 1948): 6
#12 (July 1948): 2
#13 (September 1948): 1
#14 (November 1948): 1
#15 (January 1948): 0
#16 (March 1948): 0
#17 (May 1949): 0

The only set of distinctively Baker-style layouts is from May 1948, the month following the most Baker-prominent issue of *Phantom Lady*. While the eight other stories combined include misdirecting appendages, reversed paths, and parallel saccades, #11 features all five techniques, including an otherwise missing mixed path and segment leap. The January 1949 layouts, almost certainly drawn after Baker's departure from Iger, are also revealing because while they reflect Witek's description of high baroque's "wavy or jagged lines for panel borders, circular, triangular, or other unusually shaped panels," they contain none of Baker's misdirections, further suggesting that his techniques are distinct even within the category of high baroque.[44]

Baker's misdirections are not limited to *Phantom Lady*. The "Sky Girl" excerpt from *Jumbo Comics* #83 (December 1945) in figure 5.9 demonstrates the combined use of a parallel saccade between panels 3 and 4, a reversed path between panels 5 and 6, and a segment leap between panels 6 and 7. The page also provides a test for altering Cohn's directives to account for Baker-style layouts.

Cohn's directives would probably produce one of the following orders: 1, 4, 6, 2, 5, 3, 7 or 1, 2, 3, 4, 6, 5, 7, both of which contradict Baker's intended path. Rather than following inner and outer borders as defined by complete panel frames, viewers may instead apprehend image order according only to salient areas. Top-left corners may be sufficient, while also avoiding complications and ambiguities produced by unnecessary attention to gutters. The second and third diagrams show that Baker's path and a path based on top-left panel corners are the same, while an order derived from bottom-right corners in the fourth diagram is counterintuitive.

Since not all comics panels have corners (as demonstrated by the unframed second image), paths instead may be derived from image entrance areas (typically the top left), while disregarding image exit areas (typically the bottom right). Layouts that include one or more panels with significant frame-breaking content (as seen in the first and third diagrams in figure 5.7) still conform to this approach. If so, Thierry Groensteen is incorrect when he claims that a viewer's eye "always arrives ... from another point situated" within the viewing path and that an "exit is always indicated, pointing to another" panel.[45] A viewer's eye would instead orient itself by entrance areas only. Ignoring exit areas also explains why the Baker-style misdirections do not produce significant confusion, even though they indicate incorrect exits that point to nonsequential panels. It also explains why Cohn's viewing directives fail to explain Baker's pages because Cohn's studies define the spatial

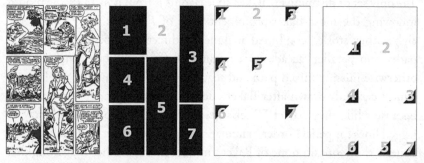

FIGURE 5.9 "Sky Girl" panel, entrance, and exit orders

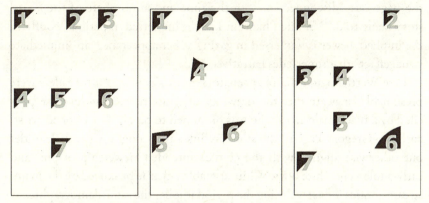

FIGURE 5.10 Layouts from figure 5.8 diagrammed by entrance order

"relationship between panels by approximating the centrepoint of a panel in relation to the centrepoint of the narratively preceding panel."[46]

Figure 5.10 applies an entrance approach to the three combination layouts diagrammed earlier in figure 5.8. The circular configurations in the bottom half of the first diagram and in the top half of the second are eliminated, as is the parallel saccade in the third. Only the order of the final two panels of the second and third diagrams are ambiguous since it is not clear whether highest or leftmost is prioritized when ordering.

Misdirectional Gaze

According to Becattini, the "ill-concealed purpose" of the protagonist of *Sky Girl* and her "series of predicaments . . . was to allow Baker to highlight the girl's long legs, regularly uncovered by pitiless turbulence to the delight of male readers. . . . Baker drew them from every conceivable angle. . . . Needless to say, he was hugely successful."[47] The description applies to Baker's work generally and to *Phantom Lady* specifically. Each page features at least one and usually multiple female figures drawn in leg-highlighting clothes, poses, and angles. Though loosely naturalistic, the images also reproduce the mid-century industry's mildly cartoonish drawing norms for female proportions, including impossibly thin waists and impossibly long legs.

Baker's images were not designed for story immersion, and rather than promoting effortless viewing flow, they invite pauses. The effect aligns with Witek's description of the "highly antic mode of storytelling" common in "high baroque," in which "the emotional effects suggested by the design of the page" are "disconnected from the tone and atmosphere of the actual story being told."[48] While Phantom Lady is immersed in perilous conflicts, the implied viewer is immersed in gazing at her appearance, an "immediate visual effect" that supersedes narrative.

Like Wertham and the 1954 senators, most *Phantom Lady* readers were presumably unaware that the drawings of white female figures were penciled by a Black male artist who was presumed to be gay. The implied artist-author—Gregory Page in the story credits—is a straight white male, older but otherwise aligned with the comic's intended viewership of pre- and early-adolescent white boys. While arguably any title produced by the mainstream comics industry during the period implies the same demographically defined creator, *Phantom Lady* and Baker's other titles do so doubly.

Laura Mulvey introduced the male gaze in her 1975 essay "Visual Pleasure and Narrative Cinema," building on Freudian scopophilia, in which a viewer takes "other people as objects, subjecting them to a controlling and curious gaze," and applying the concept to film "ordered by sexual imbalance," where "the determining male gaze projects its phantasy on to the female figure."[49] The parallel to Baker's misdirectional viewing paths is striking: "The presence of women is an indispensable element of spectacle, . . . yet her visual presence tends to work against the development of the story line, to freeze the flow of action in moments of erotic contemplation."[50] While the male gaze typically combines a male spectator's gaze with the gaze of a male character within a narrative, Mulvey also notes examples of "no mediation of the look through the eyes of the main male protagonist" but instead "the image in direct erotic rapport with the spectator," which further describes Baker's imagery.[51] Like a film aesthetic that aims "to eliminate intrusive camera presence and prevent a distancing awareness in the audience," layouts that promote effortless flow obscure their own presence and therefore the design choices of the artist.[52] Baker's misdirectional viewing instead draws attention away from the narrative world and toward the comics page, a further parallel to film directors whose "conventional close-ups of legs" destroy the illusion of depth in favor of "one-dimensional" effects that produce "the quality of a cut-out or icon rather than verisimilitude."[53]

Baker, however, contradicts the norms of the male gaze in one critical way. The gaze combines three kinds of looking: the male character's, the implied male spectator's, and the implied male creator's, which in film is the director's as embodied by the camera lens. In comics, the creative looking is the artist's. The conflation of the three into a unified gaze also projects a sexuality and racial identity onto the implied artist—one that Baker disrupts. Perception of Gregory Page as a straight white male collapses if a viewer experiences Baker's contradictory presence as gay, Black, or both. The conflated perspective also disrupts a young white male's viewing of the female figures because his literal point of view is identical to Baker's, as if the two were sharing a single area in diegetic space. The vantage places viewers inside Baker's implied body because hand-drawn comics expand the gaze beyond viewing. "Marks made on paper," writes Hillary Chute, "are an index of the body" of the artist, and Phillipe Marion similarly argues that viewers identify with a comics artist so fully that they have "the ability to redo, to remake, or at least re-experience the enunciative work produced by the author" as though physically drawing the art themselves.[54]

Experiencing white women through a Black man's body violated midcentury racial taboos, but the relationship was further complicated by Baker's presumed sexuality. Though, as Susan Bordo critiques, "the meaning of 'the gaze' varies by culture, gender, race, sexuality, etc.," *Phantom Lady* presents a specialized challenge since its surface relationships follow Mulvey's formulation and not later constructions of the female gaze or the "queer(ed)" Black gaze toward male sexual objects.[55] bell hooks critiques Mulvey by describing the experience of Black women spectators, who by refusing "to identify with white womanhood" or to "take on the phallocentric gaze of desire and possession, created a critical space where the binary opposition Mulvey posits . . . was continually deconstructed."[56] Once aware of Baker's authorial presence, the comic's intended viewers might enter a similarly deconstructed space, but rather than achieving hooks's oppositional gaze by refusing to identify with the implied straight white viewpoint, viewers are prevented from identifying with that gaze because Baker's positionality disrupts it. Awareness of questions about his sexuality could undermine the erotic effects of his images with the presumption that the acts of drawing them were not arousing to him and so reexperiencing those acts would not be arousing for a viewer. This is where misdirection once again plays an important role in disrupting an established viewing pattern.

White male viewers would also reexperience looking at and physically tracing the white female figures from the perspective of a Black man—a vantage many would have found intolerable in the time period. A year after Baker's *Phantom Lady* cover was displayed in the Senate hearings room, fourteen-year-old Emmett Till was murdered for allegedly flirting with a white woman. How would Till's murderers respond to Baker's cover image knowing that its "sexual stimulation by combining 'headlights' with a sadist's dream of tying up a woman" was a Black man's?[57] Baker's *Phantom Lady*, then, disrupts viewing in multiple senses, presenting challenges not only to layout paths but also to viewer engagement with its racialized and hyper-sexualized content.

Baker stands at a complex historical juncture. Though his earliest studio work includes African male figures in *Sheena* backgrounds, he is renowned for the white female bodies that dominate his artwork and paradoxically embody his artistic success. Unlike Jackie Ormes, an openly Black artist producing work through a Black publisher for a Black audience, or George Herriman, a passing-as-white Black artist producing work through a white publisher for a white audience, Baker was a well-regarded Black artist producing work within a white-dominated industry for a white audience that was unaware of his identity. Disguised identities were also one of that industry's norms. The *Phantom Lady* pseudonym hid other contributors, including Ruth Roche, a white female writer in a position similar to Baker's. Since Baker probably drew from Roche's and others' scripts rather than in the so-called Marvel method, in which artists have loosely equal if uncredited authorial control, his disruptive techniques suggest a further resistance to period expectations. It is a suggestive coincidence that Phantom Lady's identifying gadget is a blacklight projector that temporarily blinds her enemies by enclosing them in a beam of projected blackness. Disrupting viewing is her superpower, but being viewed is her purpose and Baker's artistic priority, one he simultaneously achieves and complicates. Baker is similarly present and absent, his blackness both obscured by and projected through his misaligned gutters and the phantom limbs that break the frames of their no-longer-segregated panels.

Baker's misdirectional viewing patterns allow for interpretations that do not reproduce hierarchies of difference but instead compel a more nuanced exploration of the multiple interpretations of his work. Black artistic expression through predominantly white aesthetics is often a necessarily covert response to the persistently negative call of "normative signifiers of blackness . . . that renders [blackness] strange, unknowable, and open to the process of signification: a queering of blackness, so to speak."[58] Replicating the visual fantasy of a white woman for the white male gaze yet "coding" the work by circumventing the schema of conventional comics diagrams positions Baker as someone who, on a conceptual level, understood the value of misdirection as both strategy and technique.

Baker's use of visual misdirection as a device that is meant to go beyond the pure understanding of comics layout nudges the reader's eye and consciousness toward a visual discourse that he could not openly have or "perform." Reminiscent of Ralph Ellison's ability to "cloak" his narrative in ways that appealed to white readers, perhaps because many did not fully understand the nuances of his arguments, Baker was equally adept, through his layouts, at turning the "purity" of the white woman into a misdirectional device, thereby drawing attention away from the supposed "impurity" of blackness.[59] By employing misdirection in his layouts, Baker effectively mounted an implicit critique of white norms.

Notes

1. Becattini and Vadeboncoeur, "Matt Baker Checklist."
2. Wertham, *Seduction of the Innocent*, 212–213.
3. Mills, *Racial Contract*, 1.
4. Mills, 53.
5. Mills, 53.
6. Becattini, "Baker of Cheesecake," 37.
7. Minh-Ha, *When the Moon Waxes Red*, 156.
8. Jain, "More than Meets the Eye," 33; Haley, "Like I Was a Man."
9. Becattini, "Baker of Cheesecake," 38.
10. Giusto, "Great Friendship," 132–133.
11. Ritbergen, "Further Ruminations," 121.
12. Crawford, "My Noose around That Pretty's Neck."
13. Hall, "Race, the Floating Signifier."
14. Earle, *Writing Queer Women of Color*, 32.
15. Foucault, "Preface to Transgression," 34.
16. Although there is no indisputable evidence confirming Baker's sexuality, his close friend Frank Giusto told the comics historian Shaun Clancy in a 2011 interview that he had advised Baker to see a psychiatrist about being gay and that upon returning from a session with the psychiatrist, Baker quipped, "the guy is queerer than I am." Giusto, "Great Friendship," 128. See also Ken Quattro's *Invisible Men: The Trailblazing Black Artists of Comic Books* (2020), in which he also cites Giusto. For further critiques of Baker's work and his personal life, see Dwain C. Pruitt's 2016 article "It Rhymes with Lust? Matt Baker and the Ironic Politics of Race, Sex and Gender in the Golden Age." While Pruitt also draws on the Clancy interview with Frank Giusto regarding speculation about Baker's sexual orientation, he notes that for the time period during which Baker and other Black artists lived, there would have been a number of tensions at play that would have been bound up in the "major components" of one's Black identity (208).
17. Witek, "Arrow and the Grid," 154.
18. Pederson and Cohn, "Changing Pages of Comics," 14.
19. McCloud, *Making Comics*, 37.
20. Cohn, *Visual Language of Comics*, 97–98.
21. McCloud, *Making Comics*, 36.
22. McCloud, 33.
23. Witek, "Arrow and the Grid," 154.

24 Hatfield, *Alternative Comics*, xiv.
25 Bateman, et al, "On the Track of Visual Style," 1.
26 Gavaler, *Superhero Comics*, 212.
27 Figure 5.1 represents page 5 of the first Phantom Lady story in *Phantom Lady* #13 (August 1947), Fox, Digital Comic Museum; page 5 of the second story in the same issue; page 2 of the first story in issue #21 (December 1948); page 8 of the second story in #20 (October 1948); page 5 of the first story in #23 (April 1949); and page 2 of the first story in #16 (December 1947).
28 Figure 5.2 represents page 4 of the second story of #18 (June 1948); page 5 of the second story in #19 (August 1948); and page 4 of the first story in #16.
29 Figure 5.4 represents page 4 of #18's second story, page 7 of #16's second story, and page 6 of #19's first story.
30 Figure 5.5 represents page 5 of #19's first story, page 7 of #20's first story, and page 3 of the first story of #22 (February 1949).
31 Witek, "Arrow and the Grid," 154.
32 Pederson and Cohn, "Changing Pages of Comics," 14.
33 Figure 5.7 represents page 8 of #19's first story, page 3 of #16's first story, and page 8 of #16's second story.
34 Witek, "Arrow and the Grid," 154.
35 Neidich, "Pierre Molinier and the Phantom Limb."
36 Witek, "Arrow and the Grid," 154.
37 Figure 5.8 represents page 9 of #18's second story; page 8 of #23's second story; page 5 of #18's second story; page 6 of #14's first story; page 6 of #16's first story; and page 7 of #17's first story.
38 Siegel and Shuster, *Superman Chronicles*.
39 Siegel and Shuster, *Superman*.
40 Kane and Finger, *Batman Chronicles*.
41 Burgos et al., *Marvel Firsts*.
42 Becattini and Vadeboncoeur, "Matt Baker Checklist," 82–83.
43 Becattini, "Baker of Cheesecake," 68.
44 Witek, "Arrow and the Grid," 154.
45 Groensteen, *System of Comics*, 48–49.
46 Pederson and Cohn, "Changing Pages of Comics," 12.
47 Becattini, "Baker of Cheesecake," 37.
48 Witek, "Arrow and the Grid," 154.
49 Mulvey, "Visual Pleasure and Narrative Cinema," 59, 62.
50 Mulvey, 62.
51 Mulvey, 65.
52 Mulvey, 68.
53 Mulvey, 62–63.
54 Chute, *Disaster Drawn*, 20; Baetens, "Revealing Traces," 150.
55 Bordo, "It's Not the Same for Women."
56 Hooks, "Oppositional Gaze," 99.
57 Wertham, *Seduction of the Innocent*, 212–213.
58 D. Murray, "Mickalene Thomas," 10.
59 Ellison's writing was imaginatively expressed and still finds critical purchase in contemporary scholarship. Indeed, in a nod to his deep love of music, Ellison's work and the complicated interiority of his characters drew heavily on the elegant "chaos" of jazz. At once elevating and perhaps unconsciously "cloaking" the signifying of the

Black aesthetic in the twentieth-century United States, it could be said that Ellison borrowed from jazz to craft literature as a counterpoint to the encoded and unrelenting cacophony of whiteness. Even Henry Louis Gates Jr. has described Ellison as "our Great Signifier, . . . naming things by indirection and troping throughout his work" ("Blackness of Blackness," 695). In this way, the lens through which we examine Matt Baker's work necessarily turns on historical and intersecting inflection points that invite contemporary readings.

6

The Art of Alvin Hollingsworth

● ● ● ● ● ● ● ● ● ● ● ● ●

BLAIR DAVIS

Alvin Hollingsworth (1928–2000) was a talented artist who worked in the comic book industry in the 1940s and 1950s before becoming a painter and a professor. One of the few Black creators to work in comics prior to the civil rights movement, Hollingsworth's career is especially notable in how he shifted from drawing comic books to using art for civic engagement. In 1963, he was part of the art collective Spiral, and by the 1970s, he taught art as a professor at Hostos Community College of the City University of New York in the South Bronx. His work within the comic book industry is itself a key piece of comics history that has gone unchronicled, but his career is also a critical object of study for the larger fields of media studies *and* cultural studies given how the trajectory of his work moved from comics to fine art; his work spans both popular culture and the visual arts, bridging the realms of so-called lowbrow and highbrow culture.

In moving from horror, crime, and jungle comics (as well as love stories targeted specifically to Black readers in the 1950 series *Negro Romance*) to paintings imbued with more overt political intent, Hollingsworth's career is

FIGURE 6.1 "Anatomical Monster" showcases Hollingworth's use of abstraction and heavy shadows (*Eerie* #11 [Avon Comics, April 1953]).

a vital example of how the comics medium could serve as a training ground for an artist who sought to do more than just entertain through lurid genre stories. Many of his stylistic traits as an avant-garde painter later in life can be traced back to his early work in comics. The horror series *Eerie*, for example, became a forum for Hollingsworth's skilled use of abstraction and distortion in drawing the human body via heavy shadows and silhouettes, such as issue 11's story "Anatomical Monster," a pattern that (in addition to being an important precursor for the work of later comics artists like Mike Mignola and Jae Lee) he would take in new directions in the 1960s and 1970s with such paintings as *Trapped*, *Voodoo*, and *Don Quixote*.

In 1971, Hollingsworth fused his penchant for abstracted human figures with his sociopolitical beliefs in his painting of an African Jesus Christ: Hollingsworth told *Ebony* magazine that the painting was intended to draw a parallel between Christ and slain Black leaders like Malcom X, serving as a "philosophical symbol of any of the modern prophets who have been trying to show us the right way": "To me, Martin Luther King and Malcolm X are such prophets."[1] A published collection about African American artists displayed at the Barnett-Aden Gallery described Hollingsworth as one of several "artists who find their inspiration in the black protest movement, the black experience in America, or the motives, symbols, and color of Africa but work within an established tradition."[2] In turn, this essay traces how the cultural and political underpinnings of Hollingsworth's paintings and other artwork were molded, for better or worse, by his experiences as an artist in the largely segregated comic book industry in the decades leading up to the civil rights movement.

So much of the work done to date about Black comic book characters and creators has looked at the social, cultural, and political contexts surrounding how comics creators and fans have treated such popular figures as Black Panther, Luke Cage, Storm, and other heroes, as well as how Black creators like Jackie Ormes, Kyle Baker, Dwayne McDuffie, and Christopher Priest have used the medium of comics to tell Black stories. But the analysis of how Black characters, artists, and writers have thrived and/or struggled, strived, resisted, or endured must go beyond just looking at questions of representation, as vital as that aim still remains. We must also examine issues of form and aesthetics in more direct ways when studying the work of Black creators. This emphasis on formal analysis places aesthetic issues at the forefront, allowing Hollingsworth's art and his artistry to be analyzed in a way that elevates the work itself by comparing the stylistic traits between his comics art and his paintings. Tracing the stylistic development of Hollingsworth's artwork across his comics and later art career allows us to examine not only how his work predates that of later comic book artists but also how his comics career influenced his subsequent work in other artforms—much of which saw him develop earlier stylistic traits with greater degrees of experimentation and to much more explicit sociopolitical ends.

Early Career

Born in New York City on February 25, 1928, Alvin Carl Hollingsworth was the son of the Caribbean immigrants Charles and Cynthia Hollingsworth.[3] Raised in Harlem, Alvin began his career in comics at a young age: he was still a junior high school student when he began working as an art assistant at Holyoke Publishing in the early 1940s.[4] Holyoke was a lower-tier publisher (which probably explains why it hired such young artists), and it was here that Hollingsworth met Joe Kubert, who was just seventeen months older than Hollingsworth. Kubert's first published artwork came in 1942 for Holyoke's *Cat-Man Comics*, a series for which Hollingsworth drew background details and did the kind of touch-up work common to the art assistant role. "My first cartoons were city scenes picturing the Empire State Building," Hollingsworth recalled later in life of his first work for Holyoke.[5]

The two teenagers became fast friends after meeting at Holyoke, with Hollingsworth regularly joining the Kubert family for dinner. Kubert's biographer Bill Schelly describes how Joe encouraged Alvin to apply to the High School of Music and Art in Manhattan, which Kubert attended. "Hollingsworth was in eighth grade at the time. Subsequently," says Schelly, "Hollingsworth did apply and was accepted at M&A for his freshman year."[6] While Schelly calls Hollingsworth "a Kubert protégé of sorts," their relationship was that of two high school friends rather than mentor-apprentice.[7] Hollingsworth and Kubert regularly honed their comics art skills in Joe's attic after eating dinner together: "'Joe was very nice,' Hollingsworth recalled. 'Every weekend while the other kids were out playing basketball, I was going over to study with Joe. Joe taught me a lot. He taught me how to cut a line [with] a razor blade . . . so the line was so sharp it looked like it was printed. He taught me a lot about how to give a picture force by having the punch look like it swept through the page.'"[8]

While Kubert's career in comics lasted far longer than Hollingsworth's, Joe recalled in a 2013 interview, "Alvin turned out to be one of the outstanding black artists. . . . Incredible artist! Painter! Used to come home with me when I lived in east New York. My mother never hesitated! . . . And he would be with us, he would sup with us. And there was no distinction at all. The fact that he was black, the fact that we were Jewish. Never any kind of thing like that."[9] Hollingsworth was one of only a few Black creators to work at comic book publishers or studios in the 1940s, along with artists like Matt Baker, Cal Massey, and Elmer C. Stoner. Baker is the best remembered today, especially for his work drawing *Phantom Lady* and the early graphic novel *It Rhymes with Lust*. While the comic book industry was certainly marked by systemic racism in this era, many publishers were integrated workplaces that saw Black and white creators working side by side. Baker's talent made him a respected figure among many of his white peers, with the artist Jack Katz saying about their time working together at the Iger-Roche Studio in the mid-1940s, "Matt was accepted, at least to his face. I don't know all that went on there, but really, Matt and I got along beautifully. I used to just praise his stuff to the ceiling." Katz saw Baker's talent as affording him more respect than other creators of color encountered: "He won by way of his art. . . . Really, none of the others could draw half as well as he could. He was treated with respect."[10]

Hollingsworth, however, had a different experience. "When I got into the field I began running into prejudice, for now I was competing for jobs," he said, noting how he encountered more discrimination after moving from his early role as an art assistant to do his own penciling and inking: "I was no longer 'helping people.'"[11] Systemic racism is also probably responsible for the changes made to the character Bronze Man created by Hollingsworth in 1946's *Blue Beetle* #42, who some comics fans believe was intended to be the first African American superhero. An anonymous indexer at the Grand Comics Database describes how Hollingsworth "meant for Bronze Man to be of African-American heritage, wearing an iron mask whenever he appeared as Bronze Man, but the published version was Caucasian and sans the mask," while the comics historian Craig Yoe writes that since "the term 'bronze' was a way to refer to African Americans" in this era, there is a strong possibility that Hollingsworth "designed him to be a black superhero," only to find that "the publisher scrapped the idea and had Bronze Man's mask and skin color changed."[12]

After Hollingsworth worked as an art assistant for a few years, his first credited work as an artist appears to be *Crime Does Not Pay* #31; its January 1944 cover date means that he was only fifteen years old at the time. Several sources note that he began in comics at age twelve, making him one of the industry's youngest creators ever. He worked on numerous crime titles including *All-Famous Police Cases*, *Fight against Crime*, *Fight against the Guilty*, *Headline Comics*, *Police against Crime*, and *Police Trap*, plus Western series like *Blazing West*, *Indian Fighter*, and *Western Outlaws*. At Fiction House, he drew stories for Jungle Comics, Rangers Comics, and Wings Comics, while at Fox Feature Syndicate, his work appeared in *Crimes by Women* and *Rulah, Jungle Goddess*, along with his Bronze Man stories for *Blue Beetle*. He also drew several romance comics, including *All-True Romance*, *Romantic Secrets*, *Young Love*, and *Young Romance*, along with Fawcett Comics' landmark 1950 series *Negro Romance*, which featured Black protagonists throughout its short-lived three-issue run (see Jacque Nodell's essay on the latter series, chapter 13 in this volume). Hollingsworth even drew a three-page profile on the jazz legend Duke Ellington for the first issue of Eastern Color Printing Co.'s *Juke Box Comics* in 1948. By 1950, his work had been featured in titles from at least a dozen publishers, making him one of the most prolific Black artists of comics' Golden Age of the 1940s and 1950s.

Hollingsworth's Style

Hollingsworth's art style evolved over the course of his comic book career, often shifting to suit the demands of a particular genre or publisher, as was common of most artists in this era. In many instances, his work had a distinctive quality, while at other times, it conformed to a series's existing look. But despite the practical need to produce material that followed certain industrial parameters, his comics output often showed traces of the stylistic tendencies that he would go on to develop much further in his avant-garde artwork later in life. In his paintings and illustrations produced in the 1960s onward, Hollingsworth used a style known as "figurative expressionism," which the museum director Terrence E. Dempsey describes as "the deliberate distortion of recognizable figures—a distortion of shape, color and space—that allows the artist (and the viewer, it is hoped) to go beyond surface reality in order to reach deeper emotional and often spiritual realities."[13] This "distortion" of physical features and human anatomy became a recurring trait of Hollingsworth's approach to many of his characters, especially in his crime and horror work in the late 1940s and 1950s. By the time he started drawing horror titles like *Eerie*, *Ghostly Weird Tales*, *Horrific*, and *Witchcraft*, his artwork demonstrated a regular interest in rendering human and nonhuman bodies in increasingly abstract ways—serving as a natural bridge between his work in genre comics in one decade and that of a figurative expressionist painter in the next.

In this way, Hollingsworth's art anticipates that of popular artists in later eras of comic book production, such as Jae Lee, Mike Mignola, and Tim Sale, all of whom eschew traditional approaches to their figures in favor of a more distorted approach. The comics scholar Scott Bukatman describes Mignola's artwork, for instance, as "increasingly non-naturalistic," seeing him as one of a number of late twentieth-century artists "working in genre comics who have pushed comics in new directions in the treatment of human figure," along with Jae Lee.[14] Dempsey further notes how figurative expressionism "was increasingly used by 20th century artists to call attention to the affective dimension (and not just the intellectual dimension) of what it means to be human," with religious or spiritual subject matter often present.[15] This is true of Mignola's occult-themed work in *Hellboy* and *B.P.R.D.*, just as it is in Hollingsworth's paintings *Madonna's Dream* and his "The Prophet" series depicting a Black Jesus Christ and other Christian figures.

Hollingsworth's artwork was featured alongside that of Matt Baker in *Rulah, Jungle Goddess*; Alvin drew a story about a backup character named Numa in 1948's issue 18, while Baker was the title character's regular artist. But while Baker is celebrated by his fans for the clean lines of his "good girl" art style with characters like Rulah and Phantom Lady, Hollingsworth's artwork was often less concerned with this kind of cleanliness.[16] While he could certainly draw pretty girls like Tiger Girl in *Fight Comics* in a way that fit in with dominant genre styles, his artwork was at its most distinctive when he favored jagged edges over round ones and weathered faces over smooth complexions. He could draw pretty, but he was better when he drew ugly.

In a word, Hollingsworth's comic book art was regularly concerned with *texture*: his penciling and inkwork creates a distinct visual style with regard to the texture of clothing, objects, and surfaces, along with the human face, an approach that he took even further in his expressionist artwork after leaving the comics industry. The artist Klaus Janson describes how in comics art, "texture refers to the visual or tactile characteristic of a surface. A solid black or white on paper is flat. It has no texture. Once the artist starts creating a grey tone," says Janson, they are "interpreting a tactile quality to create a more convincing representation of the object or surface."[17] This approach is on clear display in Hollingsworth's one-page story "The Midget Murderer" in 1948's *Crimes by Women* #2, in which a range of distinct textures are created across just six panels, from the frilliness of a woman's brassiere to her rumpled bedspread, from the heavy presence of an iron lamppost to the cracked façade of a brick wall, and from the smooth veneer of a slatted park bench to the bumpy contours of a stone prison wall.[18]

The texture conveyed by a drawn image is often the result of an artist's line work, which can vary in width, length, depth, and weight. In the 1900 book *Line and Form*, Walter Crane described how artists can use line work "to express form in a more complete way than can be done in outline alone." Artists can create different tonal qualities depending on how their lines are drawn. "The quality of our lines will depend on the quality we are seeking to express. We shall be led to vary them in seeking to express other characteristics, such as textures and surfaces," he noted.[19] Crane also described how "there are the *qualities* of line in different degrees of firmness, roughness, raggedness, or smooth and flowing. There are degrees of direction of line, curvilinear or angular. . . . Every artist, sooner or later, by means of his selective adaptive practice, finds a method in the use of line to suit to suit his own personality—to suit his own individual aim in artistic expression."[20]

Hollingsworth's approach to texture in his line work regularly involved a very scratchy style—embodying the "roughness" and "raggedness" that Crane describes as opposed to Baker's smoother lines—with lots of tiny brush strokes to fill in the details of many characters' outfits, such as the fur collar and lining of aviator jackets or the nicks and scrapes on soldiers' helmets, which were accompanied by a stippling effect using lots of tiny dots to show wear and tear in 1946's *Wings Comics* #67. The artwork by other artists in *Wings Comics* (like "Captain Wings" by Lee Elias) usually strove to resemble Milton Caniff's figures in his influential newspaper strip *Terry and the Pirates*. This is particularly true in how characters' faces are drawn with minimal line work to resemble the major players of that comic strip, an approach that avoids an abundance of extra details created by the use of ample pen lines. Kubert described Caniff's style as being marked by "heavy blacks and quick line work," while Caniff himself said that the "key" to his style was "eliminating unnecessary lines."[21]

Kubert's art, like his friend Alvin's, was marked by the type of plentiful line work that Caniff eschewed. But while Kubert's artwork was similar to that of his childhood favorite artist, Hal Foster (who drew the newspaper strips *Tarzan* and *Prince Valiant*), in using numerous lines to create a detailed musculature for each of his characters, Hollingsworth used his line work to emphasize different anatomical aspects such as bone structure and skin. Hollingsworth's faces are often less clean and more exaggerated: the bone structure of his faces is not uniformly round, with characters' jaw lines varying in shape and size (but drawn consistently within each story for individual characters). This approach to anatomical impreciseness is one that kept developing throughout his career as he moved from drawing human figures in the crime and action genres to more pronounced efforts at bodily distortion in horror comics and then finally in more abstract and expressionist ways in his later paintings such as *Chance, The Women (Amarillo)*, and *Together* and in illustrations for such books as *Black Out Loud* (1970).

Crane makes a key distinction in how the human face is drawn between the "firmness of fundamental structure (in the bones) and surface curve (of sinew and muscle)."[22] While Kubert often strove for realism in the latter, Hollingsworth deliberately exaggerated the former. In his 1946 "Suicide Smith" story from issue 67 of *Wings Comics*, a crime boss named Flash is drawn with an excessively large/rounded chin and cheekbones, creating a segmented look to his face. Similarly, in issues 106 and 107 of *Wings Comics*, Smith battles various villains whose jaws are distorted well beyond normal proportions—unnaturally long and angular in one case, excessively wide in another.

This trend can even be seen in Hollingsworth's early work for *Crime Does Not Pay* #31 via the distorted facial structure of several bandits from his story "The Million Dollar Robbery." To be sure, other artists of this era often drew their villains and crime bosses with some degree of embellishment not seen with their heroic protagonists. Hollingsworth was not alone in drawing ugly criminals that looked more like the film noir actors Rondo Hatton or Mike

Mazurki than like handsome leading men such as Alan Ladd or Dick Powell. But Hollingsworth's distorted, expressionistic style was not just a strategic departure from his regular tendencies: it was a consistent trait of his artwork across various decades and artistic media. His distorted faces never quite seem to align with any plausible degree of human anatomy. While other artists of the same era certainly drew plenty of ugly gangsters and brutish criminals, many of Hollingsworth's villains never seem quite real in their bone structure—their faces becoming rough approximations as if carved from stone, often with jagged edges and sharp points. It was this distortive tendency in depicting human figures that he took in new directions after leaving the comics business behind for other artistic venues.

Hollingsworth's interest in figurative expressionism only grew from his early work in crime and horror series through to his sketches, paintings, and other illustrations in the 1960s and beyond. He strove not for a purely clean look but rather for something more askew, more chaotic than other artists who used their line work to create a normalized world in their pages. His characters, especially his villains, were often drawn in a way that reflected their inner qualities. While Kubert drew a character like the supernatural DC villain Solomon Grundy as having a distorted, unnatural face due to his zombie-like nature, Hollingsworth often took the same approach to regular people. Even in stories in which he imitates the "quick line work" of Caniff's faces, like *Crimes by Women* #5's "Radiant Jade: The Devil Incarnate," moments of stylistic distortion still emerge. While the story of a woman who murders a Japanese colonel mostly adheres to the visual style of drawing Asian faces established by Caniff in *Terry and the Pirates* (a creative choice just as likely to have been spurred by editorial demands as by creator preference), Hollingsworth's distinct approach to drawing faces is still seen in key moments. When Jade surprises the colonel with a poisonous snake in his bed, the look of shock on his face is heightened by his distorted appearance: his forehead bulges and his eyeballs widen well beyond what is physically possible, while the whites of his eyes contain a combination of larger/heavier and smaller/thinner lines meant to convey fear and shock.[23]

Much of the stylistic nuance in how any artist's line work creates certain textures arrives when the pencil work is inked. Hollingsworth frequently inked his own artwork, a way of guaranteeing more control over the finished look. Janson notes that inking one's own work is indeed about retaining such creative control: "My penciling approach is greatly affected by who is going to do the inks. If I am inking the work myself, I try to stay rough in my drawing so that my inks have something to add instead of just tracing my penciled lines. If someone else is going to ink the pencils, I will make my drawings as tight as possible so that the inker has as little to do as possible. My goal is to keep as much control over the work I can to ensure that it reflects my own artistic sensibilities."[24] Hollingsworth inked much, if not most, of his work, which allowed the finished product to retain a style marked by deliberate and consistent line work across his comics career. He may have altered his lines to match the tone of certain genres like romance comics, but throughout much of his comics career, we see a distinctive style emerge and grow as he experimented with textural effects and bodily distortion across numerous genres.

Hollingsworth and Horror Comics

In Schelly's biography of Joe Kubert, he describes how Hollingsworth "found his niche drawing weird, semi-primitive images of floating skulls and grisly graveyards."[25] The horror genre definitely marked a turning point in Hollingsworth's career, seeing his most sustained efforts on a single series as opposed the shorter runs and single efforts done for series in other genres. While he did a four-issue stint of "Suicide Smith" stories for *Wings Comics* in 1946 and then six more issues of that series between 1949 and 1950, he drew stories in eleven straight issues of Story Comics' *Dark Mysteries* from 1952 to 1954 as well as six consecutive issues of *Mysterious Adventures* between 1951 and 1952 for the same publisher. He also drew stories for Avon Comics' *Eerie* and *Witchcraft* from 1952 to 1955, along with issues of Comic Media's *Horrific*, Minion Publishing Corp.'s *Tales of Horror*, Star Publication's *Ghostly Weird Stories*, and Trojan Magazine's *Beware* between those years. The comics horror-zine author Peter Normanton includes Hollingsworth in a list of top horror artists in the 1950s alongside EC Comics' Johnny Craig, Jack Davis, and Graham Ingels, pointing to his work at Avon Comics in particular: "the ever-astute Joseph Meyers at Avon need only put out the word and Alvin Hollingsworth would be poised, brush in hand, to produce page upon page of his unearthly visions."[26] The horror genre is where Hollingsworth did his most prolific work in comics, and it is where the stylistic parallels with his later career in fine arts are most apparent.

Through these horror tales, Hollingsworth was able to explore expressionist techniques much more readily in a way that was welcomed by the genre's subject matter, from the rotting anatomy and scrawny legs of newly resurrected zombies to the distorted faces full of shadows and black areas of various menacing figures. Much like Mignola would later do in his work on *Hellboy* (followed by the efforts of the artists who worked on such *Hellboy* spin-off series as *B.P.R.D.*, *Abe Sapien*, and *Sir Edward Gray, Witchfinder*, like Scott Allie, Gabriel Bá, Guy Davis, Paul Grist, Troy Nixey, Michael Avon Oeming, Matt Smith, Peter Snejbjerg, Ryan Sook, and Tonci Zonjic), Hollingsworth's horror comics were a forum in which he could play with shape and shadow, figure and line, while he drew all sorts of different bodies and forms, both human and monster. His work in the genre stands as a pioneering moment in the history of Black horror comics, followed by such notable artists in later decades as Billy Graham on *Vampirella*, John Jennings's *Box of Bones*, and Sanford Greene's *Bitter Root*.

The "floating skulls" that Schelly describes as a hallmark of Hollingsworth's work echo throughout Mignola's work, with skulls, skeletons, and severed heads becoming a prominent visual trope in many *Hellboy* comics. In the story "Heads," Hellboy faces off against a demonic horde of floating heads in Japan; in "King Vold," the story's titular villain holds his own severed head in his hand; Hellboy faces various flaming skeletons in "The Corpse" and fights a skeletal creature whose head is decapitated in "Wake the Devil"; skeletons and skulls are recurring images in "The Vârcolac," "Conqueror Worm," "The Third Wish," "The Island," "The Vampire of Prague," "They That Go Down to the Sea in Ships," "Darkness Calls," and "Hellboy in Hell," among others. Even the spines of the *Hellboy Library Edition* hardcover collections feature a skull at the top of each volume, in keeping with how commonly Mignola uses skulls in his work, much like Hollingsworth did decades earlier.

Hollingsworth's cover to *Witchcraft* #4, for instance, features a robed skeleton holding a staff with a skull on it while cooking a young couple in a skull-lined cauldron. His cover to #6 features a series of five floating heads—the first that of a human being and the last a skull, while the middle three images depict various states of transformation between the two states. Skulls and skeletons abound within stories from *Dark Mysteries* #10 ("The Note of Death") and #14 ("The Skeleton's Revenge"). In *Witchcraft* #4's "The Man Who Bribed Death," the grim reaper takes the form of a "skullfaced thing" wearing a top hat and overcoat who has come to collect an overdue soul.[27] Hollingsworth depicts the inner torment of the man marked for death in a dream sequence inspired by the imagery of Salvador Dalí, complete with numerous eyeballs, doorways, skulls, and a clock.

Hollingsworth's emphasis on the textural qualities of his subjects is used to new, macabre ends in such stories as "Mystery of the Moaning Statue"

FIGURE 6.2 "Kill No More" showcases Hollingsworth's shadowing technique, anticipating later work by artists like Mike Mignola (*Beware* #16 [Trojan Magazines, July 1953]).

from *Witchcraft* #6, in which a sculptress's pitted, porous statue comes to life and murders her lover. He also regularly used deep, dark shadows throughout much of his work in the horror genre, paralleling the later work of more recent artists. Characters' faces, and their eyes especially, are often obscured by heavy shadows in "Bride for the Dead" from *Mysterious Adventures* #6 and "Kill No More" from *Beware* #16 (figure 6.2). In "The Ripper's Return" in *Tales of Horror* #2, we are met with heavy shadows over lumpy, uneven faces in a way that resembles the modern artwork of Mignola, Eduardo Risso, and Tim Sale. The same lumpy textures and rich black shadows are found in "The Manikins of Death" from *Mysterious Adventures* #3, in which an artist sculpts a manikin out of clay.

The recurrent plot device of sculpture in Hollingsworth's horror tales is especially key to how we study his work, given the ways in which Mignola's artwork has been read through sculptural frameworks. Bukatman notes in *Hellboy's World* how "Mignola draws heavily on sculptural principles," such as how "small marks pepper the surfaces, be they stone, cloth, or flesh, endowing the whole world with a chiseled quality."[28] Bukatman also draws a distinct parallel between Mignola's work on *Hellboy* and the sculpture of Auguste Rodin: "Figures emerge from the negative space of an inky blackness as they emerge from the negative space of Rodin's pediments."[29] Hollingsworth's art was also marked by the same sculptural "peppering" and the same "inky blackness" on many occasions (like in "Kill No More" from *Beware* #16 in which characters' facial features disappear within the cavernous dark shadows that engulf their eyes, ears, and/or nostrils). Hollingsworth was particularly fond of using shadows to create "negative space" *within* the bodies of his characters, given his interest in figurative art, while Mignola and others took these shadowing techniques even further in juxtaposing their shadowy characters against the equally shadowy backdrops within individual panels as the horror genre evolved in the decades that followed.

Hollingsworth's early strides in figurative expressionism are found in many of his horror tales, such as in how he draws a distorted ghost in "Terror Comes in Threes" from *Dark Mysteries* #8. Similarly, the characters in "The Last Man Alive" from *Ghostly Weird Stories* #121 become an exercise in figurative distortion as their warped, contorted bodies are drawn at one point as if appearing in a fun-house mirror. In *Eerie* #11's "Anatomical Monster," a creature comes to life from a drawing of a human anatomy chart, its form half flesh, half skeletal. In "The Horror of the Walking Corpse" from *Dark Mysteries* #16, both the structural design of the titular corpse's limbs and the pen lines Hollingsworth uses to render its gnarled body are a precursor to the way he drew bodies in many later paintings and sketches—such as the lean, jutting figures of his "Don Quixote" series and the fragile, branch-like limbs of the bodies in *Family Tree*, *The Women*, and other paintings (figure 6.3). Given how several of the stories he drew about witch doctors and jungle tribes (like *Dark Mysteries* #18's "Some Die Twice") were full of racist tropes concocted by their white writers, Hollingsworth's ability to reclaim how he drew Black bodies later in his career by updating his use of figurative expressionist techniques within the new artistic media of his paintings, sketches, and multimedia projects is a rare example of a Black comics artist turning their style toward more overtly sociopolitical ends for new audiences as their career progresses.

Conclusion

Hollingsworth continued drawing comic books throughout the mid-1950s, while also working on the comic strips *Scorchy Smith*, *Martin Keel*, and *Kandy* in this period. He did work for numerous publishers in different genres in the late 1940s and into the 1950s, notably drawing for Fawcett's

FIGURE 6.3 In "Horror of the Walking Corpse," Hollingsworth's artwork anticipates his later work in figurative expressionism (*Dark Mysteries* #16 [Story Comics, February 1954]).

Negro Romance in 1950 as well as Joe Simon and Jack Kirby's romance series *Young Love* and *Young Romance*. The *Negro Romance* writer Roy Ald and Shaun Clancy say of the title's creation, "It was because of Hollingsworth that we did that series," showing how the artist was often able to tailor his work toward his own interests as his comics career progressed.[30] As Hollingsworth transitioned away from comic books, he went on to draw for men's adventure and lifestyle magazines later in the decade, including *Man's Daring Adventures* and *Relax: Prescription for Pleasure* (serving as art director for the latter). Just as he balanced his studies as a high school student in the 1940s with his comic book assignments, so too did Hollingworth pursue advanced degrees in fine art while continuing his drawing career in the 1950s: he earned a bachelor's degree in 1956 (graduating Phi Beta Kappa) and then a master's degree in 1959 from the City College of New York, followed by a PhD in the 1970s from New York University.

Hollingsworth began painting avant-garde work in the 1950s alongside his commercial work, but he credited the Spiral art collective for allowing him to commit more fully to doing fine art. Spiral was active between 1963 and 1966 in Greenwich Village in New York City and was one of the first Black artists' alliances since the Harlem Renaissance. "In the 1950s, I had done my abstract expressionist thing, and I was more French than a Frenchman," Hollingsworth recalled. "But when Spiral came along, I really got involved."[31] The art historian Courtney J. Martin describes how, "under the banner of civil rights, [the Spiral artists] sought to address aesthetic, social, and cultural concerns pertinent to the turbulent 1960s. From the summer of 1963 through 1966, they bantered about the existence of the 'Negro' artist at their weekly meetings, where they attempted to support one another artistically and emotionally."[32] In a 1966 interview with Hollingsworth, the art historian Jeanne Siegel noted how he "thinks of Spiral as a form of group therapy." Hollingsworth himself described Spiral as a forum for both individual and political expression: "It's a place for Negroes to air their own prejudices and see each other in realistic terms and realize that we have the same concerns as most bourgeois white painters."[33]

Hollingsworth's early paintings allowed him to explore some of the images that he frequently drew in comic books in new, politically motivated ways. In his "Cry City" series, which he began in 1961, Hollingsworth used mixed media to explore the effects of urban life on African American communities. "I had a statement to make and I made it," he said of the series. While Hollingsworth began his career in comics doing background work on the cityscapes that permeated various superhero titles, he was able to take a more

FIGURE 6.4 Hollingsworth explores themes of urbanism and the Black body in his sketch "Lonely Boy." (Author's collection, date unknown)

political approach in his paintings two decades later with the same subject matter. "I had grown up in a gang era. Bopping clubs and fighting chiefs were everywhere. And it seemed to me that the pressures on minorities stemmed at least partially from urbanism—the crowding, the competition, the slums, the situations and conditions that the city creates. I felt that I could make a contribution through my feeling about the city," said Hollingworth.[34]

Tim Jackson describes in *Pioneering Cartoonists of Color* how as Hollingsworth's painting career continued, his work frequently "dealt with themes such as civil rights, women's struggles, spiritual concepts, jazz, city life, time and space, and dance."[35] Indeed, his paintings regularly returned to many of same kinds of images that he drew in his comics, but in a way that allowed him to forgo the needs of genre conventions and editorial demands. After drawing women from a range of different class backgrounds in comic books and strips like *Crimes by Women* and *Kandy*, he was able to explore this dynamic through his expressionist style in such paintings and mixed media work as *Woman at High Tea*, *Hip Ain't Easy*, *Woman with Child*, *Trio*, and *Together*. His emphasis on men and women of color, begun in the pages of *Negro Romance* and *Juke Box Comics*, continued in paintings like *No*, *Fisherman*, and *Distinguished Female Publishers* (a collage of fourteen women of color who were newspaper publishers), as well as in his illustrations for the 1970 book of poetry *Black Out Loud*.[36]

Hollingsworth also wrote and drew a children's book about art for the Guggenheim Museum in 1970, titled *I'd Like the Goo-Gen-Heim*, allowing him to come full circle in how his drawings reached a younger audience after his early career in comics was supplanted by avant-garde work done for older observers. He continued in this aim of public outreach when he hosted three television series on WNBC, 1971's *You're Part of Art*, 1977's *You've Gotta Have Art*, and 1980's *The Creative Years of the Child*.[37] By this point in his life, Hollingsworth was also a professor in the Visual and Performing Arts Department at Hostos Community College of the City University of New York, where he taught from 1971 until 1998. Prior to that, he had taught at the High School of Music and Art in New York, returning decades later to the place where he and Kubert had studied together and honed their craft as comics artists.

Alvin Hollingsworth died in 2000, just two years after retiring from Hostos. The different stages of his remarkable career add up to a life fully dedicated to making and teaching art: as a preteenager in an art assistant role; as a teenager drawing comic books while going to high school; as someone who pursued two advanced degrees while drawing comic books, strips, and magazine illustrations; and as an accomplished painter who was a television host and college professor by the time he completed his PhD. While later artists like Dave McKean and Kent Williams were able to bridge the realms of comics and fine art in a concurrent way that was not as welcomed earlier on in comics history, Hollingsworth managed to weave his interests in avant-garde art into many of his comic book assignments (especially as he moved into the horror genre in the 1950s). His comics artwork serves as an important precursor to both his own fine arts career and many of the stylistic trends made popular by modern artists, proving that an interest in distorted figures, heavy shadows, scratchy lines, and uneven textures is not a recent development in the comics medium. Alvin Hollingsworth was a major artist of the Golden Age of comics, even if his work remains mostly unknown to date. Further study of his career must be a vital part of how we proceed in desegregating comics history.

Notes

1. "Artists Portray a Black Christ," 177.
2. *Barnett-Aden Collection*, 21.
3. Charles and Cynthia Hollingsworth were British West Indies citizens when they emigrated to the United States from the island that is now the country of Barbados.
4. The Bails Project's "Who's Who of American Comic Books" database lists Hollingsworth as having worked for Jack Binder's studio as well in the early 1940s (Bails, "Who's Who").
5. Interview with Vallierre Richard Auzenne, quoted in Schelly, *Man of Rock*, 51.
6. Schelly, 50.
7. Schelly, 57.
8. Schelly, 51.
9. "Making of a Master of Sequential Art," 55–56.
10. Amash, "We Considered [Comics] an Art Form."
11. Schelly, *Man of Rock*, 52.
12. *Blue Beetle* #42; Yoe, *Super Weird Heroes*, 47. Bronze Man appeared in only two issues of *Blue Beetle*, both by Hollingsworth. The character is described in the story as wearing a bronze mask when in his superhero form, but his face resembles that of a white man. When he is in civilian form as the war veteran Randy Ronald, his apparently disfigured face is always obscured or turned away from the reader—lending further credit to the notion that the unblemished white face we see when Ronald changes into Bronze Man was actually meant to be a bronze mask. Yoe adds that Bronze Man's backstory saw him captured during his service in the Air Force during World War II, whereby "the enemy subjected Randy to torture, horribly disfiguring him. The interesting conceit is that we never see Randy's face. The artist spares us that pain by posing the character from behind, off-panel, turning, or somehow covering his head. Readers are shielded from the horror, unlike the people Randy comes in contact

with.... When Randy turns into Bronze Man, he wears a metal mask. However, this mask looks like skin and shows Bronze Man's expressions just like a regular face. The coloring on the mask and hands makes the superhero appear Caucasian" (Yoe, *Super Weird Heroes*, 47). With this coloring change, the publisher denied Hollingsworth the chance to see his character appear as intended and in turn denied readers the opportunity to understand his identity as anything other than white.

13 Dempsey, "And the Word Was Made Flesh," 16. See also Schimmel and Stein, *Figurative Fifties*.
14 Bukatman, *Hellboy's World*, 9, 11.
15 Dempsey, "And the Word Was Made Flesh," 16.
16 Rowe, *"Fox Feature Syndicate,"* 46; Schelly, *American Comic Book Chronicles*, 67.
17 Janson, *DC Comics Guide to Inking Comics*, 100.
18 *Crimes by Women* #2, 19.
19 Crane, *Line and Form*, 199, 204.
20 Crane, 24.
21 Schelly, *Art of Joe Kubert*, 49; Harvey, *Meanwhile—*, 231.
22 Crane, *Line and Form*, 51.
23 *Crimes by Women* #5, 4.
24 Janson, *DC Comics Guide to Pencilling Comics*, 117.
25 Schelly, *Art of Joe Kubert*, 98.
26 Normanton, "From the Tomb Presents," 49.
27 *Witchcraft* #4, 4.
28 Bukatman, *Hellboy's World*, 163–164.
29 Bukatman, 176.
30 Clancy and Ald, "'Is This What I Want...?': Part 2," 79.
31 Hewitt, "Themes of Alvin C. Hollingsworth," 5.
32 Courtney Martin, "From the Center," 87.
33 Siegel, "Why Spiral?," 82.
34 Hewitt, "Themes of Alvin C. Hollingsworth," 5.
35 T. Jackson, *Pioneering Cartoonists of Color*, 144.
36 Adoff, *Black Out Loud*.
37 In *Encyclopedia of Black Comics*, Sheena Howard describes how *You're Part of Art* "was produced in cooperation with the Art Students League of New York" and how he "toured the East Coast while filming the ten part series, lecturing and conducting painting demonstrations" (120). See also "Hollingsworth Hosts Series on WNBC." In addition to New York, *You've Gotta Have Art*—which aired weekday mornings from 6:30 to 7:00 a.m.—was aired in Chicago, Cleveland, Los Angeles, and Washington.

7

"Hello Public!"

• • • • • • • • • • • • •

Jackie Ormes in the Print Culture of the *Pittsburgh Courier*

ELI BOONIN-VAIL

On December 21, 1946, Jackie Ormes got off the train at Union Station in Pittsburgh wearing a Black Cossack hat and a leopard-skin coat over an orange sweater and black skirt. She tied it all together with a gold metal belt. Gertrude "Toki" Schalk Johnson reported all of these details in her weekly "Toki Types" column for the *Pittsburgh Courier*, then the African American newspaper with the largest circulation in the United States. "Jackie can wear sweaters with swank, and all the form fitting little numbers that we hefties sigh for," Toki wrote, noting that "the chic and talented Mrs. O's . . . *Patty Joe 'n' Ginger* [*sic*] are such raves in *The Courier*."[1] Ormes's single-panel comic strip *Patty-Jo 'n' Ginger* had begun running in September of the previous year and would continue for a decade. It was the second of three comics that Ormes would contribute to the newspaper in her lifetime. Comics scholarship recognizes Ormes as the first widely published Black woman cartoonist. She infused her format with political bite informed at the intersections of racial and gendered identities. Ormes's accomplishments as an artist notwithstanding, Johnson's reportage on Ormes's dress must be understood as part of Ormes's print persona. Not only did Ormes model her characters after herself, but she also made the world of fashion a part of her life during and after her cartooning career.[2] For Ormes, an elegantly dressed Black woman was a political message, an act of self-presentation in line with how she drew herself. It is no coincidence that Ormes reliably drew her Black women in the latest fashions, much as Johnson does with Ormes.

Ormes's figurations of Black womanhood were a combination of refinery and cheesecake, winking at the reader while playing into the aesthetic of respectability endorsed at the *Courier*.[3] This chapter situates Ormes's comics within the context of Black women's print culture at the *Pittsburgh Courier*. While several scholars have contributed readings of Ormes that have brought aspects of the newspaper to light, none has sought to connect the work of *Courier* women journalists with Ormes's comics and life.[4] Even H. Zahra Caldwell, who has done the most comprehensive work to date connecting Ormes's comics to midcentury progressive Black journalism, largely eschews the relationship between women's writing in the pages of the *Courier* and Ormes's art in favor of pursuing Ormes's engagement with male colleagues, fellow cartoonists, and radical politics.[5] By recuperating the labor of figures like Toki Johnson and placing it alongside Ormes, we stand to expand our understanding of the comics' modes of address, their imagined audience, and the networks—of profession but also of kinship—that facilitated their promotion and exchange among a midcentury Black readership. In return, we shall see that Ormes's cartoons existed within a constellation of social writing unique to Black women's literary and journalistic production, bringing her in touch with figures ranging from Johnson to Zora Neale Hurston.

Consider the case of Ormes's excursions in column writing before and during her cartooning. Ormes's biographer Nancy Goldstein mistakes this literature as ancillary to Ormes's larger goals, writing that between the 1937 *Torchy Brown in Dixie to Harlem* and the brief 1945 *Candy*, Ormes was "still stuck writing the obligatory women's column."[6] In fact, as Goldstein knows, the women's column was a format that Ormes had been playing with since high school, when she wrote a column for the *Courier* from 1929 to 1930 under the title "Hello Public!" Jacqueline Jones Royster argues that since the nineteenth century, Black periodical presses have "held a central and vibrant place in the text production of African American women, in their use of language to speak out, and in fulfilling their desires to participate actively in establishing and implementing social and political agenda."[7] While it is true that ambitious Black women writing for Black newspapers were forced into the "woman's work" of women's columns and sections, describing such work as "obligatory" downplays the significance of this mode of literary production. Caldwell, who argues that Ormes "used her pioneering comics as a form of progressive Black journalism, using a Black female voice, and citing Black women's concerns," acknowledges that Ormes began her career as a "cub reporter" who worked largely on "minor assignments" and occasionally "harder news," framing the transition from writing to cartooning as a move toward the artist's "true passion." This transition meant that Ormes "maneuvered her way to the comics, retaining the eye of a reporter."[8] Caldwell's description of Ormes's reportorial ethos is fitting, but the irony of holding Ormes's cartooning work above her earlier written work—the work of women's columnists—is that we risk elevating one form of "low" literary culture while denigrating another. They deserve to be considered as complementary textual methods.

Women's columns produced at the *Courier* by the likes of Johnson and her colleagues Hazel Garland and Evelyn Cunningham functioned rhetorically and journalistically on varying registers—often within the same piece—oscillating between the proverbial and the quotidian, carving space for a writer to assert her own subjectivity. These forms of writing also served the vital function of maintaining Black kinship networks, keeping track of the comings and goings of countless members of an astonishing number of communities throughout the nation. One such community was the Ormes-Cyrus-Manzilta network in Salem, Ohio, of which Jackie Ormes was a part and which Johnson and Garland both tracked in their columns from the 1940s to the 1970s.[9] Jackie Ormes was stopping by Pittsburgh in December 1946 in her Black Cossack hat and leopard-skin coat before traveling on to a family gathering in Salem, as Johnson was keen to note.

The pages of the *Courier* offer opportunities for intertextual readings between women's columns and Ormes's cartoons, as in the case of one of Ormes's most celebrated *Patty-Jo 'n' Ginger* strips from October 8, 1955. On a page where ten of the twelve letters to the editor decry the acquittal of Emmett Till's slayers the previous week, Ormes ran a strip of Patty-Jo, hand on hip, emerging from her middle-class apartment's kitchen to tell her sister, "I don't want to seem touchy on the subject . . . but that new little white tea-kettle just whistled at me!" (figure 7.1).[10] Simultaneously critiquing the unjust murder of a Black child while alluding to a middle-class Black family's ability to participate in the postwar commodity economy with reference to

FIGURE 7.1 The white tea-kettle strip, *Patty-Jo 'n' Ginger*, October 8, 1955. (Copyright *Pittsburgh Courier*)

a new kitchen amenity, this strip demonstrates how, in the comics scholar Deborah Whaley's words, *Patty-Jo 'n' Ginger* was "the most forthrightly political gag that featured Black girls and women during the latter years of the Popular Front."[11] However, viewed in isolation, the October 8 panel only tells us part of the story.

This panel ran during a period when Ormes shared her page with Ollie Harrington's *Dark Laughter*. Harrington's association with Richard Wright, Chester Himes, and other prominent Black literary figures of the period has long afforded him a spotlight that was denied to Ormes.[12] Harrington's cluttered line work and frequent depictions of abject poverty contrast markedly with Ormes's clean designs of Black middle-class ascension. While Harrington directly represented the poverty and violence confronting Black Americans, Ormes's tea-kettle strip neatly demonstrates an alternative approach. Ormes couches reference to horrific violence against a Black child in a domestic scene of fashionable clothes, modernist furniture, and the innocuous body of a child.

Ormes and Harrington also shared their page with Evelyn Cunningham's "The Women" column. Cunningham's column for the day of the tea-kettle strip speaks to the predicaments of ambitious writers stuck in the women's rut by editors and publishers: "For the most part, cullud women on cullud newspapers spend most of their time going to parties, dances, cocktails, weddings, christenings, and other like adventuresome gatherings. Happily, more and more news women are getting out of the cocktail lounges and into the union halls and political arenas. Still, basically, a woman is expected to report news of women's activities. Over a period of time the social circuit becomes wearisome."[13] For Cunningham, a reporter who would go on to earn the nickname "lynching editor" and who interviewed Martin Luther King Jr. and Malcolm X, such limitations were stifling.[14] Yet her use of a women's column to dispel the myth of socially functionless women's writing and to advocate for Black women's political reporting parallels the function of Ormes's strip for that week, which challenges the innocence of a weekly gag cartoon by infusing it with a critique of racist violence. Both blur the boundaries between "low" literature and social function in Black women's print culture. Cunningham's description of the world of women's reportage at the *Courier* also describes a social world that Garland and Johnson dedicated their lives to and one that Ormes alternately covered and was a fixture in.

Cunningham's sharp prose at the start of her column echoes words that Ormes wrote as a cub reporter for the *Courier* while still in high school. Cunningham begins by telling us—in a prelude to intersectional thinking—"It's one thing being cullud. It's another thing being a cullud woman. And yet another thing being a cullud woman newspaperman." Likewise, Ormes began her May 17, 1930, column, "Public o'Mine: This being a newspaper woman is getting to be a strenuous business."[15] Whereas Cunningham was serious-minded, an eighteen-year-old Zelda Jackson (she had not yet married Earl Ormes) used the column spaces of the *Courier* as a playground for various forms of public address, giving scholars of her later comics an inroad to recognizing several rhetorical tactics familiar in her cartoons. Zelda Jackson reliably begins her column with an informal address that mimics the title of the column: "Dear Perspirin' Public" (June 21, 1930), "H'lo Pub!" (March 1, 1930), "Pst!—Public!" (January 4, 1930), and most often "Dear Public."[16] Such addresses initiate a chatty and dialogical rhetoric that Jackson consistently thematized in creative displays of whimsy. The August 2, 1930, edition adopts the form of a diary entry about attending the Deltas' dinner dance at the Orchard View Country Club. Ormes interrupts the "Dear Public" format midway through the column with a "H'lo, Diary Dear."[17] A June 21, 1930, installment pretends to be Zelda Jackson's own dictionary, dispensing with the pretense of reporting social functions and presenting a series of wordplays and alternative definitions that will be "bothersome to proper, literal people": "Ah say, Pub, won't my dictionary be a la-la?"[18] Considering that, according to Whaley, Ormes maintained a political purpose in her comics through "her use of signifyin(g)—that is, an indirect, satirical Black speech form that utilizes sounding (verbal dueling), loud talking (a direct critique formed with indirect speech), cutting (direct insult), marking (mimicry), and taunting," it is not difficult to see these early columns as, like her comics, "representative of Black vernacular culture."[19]

We may also see in her attitude toward the public a forerunner to her graphic style. Note that in nearly every installment of *Patty-Jo 'n' Ginger*, for example, some graphic element from within the frame extrudes into the caption space (figure 7.2). Often one of Ginger's stylish heels or Patty-Jo's miscellaneous toys, these figures leave their consigned spaces, breaking down the boundaries between text and paratextual surroundings on the rest of the page, beckoning outward toward a Black reading public. Compared to Harrington's cartoons on the same pages, which reliably stay within the margins, this strategy represents a different way of approaching the reader.[20] This graphic address of the public is intensified in the *Torchy Togs* paper-doll accompaniment to the color romance comic *Torchy in Heartbeats* that ran in the *Courier* alongside *Patty-Jo 'n' Ginger* from 1950 to 1954. In addition to giving Ormes the opportunity to illustrate the latest fashions, this section furthered Ormes's playful interaction with the reader. Goldstein notes that "Torchy is the only paper doll in history that speaks directly to readers, instructing them on how to dress" with such coy phrases as, "Girls! Get those scissors ready! Here are some items from my new wardrobe. Cut carefully along the heavy Black outlines so they'll fit me! And *please* ... do right by my figure, too. Go slow around the curves."[21] One instance of this occurs in a February 23, 1952, issue of *Torchy in Heartbeats*. In an installment during a story line that involves Torchy traveling on a steamship to work on a banana plantation in South America, a ship hand sexually assaults Torchy.

"Hello Public!" • 147

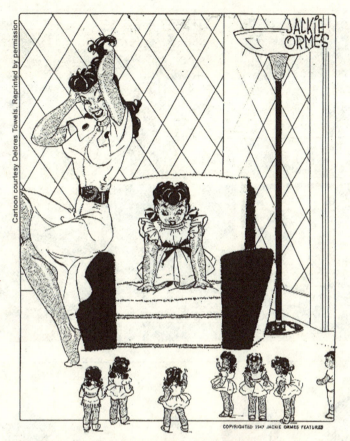

"But they're so much like me, Sis... just s'pose an idea hits 'em—
Kinda frightenin' isn't it ???"

FIGURE 7.2 A typical *Patty-Jo 'n' Ginger* strip promoting a Patty Jo doll line. Note how some of the dolls stand outside the frame and look inward. (Copyright *Pittsburgh Courier*)

Ayanna Dozier, noting the rarity of comics depictions of sexual violence against Black women, breaks down how an "innovative layout of panels conveys the turmoil of the attempted rape and the turbulent weather," but she does not connect the story to its paratextual accompaniment.[22] In a bold *Torchy Tog* beneath the assault, Torchy stares the reader dead in the eye, simply declaring, "OK?" (figure 7.3). Even as Torchy becomes a toy in the readers' hands, she expresses recognition and defiance, her face scrunched up in ambivalence. In the comic, an aggressor attempts to strip Torchy of her clothes, but here Ormes encourages the reader to dress Torchy in dignified outfits, visually and haptically positioning the reader in opposition to the

FIGURE 7.3 The *Torchy Tog* that stares back at the reader underneath an assault sequence. (Copyright *Pittsburgh Courier*)

assault.[23] Ormes thus overturns Torchy's status as passive victim by engaging in a comics version of the dialogic readerly practice familiar from her *Hello Public* days.

From the start of Ormes's cartooning career, she facilitated a reading of her comics that extended beyond the strip and into the *Courier*. A December 25, 1937, Christmas special strip of *Torchy Brown in Dixie to Harlem* features Torchy—herself modeled on Ormes—speaking on the phone to "the dizzy dame who draws [her]," who calls from Pittsburgh "invitin' [her] to *Courier* headquarters for a reunion party" (figures 7.4 and 7.5). Edward Brunner describes this strip as having a "pleasantly vertiginous logic" in which "Torchy Brown is a fictional character, even as she is here dramatized as taking a telephone call from an actual person (her 'boss'), as if she (Torchy) were real and invited to a place that we know exists—'*Courier* headquarters in Pittsburgh'—because it produces the newspaper that we hold in our hands."[24] Ormes's own relationship to *Courier* headquarters and her role as a recurring character in its social columns also enacted this vertiginous logic. A January 6, 1951, edition of "Toki Types" reports, "Here for just a day, Chicago's Earl and Jackie Ormes, to see Wini and Bill Houston, and the *Courier* folk."[25] Toki reported Jackie's comings and goings almost yearly around the holiday season from the 1940s into the '70s, to the point that she sometimes writes that she "missed seeing her," as was the case in 1952. A January 3, 1948, "Toki Types" with a very Ormesian title ("Resolutions! What . . . Again?") sends out holiday well-wishes that reinforce the newspaper's respectability politics while also once more asserting Ormes's status as a figure in constant orbit around the *Courier*: "We wish for . . . More NAACP memberships for our Daisy Lampkin . . . Less divorces among our acquaintances everywhere and more contented couples . . . More Lena Hornes who possess racial consciousness as well as talent . . . A huge financial success to Jackie Ormes and her Patty Jo dolls."[26] We will return to Ormes's work with dolls soon.

Johnson's boosterism of Ormes's career came not just in her columns but also in long-form feature articles such as the April 17, 1948, piece running under the headline "Success Depends on Persistence, Says Jackie Ormes." Here, Johnson describes Ormes as "a girl-makes-good story which is wrapped up in the pink pages of The *Courier* as far back as she can remember." The article recognizes how Ormes's *Hello Public* days led into *Torchy Brown*, "the cute little brown skinned girl whose tousled hair and pretty legs were more than faintly reminiscent of her creator."[27] At the same time, Hazel Garland in her "Things to Talk About" column promoted Earl Ormes's Chicago hotel ventures.[28] A June 19, 1954, column confirms her as having

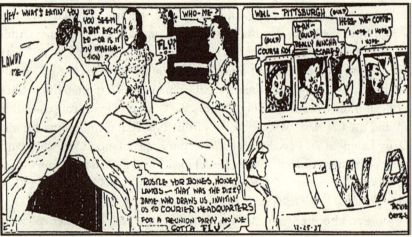

FIGURES 7.4 AND 7.5 Torchy talks to Jackie and references the *Courier*. (Copyright *Pittsburgh Courier*)

stayed for a week at "the delightful hotel managed by Earl Ormes," where she also spent time with Jackie, who "sent regards to her many friends back here [Pittsburgh]."[29] Almost exactly two years later, on June 23, 1956, Garland devoted her entire opening paragraph to Earl's management of the Sutherland and the "face-lifting during the past year or so" that made the property "rank with the best anywhere."[30]

While Garland's column did not cover the travels of the Ormeses with the same frequency as did Johnson's, by the 1970s and '80s Garland became a champion of Jackie Ormes's legacy. A fascinating 1974 column begins with Garland—now more politically engaged—writing on how the nomination of Nelson Rockefeller for vice president could affect Evelyn Cunningham: "Big East, as Evelyn was called by the gang at the old *Pittsburgh Courier* when she worked here during the early fifties, has been working for and with Nelson Rockefeller since she left the *Courier*." In the same column, Garland mentions speaking at a reception for E. Marie Coleman and a number of other "women who were doing outstanding community work when [she] started writing for the old *Courier*." Garland closes out the column mentioning, "Earl and Jackie Ormes of Chicago were in Pittsburgh last weekend and I am so sorry I missed seeing them. . . . Old *Courier* readers will remember Jackie as the lovely and talented artist who created the cartoon 'Patty-Jo.' There was also a Patty-Jo doll that every little girl adored. Some of us big ones did too."[31] Three years later, Garland wrote in "Things to Talk About" that Jackie—now a widow—was staying once again with Bill and Wini Houston. She used this visit as an opportunity to once again testify to Ormes's vital cultural role at the *Courier* "back in the forties when [Garland] joined the old *Pittsburgh Courier* staff."[32] In this way, Garland continued a tradition of celebrating and keeping track of Ormes that Johnson had initiated.

Dozier, narrowing in on the 1950–1954 window during which *Torchy in Heartbeats* ran, finds that "an investigation of the paper's articles, editorials, reports, and advertisements of that time reveals a deep focus on Black women's appearance and manners," suggesting that the *Courier* was engaged in what Lisa B. Thompson calls "circulating ideologies such as the Cult of True Womanhood and the Cult of Domesticity, which emphasized piety, purity, and submissiveness."[33] Dozier argues that Ormes "successfully worked within the system (while being surveilled [by the FBI]) to produce a wealth of politically challenging material that spoke to Black women's lived experience," in part through telling stories of "a Black woman freely traveling."[34] While she cites women's columns—particularly one of Johnson's 1951 "Toki Types," titled "Watch Your Manners"—as evidence of the constraints of respectability that Ormes's comics labored within, we might just as easily argue that such columns constituted similar sites of "working within the system." A column like the aforementioned Cunningham piece could speak plainly to a Black woman's subjectivity, while Johnson's columns documented countless people of color "freely traveling." In an era of segregation when the travel of Black people was policed under threat of violence, such documentation spoke to a network of resilience.

The *Courier*'s own relationship with respectability and the image of Black womanhood was malleable and multifaceted. Between 1920 and 1960, the newspaper ran over 120 articles endorsing female impersonation events in Pittsburgh as wholesome family fun.[35] This combination of the raucous and the genteel was not counterintuitive for the Black middle class and may help us understand Ormes's blend of political critique and chic femininity as well as the lives and writings of her sisters-in-print. An April 7, 1951, article advertised "one of the gayest, maddest variety shows this town has ever presented," where "Toki Schalk Johnson will emcee" and "Hazel Garland will torch sing her way into your heart."[36] By performing torch songs, Hazel Garland channeled Ormes's Torchy Brown and emulated the Pittsburgh native Lena Horne, described as having "racial consciousness as well as talent" by Johnson. Such shows did not cast aside the politics of respectability wholesale but retooled it into a performative negotiation of Black feminine joy. That Johnson, Ormes, and Garland functioned as both subjects and authors of reportage on such scenes suggests a vibrant women's print culture embedded within the Black community that both addressed and participated in a flexible politic of respectability. Whereas Angela M. Nelson has found a relatively uncomplicated proliferation of "Black bourgeois" ideology in the male-driven comics of the Black press in nearby Toledo, Ohio, a close investigation of the connections between Ormes and her print culture reveals a complex and playful relationship with Black middle-class ideas of gender and respectability.[37]

It was within this print culture that, from the fall of 1952 to the spring of 1953, Zora Neale Hurston worked as an investigative/imaginative reporter covering the case of Ruby McCollum, a Black middle-class housewife from Live Oak, Florida, accused of killing the white doctor C. LeRoy Adams. While the majority of reportage on the case adhered to what Tammy Evans describes as a "rhetoric of silence," in which "acts of silence in texts about Ruby McCollum 'write' reality; silence determines by default who is permitted voice, whose words are given merit, whose words are denounced, who may listen, and—above all—who must remain mute within the confines of a regional ideology dominated by myths and often enforced by intimidation," Hurston's writing represented a rhetorical act of breaking silence.[38] Borrowing from her own prose in the 1937 novel *Their Eyes Were Watching God*, Hurston reimagined "The Life Story of Mrs. Ruby J. McCollum!" in a series of sixteen articles for the *Courier*. She found that the mere details of the trial, reported throughout the white press, left out critical information: Ruby's abuse at her husband's hands, her finding comfort in an affair with Adams, Adams's relationship with Ruby turning violent, and Adams's high-level membership in the Ku Klux Klan. Writing past the gaps enacted by a vengeful white society and a fearful Black community in Live Oak, which often turned journalists away, Hurston made what she described as an "attempt at self-revelation" in Ruby's case. Her writing exposes in the pages of the *Courier* an ambivalent relationship with the notion of a Black middle-class femininity. Hurston describes McCollum as "a Negro woman with the courage to dare every fate, to boldly attack every tradition of her surroundings and even the age-old laws of every land."[39]

Roberta S. Maguire, who has catalogued the intersections between Hurston's writing on the McCollum case and passages from *Their Eyes Were Watching God*, argues that "the McCollum series functions as a challenge to all readers, including Race Men and Women, to see Ruby in her full complexity, a woman much like Janie Crawford in *Their Eyes*—Black, to be sure, but with hopes and desires transcending race."[40] Citing the use of free indirect discourse—the blurring of narrational and character voices—in both Hurston's reporting and her novel, Maguire suggests that Hurston's literary technique functioned both to "draw readers into Ruby's interior life" and to signal "a moment of transition."[41] Whereas Henry Louis Gates Jr. has argued that this technique indicates Janie's movement toward self-knowledge in *Their Eyes Were Watching God*, Maguire finds that in the McCollum writings, Hurston uses free indirect discourse to indicate Ruby's slow downward spiral toward the murder.[42] Virginia Lynn Moylan suggests that this technique and the borrowed language from *Their Eyes Were Watching God* made "the existing drama all the more titillating," adding Hurston's "characteristic rich descriptions and folksy language" to a crime saga that lurked beneath the McCollums' respectable veneer.[43] Ruby's husband, Sam, ascended to the middle class by running an illegal Bolita gambling ring out of their home. Ruby oversaw the ring's finances, eventually expanding their operation into the legitimate tobacco-farming and Black life-insurance industries.

Hurston's telling of the story complicated a flat picture of Black middle-class femininity. Letters to the editor in the *Courier* evidence a readership receptive to this complex picture. "Don't let us judge poor Ruby," wrote a reader from Florida on May 2, 1953. "Look around our own homes, for if we don't God will." Another reader from that week simply wrote in, "Let us sympathize with Ruby McCollum."[44] So many letters flooded in during this period that the *Courier* briefly created a recurring feature, "Ruby! Good or

Bad?," for readers to weigh in.[45] This column ran condemnations and pleas for compassion, occasionally featuring nuanced historical perspectives such as that of "Mrs. P.R. Small" of Lakeland, Kentucky, who wrote in that "Over eighty years ago Negro women were sold on blocks like cattle at auction. At that time, the White man picked out the Negro woman he wanted. Women's virtue was taken away from them because they were slaves. That is why our race is so well-mixed. So why condemn Ruby McCollum?"[46] At the same time, "Toki Types" was promoting Hurston's coverage of the story, as in an October 18, 1952, edition in which Johnson writes, "Zora Neale Hurston has lost none of her magic influence with words. The story of Ruby McCullum [sic], now appearing in the Courier . . . is a 'best seller' right from the tragic pages of life, as seen through the all-seeing eyes of the novelist."[47] Johnson, who had begun her literary career writing urban realist fiction in the Boston-based *Saturday Evening Quill* and pulp romance formula stories for *Love Story* and *All-Story Love* in the 1920s and 1930s, may have sensed a kindred spirit in Hurston, who combined the lived experiences of a Black woman with the literary modes of romance, pulp, and popular literature.[48]

In the same period that the *Courier* ran Hurston's McCollum coverage, Jackie Ormes produced some of her most celebrated political work. In the final story line of *Torchy in Heartbeats*, which ran from late January 1953 to September 18, 1954, Torchy pursued love with a Black doctor while also working to stop a chemical plant run by "Colonel Fuller" from polluting the water around the predominantly Black "Southville."[49] Realized in the full colors provided for by the *Courier*'s short-lived contract with the white-owned printing operation at the Smith-Mann Syndicate, this story line features some of Ormes's most detailed line work and inventive compositions while addressing environmental racism. Dozier notes that "the earlier narrative arcs of *Torchy in Heartbeats* are generally dismissed as superfluous romance threads," but she finds that these story lines contain "subtle political subversions that Ormes executed in *Torchy in Heartbeats* through her emphasis on Black women's pursuit of love and travel in a time where respectability was prominent."[50] *Heartbeats*' earliest story line from 1950 follows a desperate Torchy's attempts to escape a doomed relationship with Dan, a selfish gambler who eventually gets himself killed. Ormes's romance strips and Hurston's literary journalism thus shared narratives of Black women who felt trapped in their romantic relationships and struggled for independence, with men's gambling and two-timing playing a prominent role in both. The two function as dark mirrors of each other. In Ormes's rose-colored vision, Black female independence wins the day, with Torchy's wayward travels and eventual marriage to doctor Paul Hammond. Hurston's view of McCollum creates a bitter triumph out of cruel defeat, claiming a position of identification and resilience in the story of a doomed woman whose middle-classness became part of her undoing.[51]

That Hurston and Ormes were simultaneously envisioning Black female life differently in the pages of the *Courier* suggests that the print culture of this newspaper offered a critical location of literary expression smuggled under the guise of pulp romance, lurid reportage, and women's columns. The parallels between these two figures, while not total, are illuminating. Both have been posthumously heralded as vanguard Black female artists with contemporary resonance, as was famously the case with Alice Walker's participation in the cultural resuscitation of Hurston in the 1970s and as has more recently been the case with the Ormes Society, a contemporary coalition of Black women comics writers.[52] Interestingly, Alice Walker wrote, "Zora *belongs* in the tradition of Black women singers, rather than among 'the literati,' at least to me. There were the extreme highs and lows of life, her undaunted pursuit of adventure, passionate emotional and sexual experience, and her love of freedom."[53] Walker may very well have been describing Torchy Brown, Lena Horne, or even Hazel Garland singing a torch song herself from the pages of the *Courier*. Hurston and Ormes also shared a passion for Black female empowerment and representation beyond the page, in the material culture of doll manufacturing. Ormes labored intensively to manufacture and market a Patty-Jo doll in partnership with the Terri Lee company in 1947.[54] Though the actual production of the doll was short-lived, Ormes made collecting and promoting the dolls a lifelong project, eventually inspiring Sara Creech—a wealthy white civil rights advocate—to spearhead the creation of the later Black Sarah Lee doll. Moylan describes Hurston, a friend of Creech's, as "the doll's official godmother," claiming that "her letters of introduction had played a vital role in the doll's manufacture, and she continued to promote it with characteristic zeal among her Harlem friends."[55] Hurston and Ormes in this way found a common cause in an unlikely alternative medium, further evidencing their shared perspectives, approaches, and values as creators.

We should not oversimplify the similar values and techniques of Hurston and her contemporaries at the *Pittsburgh Courier*. Hurston had a fraught relationship with the publication, stemming at least in part from the newspaper's failure to pay her for her services rendered in the McCollum articles.[56] In a bitter May 14, 1954, letter to William Bradford Huie, a fellow writer who would eventually produce a book on the McCollum affair,

Hurston drew a sharp line between herself and the world of Black print that this chapter investigates: "Negro newspapers are loaded with would-be writers and naturally bloated with envy. They are the most brazen frauds on the American continent. Screaming about 'rights for Negroes' and lynching every Negro who shows any marked ability."[57] To conscript Hurston into the *Courier*'s orbit for the sake of easy comparison would be an injustice to the author's experience, just as to describe Jackie Ormes simply as "the Zora Neale Hurston of comics" would be to iron over the details that enrich both women's creative lives. Nevertheless, the *Courier* allowed openings for Black women to convey their lived experiences and perspectives in the most overlooked of literary places.

Understanding Ormes's comics requires more than close analysis and political contextualization. It requires an appreciation of the print culture in which she was entrenched. This is what it means to think of Ormes as "wrapped up in the pink pages of The *Courier*." Hazel Garland's "Things to Talk About" from August 22, 1981, offers a picture of this culture and the readerly experience it encouraged. Garland quotes at length a letter from Howard A. Tibbs of Newark, Ohio, "a relative of friends" of hers:

> Tibbs recalled all of the "young Turks" such as Melvin Ormes and Ray Mahoney and several others whose names he couldn't quite remember, serving as escorts for the "Debs About Town" affairs. The Debs, if you recall, was a group of beautiful young women that the late great Courier Woman's Editor, Julia B. Jones got together... Tibbs remembered leaders of the old Courier like Robert L. Vann, Ira F. Lewis, Bill Nunn, Sr., Wendell Smith, Sam Milai and Chester Washington.... He recalled the time when 'Jackie' Ormes did a comic strip called 'Patty-Jo' and Ginger and the fantastic times he used to have with Cornelius Gould, now living in Cleveland Ohio.... In closing, Tibbs wrote: "I read somewhere that those things best remembered probably never happened. But I know those things that I've mentioned happened because I was there. Our subscription to the *Courier* is the National Edition and my mother, while she lived, would search for names of people she knew from 'the Valley,' as she called it. She passed two years ago, at age 96. Betty (my wife) and I would try to cushion her disappointment, and tell her to be sure to read Hazel Garland's column, for people whose parents and often grandparents she had known. Now I'm in that same boat (smile). Please keep writing about great people and fine places."[58]

Tibbs's panoramic recollection of the *Courier*'s midcentury milieu bespeaks a vibrant and intimate print community. It suggests a reading experience much in the style of Ormes's figures who stepped just a little out of their frames. Unlike comics scholars who view Ormes's works in isolation or at best through comparison to Harrington and other Black comics artists, Tibbs identifies Ormes as a single part of a larger print universe that intersected with his own life and the lives of so many others. Garland's reprinting of the letter served to validate Tibbs's view of the *Courier*'s purpose, to keep people of color "reading about great people and fine places," announcing their lived experiences by seeing themselves and their people in print, as Tibbs describes of his mother reading Garland's column. Jackie Ormes has been written about as a toy maker, a political subversive, a fashion icon, but most of all as a cartoonist. To this should be added newspaperwoman. This is, after all, how Ormes first introduced herself to the *Pittsburgh Courier* readership in her "Hello Public!" days. Recognizing her connections with the world of Black women's journalism opens us up to a new view of her work as a cartoonist, one more in line with the historical readership practices of the *Courier*'s subscribers.

Notes

1. T. Johnson, "Toki Types: About People Here!"
2. Goldstein, "Fashion in the Funny Papers."
3. For an overview of *Courier* founder Robert L. Vann's politics of respectability, see Bunie, "*Courier* as a Social Force," in *Robert L. Vann of the "Pittsburgh Courier."* For an overview of cheesecake, a mode of gendered illustration and representation that presented the seminude female form in a socially acceptable middlebrow manner, see Meyerowitz, "Women, Cheesecake, and Borderline Material."
4. Ayanna Dozier reads Ormes's *Torchy in Heartbeats* alongside strips by her fellow cartoonists Ollie Harrington and Jay Jackson. She also draws our attention to the discourses of colorism in the paper's respectability politics, as evidenced by advertisements for hair-straightening and skin-whitening products. Ormes herself once drew an advertisement for such a hair product. Dozier, "Wayward Travels."
5. Caldwell, "I Was Anti-Everything."
6. Goldstein, *Jackie Ormes*, 32.
7. Royster, *Traces of a Stream*, 11.
8. Caldwell, "I Was Anti-Everything," 102, 118.
9. Ormes was not the only member of this network who also participated in the *Courier* family, as we shall later see.
10. While Emmett Till's death remains a pivotal moment in the history of racist violence in the United States, it is difficult to overstate the significance of the event for the Black press. Hardly any form of Black journalism—from social columns to comic strips—failed to comment on the murder. See Whitted, "Comics and Emmett Till."
11. Whaley, *Black Women in Sequence*, 62.

12. See Inge, *Dark Laughter*; Davenport, "Blowing Flames into the Souls of Black Folk"; Dolinar, *Black Cultural Front*.
13. E. Cunningham, "Women."
14. She even asked Eugene "Bull" Connor for an interview. Matthews, "Evelyn Cunningham."
15. Z. Jackson, "Hello Public," May 17, 1930.
16. Z. Jackson, "Hello Public," January 4, 1930; Z. Jackson, "Hello Public," March 1, 1930; Z. Jackson, "Hello Public," June 21, 1930.
17. Z. Jackson, "Hello Public," August 2, 1930.
18. Z. Jackson, "Hello Public," June 21, 1930.
19. Whaley, *Black Women in Sequence*, 46.
20. Whaley was the first scholar to acknowledge this characteristic of Ormes's comics, writing of a 1946 *Patty-Jo 'n' Ginger*, "This technique was a carryover from Ormes's *Torchy Brown* and increased the performative aesthetic and connection with readers. Patty-Jo and Ginger's placement outside of the box panel in Ormes's gag relays that they are venturing outside of their comic strip world and into the 'real' world of the civil rights struggle" (60).
21. Goldstein, "Trouble with Romance in Jackie Ormes's Comics," 36.
22. Dozier, "Wayward Travels," 23–26.
23. Thanks are due to Qiana Whitted for this insight.
24. Brunner, "Shuh! Ain't Nothin' to It," 27. Brunner also points out that in a later strip, Torchy performs at the Cotton Club, where she is hailed as "sensational" by the *Courier* columnist Billy Rowe, whom Torchy picks out of the crowd by name.
25. Wini was Winifred Houston, Earl's sister. She and her husband, William, both worked for the *Courier* and lived in Pittsburgh after Jackie and Earl Ormes relocated to Chicago. Goldstein, *Jackie Ormes*, 18; T. Johnson, "Toki Types: On the Credit Side."
26. T. Johnson, "Toki Types: Resolutions!"
27. T. Johnson, "Success Depends on Persistence."
28. Earl Ormes managed the DuSable hotel before taking over the Sutherland in 1952, which had previously been for Whites only. Jackie and Earl would have been living in the hotel at the time of Garland's visits. Goldstein, *Jackie Ormes*, 22–23.
29. Garland, "Things to Talk About," June 19, 1954.
30. Garland, "Things to Talk About: About People and Places."
31. Garland, "Things to Talk About," August 31, 1974.
32. Garland, "Visit with Jackie Ormes."
33. Dozier, "Wayward Travels," 13, quoting Thompson, *Beyond the Black Lady*, 3.
34. Dozier, "Wayward Travels," 27.
35. Grantmyre, "They Lived Their Life and They Didn't Bother Anybody," 1087.
36. "Top Talent Featured in 'Stars on Parade.'"
37. Angela Nelson, "Middle-Class Ideology in African American Postwar Comic Strips."
38. T. Evans, *Silencing of Ruby McCollum*, 19.
39. Hurston, "Mrs. Ruby J. McCollum!"
40. Maguire, "From Fiction to Fact," 22.
41. Maguire, 26.
42. Gates, "Zora Neale Hurston and the Speakerly Text," in *Signifying Monkey*, cited in Maguire, "From Fiction to Fact," 26.
43. Moylan, *Zora Neale Hurston's Final Decade*, 120–121.
44. "Let Us Sympathize with Ruby McCollum."

45 "Ruby! Good or Bad?," June 13, 1953.
46 "Ruby! Good or Bad?," June 27, 1953.
47 T. Johnson, "Toki Types: Ask for What You Want."
48 Almost nothing has been written of Schalk's literary career, but Amber Harris Leichner has analyzed how "her constructions of gender, class, and race" are "at once fixed and fluid." Leichner also provides an account of Schalk's transition from fiction to work at the *Courier* (where she met her husband and became Johnson). See Leichner, "To Bend without Breaking."
49 Goldstein, *Jackie Ormes*, 138.
50 Dozier, "Wayward Travels," 20–21.
51 According to Moylan, McCollum was granted retrial in July 1954, but by this time, her mental state had deteriorated such that she was committed to a state mental hospital in Chattahoochee, where she remained for twenty years before being released in 1974. She died a recluse in 1992. Moylan, *Zora Neale Hurston's Final Decade*, 129.
52 Whaley, *Black Women in Sequence*, 62–66.
53 A. Walker, "Zora Neale Hurston," 19.
54 Goldstein, *Jackie Ormes*, 159–176.
55 Moylan, *Zora Neale Hurston's Final Decade*, 73.
56 Moylan, 125.
57 Hurston to Huie, May 14, 1954, in *Zora Neale Hurston*, 709.
58 Garland, "Things To Talk About," August 22, 1981.

Part III

Comics Readership and Respectability Politics

● ● ● ● ● ● ● ● ● ● ● ● ● ●

8

"Never Any Dirty Ones"

● ● ● ● ● ● ● ● ● ● ● ● ●

Comics Readership among African American Youth in the Mid-Twentieth Century

CAROL L. TILLEY

Dickie Dare was not the stuff of legends. The eponymously named comic strip, created by Milton Caniff in 1933 and soon handed over to Coulton Waugh and other artists, was a serviceable adventure strip. *Dickie Dare* did not lack ardent fans, but it had neither a radio serial nor Big Little Books to continue the story of the twelve-year-old Dare, who traveled the world with his adult mentor, Dan Flynn, and dog, Wags. A 1934 reader's poll in the *Salt Lake Tribune* put the strip tied for twelfth place with *Alley Oop* out of nineteen contenders. That poet Amiri Baraka (born LeRoi Jones in 1934) invoked *Dickie Dare* before cascading through mentions of Captain Midnight, the Lone Ranger, and Superman in his poetry demonstrates that

Baraka was a child of the comics: "People laugh when I tell them about Dickie Dare!"[1]

Baraka's affection for comics was not unique among his Black creative contemporaries. The poet Lucille Clifton, born in 1936, wrote four short poems to Superman and his everyday counterpart, Clark Kent. The guitarist, songwriter, and performer Jimi Hendrix, born in 1942, enjoyed reading comics about Batman and Donald Duck. Walter Dean Myers, a prolific writer of children's books who was born in 1937, had to hide his comic book reading after a neighbor convinced his mother that comics were "a roadmap to the jailhouse."[2] The author Toni Cade Bambara, who was born in 1939, had "an indiscriminate appetite for print" that led her to devour comic books along with shelves of library books.[3] The feminist writer Audre Lorde, born in 1934, reminisced about reading the Sunday funnies and trading comics with neighborhood kids. She even described visiting a used-comics shop in Washington Heights with her sisters. While they searched out copies of coverless *Captain Marvel* comics, Lorde was groped by the white shop owner as she tried to look for *Bugs Bunny* and *Porky Pig* issues for herself.[4]

Lorde, Baraka, and the others were all part of the generation of children—those born in the United States in the 1930s through the 1950s—who were reared alongside and through comics. This period was the apex of comics culture, as comic books (magazines), which began in the 1930s as a novelty or promotional item, grew in sales from ten million new copies each month in 1940 to more than one hundred million new copies monthly by the early 1950s. Children were the largest market for comic magazines, whose dime price made them more affordable than children's books. Publishers and marketers estimated that each issue was read by as many as five or more people beyond the purchaser, through resales, trades, and general sharing. Comics also appeared in strip form in daily and Sunday newspapers, which sent comics readership even higher, as nearly all households purchased or subscribed to at least one paper. Adding in comics crossovers to Big Little Books and similar mass-produced, chunky, illustrated books, movie serials, radio serials, television serials, toys, and clothes, it becomes clear that comics were inescapable.[5]

The scholarship that views the comics readership experience of this period retrospectively, as well as the most visible then-contemporary studies, nearly always views it through the lens of whiteness. My research is no exception. As a white comics scholar, I have found it all too easy to approach my historical investigations of readership without considering the race of the readers I study except in a cursory manner. The voices of young people that

I have found in archival materials began to signal to me what was missing from my work. A chance encounter in August 2018 helped turn that signal into a siren. I was hosting the inaugural conference of the Comics Studies Society, and our first day was a community day in which the talks and activities were open at no charge to anyone who wanted to attend. Throughout the day, I greeted attendees, including an older Black woman who had come out of curiosity. She asked if she could return the following day for a talk on Black women in comics history. Consequently I invited her to be my conference guest, and she attended the full conference. When we spoke at its conclusion, she told me how exciting it had been to learn about Jackie Ormes. "I grew up reading *Archie* comics," she said. "How I wish I had known there were comics for someone like me."

In this chapter, I synthesize and analyze scattered historical evidence of comics reading by Black youth in the United States during the 1930s through the 1950s. I do this by creating three brief counterstories, based in primary sources, shaped and interpreted in ways that privilege the lived experiences of Black youth and their engagement with comics. These counterstories, based on ideas developed by Daniel Solórzano and Tara Yosso, foreground these young readers' blackness, while integrating the influence of geography, socioeconomic status, education, family, and community.[6] Each focuses on a different aspect of reading—making meaning from comics, assimilating and subverting, pathologizing—and raises more questions than I answer. As a white scholar, I rely on research by Black scholars, wherever possible, to help me situate these insights about comics readership in the broader contexts of African American print cultures and lived experiences. Sometimes this is made easier by the sources of these data: Black youth, students, scholars, writers, and photographers.

The Southwest DC Boys: Reading Comics, Reading Their World

At a surface descriptive level, it is enough to state that the photograph by Gordon Parks shown in figure 8.1 documents two young Black boys reading comics somewhere in southwest Washington, DC, in November 1942. Nothing is incorrect in this reading: it recapitulates the metadata provided by Parks and the Library of Congress and provides a data point to document Black youth reading comics. But in reading this photograph as a cultural text, such as in the manner proposed by the historian Alan Trachtenberg and

FIGURE 8.1 Gordon Parks, *Washington, D.C. Two Negro Boys Reading the Funnies on a Doorstep*, November 1942. (Library of Congress)

his followers, richer details and questions emerge that can inform our understanding of the role comics played in the lives of Black youth.[7] Moreover, it allows us to build toward a more robust counterstory. Extant, publicly available photographic examples of white youth reading comics during this era are more common than those for Black youth, making it even more critical to pay close attention to what we can learn from the images that persist.

The Library of Congress holds three extant photographs taken in November 1942 by Gordon Parks showing two boys sitting on the stoop near the entrance of a commercial building. They are engrossed in reading comic books, their eyes focused and mouths unsmiling, as comfortable as they could be on a brisk but sunny day in their landscape of stone, brick, concrete, peeling paint, and wire-mesh-covered glass. Aside from the comic books each has in his hands, at least one appears to be on the ground between them. A sign for a public pay phone is on the wall behind them, and in the photo where the boys appear together, a men's bicycle with a leather seat and rear cargo rack sits in the foreground. The younger of the two boys appears to be around ten years old. Even though it was November and chilly enough to wear a zipped-up leather coat and striped knit hat, the shorts he wears expose his scuffed, scabbed legs and well-worn canvas shoes. The older boy is perhaps twelve and wears dungarees, a shirt, a zippered light jacket, and a long, lined wool coat, which gives the illusion in one photo that he is sitting on a checkered blanket.

Parks, shy of his thirtieth birthday, captured the images of these two boys for his job chronicling social conditions in Washington, DC, as a photographer for the Farm Security Administration (FSA). An exact location is not provided, only that he took it in the southwest area of DC. Other nearby images in Parks's negatives show the Wharf, a splashy tourist area today. In 1942, however, DC's Southwest Waterfront was a primarily poor and working-class Black neighborhood, which the government soon demolished to make way for housing projects and highways. It was an early experiment in urban renewal that acted more like "Negro removal."[8] Parks had two school-aged children at home, and in his 2005 memoir, he recalled that racial conflict in the city meant that he "could not think of Washington as their permanent home."[9] He described a riot that broke out at a local Louis Armstrong concert in July 1942, only a few months before Parks took these photographs, which had raised tensions between Black residents and white police: the police "were looking for Black heads to beat." Months of protest and violence followed, and Parks continued to spend "hours recording the plight of Black people living on the back streets that Washington assigned them to."[10]

The one identifiable comic book in the photographs is *Police Comics* #9 (Quality Comics, May 1942).[11] It is opened to the Phantom Lady story in that issue and appears in all three photos, once in the hands of the younger boy and twice with the older one. The pages are curled, and small tears are visible in the *Police Comics* copy; the other unidentified comic book's cover has separated from the interior, and its pages are curled too. That the boys are reading "Phantom Lady" is intriguing, as Sandra Knight, the heroine's alter ego, is the daughter of a U.S. senator and the stories often take place in Washington, DC. In this issue's story, she witnesses her father being shot as part of a "Jap" sabotage plot. Her special "black light" helps her uncover the truth and capture the man who wounded her father. Other stories in the issue feature characters such as Plastic Man, in a story featuring white men held captive and forced to work as "slaves," and the Firebrand, who rescues a white man and woman who are being hanged to death slowly on melting blocks of wax. Half of the stories are focused on the war, the other half on crime. The exposition in the second panel of the "Manhunter" story reads, "On the water front of Empire City, squats the 'Swamp,' . . . evil, sinister! A place of muffled footsteps, . . . a strangling gurgle, and another corpse in the morning." The next panel reinforces the message: "No honest man ever tarries [there] after sundown."

Foregrounding even this small amount of context helps humanize the boys, grounding them more firmly in a place and time, while also generating questions for which answers might be theorized but probably never confirmed. For instance, the photographs are not sequentially numbered on the roll, implying that Parks returned to the boys. What drew him back? Parks did not often photograph children on their own: What made him choose them? Did he speak with the boys? Was he reminded of his own children? Were his children comics readers? How did being a Black man affect Parks's choice to take these particular images? Where did the boys acquire the comics, which were not new? Did they already have them at home, grabbing them for their day out? Maybe they acquired them from the paper-salvage collector appearing in other photographs by Parks on that film roll. Why did they choose the wharf area for reading? Were the boys brothers? Friends? Is this how they usually spent their free time?

What about the boys' choice of reading? Some adults during this era believed comics served primarily as escapist entertainment, but that is not always what research revealed. For instance, the librarians Gweneira Williams and Jane Wilson observed anecdotally from conversations with young readers that "youngsters want to read of the rumbling realities that are threatening our world; they take part in these 'realities' by proxy, with Superman and Captain America."[12] The Black sociologist E. Franklin Frazier, who studied Black youth in Washington, DC, discussed a lower-class Black teenage girl he named Almina. She noted reading pulp magazines such as *True Romances*, but Almina clarified that she read for "enjoyment not to escape from reality, since she never identifies herself with the heroines of stories, nor does she 'have time' for building air castles."[13] Did the boys in Parks's photos make a connection between their city and neighborhood and the stories in *Police Comics* #9? To their minds, was their Southwest Waterfront neighborhood a swampy, sinister place?[14] Did the panels about slavery and lynching draw their attention more than others? Were they reading for escape, for entertainment, or to establish greater agency in the world around them?

The Indianapolis Girls: Comics and the American Creed

In the photograph in figure 8.2, from the *Indianapolis Recorder* published in late summer 1948, five Black girls in their tweens or early teens sit in the grass reading comics. The occasion was the newspaper's eleventh annual picnic, a mix of reward for its young newspaper carriers and an opportunity to provide a recreational experience to needy youth. The accompanying story described the day, noting that more than six hundred young people "not only enjoyed the exhilarating air of the open countryside . . . but an untrammeled opportunity to play games, romp, skip, hop and jump to their hearts' content." Coca-Cola provided both drinks and a truck with a sound system to play music, while other donors supplied hot dogs, ice cream, and prizes. Seven photos showed scenes of young people dancing, playing baseball, and drinking bottles of Coca-Cola. The image of the girls is captioned, "some of the girls preferred to read the commies under shade trees."[15] While the day was organized for fun, at least two adults gave talks that focused on "advancing the worthy aspirations and ambitions of Negro people" and the role of Black newspapers like the *Recorder* in helping readers understand how events affect "the lives and destiny of members of their race."[16]

FIGURE 8.2 *Girls at the Recorder Picnic*, September 4, 1948. (*Indianapolis Recorder* Collection, Indiana Historical Society)

The picnic was held on a farm in far western Marion County about ten miles from many of the city's heavily redlined Black neighborhoods. Ten buses escorted by four law enforcement officers transported the participants there and back. The pleasure of basking in a few hours of recreation, food, and music amid trees and open green spaces was probably a welcome respite for Black youth. Although Indianapolis is geographically north of the Mason-Dixon line, its Riverside Amusement Park grudgingly opened for Black patronage a single day annually, while one inconveniently located public pool served the city's sixty thousand Black residents.[17] The city's public schools also remained segregated, despite years of intense pressure from the local Black community. A financially and socially exclusive white-run organization called the Citizens' School Committee ensured that the separate and unequal status quo remained intact.[18] Thus, the picnic's dual purpose of providing recreation and racial uplift seems most appropriate in this social context where Black youths' opportunities were too often constrained by white supremacy.

In the photographs I have located of young Black readers from this period, the image from the *Recorder* in figure 8.2 and the joyous one by Teenie Harris of a young Black girl at a Pittsburgh newsstand are the only two featuring female-appearing subjects. A close examination of the *Recorder* photograph reveals that the second girl from the left is reading an issue that included the characters Nancy and Fritzi, while the second girl from the right is reading a copy of *Detective Comics*.[19] Were these gifts from the drugstores or other sponsors that provided support to the picnic's organizers, or did the girls bring them along? Were the comics new, last month's issues left unsold, or secondhand swapped? Was reading comics a normative practice or an opportunistic one? The middle three girls seem rapt in the stories, one with a broad smile, another with scowling focus, and the last with her left cheek raised in the hint of a smile. The girl nearest the photographer, who unlike her dress-wearing companions is attired in wide-legged dungarees, a striped T-shirt and leather shoes, has let her comic book fall to her lap. She glares at him in apparent irritation for this unwelcome intrusion.[20]

A few studies from this period offer some insights on Black girls' comics readership. In a 1949 thesis, Derotha Allen studied the leisure activities of fifty Black ninth-grade girls in Los Angeles, with the goal of creating recreational programs. Through an analysis of the girls' diary logs, Allen found that "reading was not very popular with girls. The variety of reading materials seem to be very limited. Comic books took precedence over all other reading material. Only four girls visited the library during the week."[21] In a 1947 study of forty-four Black teen girls served by a school welfare center in South Central Los Angeles, Vivian White concluded that although the majority of girls did not read books and only five had library cards, all but two read comic strips and three-quarters read comic books.[22] No titles are provided, but nearly half of the girls listened to the *Superman* and *Dick Tracy* radio programs, perhaps indicating a similar preference in comics titles. In 1947, Vernetta Adlee Madison surveyed three hundred Black high school students in Norfolk, Virginia, to inform planning for programs to combat a perceived rise in delinquency.[23] While 70 percent of the boys indicated an interest in comic books, 90 percent of the girls did. No other magazine was more popular among boys, but girls expressed a nearly unanimous appreciation for love stories (it is unclear whether they were referring to the pulp magazine *Love Story* or a category of titles). While these studies are not a full accounting of Black girls' literary and literacy practices, they indicate that comics were integral to them.

In the 1944 report *An American Dilemma: The Negro Problem and Modern Democracy*, commissioned by the Carnegie Corporation, the economist Gunnar Myrdal wrote, "America is, however, prominent in the type of passive mass education through such agencies as the radio, press, popular magazines and movies.... Through these media, [Negroes] are made more American."[24] This passage is situated in a chapter on education and formal schooling, in which Myrdal noted the lack of prestige afforded *learning* in the United States and the relative absence of systematic civic education. Myrdal's focus here was primarily on adults, and he mentioned "popular magazines," not comics. Yet his supposition that mass media and popular texts can promote shared ideals and an acceptance of his theorized "American Creed" based in democracy and equal opportunities leads me to consider comics reading as part of the broader literary, literacy, and civic practices of Black youth. As the media and comics scholar Rebecca Wanzo argues, "representational struggles often occur not in attempts at the realistic but in fantastic representations of 'real Americanness' in history, film, and news media," with caricature being "a language used to demonstrate a citizen's value."[25] Reading comics placed Black youth in a space to negotiate their individual and collective identities in relationship to the American Creed.

So what can we make of the *Recorder* girls and their comics? The photograph and the setting designate their comics reading as recreational, an escape from the city, its concrete, and the ubiquitous white gaze. Yet the accompanying story shared how picnickers also cheered the talk that reminded these youth that they "will some day take an important place" in advancing the cause of Black people.[26] What ideals did Black girls learn from Batman and Robin stories and Tootsie Pop advertisements? What did it mean to them as readers to negotiate their identities via comics in which few Black characters returned their gazes?[27] How did engaging with stories so deeply embedded in white lives mesh with Black experiences with white supremacy? Was white supremacy as shared—intentionally or not—via the pages and panels of comic books a more potent message about shared American ideals than the messages of uplift and interracial understanding found in the pages and panels of *Negro Heroes* #2, the "comic book ... that should be in every Negro home" that was released earlier in the summer of 1948?[28]

Ralph in Queens: Pathologies of Reading

A grainy black-and-white microfilm image of a 1955 photograph published in the *Chicago Defender* on September 17 of that year shows a single bed pushed against a wall, covers askew, curtains ajar, pillows bare of cases, and a pile of objects barely identifiable as magazines and newspapers. The caption reads, "STILL UNMADE and unslept in since August 28 is the bed Emmett Louis Till was taken from that night. Only one member of the Wright family has slept in the house since that night. Several comic books and papers remain on the bed." Six days after this photograph was published, a jury acquitted the men who took Emmett Till from this Mississippi bed in which he slept with his cousin Simeon and murdered him. Two weeks later, a *Defender* article confirmed that Till was indeed a comic book reader. It quoted one of Till's Chicago neighbors, who said the fourteen-year old Till read "Little Lulu, Superman and Space Patrol. Never any dirty ones or nasty pictures."[29] That the neighbor carefully qualified the kind of comics Till read indicated the precarities of both comics and Black boyhood.

Many adults—mostly white—placed comics under increasing scrutiny during the 1940s and 1950s. The adults' concerns followed familiar patterns of moral panics around media, as they feared that reading comics would corrupt youth in various moral, sexual, and cognitive aspects. Fredric Wertham, a New York City psychiatrist, deployed his substantial experiences in both mental hygiene and forensic psychiatry to lead significant public outcry about comics beginning in 1947. His book *Seduction of the Innocent* (1954) synthesized his arguments about and clinical research around comics and youth. In research published in 2012, I provided evidence from Wertham's

STILL UNMADE and un-slept in since August 28 is the bed Emmett Louis Till was taken from that night. Only one member of the Wright family has slept in the house since that night. Several comic books and papers remain on the bed.

FIGURE 8.3 Still unmade bed. (*Chicago Defender*, September 17, 1955, national ed.)

archival record demonstrating the falsifications he perpetrated in *Seduction*. Although his published presentation of clinical cases is problematic, Wertham's case records and notes can enlarge our understanding of Black youths' experiences with comics.

Readers meet Ralph in *Seduction*'s chapter on the effects that reading comics has on young people, his one-paragraph story bookended by comments about how comics have made brutality and torture commonplace among children.[30] A year before white men kidnapped Emmett Till, beating and shooting him, then hanging a cotton-gin fan around his neck with barbed wire and dumping his body into the Tallahatchie River, Wertham wrote about Ralph,

> A Lafargue social worker investigated the case of an eleven-year-old boy who "played" with a boy several years younger. He put a rope around his neck, drawing it so tight that his neck became swollen, and the little boy almost strangled. His father happened to catch them and was able to prevent the incident from turning into a catastrophe. About a month later the eleven-year-old beat the younger child so that his mouth was all bloody. He did not know that one should not hit a younger and smaller boy. What he did know was that this sort of thing was done in innumerable comic-book stories about murders and robberies.[31]

Wertham's account is based on one typed page plus two scrawled notes that are extant in his archival record.[32] The typed page documenting Ralph's story carries a spring 1948 date, so these events are already six years in the past at the time of *Seduction*'s publication and correspond to the early period of Wertham's interest in the broad effects of comics in children's lives. In late March 1948, *Collier's* magazine published an article titled "Horror in the Nursery" by Judith Crist, one of Wertham's initial advocates in his anticomics work, that highlighted Wertham and his efforts to curtail the harmful effects of comics reading. This article followed a number of other articles and events in the New York City area in winter and spring 1948 that provided a platform for Wertham to share his views. Only a couple of years earlier, Wertham's efforts to provide psychiatric services to Black residents of Harlem through the recently established Lafargue Clinic had made local and national news.[33] Thus, he was visible and widely known in the greater New York City area as someone interested both in the mental health of Black people and the purported negative effects of comics reading.

This context helps explain the origin of Ralph's story, which was not because a Lafargue social worker investigated the case, as Wertham contended. The typed document about Ralph originated with a social worker for the Salvation Army, who passed it along to a volunteer at Lafargue. That volunteer provided it to Wertham sometime after the end of March in the spring of 1948. The typed document bears a penciled note from Wertham at the top—"not yet used. v[ery] good"—while prolific underlining and crosshatching in red pen indicate that Wertham incorporated elements of the report into *Seduction*. While Wertham's account of the strangling and beating incidents are generally consistent with the written report he was provided, he failed to provide an accurate context for the incident.

Ralph was actually thirteen years old, not eleven. He was Black and, as the document states, part of a "stable Negro family," which most probably refers to him being part of a family headed by both parents and not that the family was financially stable. According to 1940 Census and World War II draft records, his father was a handyman for a restaurant located in Manhattan's Financial District. The family's household income in 2020 dollars was approximately $21,000. Both parents had eighth-grade educations and had immigrated from southern states: his father from North Carolina and his mother from Georgia. Their address on both draft records and the document in Wertham's files places the family as residing in South Jamaica Houses, an integrated housing project completed in 1940, built in a Black neighborhood, and managed by the New York City Housing Authority.[34]

Of course, Ralph's father may have changed jobs by 1948, but the family's economic circumstances could not have changed significantly since they remained in public housing.

Ralph had a congenital heart condition and severe myopathy. The social worker made no indication that his eyesight was corrected with glasses. Either way, a Black nearsighted teenager with a chronic health problem, living in an urban housing project, had probably experienced his own share of bullying. Perhaps he simply wanted the experience of treating someone else in the way he had been treated? Or maybe, at least with regard to the beating, he was indeed retaliating for being hit by a football, as he had reported. The social worker documented little information about the boy whom Ralph purportedly abused, only that he was a neighbor's child, smaller and several years younger than Ralph, who lived downstairs. In three separate sentences, the social worker described the younger boy as Ralph's friend, implying that their relationship was not one between a bully and his victim. Ralph was reluctant to speak to the woman at Salvation Army, so most of the details of the two incidents were relayed by his mother, who had witnessed neither one. The social worker noted that "Ralph's face was expressionless during the interviews."[35]

The Salvation Army woman questioned Ralph's mother about whether he read comic books. His mother "appeared startled and wondered if that were bad."[36] In this way, his mother was like millions of other parents during this era. The ubiquity of comics both generally and in the hands of young readers made many parents somewhat blind to their existence: comic books were simply part of the landscape. Survey research and studies such as the one by Sarah Lean Bivins (1954) indicate that parents purchased comics for their children, and perhaps Ralph's mother did this.[37] She reported that he read *Crime Does Not Pay* and *Gang Busters*, which were both popular titles emblematic of the crime comics genre that grew immensely popular in the last half of the 1940s. The first title was in the midst of its successful thirteen-year run, while the latter—which was based on a radio program—was relatively new in 1948, when Ralph's visit to the Salvation Army occurred. The crime genre was widespread across media: this was the era of detective radio shows, film noir, hard-boiled crime paperbacks, and pulp crime magazines. If Ralph had not read crime comics, chances are good he would have encountered similar stories in other media. When he was asked directly what comics he read, Ralph said he liked *Batman* and *Superman*. As Wertham did in *Seduction*, Ralph mentioned the murders and robberies contained in these books. Unlike Wertham, Ralph clearly emphasized that these superhero titles were focused on the titular characters capturing murderers and robbers.

On the basis of such a slight record and the distance of more than seventy years, one cannot adequately or responsibly determine any sort of cause-and-effect relationship between Ralph's professed comics reading and his claimed abusive behavior. Instead Ralph—like Emmett Till and so many other Black youth—was engaging in a pastime embraced by millions of young people during those decades. Wertham chose in Ralph's case to pathologize his comics reading, arguing that it was indicative of the lynching-as-play in which Ralph purportedly engaged.[38] Yet, that same act of comics reading becomes in the neighbor's description of Emmett Till a means of humanizing him or, as the comics scholar Qiana Whitted writes, of "reclaim[ing] his immaturity as a teenager."[39] That reclamation should be unnecessary except, as the literary scholar Habiba Ibrahim reminds us vis-à-vis the work of Frantz Fanon, "adulthood ... [was] shackled to the necks" of Emmett Till, Ralph, and countless other Black youth.[40]

Looking Ahead to More Counterstories

In this essay's opening, I invoked a handful of Black cultural icons to illustrate how comics reading was normative for Black youth born in the mid-twentieth century. But each of these examples is also an invitation for creating a counterstory. Take Amiri Baraka. He was not just a comics reader who invoked *Dickie Dare* in a poem he wrote in adulthood. Baraka taught himself to read from a comic book, while he was confined at home during kindergarten because of illness. In his memoir, Baraka recalled that the comic was titled *Targeteer*, which does not seem to have existed, but there was *Target Comics*.[41] Its first issue had a cover date of February 1940, and the characters Target and his companions the Targeteers were introduced in issues later that year. Like a lot of early comics, the Target, Spacehawk, and other stories in this series were loquacious with words that must have been baffling to a new reader: "diligent," "futile," "masquerade," "menaced," "spectators."[42] Even if Baraka's memory was not wholly accurate, he chose this particular comic series to identify as the birthplace for his literate self. Target and the Targeteer had meaning for Baraka.

While the evidence that these comics were important to Baraka comes from him—albeit the adult, not the child, him—most of the documentary evidence that scholars encounter regarding historical children is mediated by external adults—for instance, Ralph's story, relayed primarily by his mother, filtered through the lens of a probably white female social worker, and then rhetorically transformed by a powerful white physician into an example of the harm wrought by comics reading. This kind of mediation exemplifies a vital truth at the core of my attempts to provide these historical counterstories. Simply, "like many sources employed by historians of children and youth, and particularly the least powerfully located children and youth, others speak" for them.[43] For this essay, those "others" include the photographers, journalists, and researchers whose texts capture historical instances of Black youth engaging with comics. Just as Wertham subtly transformed Ralph's story to advance his own aims, the other adults with whom these texts and data points originate used children's experiences to achieve their own documentary and explanatory purposes. None of them allow us to interact directly with the children who are the foci of their efforts. And through this essay, I am adding my own editorial intentions and imagination to the records of these historical children's experiences.[44]

My hope is that the counterstories in this essay provide a useful starting point for the construction and reclamation of more and richer stories about historical Black children as comics readers. Digitization projects make it easier to read sideways, upside down, and into new archives, as the scholars Tammy-Cherelle Owens and Marcia Chatelain discuss in a roundtable on the Black girlhood historiography.[45] But more than access to resources, scholars who want to foreground the lived experiences of historical children—nearly all of whom, regardless of race, are marginalized within the documentary record—must be willing to listen to what these children have to tell us. We must draw on our own empathetic understanding of what it means to be a child, not to appropriate their experiences as our own but to enter into conversation. I may be a white, middle-aged woman, writing seventy years in the future, but when I look at the dungaree-wearing girl in the *Recorder* photograph, I am certain she has stories.

Notes

1 Baraka, "Look for You Yesterday, Here You Come Today," in *S O S*, 14–16.
2 Clifton, *Book of Light*; Hendrix and Mitchell, *Jimi Hendrix*; Burshtein, *Walter Dean Myers*, 26.
3 Holmes, *Joyous Revolt*, 12.
4 Lorde, *Zami*.
5 For more information on midcentury comics and readership, see Gabilliet, *Of Comics*

and Men; Tilley, "Seducing the Innocent"; Tilley, "Comics"; Wright, *Comic Book Nation*.
6   Solórzano and Yosso, "Critical Race Methodology."
7   Trachtenberg, *Reading American Photographs*.
8   Russello Ammon, "Commemoration amid Criticism," 177; Parks, *Hungry Heart*, 66. Per Downey, "1954 Court Case," the Southwest neighborhood was targeted in part because "the Southwest area became [the development plan's] early focus. About 58 percent of the houses there had outdoor toilets, 29 percent lacked electricity, 82 percent had no wash basins or laundry tubs, 94 percent lacked central heating. About 64 percent of the buildings were deemed too dilapidated to repair. The tuberculosis death rate in the area was more than double the city average."
9   Parks, *Hungry Heart*, 66.
10 Parks, 68.
11 You can view a full scan of *Police Comics* #9, which is in the public domain, at Comic Book Plus, accessed October 14, 2022, https://comicbookplus.com/?dlid=19828.
12 Williams and Wilson, "They Like It Rough," 204.
13 Frazier, *Negro Youth at the Crossways*, 246. LaKisha Michelle Simmons, in *Crescent City Girls*, offers additional insight into how confessional and romance magazines functioned in the lives of Black girls. These magazines served as sources of information about sexuality and romance, topics that young readers' mothers may have been reluctant to address. Just as comics were conduits for children to learn about harder realities, *True Romances* and similar magazines offered vicarious insights into adulthood.
14 Freddie, one of the Black teenagers from Washington, DC, who is featured in Frazier's *Negro Youth at the Crossways*, makes this comment about the Southwest neighborhood: "I sure wouldn't want to be a policeman even off duty without a gun. Not as bad as the 'niggers' are down here" (xvi).
15 "600 Newsies Have the Time of Their Lives," 3. I have encountered the term "commies" as slang for comics only here.
16 "600 Newsies Have the Time of Their Lives," 1, 3.
17 Mullins, "Romanticizing Racist Landscapes"; Mullins, "Race and the Color Line."
18 Steele, *Making a Mass Institution*.
19 Nancy appeared in several comic books at the time, including *Tip Top Comics*, *Comics on Parade*, and *Sparkler*. Stories featuring Nancy—a white child, with a curly, textured helmet of hair—often involved sight gags and wordplay and featured her pal Sluggo, a white boy whose speech and dress place him at a lower socioeconomic level than Nancy. *Detective Comics* was the anthology title that ran Batman and Robin stories, alongside others that in 1948 featured characters including the Boy Commandos, Slam Bradley, and Robotman.
20 "600 Newsies Have the Time of Their Lives"; "Girls at the Recorder Picnic" (the published newspaper credits staff photographer Thom Ervin).
21 Allen, "Leisure Time Activities of a Selected Group of Negro Girls," 32.
22 V. White, "Social Contributions of a Welfare Center for Negro Girls."
23 Madison, "Study of Recreational Opportunities for Negro Children."
24 Myrdal, *American Dilemma*, 886.
25 Wanzo, *Content of Our Caricature*, 4.
26 "600 Newsies Have the Time of Their Lives," 1.
27 In 1948, few Black characters—stereotypically caricatured or otherwise—could be found in comic books. One of the most egregiously drawn characters, Captain

Marvel's valet, Steamboat, departed in 1945 after a group of New York children who were part of a Youthbuilders civic club successfully petitioned the publisher (cf. Tilley, "Comics"), although Will Eisner's character Ebony remained part of *The Spirit* until 1949.

28   "Editorial: Negro Heroes," 3.
29   Barrow, "Here's a Picture of Emmett Till," 4.
30   Although these records are publicly accessible, I have omitted the children's surname and provided only partial file dates to protect their and their families' privacy. In this instance, as will be revealed in the next paragraphs, this particular case originated outside Wertham's private and clinical practices.
31   Wertham, *Seduction of the Innocent*, 109–110.
32   Ralph N—April 1948, box 110, folder 2, Fredric Wertham Papers, Manuscripts Division, Library of Congress, Washington, DC.
33   For additional information, see Mendes, *Under the Strain of Color*.
34   New York City Housing Authority, "Project Statistics July 1947"; "South Jamaica Houses."
35   Ralph N—April 1948, box 110, folder 2, Fredric Wertham Papers, Manuscripts Division, Library of Congress, Washington, DC.
36   Ralph N—April 1948.
37   Bivens, "Comparative Study of the Reading Interests."
38   Wertham's particular pathologizing in this case is unreliable as well, given his lack of firsthand understanding of the particulars of Ralph's case as well as his belief that "neutrality—especially when hidden under the cloak of scientific objectivity—... is the devil's ally" (Wertham, *Seduction of the Innocent*, 351).
39   Whitted, "Comics and Emmett Till," 71. In an interview recorded decades after Till's murder, his classmate Magnolia Cooksey recalled seeing Till's body in the casket and that it appeared "like it was from a mystery science fiction ... comic book" (Cooksey, interview). I mention this recollection here because while invoking comic book reading served to humanize Till, the violence done to him by his white murderers rendered his body fantastically grotesque, reminiscent of the monstrous creatures in early 1950s horror and science fiction comics that Wertham and other, mainly white anticomics advocates sought to regulate.
40   Ibrahim, *Black Age*, 17.
41   Baraka, *Autobiography of LeRoi Jones*, 10.
42   These words are taken from the Target story appearing in *Target Comics* #11 (December 1940).
43   Gleason, "Avoiding the Agency Trap," 454. See also Ferrière, "Voice of the Innocent."
44   See, for instance, Little, "What Is Historical Imagination?"
45   Field et al., "History of Black Girlhood."

9

All-Negro Comics and Counterhistories of Race in the Golden Age

●●●●●●●●●●●●●●

QIANA WHITTED

Detective Ace Harlem may have a sharp eye for detail on the job, but the Zoot Chain Killers have him stumped. Once he inspects the strangled body at Pop's Bar-B-Que Shack, Ace declares, "Never saw anything like this before!" and after speaking with a witness, he thinks to himself, "This is certainly a new one to me!"[1] The provocation of the strange case continues to baffle the expert African American detective, dressed in a sharp double-breasted suit, trench coat, and fedora as he approaches the fingerprint expert's office and admits, "First time I ever tackled one like this!" (10). Clues will ultimately lead Ace from police forensics and an urban root doctor to the top floor of a tenement building, but by the time he tracks down the two culprits, greed has set them against each other; one is murdered, the other accidentally hanged by his own zoot-suit chain. Ace greets

FIGURE 9.1 Ace Harlem in *All-Negro Comics*, 1947.

this unexpected act of retribution with awe, tossing back a quip to a fellow officer: "Never saw a case solve itself so quick before. Those two took care of themselves!" (17; figure 9.1).

The startling novelty of Ace Harlem's case brings into relief what may have been even more surprising about the comic book in which his sleuthing appeared. Written by the Philadelphia journalist Orrin Cromwell Evans and drawn by the artist John H. Terrell, "Ace Harlem" is the first of six features that debuted in the inaugural issue of *All-Negro Comics* in the summer of 1947.[2] The title is celebrated as the first comic book to be written, illustrated, and published by and about African Americans in the United States. Only issue 1 of the series was printed and sold, featuring a full-color anthology of crime, adventure, fantasy, and humor stories that were created to disrupt the popular and profitable racial caricatures that continued to circulate in the comic book industry after World War II. Evans seized an opportunity to offer Black readers an alternative when he partnered with his former colleagues at the *Philadelphia Record* newspaper to form the company that would publish *All-Negro Comics*.[3]

Beneath the headline of Evans's opening editorial—"Presenting Another FIRST in Negro History"—he declares that the drawings are original, that the humor and fantasy are "good" and "clean," and that the pages will satisfy comics consumers with "fast action." Evans scripted the stories and recruited the talents of the freelance cartoonist Terrell along with students from the Philadelphia Museum of Art School: William H. Smith, Leonard Cooper, and his brother, George J. Evans Jr. With their contributions, the publisher was able to boast that "every brush stroke and pen line in the drawings on these pages are by Negro artists" (1).

Ace's story was followed by a playful sojourn in the make-believe world of the Dew Dillies, cherubic creatures of the sea and sky, while in another tale, a young African American scientist named Lion Man protects the African Gold Coast and its volatile uranium deposits from outsiders. In the closing story, Sugarfoot and his companion, Snake Oil, travel the rails in search of adventure and a hot meal. Alongside these features are two one-page comic strips and cartoon art featuring "Hep Chicks on Parade" and "Lil' Eggie." The short story "Ezekiel's Manhunt" served as the two pages of printed material required by the post office. The title sought to represent a panoramic view of Black experiences, and as the comics scholar Blair Davis explains, "*All-Negro Comics* offers its readers a wide range of character types and backgrounds: urban and rural, domestic and international, highly educated and unschooled alike. The book's stories are set in both busy city streets and pastoral settings, in the open wilderness and in cramped apartment buildings. The various characters speak with different dialects and levels of diction. Some cannot afford their next meal, while others are at the top of their professions."[4] The debut issue captured substantial media attention, with announcements and interviews in *Time*, *Washington Post*, *Collier's*, *Atlanta Daily World*, *Chicago Defender*, and the *Baltimore Afro-American*. The press marveled at Evans's initiative and remarked on the wonders of "America's first Negro comic book" in ways that resembled detective Ace Harlem's frequent words of astonishment. Even Eleanor Roosevelt, in her syndicated "My Day" column, wrote, "I must say that, as I glanced through the pages of this newcomer, I felt that it compared very favorably with the best of the comic books. In some features it is really better."[5]

Nevertheless, the African American writer and conservative critic George S. Schuyler was among the few reviewers to situate the significance of Evans's innovative effort within a broader social and cultural context. Writing for the *Pittsburgh Courier*, Schuyler observes,

> Of course Negro comics are not new. They have appeared in most of our leading weekly newspapers and in this connection *The Pittsburgh Courier* was a pioneer. One of the most popular comic strips in journalism is W.L. Holloway's "Sunny Boy Sam," which has appeared in this newspaper for more than a generation. But an all-cartoon magazine aimed at the Negro market is something new.

> Which causes one to wonder about the limits of Negro achievement in this civilization. Frankly, what is it that we cannot do here, if we try hard enough and stick long enough? There is much beefing and lugubrious moaning about how "underprivileged" we are, and this gives us a wonderful opportunity to sit back, do nothing and feel sorry for ourselves.
>
> But frankly what is it we are not privileged to do? What obstacles can we not get around if we want to get around them sufficiently to put forth the necessary effort?[6]

Schuyler describes the colorful images in *All-Negro Comics* as "well-drawn," and he emphasizes, too, the wholesome aim and accessibility of the stories for young people. But it is the entrepreneurial initiative that Schuyler finds most inspiring about Evans and his comic. He indexes what Evans accomplished in a way that connects the series's launch to the collective determination of a people who he insists can and should refuse to allow racism to stall their aspirations, leading the *Courier* columnist to conclude, "What we want we can get—and without begging."[7] To Schuyler, this comic book is illustrative of the limitless potential of African American striving.

Yet if the notions of "progress" and "pioneering spirit" that Schuyler invokes in his column are the starting points for a critical consideration of *All-Negro Comics*, how, then, do readers reckon with the series's failure? What are we to make of the individuals and the institutions and the social practices of the comic book industry that worked to *unimagine* what Evans and his collaborators created? This chapter's analysis responds to these questions by placing *All-Negro Comics* and its artistic and narrative choices at the center of a disruptive counterhistory of the comic book industry's Golden Age of success. While I examine the stories in the first and only extant issue of the series, the larger aim is to call attention to the gaps left open by the installments that were to come. My reading posits *All-Negro Comics* #2 as emblematic of this effort; its haunting absence echoes all the unrealized comic books of the era that attempted to underscore Black lives, that became ensnared in the power differentials behind comic book production, distribution, and sales, and that "put forth the necessary effort" only to be denied the privileges of serialization. At the heart of this thought experiment is my attempt to demonstrate the real, material ramifications of what Michael Hanchard refers to as "racial time" on the development of comics books in the United States.[8] *All-Negro Comics* offers us a space to inhabit this complicated history more fully and to make room beside the milestone firsts to name and to grieve all the stories that have been lost.

All-New, All-Negro

When Schuyler wrote in 1947 that "of course Negro comics are not new," he was clarifying a distinction about form and readership. Wilbert L. Holloway's "Sunny Boy Sam," the newspaper comic strip that debuted in 1928, was the longest-running serial comic in the *Courier*, second in the Black press only to "Bungleton Green," created by Leslie Rogers for the *Chicago Defender* in 1920. In Tim Jackson's *Pioneering Cartoonists of Color*, he dubs the subsequent period between 1940 and 1949 "The Cartoon Renaissance," detailing nearly fifty comic strips and single-panel cartoons that appeared in African American newspapers and were targeted to their regular subscribers.[9] Holloway would be joined by a host of other cartoonists in the 1940s, including E. Simms Campbell, Ollie Harrington, and Jackie Ormes, who created their own comic strips. But *All-Negro Comics* was a comic book, referred to by Schuyler as "an all-cartoon magazine." He rightly pointed out that these kinds of saddle-stitched serials were not typically "aimed at the Negro market," much less drawn by Black artists. And the few African Americans who were active in the comic book industry in the 1940s, such as Elmer Stoner, Matt Baker, Alvin Hollingsworth, and Ezra Jackson, were seldom afforded the opportunity to illustrate stories about Black people.[10]

Appearing only a few months before the publication of *All-Negro Comics* was a comic book called *Negro Heroes*, a collaboration between Parents' Magazine Press, the Urban League, and Delta Sigma Theta Sorority that also claimed the distinction of being "the first all-Negro comic magazine."[11] The two-issue omnibus reprinted previously published material from other biographical comics (and even featured an editorial note by the world champion boxer Joe Louis). *All-Negro Comics*, by contrast, featured new characters in original stories completely written and illustrated by African Americans. Christopher J. Hayton and David L. Albright also point out that Evans did not have access to the same financial resources or to an established publisher's distribution network, however, and while the first issue of *All-Negro Comics* was longer than some of its competitors, with forty-eight interior pages, it sold for fifteen cents, when most cost a dime.[12]

Correspondence from Evans's distributor, National News Co., reveals that in the fall of 1947, half of the three thousand copies of *All-Negro Comics* distributed in Chicago were returned, "which indicates that the sale thus far has been very slow." The company's president suggested ways that Evans could better publicize the title to newsstand vendors and agreed to devote more effort to promoting the comic by sending sales letters and sample copies to outlets in "four states in the deep south."[13] Evans also enlisted student salespeople and offered to send the issue to schools that served African American youth, giving them and their principals the opportunity to make a small profit and ensuring more reliable direct distribution for future monthly installments. In a letter to a Tennessee school principal in October 1947, Evans made his pitch, noting, "our plan to Negro schools for sale of the books to the students and to homes has been remarkably successful."[14] References to these efforts, combined with the available circulation numbers, suggest that the print run of *All-Negro Comics* was probably much fewer than the 170,000 copies printed for *Negro Heroes* earlier that year, despite Evans's initial claim that 300,000 would be distributed across the United States and the West Indies.[15]

Whether *All-Negro Comics* circulated on newsstands or mostly in school rooms, the title boldly piqued the reader's interest and took advantage of the decade's trend in targeting a single subject through the "All" comics compilation style (e.g., *All Teen Comics*, *All-Star Comics*, *All-American Comics*, *All Funny Comics*, *All Top Comics*, and *All Great Comics*, just to name a few titles from July 1947 alone).[16] To attract attention in a congested market, Evans and his collaborators implemented a familiar assortment of visual and verbal strategies, including conspicuous branding, an ensemble cast, promotional teasers, and direct appeals to readers. Across the top of a solid black cover, a red banner unfolds beneath the bright yellow words of the title (figure 9.2). Pictured at the center are the comic's signature characters: Ace Harlem chases after Lion Man's young ward, Bubba, while the child's arrows spray through the wing of a Dew Dillie and into Snake Oil's banjo. The scene is drawn in such a way that it appears to blast through a solid black page, folding back torn leaves of the cover and filling the empty space with "All-Negro" colors. The tableau sets the stage for an arrival that is affirmed by Evans's declaration of the comic as a "first" and the all-caps promotional teaser on the back page that announces, "IT'S NEW!"

Ace Harlem is positioned prominently as the narrative analogue to these sentiments. Inside the comic's back-cover promotion, he is pictured as a spokesman, pointing directly at readers with these words of advice: "Remember—Crime doesn't pay, kids! Stick to the church, and use up your energy in good clean sports" (51). In his opening story, he serves as our ambassador through the story world of his comic. The artist John Terrell allows us to look over Ace's shoulder as the detective "takes in everything—at a glance!" including the clues in the case of the Zoot Chain Killers. Yet the "new" and "never seen before" textual cues are more than just a genre

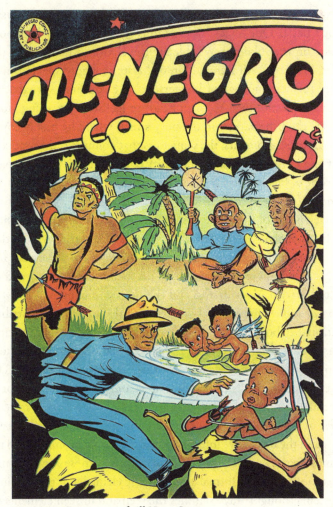

FIGURE 9.2 Front cover of *All-Negro Comics*.

convention deployed to sustain the story's suspense. These moments are also a way of staging an encounter between form and content, where the short-form comic strip meets the long-form all-cartoon magazine. The surprises are marked by scene transitions that signal the stop and start of each episode in the story's pacing, much like a newspaper serial. Some of these breaks are marked by narrative boxes that recap prior events and character taglines. Panel transitions lead to page turns that stitch these installments together into a full-length comic book for readers who were more accustomed to following characters like Ace in weekly installments in the *Pittsburgh Courier*.

Along the way, a succession of interior and exterior scenes transports us into Pop's Bar-B-Que Shack, where Louis Jordan's "Open the Door, Richard" spins on the Juke Box. Visible are the elixirs and charms of the local herbalist, "Doctor" Ali Ben, a Man of Mystery, whose speech shifts from the more formal language of his persona to a southern vernacular under Ace's tough questioning. Ace next heads to Jackson's Boarding House, the one beside the fish market on the busy street, where he finally corners the culprits. In these moments, the sequences that connect the narrative are significant as a cross-section of community comes into view that expands the visual scope of blackness in comics. Such creative choices would elicit praise from the *Baltimore Afro-American* commentator who was eager to see the "casual viewpoint of the average Afro-American," in which "daily situations arising from open or latent Jim Crow" could be dramatized. On the other hand, another reviewer from the *Chicago Defender* characterized *All-Negro Comics* as a "commercial venture with no social story to tell" and directly contrasted it with *Negro Heroes* and the 1946 comic book *Joe Worker and the Story of Labor*, published by Commercial Comics and distributed by the National Labor Service.[17] These differences of opinion anticipate the frictions between the "entertaining" and "educational" aims of comics that would play out in the decade to come through companies like EC Comics that entwined the thrills of horror, crime, and science fiction storytelling with social and political commentary. The *All-Negro Comics* reviews are a reminder of how the politics of racial representation inform the visual connections and the discursive inferences that the comic prompts us to make.

Comics studies scholarship can also connect these kinds of narrative interpretations with the formal and aesthetic elements of the medium. Barbara Postema thoughtfully examines the seen and unseen elements of comics sequence that generate readerly anticipation and construct meaning through image and text. Drawing on Thierry Groensteen's notion of "iconic solidarity" as well as Scott McCloud's formulations of closure, Postema explains that "the panels on a comics page, when they form a sequence, are bound together because each panel presupposes the one before and after it."[18] She also notes that "each panel, as a signifier, gives a certain amount of information, which is re-evaluated with each new panel, if necessary by revisiting earlier panels. Comics call for a process of retroactive resignification, where one must continually loop back to reconsider meanings and make new meanings as one goes forward in the text."[19] What helps to hold these panels together are the blank spaces or "gaps" created by frames (which the panels encapsulate) and gutters (the space between the panels). These gaps are integral to the sequences that make up comics. What turns a single moment into a combination of moments, Postema argues, is "all based on unvisualized connections between the panels."[20] Her notion of "retroactive resignification" provides fresh insight into not only our reading process but Ace Harlem's. As the one who "takes in everything—at a glance," he is our stand-in, our focalizer through each scene, and as a representative of the law, his discerning eye is primed to piece together the "unvisualized connections" and impose a sense of order on the unruly unknowns before him. Ace embodies both the possibility and the anxiety of comics reading in this unprecedented moment.

The decision to make Ace a crimefighter also suggests an attempt to disrupt the antagonism between African Americans and law enforcement by highlighting instead "the outstanding contributions of thousands of fearless, intelligent Negro police officers engaged in a constant fight against crime," as Evans writes in his editorial (2). Ace's debut frames his authority and moral character in the tradition of Chester Gould's Dick Tracy or Will Eisner's the Spirit.[21] Yet just as with these well-known comic-strip detectives, race continues to be implicated in the urban clash against disorder and deviance, with the "two vicious young hep-cats" conveying vain self-interest, greed, and a careless criminality. The intergenerational tensions that they represent are animated through their zoot suits—the long, elaborately tailored drape suits of the 1930s and 1940s.[22] As the fashionable attire gained in popularity among African Americans as a resistant mode of style in the city, it also acquired negative connotations among law enforcement that extend in the comic to the sinister use of the long, swinging watch chain as a murder weapon. One reporter for *Time* commented on the characterization of the bad guys in "Ace Harlem," noting that "the villains were a couple of zoot-suited, jive-talking Negro muggers, whose presence in anyone else's comics might have brought up complaints of racial 'distortion.' Since it was all in the family, Evans thought no Negro readers would mind."[23]

Herein lies another danger for the collaborators of *All-Negro Comics*, as their efforts to build compelling character types run the risk of perpetuating the exaggerations and misrepresentations of caricature. How does a comic designed to defy racist images avoid enabling the distortions that are so deeply embedded in the form's narrative and aesthetic traditions?

All in the Family

Caricature, to borrow Schuyler's phrase, is the other way in which "Negro comics are not new." The lens of racial stereotype has a wide scope in the comics industry and a long history of prompting and bolstering an already pervasive material culture in which blackness is exploited as a vehicle for ridicule, shame, pity, and fear. From washing powder and syrup advertisements to the illustrations in reading primers for small children, visual and verbal representations of Black people as buffoons and savages continued to circulate in the 1940s. Captain Marvel's Black valet and sidekick, Steamboat, was a fixture in the popular comic book series until 1945, while one of Bucky Barnes's companions in Timely's *Young Allies* and *Kid Komics* was Whitewash Jones, a zoot-suited Black teen with the balloon lips of minstrel caricatures and a love for watermelon. Readers who picked up Dell Comics' *The New Funnies* in 1947 would have encountered the antics of Li'l Eightball, a boy with a shiny, round black head, alongside the funny animal adventures of Woody Woodpecker and Andy Panda.

Evans knew that African Americans, young people especially, counted themselves among these comic book readers and enthusiastically embraced the medium, even as they critiqued its racist representations. According to the *Time* article, he stated that "Negroes are usually ridiculed and their way of life distorted in comics drawn by white men," suggesting that his own comic would steer clear of such pitfalls, not only by employing Black creators but also through narrative sequences that were grounded in shared cultural and social realities.[24] What is perhaps most daring, in this regard, is Evans's decision to immerse his characters in fictional genres—including slapstick comedy and adventure—that had frequently been used to denigrate people of color. Comic book publishers tended to answer such complaints with titles like *Negro Heroes*, which focused on historical leaders and sports figures and sought to avoid "distortions" by adhering to facts and stats. Instead, the first issue of *All-Negro Comics* invited readers to see a glimpse of themselves in the comic's escapist storytelling, to laugh, to gasp in awe and shock. This, too, is part of the retroactive resignification process that comics enable. Sidestepping the problematic traditions that comics like *The New Funnies* endorsed and the solutions touted by *Negro Heroes*, Evans and his collaborators hoped that readers who spent their fifteen cents on *All-Negro Comics* would know "at a glance" what was new.[25]

One genre noticeably missing from Evans's anthology comic is superheroes, at least with regard to costumed characters with alien, supernatural, or technological sources of power. Davis makes a compelling case for why Lion Man should be classified as a superhero based on "his heightened abilities and role as a defender of Africa's Gold Coast."[26] Importantly, like his Marvel Comics successor Black Panther, Lion Man's creators tapped into the tropes of imperial "jungle" comics, popularized by Edgar Rice Burroughs's Tarzan adventures as well as comics published by Fiction House and Fox Features Syndicate that dramatized the exploits of white adventurers in remote lands facing off against angry natives, ferocious animals, and greedy hunters. Evans makes a point to identify Lion Man as an "American-born, college educated" scientist who works for the newly formed United Nations to watch over a place called Magic Mountain in West Africa, where the "world's largest deposit of uranium" contains "enough to make an atom bomb that could destroy the world" (30). These Cold War–era concerns link Lion Man not only to debates over sovereignty and geopolitical containment but also to the revolutionaries who were rejecting colonial rule across the African continent.

Davis notes that "while the representations of black characters in most jungle stories of the period are born out of ignorance, Evans signals early on that his creators are using the jungle as a backdrop to tell an African story, rather than simply using the word 'jungle' to conjure up sensational (and colonialist) images in the reader's mind."[27] Indeed, the story is anchored around the way Lion Man uses his smarts and his strength to best intruders. When the "evil" Dr. Blut Sangro arrives at Magic Mountain with his pith helmet and hidden pistol and "raises his hand in mock friendship," his nefarious intentions are clear (35). The "dirty trick" that he uses in hand-to-hand combat with Lion Man further reinforces the qualities of the "warlike nation" that he represents (37, 39). At the same time, Evans and the artist George "Geo" Evans, Jr. also make critical choices in depicting their hero's relationship with a young orphan named Bubba, using the Black boy as comic relief in ways that perpetuate familiar reductionist types. Bubba is as rambunctious as Dennis the Menace and is prominently featured in the story trailing behind his unsmiling benefactor, playing jokes and stumbling into trouble. The contrasts between Bubba and Lion Man are only heightened by the young boy's clashes with the outsiders on Magic Mountain. When Dr. Sangro sees that Bubba has mistakenly fallen into an animal trap, he stands over the pit in the ground and asks, "What have we here? Some new kind of animal?" (35; figure 9.3).

Caricatures of careless, undisciplined Black children have appeared in cartoon art since the nineteenth century. The earliest of these stereotypes depict grinning Black boys and girls—mischievous, clumsy, and often naked—with

FIGURE 9.3 Bubba falls into a trap in "Lion Man" from *All-Negro Comics*.

the sole purpose of bringing chaos to the people around them. At times, they are analogized with animals or ridiculed as bait for alligators and lions. The comics scholar Lara Saguisag explains that Progressive-era depictions of this "child coon" or "pickaninny" caricature "implied the inherent corruption of black children as well as the permanent childishness of African American adults," while Rebecca Wanzo calls attention to the far-reaching consequences of the cognitive dissonance that results from the way "black children have been a binary other to romanticized depictions of white children" in more recent comics.[28] It is not difficult to see how the depiction of Bubba, with his pantomime facial expressions and gestures, could be associated with the aesthetic practices of racial caricature in the United States. Nevertheless, Evans's editorial frames "Lion Man" as an opportunity to "give American Negroes a reflection of their natural spirit of adventure and a finer appreciation of their African heritage"—remarks that arguably connect Bubba to specific cultural traditions that associate the child's unpredictability, resourcefulness, and sense of play with a trickster figure. As a result, characters like Bubba (or the Zoot Chain Killers of "Ace Harlem") expose crucial fault lines between multiple, and sometimes opposing, ways of reading blackness in the comic. They illustrate how the collaborators behind *All-Negro Comics* attempted to wrestle free of racial stereotypes while working within the boundaries of genre and convention.

"Dew Dillies," another story from the comic, locates Black children in a world of fantasy that calls attention to the challenges of companionship in a different way. The narrative introduces a duo of imaginary "little people" named Bubbles and Bibber, a girl with fins who lives in the sea and a boy with wings who takes to the sky. Both have oversized heads, long eyelashes, and the chubby bodies of toddlers as they curl up on the lily pads of a pond or pick flowers. Their attempts to play together are frustrated when Bibber struggles to breathe under water and Bubbles refuses the clam on a half shell for lunch for fear of eating a second cousin. At one point, Bibber defends a goose from what appears to be a hostile alligator-like Dew Dillie (or "Goolygator") with a punch to the jaw that he learned from Joe Louis (figure 9.4). Although the differences between Bubbles and Bibber have not been resolved by the end of the story, the final panel closes with the pair feasting on fruit in a bucolic space between the pond and the forest, enjoying a fleeting moment of pleasure and abundance (27).

FIGURE 9.4 Bibber fights the Goolygator in "Dew Dillies" from *All-Negro Comics*.

Stories such as "Dew Dillies" would have undoubtedly contributed to the perception that *All-Negro Comics* had no social story to tell. The idea that the comic was designed for Black audiences—or "all in the family"—was all the more reason why some of these very readers expected the stories to explicitly name racism and injustice in plot points that make the need for equal rights unequivocal. Yet the comic's artistic choices suggest that these urgent issues can be engaged through matters of visual style, perspective, and composition too. In the case of "Dew Dillies," Evans and the artist Leonard Cooper repurpose features that are attributed to the pickanniny, altering what Wanzo refers to as the "situational context" of the way blackness is traditionally caricatured, in order to restore the sense of innocence and hopefulness that has been the domain of white children in comics.[29] Here Wanzo's work offers a useful set of critical tools to unpack why and how racial caricature may be "redeployed" by Black cartoonists, often to mark "an absence of rights or alienation from the nation."[30] She notes that "the tradition of people of African American descent using racial caricature or derided representations is long. Because there are such varied uses, they demonstrate that the racist or racialized representations are part of a vocabulary of black comics aesthetics that speak to the aesthetic questions of the moment while linking aesthetic traditions across time."[31] In this regard, the charmed worldbuilding of "Dew Dillies" demonstrates an early reclamation of what Wanzo identifies as Western "cute aesthetics," while the source of the narrative conflict relies on a system of contrasts between Bubbles and Bibber that have complex social implications.[32] The reprieve that the friends achieve at the story's close is an optimistic glimpse into the future, but one created with the knowledge that the wings and the fins that make them unique can also keep them apart. Questions about the costs of (in)compatibility continue to emerge even in a fantasy realm. Further, readers are to understand that children are the primary recipients of this vision; only they can see and learn from the lessons of the Dew Dillies. For adults, it may be too late.

Finally, it is also important to note the ways in which women fail to benefit from the first issue's capacious exploration of Black life. The one-page installment of "Lil' Eggie" by Terrell features the title character, Egbert, being browbeaten by his angry wife over a missing dollar from his weekly pay. The broad humor and pacing of the story's domestic squabble adhere closely to long-running comic strips such as *Bringing Up Father*, *Barney Google*, and *Blondie* and relocate the familiar character types of the domineering wife and henpecked husband to an African American middle-class context. Likewise, the women who are the focus of the single-panel features

FIGURE 9.5 Sugarfoot and Snake Oil greet Ample-Mae in "Sugarfoot" from *All-Negro Comics*.

in "Hep Chicks on Parade" exhibit a sense of brash self-importance that, along with their ornate fashion, shocks and baffles the people around them. In one of the images, a Black woman lifts her chin defiantly as she stands before a judge, while beside her a man grabs his backside and glares at the sharp edge of her tall, flame-shaped hat. The caption beneath reads, "But your honor, *he* sat on *my* hat!" (41). Women and their incongruous, strong opinions are the main source of the humor and spectacle in these instances.

In another example, the comic's last story, "Sugarfoot," illustrated by William H. Smith (signed "Cravat"), follows a pair of hungry musicians who wander the countryside until a farmer agrees to give them dinner in exchange for a performance. Once Sugarfoot and his friend Snake Oil arrive at the farmer's home, their enthusiasm for the meal shifts quickly to the farmer's daughter, Ample-Mae. Sugarfoot declares, "What curvesome aroma! What luscious cookery!" and the comic's perspective never strays far from the young woman's body, displayed prominently in panel after panel in a tight-fitting green dress (47). Snake Oil takes note of her response to nearly every question ("I'm Ample") with the observation, "You're dumb too!" (46; figure 9.5). Ultimately women of all stages and stations of life in *All-Negro Comics* are fixed in one-dimensional secondary roles for the benefit of the male gaze. And while a few characters like Ample are given names, most function to support the work of each story's protagonist in the most generic sense, like the young woman who calls the police in "Ace Harlem" and serves as the case's first witness but is only called "honey." In other instances, what could initially be viewed as assertiveness on the part of the women characters becomes a punch line that prompts the reader's contempt. When Bibber takes a nap, the narrator of "Dew Dillies" spies Bubbles in the forest and wonders aloud if she will be preparing dinner, only to clarify, "Shucks no! Pickin' flowers. Just like a woman!" (20).

To fully appreciate, then, what Evans and his collaborators hoped to accomplish with their comic, it is crucial that scholars consider the promise and the problems that informed the creative process. Questions about gender dynamics and the role of caricature in shaping the representations of blackness in *All-Negro Comics* further contribute to the thematic tensions that animate the action and humor in the stories. Likewise, with its diegetic references to World War II, atom bombs, and Joe Louis, not to mention the nods to popular music and fashion of the late 1940s, it is clear that Evans hoped to build a series that would recall familiar genre conventions, while actively taking part in the real-time conversations among Black readers.

All-Negro Comics #2

Today, Evans's comic also serves as a reminder that what's *new* in comics is only as important as what's *next*—especially for an art form that relies on sequential narrative to make meaning. Located throughout *All-Negro Comics* are paratextual signposts that seek to generate excitement in readers about the future of the series, starting with the editorial note and its reference to the forthcoming monthly historical calendar. There are also gestures within the stories to upcoming installments: "Look for Ace Harlem in the next issue of *All-Negro Comics*," declares the narrator of the first story (figure 9.1). Similarly, "Lion Man" ends with a cliff-hanger: "Will Dr. Sangro and his warlike nation try again? Watch for the further adventures of Lion Man in the next issues of *All-Negro Comics*" (38). Snake Oil tells Sugarfoot on the way to catch the train in their story: "This is a heck of a way to start life in de comics!" (42). And both of the full-page closing teasers invite readers to "look for Ace Harlem—Sugarfoot—Snake Oil in—NEXT ISSUE" and boast that those who return will find "the picture story—in color—of Negro trailblazers and champions in the sports world beginning in the next issue of—ALL-NEGRO COMICS."

But there was no next issue of *All-Negro Comics*. The second issue, if it was written, if it was drawn, was never published. A 1997 account by the comics historian Tom Christopher is widely used as the main source material for our current knowledge about the second issue, the details of which continue to circulate in more recent overviews by Tim Jackson and Ken Quattro. Christopher writes:

A second issue was planned and the art completed, but when Orrin was ready to publish he found that his source for newsprint would no longer sell to him, nor would any of the other vendors he contacted. Though Orrin was unyielding in his support of integration and civil rights he was moderate in his methods of achieving these goals. He believed in the general fairness of the system he had been born into. He was not a man given to conspiratorial thinking, but his family remembers that his belief was that there was pressure being placed on the newsprint wholesalers by bigger publishers and distributors who didn't welcome any intrusions on their established territories.[33]

Sheena C. Howard and Ronald L. Jackson II refer to Evans as "the progenitor of Black comic books" to pay tribute to all that the Philadelphia publisher accomplished, yet the honorific is arguably even more apt given the setbacks that he experienced in the wake of his series's debut.[34] *All-Negro Comics* would not be the first comic of its kind to be abruptly discontinued or to be confined to a single issue or two. Historically, comic books reached their zenith in circulation and profit during the period known as the Golden Age, starting in the late 1930s, with publishers vying in unprecedented ways for a slice of an industry that was reported to bring in a billion dollars by 1953.[35] Business boomed in ways that, for a time, seemed to reward both the innovators and imitators.

Nonetheless, as Michel Foucault reminds us, "the history of some is not the history of others."[36] It was rare for comic books featuring African Americans as main characters to last more than a few issues, leaving us with a history that is dominated by fits and starts. While Parents' Magazine Press published eighty-four issues of its biographical series *True Comics* during the 1940s, only two were devoted to *Negro Heroes*. Fawcett Comics halted *Negro Romance* after issue 3 in 1950 (a fourth issue, published by Charlton Comics in 1955, was a reprint). The six installments of *Jackie Robinson* that started in 1949 were noteworthy as part of Fawcett's "Baseball Hero" sports comic line; more common were the company's one-shot comics that occasionally included athletes of color such as *Roy Campanella* (1950) or the two issues of *Joe Louis: Champion of Champions* (1950).[37] More explicit social protest comics like *The Challenger* series from Interfaith Publications lasted four issues, while the aforementioned *Joe Worker and the Story of Labor* (1946) or *Martin Luther King, Jr. and the Montgomery Story* (1958) were subsidized by civic and religious organizations for single issues. The company that attained the most success in publishing comics about social discrimination, EC Comics, was kept afloat by the profit it generated from horror and crime comics. Still, a notorious clash over the visibility of a Black man's face in "Judgment Day!"—a science fiction comic about racial discrimination—marks the demise of the EC's comic book division in 1955.[38]

To be clear, comic book series were routinely delayed and canceled. During the period in which *All-Negro Comics* was produced, it was not unusual for a run to be pulled midstream as publishers carefully tracked resources, rates of distribution, and competitors from month to month. Golden Age publishers were willing to give comic books featuring African Americans a chance in an attempt to serve a wider audience (and to generate greater revenue), but these were experiments, not long-term investments deserving of large marketing budgets or targeted distribution strategies. Evans's correspondence suggests that encouraging vendors to sell and promote his comic was an uphill battle, despite his extensive contacts across media; however, in his enterprising efforts to reach Black schools and neighborhoods and to enlist their young readers as salespeople, he specifically stated that the comic was "soon to be issued on a regular monthly basis." His letter bids farewell to potential buyers with the words, "Hoping this is the beginning of a long, desirable relationship...."[39] In other words, his comic was designed to be an ongoing serial.

Yet the story of what happened to *All-Negro Comics*, as Tim Jackson points out, was not tied solely to underperforming sales or to war-era shortages of paper but more likely to systematic discriminatory practices, to racial bigotry and fear of competition.[40] In such an environment, traditional avenues of printing and distribution are not simply services that anyone can purchase. Schuyler, in his *Courier* column, followed his opinions about the high quality and reasonable price of the comic with the observation that its debut "causes one to wonder why this has not be done before.... So far as I know, there is no law anywhere in the U.S.A. prohibiting the publication and sale of comic books designed for Negro youth."[41] And indeed, there was no such law. But considering the unspoken institutional barriers that Black creative professionals faced from editors, publishers, and distributors during this period, Schuyler's dogged individualism comes across as profoundly inadequate and willfully naïve.[42] It was not just that Evans did not possess the economic and social currency needed to gain access to newsprint but also that the vendors who refused to do business with him collectively deprived his periodical of an even more valuable resource: *time*—time to build on the first issue's success, to finance the creative talent, and to sustain the audience's anticipation; time to keep the comic on the newsstand before it was pulled to make room for new titles; time to make good on the promise of what's next. Evans's experience demonstrates, in other words, that serialization for an all-cartoon magazine could be a privilege—an exclusive advantage that *All-Negro Comics* was denied.

In the political theorist's Michael Hanchard's foundational discussion of "racial time," he explains how the experiencing of temporal disruptions have historically served as social and political manifestations of inequality for people of African descent. These kinds of "impositions on human time" are a central part of understanding the generational impact of both the large-scale systems of oppression and the everyday interactions between people of different social groups.[43] More specifically, "racial time is defined as the inequalities of temporality that result from power relations between racially dominant and subordinate groups. Unequal relationships between dominate and subordinate groups produce unequal temporal access to institutions, goods, services, resources, power, and knowledge, which members of both groups recognize."[44] For example, nineteenth-century white enslavers' so-called purchase of the bodies and labor of African people included ownership of every moment of their time. This concept also extends to the realities of "waiting," as Hanchard notes in his discussion of racial time during the segregation era, when "to be black in the United States meant that one had to wait for nearly everything."[45] And with waiting comes the realization that the goods and services that Black people receive would only be available after white people had benefited from them first. As Wanzo points out, "racialized time is a means of keeping African Americans from participating in the traditionally mandated project of nation building through self-determination."[46] It also means that dismantling these systems requires subordinate groups to reclaim and reappropriate time for their own purposes and at their own pace—to stop the clock, for instance, by taking the so-called wrong seat on a bus or at a lunch counter.

The delays, obstructions, and cancellations that shape the growth and development of comic books by and about African Americans also demonstrate the structural effects of racial time. Knowing this requires us as critics to define success for these comics in a different way, one that unsettles linear standards of progress that rejoice in the first issue that Evans published without acknowledging the industry-wide impediments that would leave readers waiting indefinitely for a second. Nearly seven decades later, in 2014, Evans was inducted into the Will Eisner Hall of Fame by Comic-Con International, with the accompanying biography noting, "although only one issue was published, its existence was a historic achievement."[47] Ensnared by the expectations of serialization and sequentiality, the narrative cliff-hangers that were once designed to build anticipation in *All-Negro Comics* reveal instead an absence; the full-page teasers now forecast a state of interruption that is perhaps the most fitting counterhistory of race in comics of the Golden Age. It is as if the solid black cover that was blank before Ace Harlem, Lion Man, and the Dew Dillies broke through has been emptied out again, leaving a gap that overflows with unvisualized connections.

And what of *All-Negro Comics* #2? What unexpected surprises awaited Ace Harlem, famed Negro detective, around the corner? Where might Sugarfoot and Snake Oil have traveled next? Perhaps Joe Louis, himself, would make an appearance in the subsequent tales of "fast action, African adventure, good clean humor and fantasy" (1). Our willingness to imagine the pages of a second issue, to speculate about what this comic was and could have been, suggests another approach to the social inequalities of temporality that deserve more scrutiny. To this end, the work of the poet Kevin Young offers revelatory insight into how the artifacts that have been affected by racial time can be named in creative and curatorial ways. Young conceptualizes the vanished constructs of Black cultural forms through what he calls a "shadow book": "a book that we don't have, but know of, a book that may haunt the very book we have in our hands."[48] Of the three kinds of shadow books that Young catalogs, the one designated as the *lost*, "the rarest and most common—written and now gone"—best describes that unpublished second issue of *All-Negro Comics*.[49] He explains,

> Elusive as beauty and as necessary, these lost shadow books include the autobiography of Joe Wood, the complete writings of Philippe Wamba, the lost second book of Phillis Wheatley, James Baldwin's no longer extant first book about storefront churches in Harlem, the accidentally burned writings of Fenton Johnson, the purposefully burned writings of Lucille Clifton's mother—and others not so literal, lost to time, from the recording of the sound of Buddy Bolden's horn, and the first jazz in New Orleans, and later, in many senses, the actual autobiography of Billie Holiday. These shadow books are what keep me up at night, ghost limbs, books that could be and have been, but aren't anymore.[50]

Shadow books serve as an important symbol in Young's view for African American writing and creativity that is "denied existence," whether real or imagined, hidden, destroyed, or unfinished. His reference to ghost limbs is an especially fitting way to convey an awareness of the fullness and function of books that nonetheless lack material substance, leaving us bereft over what has been lost. He goes on to note, "In some crucial ways, the lost shadow book is the book that blackness writes every day. The book that memory, time, accident, and the more active forms of oppression prevent from being read."[51] Just as Foucault invites us to visualize the historical discourse that has been "carefully, deliberately, and wickedly mispresented" as emerging "from within the shadows," so too does Young's ruminations about a deeper, more ephemeral shadow book conclude with a call for cultural reclamation and recovery.[52]

The artist and cultural studies scholar John Jennings continues to embrace this approach through his comic art. Inspired by Young's formulation, Jennings observes, "If *All-Negro Comics #2* is a shadow book, imagine what kind of stories could have been created over the years if the *All-Negro Comics* series and Lion Man survived and thrived over the last seventy-three years."[53] The result is a second Lion Man story that Jennings developed with collaborators David Brame, Solomon Robinson, Jeremy Marshall, and Michael Norton Dando, which reimagines the hero's battles against the colonizer Sangro. This latest telling imagines Lion Man as the alter ego of the scientist named Dr. Orrin, who, with the aid of a magical machine and his technological assistant B.U.B.B.A., dons the mantle of Lion Man, "Master of Demons," to protect sleeping souls in a vivid mythical dreamscape. Lion Man's distinctive headband has become his costume's belt in this version, with the red and golden colors extending like flame from his mask, cape, and sword. Such recuperative efforts encourage new generations of readers to take up the stories that were left behind.[54]

All-Negro Comics is an important breakthrough in the desegregation of modern comic books. It demonstrates that the process of retroactive resignification that is fundamental to the comics form itself can operate both thematically and culturally in our ongoing interpretation of the series's impact. The rare first issue calls our attention to the kinds of stories that African American comic book readers believed needed to be told during the 1940s, while the title's tragic setback also provides a glimpse into what the Golden Age of comics could have been. Set alongside the library of shadow books that Young catalogs as part of an enduring Black cultural imaginary is a newsstand, one stocked with all the unfinished and abandoned all-cartoon magazines still waiting to be read.

Ironically enough, a newsstand appears on the back page of *All-Negro Comics* #1 (figure 9.6). The iconic sidewalk kiosk is pictured against an outline of city buildings beneath a deep-orange sky. What appears to be a white man in an automobile passes by in the background, but the people in and around the newsstand are all Black characters from the series that Orrin C.

202 • Qiana Whitted

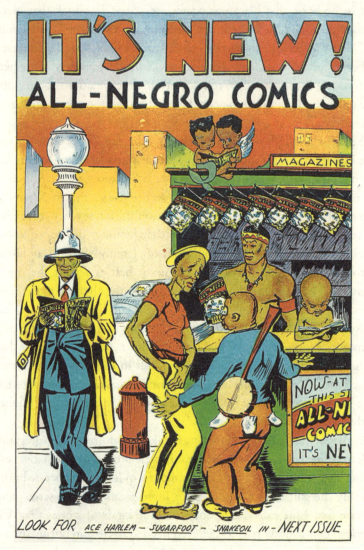

FIGURE 9.6 The back cover of *All-Negro Comics*.

Evans created. Lion Man stands next to Bubba behind a counter, where it appears that only copies of *All-Negro Comics* are available for sale. Except for Sugarfoot and Snake Oil, whose empty pockets have been turned inside out, the entire cast is engrossed in copies of their own comic. The pair of Dew Dillies share a copy from their seat above the shelves. Ace Harlem leans against a nearby light post, one foot crossed over the other, as he turns the pages. This closing image is designed to serve a promotional purpose, of course, to acquaint readers with the characters and their fully realized worlds as an extension of the product's brand. It also recalls an actual photograph, featured on this book's cover, of a young girl reading comics in front of the crowded shelves of a Black-owned confectionary store in Pittsburgh—a photo taken by Charles "Teenie" Harris in 1947, the same year that *All-Negro Comics* was published. And much like in that photo, the illustrated scene usurps a space reserved for public transactions between sales clerks and customers and instead imagines an intimate moment of joy, companionship, and creative exchange. Stacks of the issue are for sale at the counter, and with no clerks visible, there is no one standing between the comic book and its audience. The picture calls forth the kind of spatial and temporal simultaneity that projects into the future a moment free from our historical frameworks of racial time. Evans's newsstand is a fitting home for the stories of *All-Negro Comics* and a powerful elegy for all the shadow comic books of the Golden Age.

Notes

1. Orrin C. Evans, Leonard Cooper, George J. Evans Jr., William H. Smith, and John H. Terrell, *All-Negro Comics #1* (June 1947), 7, 8. Subsequent references to *All-Negro Comics* are cited parenthetically in the text.
2. The issue date on *All-Negro Comics* is printed as June 1947. The newspaper listings indicate that the comic was first distributed in July. Copyright records also list July 15, 1947. For more information, read Quattro, *Invisible Men*, 210.
3. "Press: Ace Harlem to the Rescue."
4. Davis, "*All-Negro Comics*," 285.
5. Roosevelt, "My Day."
6. Schuyler, "Views and Reviews," 7.
7. Schuyler, 7.
8. Hanchard, "Afro-Modernity," 252.
9. T. Jackson, *Pioneering Cartoonists of Color*, 52–81.
10. For more on the artist Matt Baker's work, read Chris Gavaler and Monalesia Earle's chapter 5 in this volume. For more on the artist Al Hollingsworth's work on comic books, read Blair Davis's chapter 6 and Jacque Nodell's chapter 13 on *Negro Romance*, in this volume.
11. "Urban League Publishes Comic Book of Heroes," 13.
12. Hayton and Albright, "Military Vanguard for Desegregation."
13. Carroll M. Ellis to Orrin C. Evans, October 28, 1947, box 13, folder 8, Emory University African American Miscellany Collection, 1848–2017, Manuscript Collection No. 1032, Atlanta, GA. Special thanks to Carol Tilley for bringing the letters to and from Evans to my attention.
14. Orrin C. Evans to Mattie Boyd, October 31, 1947, Small Manuscripts, MUM00400, Small Manuscripts 1998, box 1, folder 4: *All-Negro Comics* (letter & order form), University of Mississippi Archives, University, MS.

15 Lyons, "'Pit' Gets Genn."
16 Davis also states, "By drawing on an established rhetorical tradition for the book's title, Evans hoped to bolster *All-Negro Comics*' sales at the newsstands" ("*All-Negro Comics*," 280).
17 Quattro, *Invisible Men*, 214.
18 Postema, *Narrative Structure in Comics*, 55.
19 Postema, 50.
20 Postema, 58.
21 Interestingly, a few months before *All-Negro Comics* debuted in 1947, Eisner introduced a Black detective named Lt. Oren Grey to *The Spirit*, apparently as a more realistic contrast to the racist caricature and series regular Ebony White. For more on Grey's two appearances in the Sunday comic strip, read Andrew Kunka's chapter 3 in this volume.
22 Zoot suits, tailored to create wide shoulders, a high narrow waist, and tapered ankles, were popular among young working-class African Americans and Mexican American Pachucos in the 1930s and 1940s. Read Peiss, *Zoot Suit*.
23 "Press: Ace Harlem to the Rescue."
24 "Press: Ace Harlem to the Rescue."
25 Evans did reference a forthcoming "big educational feature" in his opening editorial and implied that future issues would contain stories about "Negro trailblazers and champions in the sports world," which would have placed the series in more direct competition with titles like *Negro Heroes*.
26 Davis, "*All-Negro Comics*," 287.
27 Davis, 283.
28 Saguisag, *Incorrigibles and Innocents*, 56–57; Wanzo, *Content of Our Caricature*, 139.
29 While Grand Comics Database and the comics historian Ken Quattro identify the artist who signed "Cooper" as Leonard Cooper, at least one source speculates that the "Dew Dillies" artist could have been Joan Bacchus Maynard (née Cooper), a writer and penciller best known for her work on Bertram A. Fitzgerald's *Golden Legacy* history comics series. The claim appears to be based on the idea that "its babyish pixie characters and cutesy style lends itself to a theoretical female creator." For more information, read "Joan Bacchus."
30 Wanzo, *Content of Our Caricature*, 35.
31 Wanzo, 69.
32 Wanzo, 142.
33 Christopher, "Orrin C. Evans and the Story of *All-Negro Comics*."
34 Howard and Jackson, introduction to *Black Comics*, 3–4. Howard and Jackson also assert that Evans published *All-Negro Comics* "in spite of threats on his life," though Christopher dates the death threats to his tenure at the *Philadelphia Record* as one of the first Black journalists at the newspaper whose assignments included reporting on segregation in the armed forces. Howard and Jackson, introduction to *Black Comics*, 4; Christopher, "Orrin C. Evans and the Story of *All-Negro Comics*."
35 Wright, *Comic Book Nation*, 155.
36 In Michel Foucault's series of lectures "Society Must Be Defended," he observes that in contrast to sovereign histories that preserve hegemonic ideas of power, glory, and heroism, the notion of counterhistorical discourse introduces multiple perspectives that disrupt the power dynamics of totalizing narratives. As José Medina states, "Official histories create and maintain the unity and continuity of a political body by imposing an interpretation on a shared past and, at the same time, by silencing

alternative interpretations of historical experiences. Counter-histories try to undo these silences and to undermine the unity and continuity that official histories produce." Foucault, *"Society Must Be Defended,"* 69; Medina, "Toward a Foucaultian Epistemology of Resistance," 14.

37 For more on *Roy Campanella* and Fawcett sports comics, read Brian Cremins's chapter 10 in this volume.
38 Dell's Western comic *Lobo* was also said to have been canceled after the second issue because of reports that some vendors who saw the main character's Black face on the cover returned it unsold. However, this account has been disputed in recent years. For more information about *Lobo*, read Mike Lemon's chapter 15 in this volume.
39 Evans to Boyd, October 31, 1947.
40 T. Jackson, *Pioneering Cartoonists of Color*, 80–81.
41 Schuyler, "Views and Reviews," 7.
42 Likewise, in Hayton and Albright's discussion of *All-Negro Comics*, they point out that "in a de facto segregated society even in the North, African American entrepreneurship clearly faced obstacles presented by institutional racism." The authors also speculate that the issue's high cover price and the sexually suggestive material of "Sugarfoot" could have also depressed sales of the comic. Hayton and Albright, "Military Vanguard."
43 Hanchard, "Afro-Modernity," 249.
44 Hanchard, 253.
45 Hanchard, 263.
46 Wanzo, *Content of Our Caricature*, 76.
47 Comic-Con International, "Orrin C. Evans."
48 K. Young, *Grey Album*, 11.
49 K. Young, 13.
50 K. Young, 14.
51 K. Young, 14.
52 Foucault, *"Society Must Be Defended,"* 72, 70.
53 J. Jennings, "Black One Shot."
54 As of this writing, a team led by editor Chris Robinson is preparing to reprint a seventy-fifth-anniversary edition of *All-Negro Comics* in 2023 with digitally remastered pages and new stories by contemporary Black creators featuring the comic book's characters. The project's Kickstarter page is at https://www.kickstarter.com/projects/allnegrocomics/all-negro-comics-75th-anniversary-edition/description.

"This Business of White and Black"

Captain Marvel's Steamboat, the Youthbuilders, and Fawcett's *Roy Campanella, Baseball Hero*

BRIAN CREMINS

In early September 1958, only eight months after the car accident that nearly took his life, Roy Campanella and his wife, Ruthe, at the invitation of their friend Nat King Cole, enjoyed an evening at the Copacabana in New York City. Since early May, Campanella, the beloved catcher for the Brooklyn Dodgers, had been a patient at Dr. Howard Rusk's Institute of Physical Medicine and Rehabilitation. That summer, as he struggled to accept the paralysis that afflicted his legs and his hands, Campanella also confronted the loneliness and depression that haunted him. Having begun his career as a baseball player while still a teenager in the 1930s, and coming from a close-knit Italian American and African American family, he found himself ill-equipped to handle the isolation and fear of learning to use his arms again, to feed himself, and, with the help of his nurses, even to catch a ball. Finally, during the first week of September, his doctors delivered the message that he had been waiting months to hear: it was time for him to spend the weekend at home with Ruthe and their children at their home on Long Island Sound. "As long as I live," he recalled in his 1959 autobiography *It's Good to Be Alive*, "I'll never be able to describe how I felt when I heard the news." Less than a week later, he was confident enough to hold his "first press conference" since the accident, a gathering of "reporters, radio, newsreel and camera men." They asked him about the accident, about his health, about the "future" of his life and his career. With a strict physical therapy schedule—one that at times seemed even more daunting than his old routine of getting in shape for spring training with the Dodgers—did he have any time, they wondered, for "relaxation"? "I listen to the radio most days," he explained, "watch TV at night, and read the papers and the Bible." However, he added, "I never was a comic book man."[1]

A decade earlier, Campanella, along with his Dodgers teammates Jackie Robinson and Don Newcombe, had appeared in titles published by Fawcett Publications, a company best remembered today for comics featuring Billy Batson's magical alter ego Captain Marvel and the other members of the Marvel Family (Mary Marvel, Captain Marvel Jr., and Uncle Marvel, to name just a few). The *Jackie Robinson* series, which began in 1949, would last for six issues, ending in 1952. Meanwhile, Fawcett's *Roy Campanella, Baseball Hero* (1950), like other one-shots featuring players including Larry Doby, Phil Rizzuto, and Yogi Berra, is remarkable not only as an example of Campanella's popularity and significance in the popular culture of the early 1950s but also for its hybrid quality.[2] While these comics retain visual and narrative elements that would have been familiar to readers of Fawcett's superhero titles, they also introduce a kind of realism that reflected changing tastes in the postwar comics industry. As superhero comics declined in popularity, readers turned to romance, crime, and horror titles. Sensitive to the changes sweeping the marketplace and hopeful to find a way to bolster the popularity of the company's flagship hero, *Captain Marvel* writer Otto Binder wrote a memo in 1952 noting that "stories should have *more of Billy Batson* and his doings and problems": "I'm trying to get more BB in."[3] While Binder and *Captain Marvel* artists C. C. Beck and Pete Costanza never quite managed to transform *Captain Marvel Adventures* into a comic book with a focus on young Billy's "doings and problems," by 1952, Fawcett had already experienced significant editorial shifts, ones inspired by a visit to their offices by a group of New York City middle-school students in the spring of 1945.

By introducing heroes drawn from real life, from newsreels and TV broadcasts and from the sports pages, Fawcett seized an opportunity not only to shore up its rapidly deteriorating place in the market but also to make amends for Billy Batson's valet Steamboat, one of the most grotesque racial caricatures to appear in the pages of superhero comics during the early 1940s. The students who visited Fawcett executive editor Will Lieberson's office in 1945 expressed their dismay and disgust for Steamboat, advocating for his removal. They succeeded, not only in urging Lieberson to issue a directive to eliminate the character but also in bringing about a change in the editorial and creative culture at Fawcett. By advocating for themselves, these students paved the way for comics like *Roy Campanella, Baseball Hero*, a title remarkable not only for its nuanced portrayal of Campanella's interracial family but also for the quality of its writing and its art. Just ten years after this comic appeared on newsstands, and just shy of two years after his accident, Campanella starred in an episode of the popular television show *Lassie*, in which he served as a guest coach for Timmy's baseball team (figure 10.1). As a public figure who saw it as his responsibility to inspire the kids who looked up to him, Campanella no doubt would have appreciated Fawcett's attempt to transform him from a real-life baseball legend into a superhero, one with attributes that recalled the best of Fawcett's 1940s comics while at the same time pointing the way to a more just and diverse future.

Published at the height of what Qiana Whitted and other scholars refer to as the Atomic Age of comics, Fawcett's one-shot Campanella comic drew on writing talent from outside the field to ensure both credibility and accuracy.[4] Written by journalist Charles Dexter, who in the 1960s coauthored *Baseball Has Done It* with Jackie Robinson, and expertly drawn and paced by Paul Parker, the comic is part biography, part fan magazine, and part baseball handbook, with scenes, for example, of how to catch a ball with the same flair and skill as Campy himself.[5] Also notable is Dexter and Parker's emphasis on highlighting scenes featuring Campanella's parents, John, the son of Sicilian immigrants who had arrived in the United States in the late 1880s, and Ida Mercer Campanella, whose family moved from Maryland to Delaware before finally settling in Philadelphia. Although, as Campanella's biographer Neil Lanctot points out, "no Pennsylvania statutes prevented John Campanella from marrying a black woman," he and Ida had faced "ostracism and condemnation from both families, particularly the

FIGURE 10.1 A Roy Campanella Topps baseball card from 1959, the same year that the Brooklyn Dodger appeared on the popular television series *Lassie*.

Campanellas, who virtually disowned John."[6] While young Roy's questions about his father's ethnicity play a much greater role, for example, in director Michael Landon's 1974 TV film *It's Good to Be Alive*, starring Paul Winfield and Ruby Dee, what that film and Fawcett's comic share in common is an emphasis on the nature of family, a theme that had played a central role in Fawcett's most popular comics since Captain Marvel's first appearance in *Whiz Comics* #2 in 1940.[7] Although grounded in careful research on Campanella's life and times, his comic book avatar shares a great deal in common with Billy Batson, another young man who, in his first appearance in 1940, is searching not only for his destiny but also for a new home. Unlike other heroes of the Golden Age, Billy from his very first appearance was part of an ensemble cast, one that included the wizard Shazam; his boss, Mr. Morris;

and, as Captain Marvel's popularity grew, his sister, Mary, along with his friend Freddy Freeman. A brief history of Captain Marvel will provide additional examples of how *Roy Campanella, Baseball Hero* broke new ground for Fawcett while at the same time building on the foundation of the popular superhero titles that had established Fawcett as a publisher to be reckoned with in the 1940s.

Just four years after Eastern Color Printing in Waterbury, Connecticut, started publishing the first comic books in 1934, the success of Jerry Siegel and Joe Shuster's Superman in *Action Comics* #1 (1938) sent other companies scrambling to introduce their own brightly colored heroes.[8] Unlike many of the other upstart publishers of the day, by 1939, Fawcett, founded in 1920 in Minnesota by Wilford Fawcett, was well established and respected, best known for popular magazines like *Mechanix Illustrated* and *True Confessions*.[9] Sensing an opportunity to capture the imaginations and the spare change of this new market of readers, Fawcett editor Ralph Daigh approached his colleague Bill Parker, an experienced newspaperman who had begun working on the company's *Movie Story Magazine* in 1937.[10] Daigh assigned Parker with the task of coming up with an idea for a comic book. Drawing in part on his fond boyhood memories of reading the stories of King Arthur, Parker came up with two of the most iconic characters of the 1940s: a young man with a secret destiny and an old wizard looking to pass on his knowledge to a new generation. As Parker refined his ideas, Fawcett art director Al Allard assigned C. C. Beck, a Minnesota native himself and one of Fawcett's staff illustrators, to begin character designs. After further changes, Parker and Beck's Captain Thunder, at the suggestion of Beck's fellow artist Pete Costanza, became Captain Marvelous, a name finally shortened to Captain Marvel. The character and his alter ego, Billy Batson, an orphaned newsboy given incredible powers by the wizard Shazam, made their debut in *Whiz Comics* #2 (1940). A property owned by DC Comics since the 1970s, Captain Marvel is now known simply as Shazam and recently appeared in the 2019 film of the same name starring Zachary Levi and directed by David F. Sandberg.[11]

The hero, dressed in a bright-red, form-fitting costume with a white cape and a yellow lightning bolt on his chest, turned out be just as popular with comic book readers as Superman and as Bill Finger and Bob Kane's Batman, introduced in *Detective Comics* #27 in 1939. Readers who first encountered Billy Batson and his alter ego in the early 1940s often recall him with great affection, especially because he was so distinct from the other popular comic books heroes of the period. In a 2014 interview, Harlan Ellison credited these Fawcett comics as an inspiration for his long career as a science fiction writer and essayist. Like other comic book fans born in the mid-1930s, Ellison delighted in Captain Marvel's adventures, drawn in Beck's distinctive and often minimalist style.[12] The young Ellison also appreciated the literary qualities of the Captain Marvel stories, especially once Otto Binder began freelancing for Fawcett. Binder, a pulp science fiction writer who had also worked as an agent for Robert E. Howard and H. P. Lovecraft, developed a strong sense of what kinds of adventures his young readers most enjoyed. In a 1952 letter he wrote to editor and science fiction historian Sam Moskowitz, Binder noted that the bulk of Fawcett's readership, according to market studies the company had done, "ranged from [ages] 6 to 18, but the group from 9 to 14 far outweighed them all."[13] Thanks to Binder's clever and sometimes didactic plots, ones that took inspiration from Robert Louis Stevenson, Charles Dickens, "Jonathan Swift's satires of political situations," and Lewis Carroll, he and Beck made the perfect team, as the artist also drew on nineteenth-century literature and science fiction for inspiration.[14] A voracious reader, the young Ellison picked up on these various literary allusions and, in Billy Batson, discovered a role model: "There was a legitimate, mythological tie-in to Captain Marvel and Billy Batson," Ellison recalled. "So I was able to identify with Billy's world because I was a small, lone boy in a small town in Ohio"—a boy often bullied by his antisemitic peers in Painesville.[15]

In an essay written by cartoonist and comics herstorian Trina Robbins shortly after her friend and mentor C. C. Beck's death in late 1989, she also recalled her fondness for Billy Batson's sister Mary, cocreated by Binder and Fawcett artist Marc Swayze: "My childhood discovery of C. C.'s Captain Marvel was based solely on the fact that he happened to be Mary Marvel's brother. Most superheroes bored me, and I confined my comics reading only to those books which starred female characters." She also admired Beck and his assistants' simple but dynamic work: "I couldn't resist the crisp, clean drawing style and whimsical array of characters," she explained, adding, "Captain Marvel became the only superhero comic I read as a girl, and a pretty major inspiration for my own art style."[16] Journalist and novelist Pete Hamill, another New York native like Robbins, writes movingly in his 1994 memoir *A Drinking Life* about his affection for Superman, Captain America, the Human Torch, and the Sub-Mariner, but he associates his most vivid memories with Captain Marvel Jr., introduced in 1941 by writer France Herron and celebrated Golden Age artist Mac Raboy.[17] For Hamill, reading about these comic book heroes provided an outlet to express his concern for his father, who, like Captain Marvel Jr.'s alter ego, Freddy Freeman, was also disabled. What if, Hamill wondered, his "father had a secret word" just like Billy, Mary, and Freddy, one that could cure his alcoholism? Early in his memoir, Hamill recalls these boyhood daydreams: "A lightning bolt would split the sky and there he would be: two legs, young, whole . . ."[18] Another group of New York City children also counted themselves as fans of Captain Marvel, but, unlike Ellison, Robbins, and Hamill, they found their ability to relate to these characters compromised by Steamboat, Billy Batson's sidekick. Steamboat, whose large eyes, prominent lips, and hapless behavior mark him as a "coon" figure common in Hollywood films of the era, made his debut in *America's Greatest Comics* #2 (1942) and appeared regularly as a comic foil in Billy's adventures until the fall of 1945.[19]

Earlier in 1945, these students from Harlem, all part of a program called Youthbuilders, decided to make their dissatisfaction with Steamboat known. In an article published in the *New York Post* in the summer of 1948, journalist Fern Marja provided a brief history of the Youthbuilders, established "in 1938 as a private organization by an inter-faith group" in New York City before expanding to public schools in cities across the country. Students who took part in the program discussed topics ranging from "atomic energy" and "Jim Crow" to "the Marshall Plan," postwar housing challenges, and even controversies over "vivisection." These are the kinds of topics, Marja explains, that participants, often children from immigrant families or African American kids whose parents or grandparents had migrated to northern cities from the South, wrestled with as they "[reached] out for ideas" and "[peppered] adults with eager questions and shining suggestions." The goal was for these students, as Marja puts it, to "[soak] up democracy" and to "[learn] the relationship between what happens in the world and what happens on their own block."[20] Sabra Holbrook, the social worker who helped to establish Youthbuilders, details the program's inclusive, democratic, antifascist philosophy in her 1943 book *Children Object*. In its closing chapter, she offers practical advice and lesson plans for teachers who would like to bring a Youthbuilders chapter to their schools. Successful activities, she writes, will involve a "pattern of activity" that includes "first, *free discussion*; second, *exciting investigation*; and third, *concerted action*."[21] Later in the chapter, she includes a summary of the democratic principles that serve as the foundation for these activities: "Democracy holds that the welfare of each citizen is dependent on the welfare of all citizens, that no citizen is free while another is enslaved, that the rights of each can be maintained only by defending the rights of all."[22] Today, Holbrook and the Youthbuilders are best remembered because of the students from Junior High School 120 and their visit to Lieberson's office. Articles that appeared in the African American press in 1945 offer an account of their conversation with him.

The headline that introduces an Associated Negro Press article from the *Chicago Defender* on May 5, 1945, informs readers of a "Negro Villain in Comic Book Killed by Youngsters." After introducing the Youthbuilders in the first paragraph, the reporter describes Steamboat "as an ape-like creature with all the coarse Negroid features, including a southern drawl," a largely accurate depiction of Billy Batson's often befuddled companion.[23] While Steamboat may not have been the "villain" of the series, he embodied the same stereotypes as other racial caricatures from the era, including Will Eisner's Ebony White from *The Spirit*. Steamboat and Ebony White are the kinds of figures that novelist and cartoonist Charles Johnson has referred to as "Ur-images of blacks" that remain both disturbing and notable as "a testament to the failure of the imagination (and often of empathy, too)," images that "tell us nothing about black people but *every*thing about what white audiences approved and felt comfortable with in pop culture" before the civil rights movement began gaining momentum in the 1950s.[24] The young men and women who spoke with Lieberson identified in concrete terms this "failure of the imagination" and its social, political, and cultural consequences. "The strip was fine, the youngsters all agreed," writes the ANP reporter, "but such a character will go far to break down all that anti-bias groups are trying to establish." In Lieberson's response to the students, he at first made the argument "that white characters too were depicted in all sorts of ways for the sake of humor," but, as the reporter notes, the students immediately "retorted that white characters were both heroes and villains [in *Captain Marvel Adventures*] while 'Steamboat,' a buffoon, was the only Negro in the strip."[25] Here, the Youthbuilders engaged Lieberson in what Holbrook described as the "free discussion" and "exciting investigation" portion of the program. In an interview conducted decades later with Matt Lage, Lieberson stated, "I always found the character objectionable and when I took over [Fawcett editor] Rod Reed's position I exercised my prerogative as executive editor and ordered him out of all future scripts."[26] The most striking moment in the ANP article takes place in its final paragraph, where a young man "produced an enlarged portrait of 'Steamboat' and said, 'This is not the Negro race, but your one-and-a half million readers will think it so."[27] The character made a final appearance just months later in a story called "Capt. Marvel and the World's Mightiest Dream," published in *Captain Marvel Adventures* #48 (August–September 1945). The Youthbuilders had reached the final, most important step in their project, the moment when all of that "discussion" and "investigation" resulted in "*concerted action*."

For the Youthbuilders, Steamboat's removal proved to be a major victory. An article published in a 1948 issue of the *National Municipal Review* celebrated Steamboat's demise as one of the program's great accomplishments. Elsie Parker notes in her article that "it was a Youthbuilders club which persuaded the publisher of a comic strip to cease portraying the hero as a white boy and the villain as a Negro."[28] What remains most telling about Steamboat's appearances and eventual disappearance is that, as Chip Kidd points out in his book on Captain Marvel and Fawcett, the company had in 1942 established a "Code of Ethics" that should have prevented the creation of the character in the first place.[29] "No comic shall use dialects and devices in a way to indicate ridicule or intolerance of racial groups," reads the seventh item on the list, which also warned Fawcett's editors, writers, and artists against any portrayals of "policemen, judges, officials, and respected institutions" in a negative light. This in-house Code also reminded creators that they were not to include "wanton, sexy drawings," "scenes of actual sadistic torture," "vulgar language," or any glorification of "divorce" in the pages of a Fawcett comic book.[30] Nevertheless, as Kidd notes, the Code did not prevent Steamboat from appearing on a regular basis in *Captain Marvel Adventures* between 1942 and 1945. The character was, to borrow Rebecca Wanzo's description of Black figures who appear in "the editorial cartoon archive" of the nineteenth century, yet another example of "a frozen, noble black subject, whose actions are not radical and who sublimates rage."[31] Steamboat, after all, was not a villain but a member of Billy's supporting cast, a bumbling sidekick introduced for comic relief.

While Steamboat, as comics historian Richard Lupoff points out, "was the exemplification of the racial stereotype of the era," he also appeared in Billy's adventures as a "friendly and sympathetic" character; we even meet his grandmother in issue 22 of *Captain Marvel Adventures* (1943).[32] Nonetheless, aside from his grotesque appearance, he remains subordinate to Billy and to other white heroes in the comics, with little to no agency of his own. To draw on Wanzo's terms again, he often acts in a "noble" manner, as, for example, when he uncovers the true nature of the villain Mr. Mind in the popular "Monster Society of Evil" serial published in 1943.[33] But he exists only to serve Billy; his acts of heroism are the inadvertent results of his comic bungling. Before Captain Marvel understands what kind of world-conquering foe he is up against, Steamboat discovers that Mr. Mind is in fact a tiny worm with a miniature tube radio around its neck. He only makes this discovery, however, after he takes a bite out of an apple and finds the diabolical villain inside. Why was Steamboat not given a more active, heroic role in this moment? "Part of the story of racial integration in superhero comics has continued to be the idea that nonwhite characters challenged identification and marketability," Wanzo notes. "The black experience calls attention not only to what the superhero serves, but to how racially marked their identities really are."[34] The Youthbuilders, however, found what Charles Johnson calls this "failure of the imagination" unacceptable, and their conversation with Lieberson resulted in a course correction not only for Binder and Beck but also for Fawcett's line of comic books.

After the war, Binder and Beck often condemned bigotry in their work, most notably in the story "Captain Marvel and Mr. Tawny's New Home," which appeared in *Captain Marvel Adventures* #90 (November 1948).[35] However, they did so not with Black characters but in an allegorical tale featuring Mr. Tawny, the talking tiger who befriends Billy. In *Captain Marvel Adventures* #90, Mr. Tawny, who works as a guide at a natural history museum, faces a group of bigots dressed like Klan members who threaten to burn his suburban home before Captain Marvel comes to the rescue. While Binder and Beck could often be progressive in their politics, they, like other white creators of the era, appeared unwilling to introduce African American characters as complex and human as their white counterparts. Immediate postwar attempts by established and successful publishers like "Fawcett, Parents' Magazine Press, and National Comics Publications," Qiana Whitted writes, to "challenge social inequality," while significant and well intentioned, "were sporadic, short-lived, and often undertaken with significant financial risk in a market where crude racial, ethnic, and religious caricatures were popular and profitable."[36] For Fawcett, comics about established, real-life heroes like Robinson no doubt appeared much less risky than introducing an African American superhero, in part because the publisher was now attempting to attract a new market of readers: baseball fans and aspiring players.

Although I have not located any archival evidence that enables me to draw a direct line of influence from the Youthbuilders' visit with Lieberson to the creation of titles like *Negro Romance* or the *Roy Campanella* and *Jackie Robinson* comics, it is clear that a significant transformation took place at Fawcett, not only in the types of comic books it published but also in how the company's editors, writers, and artists depicted African American characters. Fawcett historian P. C. Hamerlinck points out that "by the springtime of 1946 Lieberson was running a full-page 'special announcement' (introduced by Captain and Mary Marvel) in all Fawcett comic books to 'All Boys and Girls of America of Every Race, Creed and Color' on the virtues of fair play in life, not picking on minorities, and other sound advice to help make the world a better place to live in, delivered by Edmund G. ('Pat') Brown, district attorney of San Francisco."[37] This announcement and Binder and Beck's "Captain Marvel and Mr. Tawny's New Home" provide early examples of the impact that these students had on the company and on its editorial policies. While titles like *Jackie Robinson* and *Roy Campanella* offered readers the nuanced, fully human depiction of an African American hero that *Captain Marvel Adventures* never attempted, Charles Dexter, consciously or not, borrowed elements from Billy Batson's origin story and personality for his portrayals of both men. Perhaps Lieberson and other members of his editorial staff—including *Captain Marvel Adventures* editor Wendell Crowley and art editor Al Jetter, both of whom worked on the *Jackie Robinson* series—saw in Robinson a new hero, one with the potential to be as popular in sales as Captain Marvel had been in the 1940s.

On the first page of *Jackie Robinson* #1, the opening caption even alludes to Fawcett's other titles, describing the star athlete as the "*Marvel of the Baseball Diamond*," a player so gifted that he is "a new Ty Cobb," a young man who "has overcome all handicaps to become a symbol of the fighting spirit of the American boy!"[38] Given Fawcett's previous success with superhero comics, it is no wonder that it borrowed what had been a winning formula for these new titles: Jackie Robinson was once, just like Billy Batson, an "all-American kid," one who discovered his destiny early in his life, as did Robinson's teammate Roy Campanella.[39] Given Fawcett's success with large ensemble casts in titles like *Captain Marvel Adventures* and *Whiz Comics*, Campanella's story must have been especially compelling, since it enabled Dexter and Parker to continue the company's formula of introducing a close-knit and supportive family of characters.

Like Fawcett's other sports comics and like its short-lived series *Negro Romance* (1950), *Roy Campanella, Baseball Hero* features a photo cover with Campanella in action at bat and behind home plate. The back cover also features a colorized photo with a note reading, "To all my fans," followed by his signature. On the inner front cover is another portrait of Campanella that introduces a letter that, as the salutation puts it, is for his "Loyal Fans": "When you read this story of my career, you'll find that I'm a pretty happy guy," the letter begins before adding that, despite his success, "there were times when it looked as if I'd never find that pot of gold at the rainbow's end."[40] This letter, filled with language that echoes Fawcett's in-house "important announcement" from 1946, establishes the themes of the narrative that follows, which tells the story of Campanella's ups and downs as he made his way from the Negro Leagues to the minor leagues and finally to the Brooklyn Dodgers in 1948. Dexter strikes a balance in his script between scenes of family life with dramatic depictions of highlights from Campanella's career up to 1950. Artist Paul Parker, who in addition to his work for other comics publishers of the era served as a reporter for New York radio station WINS, draws the comic with the same flair that Clem Weisbecker brought to the *Jackie Robinson* series.[41] In Parker's and Weisbecker's art, we can see the influence of late nineteenth-century newspaper comics, especially those that cartoonist Eddie Campbell describes in his book *The Goat Getters*. As both he and scholar Amy McCrory have pointed out, sports comics and illustrations featured in late nineteenth- and early twentieth-century U.S. newspapers provided a visual vocabulary for the comic books that began appearing on newsstands in the 1930s. Even the sports rhetoric of Fawcett's house ad has distinct roots in those turn-of-the-century newspaper conventions. After all, as McCrory points out in an essay on artist Thomas Aloysius Dorgan, "sports themes have long been intermixed with other genres," notably in the work of "American editorial cartoonists of the mid-1800s [who] routinely depicted Presidential elections in the guise of sporting events," or in early newspaper cartoons that mixed "other genres often regarded as exclusive, such as 'editorial,' 'gag,' and 'domestic'" comics.[42] Building on McCrory's work, Campbell takes these observations a step further with examples from comics published by Marvel in the early 1960s. Although, as Campbell admits, today "the sports cartoon has slipped from the popular memory" for readers and for scholars alike, "in its classic mode, it mashed up the serious, the humorous and the photographic" so successfully that its impact shaped the superhero comics of the Golden and Silver Ages. Campbell argues that "early comic book artists" learned "dynamic anatomy" from sports comics and not from "regular literary illustration, or even the pulp magazines" of the 1930s. Campbell offers "the blocky fighting figures of Jack Kirby in the mid-1960s" as evidence for these claims.[43] Parker's work on the second page of *Roy Campanella, Baseball Hero* provides additional examples of what Campbell calls the "dynamic anatomy" that makes sports comics at their best so vital and fascinating.

Page 2 of *Roy Campanella* displays the same mixing of genres that McCrory has identified as being so remarkable in nineteenth-century newspaper cartoons (figure 10.2). On pages 2 and 3, Dexter and Parker alternate quiet, domestic scenes with action that no doubt would have appealed to

"This Business of White and Black" • 219

Captain Marvel or Mary Marvel fans. While the first page of the comic book describes Campanella and touts his achievements on the field, this second page—where the book's narrative begins—introduces Campanella's Italian American father in its first caption. These words appear against a scroll-like

FIGURE 10.2 Page 2 of *Roy Campanella, Baseball Hero*, script by Charles Dexter and art by Paul Parker. (Fawcett Publications, 1950)

background, indicating that we are about to take a trip back in time: "John Campanella was pleased as a pumpkin when Roy, his second son, was born just before Thanksgiving 1921!" begins the narration, adding that "Roy was a roly-poly baby with a merry smile!" In the next two panels, Dexter and Parker establish one of the key differences between Campanella and his second-born child. John Campanella provided for his wife, Ida, and his growing family by selling vegetables. Against a backdrop of brick buildings bathed in yellow sunlight, Parker draws John and his son as they exclaim, "Fresh vegetables! Fruit!" and "Oranges! Potatoes! Tomatoes!" In the next panel, however, Dexter and Parker reveal that Roy, despite his love and his respect for his father, has a very different career goal in mind. "Roy's job was to store away unsold vegetables every night!" the next caption explains. "But instead . . ." Standing over several crates, Roy shouts, "Strike two!" as he pitches an orange against a wooden post.[44]

At first, John expresses his frustration with his son: "Why did you spoil the oranges, Roy? *Speak up!*" he scolds his son after discovering that Roy has been practicing his pitching skills with leftover produce. In this panel, its background color bright red to emphasize John's frustration and Roy's ambition, the son willfully replies, "I won't do it again, Papa, if you will buy me a *ball!*" In the next image, Dexter informs us that John agreed to buy Roy "a hard rubber ball," an item that turns out to be just as magical as Billy Batson's word "Shazam," which transforms him from a regular kid into a superhero. "Wow! He's the best punchball player around!" says one of Roy's friends as they watch in amazement while Roy pitches the ball, sending it so far that it crashes into the window of a brick building that looms over an empty lot. "We'd better beat it!" shouts one of Roy's friends in the page's final panel.

John and Ida's interracial marriage is simply a given in Dexter's script and in Parker's drawings. On the next page of the comic, we see Roy having dinner with John and Ida (figure 10.3). The subtle use of different skin tones on these opening pages provides details on Campanella's family for readers not familiar with his life outside of baseball. While the colorist has used a light brown for Roy and his mom, John's skin has a reddish tone, with hints of orange. At the top of page 3, Ida and John express their misgivings about Roy's career goals. In the second panel of the page, Parker draws a cozy domestic scene, complete with green drapes, a bowl of fruit sitting atop a tan hutch, and a mirror that nearly frames Ida's profile. Ida notices that her son has injured his hands after taking a fall on the front stoop. He had recklessly run home after breaking the window on the previous page. "What's the matter with the spaghetti, Roy?" she asks, holding a fork over

"This Business of White and Black" • 221

FIGURE 10.3 Roy has dinner with his parents Ida and John on page 3 of *Roy Campanella, Baseball Hero*, script by Charles Dexter and art by Paul Parker. (Fawcett Publications, 1950)

her plate. To the right of the panel, his father sits with a cup of coffee in his hands. "You got hurt playing ball, eh?" he asks his son. The caption that sits at the base of the panel informs us that "Roy obeyed his father! For two years he played no ball." This panel, like the one on page 2 that features John and Roy in their horse-drawn carriage (figure 10.2), accomplishes in only two pages what it takes Campanella himself several passages to explain in his autobiography.

At the close of chapter 4 of *It's Good to Be Alive*, Campanella recalls a conversation he had with his mother after other boys had bullied him. Speaking first of his sister, he writes, "Doris and I faced a lot that ordinary kids wouldn't go through. Many's the time we had to punch our way home," he remembers, but "it wasn't only the white kids who called us 'halfbreed.' We caught it from both sides, white and colored."[45] After what he calls an "extra rough" fight with a group of other kids who ridiculed him, he experiences an epiphany that will be familiar to readers of other twentieth-century African American autobiographical narratives, notably W.E.B. Du Bois's encounter in *The Souls of Black Folk* with the little girl in his class who will not accept his valentine because he is Black and she is white. Campanella remembers his confusion and uncertainty. What makes him so different from the other kids in his neighborhood? "I just couldn't get it out of my mind. What *about* having a white father and a Negro mother? Was it good or bad? Was it a crime? Was it something to be ashamed of? I didn't feel ashamed. Then why did the other kids make fun of me? Why was I different? I had to find out."[46] Dexter and Parker's understated presentation of Campanella's closeness to his parents, as well as their love for each other, offers a powerful condemnation of the prejudice that the Campanellas and their son and daughter experienced. As a newspaper reporter, Dexter lays out the facts for his readers, dispensing with any heavy-handedness in his script. While he was not an experienced comics writer like Binder and Fawcett's other freelancers, he understood that he had to let Parker's pictures do the talking. Family scenes like those that open *Roy Campanella* would have announced to anxious parents that this comic, unlike so many of the others that glutted newsstands at the time, was a quality book designed to reinforce the values expressed by the letter attributed to Campanella on the inside front cover. On the last page of the comic, Dexter and Parker bring the book full circle, with closing panels reminiscent of the ones that open the narrative.

In the fourth panel of that final page (figure 10.4), Dexter and Parker reveal that Campanella's dreams have at last come true. He is seated at another dining-room table. Ida walks out from the kitchen with the evening meal. "And I told Roy not to play ball!" she says, a reminder of the dinner-time conversation that opened the comic just pages earlier. The entire comic book, in fact, might be read in the voice of Campanella's parents as they reminisce about their son's achievements. As John Campanella's daughter-in-law and his grandsons David and Roy Jr. listen to these stories, he looks at his son and exclaims, "You're too big to spank now, Roy. Ha ha!" Dexter and Parker have designed this final page of the comic to provide a complete sense of who Campanella was in 1950.

Each tier of the six-panel page displays for the reader a different aspect of Campanella's life and success, a full portrait of him as a ballplayer, son, father, and mentor. Once again, he is depicted not as a solitary hero but as a key member of a much larger network of family, friends, and colleagues, in much the same way that Billy Batson was often depicted in Beck and Binder's stories for *Captain Marvel Adventures*. First, a caption in the page's second panel tells us, he "visited the Yankee dressing room!" not long after the Dodgers lost the World Series to their rivals. Here we see Campanella's good-natured sportsmanship, a hallmark of his career. Joe DiMaggio admits that, although the Yankees won, "You made it tough for us, Roy!" Just before the dinner scene with the Campanella family, a small group of boys—two white children in baseball caps and an African American child in a red sweater—ask Roy to sign their autograph books. "These are the fans I love the best, Ruth!" he exclaims. Just as these baseball and family scenes echo the panels that open the comic, the final two images that bring his story to a close remind the reader of the broken window that, several pages earlier, marked the beginning of Campanella's career.

"This Business of White and Black" • 223

FIGURE 10.4 The final page of *Roy Campanella, Baseball Hero*, script by Charles Dexter and art by Paul Parker. (Fawcett Publications, 1950)

It's another street scene, this time presumably in New York City. A police officer gestures toward two young men playing baseball in the middle of an intersection. Campanella, his face framed by the red-brick building to his right, looks dapper in a tan fedora and in the same blue overcoat that he wore to visit DiMaggio and Joe Page after the final World Series game. Suddenly, he speaks aloud to himself—and to the reader. This is the final lesson that this comic book version of Roy Campanella will share with readers: "Every growing boy needs a playground, a park, and a gymnasium." In the final panel, we see Campanella and Robinson visiting "the YMCA to instruct the sports hungry boys of Harlem!" Beneath a drawing of the teammates working with a small group of enthusiastic kids, Dexter's final caption sums up the themes that he and Parker established in the opening pages of the comic. Dexter's closing sentence, printed on a vibrant, almost pink background, suggests that Campanella's story is just as epic and legendary as Billy Batson's origin story: "His career is a saga of American sports, the rise of a Negro Youth to enduring fame in the hearts of millions!"

I do not know what Sabra Holbrook or the Youthbuilders thought of these comics. Perhaps, were any of the young men and women who had visited Lieberson's office in 1945 still reading comics in 1950, they might have recognized in the pages of these sports titles the transformation in art and writing that they had advocated for five years earlier. And although Campanella himself, as he admits in his autobiography, did not have much use for comic books, he no doubt would have admired the nuanced way in which Dexter and Parker brought his story to life for the young readers that he and Robinson sought to inspire in New York and across the country. As Campanella reflects on his early days as a baseball player in his autobiography, he recalls a conversation he overheard between his mother and his father, both of whom were concerned that the game's color line would dash their son's hopes. "This business of white and black," John Campanella remarks. "For you and me, honey, I wouldn't change it one bit. We've been able to raise four fine kids. God willing, they're going to work out fine . . . and be happy."[47] John and Ida Campanella lived long enough to see their son, despite these complex questions of "white and black," become a success. Campanella's greatest legacy, aside from his stellar career with the Dodgers, lies in the quiet strength he gained from his parents, his wife, his children, and his fellow players. In this comic, Campanella's pragmatic, plain-spoken optimism, the trait that most endeared him to his fans, shines through. *Roy Campanella, Baseball Hero* is a footnote in his story, but a worthy one, a comic book that offers an intimate look at how race and class impacted this American family in the first half of the last century.

Notes

1. Campanella, *It's Good to Be Alive*, 213, 220, 232–235.
2. In *Fawcett Companion*, P. C. Hamerlinck includes a list of Fawcett's early-1950s sports comics (158). For a short history of Fawcett's Captain Marvel and related characters, read the introduction of Cremins, *Captain Marvel and the Art of Nostalgia*.
3. Otto Binder, "Questions—on what to do about CMA from now on . . ." (emphasis in original). This memo, housed in Binder's papers at the Cushing Memorial Library at Texas A&M University, most likely was never submitted to Fawcett's editors. It accompanies a letter to science fiction fan, historian, and editor Sam Moskowitz, dated October 15, 1952. Binder appears to have crossed out the notes in pencil with a large *X*.
4. Whitted, *EC Comics*, 13.
5. For additional information on Lewis F. Levenson, who wrote under the pen name "Charles Dexter," read Cremins, "You've Got to Be Yourself!," 74. I would like to thank P. C. Hamerlinck and David Saunders for their help in tracking down more information on Levenson and his writing career. Historian Michael Lee Lanning also mentions the work of "sportswriter Charles Dexter" in his brief reference to Fawcett in *The Court-Martial of Jackie Robinson*. The late Jerry Bails's website "Who's Who of American Comic Books 1928–1999" includes additional credits for Paul Parker: http://www.bailsprojects.com/bio.aspx?Name=PARKER%2c+PAUL. Thanks to P. C. Hamerlinck for providing me with this information on Parker and on *Jackie Robinson* artist Clem Weisbecker.
6. Lanctot, *Campy*, 5–6.
7. Mark Best provides an insightful look at these themes in his essay "Domesticity, Homosociality, and Male Power in Superhero Comics of the 1950s." As Best points out, Otto Binder continued to explore the idea of family in his popular and influential writing on Superman. Binder's work on Siegel and Shuster's hero followed Fawcett's exit from the comics industry in late 1953, as the company began the process of settling the copyright-infringement suit brought by National. Binder would go on to cocreate characters including Supergirl and Superboy's dog, Krypto.
8. For more information on the origin of comic books in the United States and on Eastern Color's role in particular, read Wright, *Comic Book Nation*, 3–4.
9. Haag and Potter, "Captain Billy's Whiz Bang," 8; and Hamerlinck, "Fawcetts Could Do It as Well, or Better, than Anybody," 10.
10. Cremins, *Captain Marvel and the Art of Nostalgia*, 14. The introduction goes into more detail on Parker and Beck's creation of Captain Marvel as well as on the success of *Whiz Comics* #2.
11. For more on the complex legal history of Fawcett's Captain Marvel, including details on National's copyright-infringement lawsuit and Marvel Comics' character of the same name, read the introduction and chapter 5 of Cremins, *Captain Marvel and the Art of Nostalgia*.
12. In *Champions of the Oppressed?*, Christopher Murray provides additional reflections on Captain Marvel's appeal to young readers in the United States during World War II (26–28). At the height of the character's popularity, Beck was in charge of a team of assistants to keep up with demand. By the early 1950s, he and Pete Costanza collaborated with writer Otto Binder on stories for *Captain Marvel Adventures*, producing some of the best work of their careers and some of the most fascinating comics of the early 1950s, most notably in the tales featuring Billy's friend Mr. Tawny.

13 Otto Binder to Sam Moskowitz, October 15, 1952. Copy courtesy of the Cushing Memorial Library, Texas A&M University.
14 Otto Binder, quoted in Lage, "We Were More or Less Inspired," 64. In an interview with Jim Steranko, Beck remarked, "I never read comic books because most of them were tasteless. I considered my magazines to be illustrated boy's adventures and handled the art accordingly" (*Steranko History of Comics 2*, 11).
15 Cremins and Ellison, "Nay, Never Will I Serve Thee, Mr. Mind," 5–6.
16 Robbins, "C. C. Beck."
17 Hamill, *Drinking Life*, 18.
18 Hamill, 24.
19 Bogle, *Toms, Coons, Mulattoes, Mammies, and Bucks*, 7–8.
20 Marja, "Youthbuilders Teach Kids to Use Tools of Democracy."
21 Holbrook, *Children Object*, 167 (emphasis in original).
22 Holbrook, 177.
23 "Negro Villain in Comic Book Killed by Youngsters." For additional information on Steamboat and the Youthbuilders, read chapter 4 of Cremins, *Captain Marvel and the Art of Nostalgia*.
24 C. Johnson, foreword to *Black Images in the Comics*, 13.
25 "Negro Villain in Comic Book Killed by Youngsters."
26 Will Lieberson, quoted in Lage, "Visual Expression," 94.
27 "Negro Villain in Comic Book Killed by Youngsters."
28 Parker, "Youthbuilders' Experiment," 391–392.
29 Kidd and Spear, *Shazam!*, n.p.
30 In *Shazam!*, Kidd and Spear include a list of Fawcett's in-house rules. Hamerlinck also includes a copy of the Code of Ethics in "Fawcett Writing Rules: The Actual 1942 Writing Guidelines for Various Fawcett Comic Characters" in *Fawcett Companion*, 24.
31 Wanzo, *Content of Our Caricature*, 25.
32 Lupoff, "Big Red Cheese," 70.
33 Read *Captain Marvel Adventures* #27 for Steamboat's discovery of Mr. Mind. P. C. Hamerlinck writes in more detail about Steamboat's appearances in the "Monster Society of Evil" serial in "Steamboat—Part II," 89.
34 Wanzo, *Content of Our Caricature*, 15.
35 For more details on the ways in which Binder and Beck employed the character to teach moral lessons, sometimes more politically progressive ones, to readers in the late 1940s and early 1950s, read Pierce, "One of the Most Real Characters Ever to Appear," 31.
36 Pierce, 6–7.
37 Hamerlinck, "Steamboat—Part II," 94.
38 Dexter and Weisbecker, *Jackie Robinson, Baseball Hero* #1 (emphasis in the original).
39 For more details on the connections between *Jackie Robinson, Baseball Hero* #1 and Billy's origin story, read Cremins, "You've Got to Be Yourself!," 76–77.
40 Dexter and Parker, *Roy Campanella, Baseball Hero*, inside front cover.
41 Bails, "Parker, Paul," in "Who's Who of American Comic Books 1928–1999."
42 McCrory, "Sports Cartoons in Context," 48.
43 Campbell, *Goat Getters*, 7.
44 Dexter and Parker, *Roy Campanella, Baseball Hero*.
45 Campanella, *It's Good to Be Alive*, 36.
46 Campanella, 36.
47 Campanella, 71–72.

Al Hollingsworth's *Kandy*

• • • • • • • • • • • • •

Race, Colorism, and Romance in African American Newspaper Comics

MORA J. BEAUCHAMP-BYRD

Al Hollingsworth, also known in various stages of his career as A. C. Hollingsworth, Alvin C. Hollingsworth, or Alvin Holly, was a founding member of Spiral, the influential African American art collective.[1] Spiral was established in 1963 in the New York City studio of the renowned American artist Romare Bearden, and its members sought to address civil rights concerns without being restricted by formulaic aesthetic strategies. In addition to Hollingsworth, its members included Charles Alston, Emma Amos, Norman Lewis, Richard Mayhew, and Hale Woodruff. Hollingsworth's paintings and collages of the late 1950s through the '70s included glyph-like cityscapes and images of elongated, contemplative women, sometimes with radiant Afros, centered in sparse, landscape environments. These works, such as *Trapped* from 1965, evince a broad range of formal and ideological influences, including Cubism, German Expressionism, Surrealism, Neue Sachlichkeit, existentialist thought, Art Brut, Abstract Expressionism, Black Power imagery, and the Black Arts Movement (BAM).[2]

Yet Hollingsworth's involvement with Spiral, and with the realm considered "fine art," might be described as a *second* phase in his lengthy career. He is arguably best known as a prolific and highly regarded cartoonist and illustrator during the period known as the Golden Age of comics that begins with the arrival of Superman in *Action Comics* #1 in 1938 and extends through the mid-1950s. The Golden Age was characterized by the increasing popularity of comic books (and newspaper strips) featuring superheroes, funny animal, teen humor, horror, science fiction, romance comics, and other genres.[3] Hollingsworth produced a sizeable body of work for the era's syndicated newspaper comic strips as well as crime, horror, jungle goddess, and war comic books for Fawcett, Fiction House, and other major publishers.[4] The historian David Hadju has described Hollingsworth as "a meticulous penciller who worked extensively in romance comics."[5] During the 1940s and '50s, along with Matt Baker, Hollingsworth formed part of a relatively small group of male African American cartoonists working in mainstream comic book publishing, until his mid-1950s shift from comics to a "fine art" realm.

In 1955, Hollingsworth produced a black-and-white continuity strip called *Kandy* for the Smith-Mann Syndicate, which distributed comics for the *Pittsburgh Courier*, the leading African American newspaper at the time. An action-driven, romance, adventure, and sports strip, it centered on a young, attractive female engineer called Kandy Mackay, coowner of a professional auto-racing business with her nurturing father, Pops, and her suitor, Rod Stone, a race-car driver (figure 11.1). Notably, *Kandy* appeared to replace an earlier, long-running, and highly popular romance/adventure strip called *Torchy Brown in Heartbeats* by the pioneering cartoonist Jackie Ormes (1911–1985). Ormes has often been referred to as "the first African American female cartoonist" and the first to produce a syndicated comic series.[6] She developed several strips for African American newspapers from 1937 through the mid-1950s, and *Torchy*, her final strip for the *Courier*, reintroduced a character featured in an earlier strip.[7]

Strikingly, Hollingsworth's titular character closely resembles DC Comics' dark-haired Wonder Woman and other "Good Girl"–styled female figures that were primarily white and appeared frequently in mainstream

FIGURE 11.1 *Kandy* by Alvin Hollingsworth, April 30, 1955. (Copyright *Pittsburgh Courier*)

newspapers and comic books during the Golden Age. "Good Girl" figures may be defined as curvaceous, long-legged, and often suggestive images of women that pictorially evolved from pinup girls. Pinups of the 1940s and '50s were featured in advertisements, on magazine covers, and in calendars, for example.[8] Pinups were popularized in the '40s and '50s but have roots in the 1890s; the name derives from service members' (and others') practice of pinning up, or adhering, these images to a wall. Whether drawings, paintings, or extracted magazine pages, they were also referred to as "cheesecake" images, and they were meant to exemplify an image of a beautiful and perfectly proportioned ideal, "the perfect woman."[9] This essay will ask, Why did Hollingsworth depict Kandy as a racially indeterminate, and/or white-passing "Good Girl" figure for an African American romance strip? The character of Kandy is fashioned in an aesthetics seemingly born of colorism, defined as discrimination against darker skin and/or a preference for a lighter complexion or an appearance of racial mixture, particularly among individuals within the same racial or ethnic group.[10] I am proposing that Hollingsworth's rendering of Kandy in this fashion was greatly informed by his primary working environment, the world of mainstream, Golden Age comics. Kandy's appearance was also shaped by other environmental factors, including a colorism that was actively present in African American media, much of it driven by the respectability politics of the *Courier* and other publications that largely catered to an African American middle class. Physically, Kandy also appeared to be modeled after the celebrated African American actress and musician Lena Horne, and I place a particular focus on assessing how Hollingsworth may have been impacted by the ubiquitous presence of Horne during this period.

A consideration of physiognomic difference in *Kandy* reveals a great deal about idealized beauty standards of the time, both within African American communities and in a larger American context. Primarily a genre-based study, this essay joins Jacque Nodell's chapter 13 in this volume by documenting an underexplored area of comics scholarship: African American romance narratives during the Golden Age of comics. I provide a brief overview of Hollingsworth's life and career and then place his use of colorism in context, turning to a brief history of the *Pittsburgh Courier* and the role of its comics offerings. I also explore *Kandy*'s possible pictorial and conceptual engagement with the strip that it was perhaps meant to replace, Ormes's *Torchy in Heartbeats*.

Al Hollingsworth and the Golden Age of Comics

Born in New York City in 1928, Al Hollingsworth was a prolific cartoonist, illustrator, painter, author, and art professor. He began his career early, working as a teenager at Holyoke Publishing Company, where he met Joe Kubert, who later became well known as an artist and editor at DC Comics.[11] Hollingsworth graduated from the High School of Music and Art in New York City, which he attended at the suggestion of Kubert. He attended City College of New York, graduating Phi Beta Kappa with a BA in 1956 and later completing an MA in 1959. He also studied at the Art Students League of New York from 1950 to 1952, and his instructors included the respected modernist Yasuo Kuniyoshi, whose abstractions drew from Japanese art, eighteenth- and nineteenth-century American folk art, and European modernist styles in a series of unique still lifes, somber landscapes, and portraits of pensive women. These works certainly seem to have influenced Hollingsworth's paintings and collages.

Hollingsworth's comic book credits include illustrations for Aviation Press, Holyoke (*Captain Aero Comics*), Fiction House (*Wings Comics* and "Suicide Smith"), Avon Comics (*Witchcraft*), Superior Publishers Limited (*The Mask of Dr. Fu Manchu*), Lev Gleason (*Boy Loves Girl*), and work on Fox Comics' "Numa" in *Rulah, Jungle Goddess*. In later years, he taught painting at the Art Students League, then at Hostos Community College, part of the City University of New York, where he was promoted to full professor of visual and performing arts, retiring in 1998.

The Look of Love: Al Hollingsworth, Physiognomy, and Golden Age "Good Girls"

With regard to style, Hollingsworth's *Kandy* is executed in the realist style of adventure newspaper comic strips that gained popularity in the 1930s. *Kandy*'s aesthetic is fashioned in a style reminiscent of Milton Caniff's *Steve Canyon*, an adventure strip first introduced in 1947 and focused on a narrative about a pilot and veteran who manages his own air-freight business.[12] Caniff, known as "the Rembrandt of the Comic Strip," was particularly astute at expanding the stylistic conventions of the adventure strip, actively refining the genre's use of high-speed plots and scenes; filmic compositions; bold, expressive shapes, shadows, and gestures; dramatic tension; and, at times, sexual intrigue.[13] Adventure comics represented a pointed departure from "funnies"-styled, humor-based comics like *Barney Google* and *Bringing Up Father* that appeared to cater to a younger readership. Brian Walker has written of how, in the late 1930s, and with the increasing employment of magazine illustrators such as Hal Foster (*Tarzan* and *Prince Valiant*) and Alex Raymond (*Flash Gordon*) as cartoonists, "the adventure strip introduced a new look, . . . [featuring] realistically rendered characters and settings."[14] *Kandy*'s dramatic and representational style fits squarely into a traditional adventure-comics aesthetic.

Hollingsworth's image of Kandy also mirrors idealized white "Good Girl" representations in mainstream newspapers and comic books. Conspicuously, when comparing Kandy's appearance to that of her romantic partner, Rod Stone, and the rounded visage of her father, Pops Mackay, there are distinct differences: Kandy's features are certainly Anglicized (figure 11.2). Why did Hollingsworth depict Kandy with this particular look, one that is strikingly identical to his images of white brunette women in mainstream Golden Age comics?

In the sequential format of a comic strip with multiple panels, physiognomy becomes ever more significant for marking distinctions between the characters. Viewers often observe these characters from every angle, sometimes close up, and their faces, hair, and entire corporeal presence may be registered or catalogued, panel by panel, and pictorially bound to their respective identities and narrative arcs. Physiognomic distinction was often employed, to great effect (and in a pseudoscientific fashion), in Chester Gould's *Dick Tracy* and, to some extent, in Caniff's *Steve Canyon*. Facial structure was used to indicate personality, intellect, emotional or psychological states, and the integrity or essential "character" of a character. As Walker

232 • Mora J. Beauchamp-Byrd

FIGURE 11.2 *Kandy* by Alvin Hollingsworth, July 9, 1955. (Copyright *Pittsburgh Courier*)

has noted of Dick Tracy, "the epic battle of good versus evil was symbolized by the contrast between Tracy's square-jawed profile and the hideously deformed faces of Gould's grotesque gallery of villains."[15] Gould presented a catalogue of bizarre villains such as Prune Face, Mole, and "Little Face" Finny that were contrasted with the perfectly proportioned, hard-edged visage of Tracy. While Gould and Caniff resorted to facial structure and deformity to indicate morality and character, for example, how did Hollingsworth use the face of Kandy? What was her appearance meant to signify in a romance-based comic, for a newspaper that catered to a primarily African American and decidedly middle-class readership?

In the context of gender, Hollingsworth's image of Kandy reveals more about the period's racial and gender-based ideals of beauty than it does about character. Kandy is depicted as a tall, willowy figure with cascading, wavy, dark hair, rendered through a series of graceful, wispy lines. Her nose, pert and delicately drawn, is slightly tilted up, positioned just above a mere hint of a mouth. Notably, Hollingsworth treats Kandy's hair in the same manner that he customarily depicts white female characters. In his oeuvre, the hair has a vibrant life of its own. Hollingsworth emphasizes snake-like swirls of lush waves that billow out or upward as his female characters navigate across a series of panels. In addition, in keeping with gender-based distinctions in any romance-centered narrative, a number of panels feature a profile view of the couple. Rod's square jaw and near-geometric features are highlighted as he faces Kandy, who is, by contrast, defined by a series of delicate, flowing lyrical lines.

It cannot be overstated that Kandy's representation is decidedly shaped by Hollingsworth's prolific and lengthy tenure in mainstream Golden Age comics and his facility with rendering "Good Girl" figures of this period. Historically, numerous Golden Age publishers had largely shifted from pulp fiction, including true crime and film noir, to comics. As David Hadju noted of the late 1920s and early 1930s, comics began to draw "more explicitly from the pulp magazines of the time, such as *Amazing Stories* and *Dime Detective Magazine*, whose... sensational adventure stories, dynamically told, had proven appealing to the adolescent boys and working-class men who were also core readers of the comics pages."[16]

Kandy's hybridized genre, a combination of romance, adventure, crime, and sports, may also lead back to Hollingsworth's grounding in the world of mainstream Golden Age comics. His penchant for experimentation and use of dramatic narrative, as well as his expressive formal style, certainly underscore his association with a number of publishers, including Fawcett, a major Golden Age–era publisher best known for a broad range of popular genres, including superheroes like Captain Marvel and the Golden Arrow, early-1950s horror comics, teenage humor (*Otis and Babs*), and funny animal, romance, war, and Western comics such as *Sweethearts*, *Soldier Comics*, and *Lash LaRue*.

Colorism, Lena Horne, and African American Media in the Mid-Twentieth Century

It may also be pertinent to ask, Does Kandy merely tap into and/or function as a reinforcement of a colorism that was already prevalent in African American media at the time? In the mid-twentieth century, African American media, including magazines, films, and the cover of African American romance magazines and romance comics, for example, also reveal a preference for light-skinned women with naturally straight or straightened hair.

With regard to popular African American female celebrities during this period, Kandy most closely bears a likeness to the American actress, dancer,

FIGURE 11.3 Lena Horne on the cover of *The Crisis*, February 1941.

singer and civil rights activist Lena Horne (figure 11.3).[17] Horne might be described as having been light beige or olive toned in complexion, with lengthy, wavy, dark hair and features that closely mirror Hollingsworth's depiction of Kandy. In fact, in 1948, approximately six years before introducing *Kandy*, Hollingsworth produced a narrative in the comic book series called *Juke Box*, published in *Famous Funnies*, that featured a biography of Lena Horne.[18] Hollingsworth's biography appeared in the second edition of the series, and the image of Horne bears more than a passing resemblance to Kandy. Yet Horne's complexion in *Juke Box* is difficult to assess, due to what appears to be color-based technological challenges. In any event, Horne is presented in a range of tones, alternating between yellow-greenish, beige, and darker shades of brown.[19] Still, she is certainly distinguished from the pinkish coloring used for white characters, as well as the darker brown hues used for African American figures in the narrative.

Interestingly, during the 1940s, Horne was featured in several media outlets that employed her image for their own respective aims regarding racial uplift and progress. *The Crisis*, published by the National Association for the Advancement of Colored People (NAACP), tapped into Horne's increasing fame during World War II and attempted to present her as "a symbol of bourgeois respectability."[20] *The Crisis* was the official publication that espoused the ideas of the NAACP, a civil rights organization founded in 1909 by an interracial group that sought to actively push for civil rights, to fight for integration by revealing and seeking to obliterate injustices through legal strategies, and to present an image of middle-class respectability. The organization's aims were aligned with those African Americans who felt that exhibiting evidence of middle-class values would, as discussed by the scholar August Meier, "impress whites so favorably that they would be freely accorded their rights."[21] As pointed out by Megan E. Williams, Walter White, then executive secretary of the NAACP, felt that Horne, as a *Crisis* cover girl, would be an "interesting weapon" in the organization's efforts to "depict the Negro in films as a normal human being and an integral part of the life of America and of the world."[22] *Crisis* cover girls of the 1940s were largely college or university students or graduates (and beauty-contest winners) who were meant to embody W.E.B. Du Bois's emphasis on education for African Americans, including the idea of the "Talented Tenth," an elitist hierarchy that privileged highly educated African American leaders.[23]

Ebony magazine, on the other hand, sought to model itself after the mainstream *Life* magazine and presented the well-known Horne as an example of Black womanhood that it perceived as "uplifting African American readers and educating white readers."[24] In a 1947 editorial, *Ebony* stated that its aims included providing a version of "the Negro's everyday life," as a means of providing an image of "an ordinary human being, . . . not a freak or stereotype, not a debate or a resolution."[25] *Ebony* preferred to focus on female entertainers, rejecting a focus on Black women who were working in the service industry and highlighting African American women who were "entertainers, doctors and judges."[26]

Horne, in fact, was featured on the cover of *Ebony* magazine more than any other female personality in its first four years. She functioned as a broadly acceptable pinup girl who, according to *Ebony*, proved that "Negro girls are beautiful too"; *Ebony* noted that "pinup pictures of Lena are plastered on barracks and pup tents around the world."[27] The magazine's selection of Horne and other young women as cover girls evinced a preference for women with light skin, a practice that was often critiqued by *Crisis* readers in numerous letters to the editor.[28] Notably, it is important to point out that *Ebony* featured hair straighteners and skin lighteners in its advertisements as well, including products such as Nadinola Bleaching Cream, a skin lightener.

Comics and the *Pittsburgh Courier*

The *Pittsburgh Courier* was founded in 1907 by Edwin N. Harleston, a native of Charleston, South Carolina, who worked as a security guard at the H. J. Heinz Company in Pittsburgh. Harleston initially distributed the paper as a flier for several years, but by the 1930s, the *Courier* had become one of the most highly visible and widely distributed African American newspapers in the nation.[29] By the end of the 1940s, its readership had exceeded 350,000.[30] From the *Courier*'s inception, as pointed out by David Hopkins, it focused on a dual mission: (1) to highlight the "everydayness" (or normalcy) of African American life and (2) to highlight race-related discrimination in the United States in hopes of fostering progressive change in housing, health, education, and other quality-of-life imperatives.[31] As part of the latter, the *Courier* also provided financial and wealth-building education and encouraged its readers to engage in charitable endeavors and other forms of civic responsibility, including encouraging them to support the National Urban League and the NAACP.[32] In 1948, James Baldwin referred to the *Courier* as a "high class paper," a reiteration of the paper's association with an African American middle-class audience.[33]

During this period, African American newspapers like the *Courier*, the *Chicago Defender*, and the *Atlanta World* were distributed on a weekly basis. The most current news was provided by mainstream newspapers, while African American periodicals focused on social and political affairs, documenting businesses, education, sports, and other local issues directly related to African Americans. These programmatic initiatives provided an outlet for networking, identity formation, and relatively subtle directives regarding how to function properly as productive and progressive members of an African American middle class.

The *Courier* began publishing comic strips in 1928 with an array of black-and-white, strategically selected and commissioned strips, including *Sunny Boy Sam*, a slapstick/gag-styled strip that initially appeared, in black and white, in the newspaper's pages in 1928. Wilbert Holloway drew *Sunny Boy* for forty-one years. A male-centered strip that ran through the 1970s, it focused on a kind of urban, quick-gag comedy and sometimes drew on race-based stereotypes. Others included Ted Shearer and E. Simms Campbell's one-panel gag comics and Sam Milai's *Society Sue* and *Bucky* strips. *Bucky* operated in the "precocious child" genre of comics, and *Society Sue and Family* featured a middle-class African American family dominated by a father figure who was a bit uncouth and a story line with narrative similarities to George McManus's highly popular *Bringing Up Father*, which appeared in mainstream newspapers. Ollie Harrington's *Jive Gray*, an adventure strip modeled after Caniff's *Terry and the Pirates*, arrived on the *Courier* pages in 1943.[34]

Jackie Ormes produced a single-panel gag strip called *Patty-Jo 'n' Ginger*, published in the *Courier* from 1945 through 1956. The strip focused on a precocious young girl and her stylish older sister, and while lighthearted in tone and punctuated by visual and verbal gags, *Patty-Jo 'n' Ginger* often tackled serious issues such as voting rights, segregation, McCarthyism, and union strikes.[35] By 1937, Ormes's continuity strip character, Torchy Brown, was appearing in *Dixie to Harlem*, a narrative about a teenager from Mississippi who travels to Harlem to perform at the Cotton Club. The largely self-taught Ormes was, according to her biographer Nancy Goldstein, considered to be by "cartoon historians . . . the first African American woman newspaper cartoonist." Goldstein qualifies this assertion, noting that Ormes was "certainly the first who compares to contemporaneous syndicated cartoonists."[36] Impressively, unlike many cartoonists of the time, Ormes drafted her own story lines, penciled (or drew) all her figures, produced her own lettering (text), and, presumably, applied her own coloring (for the *Courier* color comics section).

On August 26, 1950, the *Pittsburgh Courier* announced a "first" in the African American press, the New York City launch of a sixteen-page magazine called *Carousel*. It featured an eight-page, full-color comics section/insert in the *Courier*, the leading African American newspaper for much of the twentieth century. The launch was held at the legendary Ambassador Hotel, and an article in *Editor & Publisher* noted that "New York newspaper and magazine men expressed special interest in the comic section. All the heroes and heroines, businessmen, soldiers, cowboys, athletes, private-eyes, pilots and glamor girls, were Negroes." As described by George S. Schuyler, associate editor at the *Courier*, "These are not new comics. . . . They have been presented over the years in our columns, and our readers are thoroughly familiar with them. It is the addition of color that makes them more appealing."[37] The *Courier* color comics section was the first to be included in a syndicated African American newspaper. Published from August 1950 through August 1954, it was fashioned in the vein of Will Eisner's groundbreaking *Spirit* section, a sixteen-page, tabloid-sized, color comic book introduced in June 1940 in the mainstream *Register* and *Tribune Syndicate* newspapers. The *Spirit* section was centered around *The Spirit*, Eisner's canonical masked-crimefighter strip.[38]

The *Courier*'s color comics featured African Americans as protagonists in a broad range of Golden Age–fashioned comic genres. In addition to the aforementioned *Sunny Boy Sam* and Ormes's *Torchy*, a romance/adventure hybrid, also featured was a sports-themed narrative called *Don Powers*, produced by Sam Milai. Milai joined the *Pittsburgh Courier* as a staff artist in May 1937, working alongside Wilbert Holloway, and he produced black-and-white editorial cartoons and the aforementioned *Bucky* and *Society Sue* in earlier phases of the *Courier*'s history. Carl Pfeufer provided a Western called *The Chisholm Kid* and, briefly, *Neil Knight of the Air*. The latter strip was initially presented as an aviation narrative, and then, as wartime themes decreased in U.S. newspaper strips, it shifted to a space/science-fiction-themed narrative.[39] Edd Ashe's *Guy Fortune*, a secret-agent-themed narrative strip, and *Mark Hunt*, a detective adventure narrative, both featured decidedly nonstereotypical characters that echoed the style of mainstream newspaper strips. Ashe and Pfeufer were among several white cartoonists who worked for mainstream newspapers and produced syndicated strips that were specifically geared to the *Courier*'s African American audience.[40] These comics all addressed some component of the *Courier*'s larger aims, issues of representation, and the "everydayness" of African American life. Although some of the *Courier*'s earlier strips continued stereotypical ideas regarding African Americans, Ormes's *Torchy in Heartbeats*, *Kandy*, and the other 1950s strips played a significant role in reinforcing a range of the newspaper's social, cultural, and political aims.

From *Torchy* to *Kandy*?

Was *Kandy* really meant to replace and serve as a pictorial and genre-based link to Ormes's *Torchy in Heartbeats*, an equally unique offering with regard to genre and nontraditional gender-based expectations? If *Kandy* is to be considered a replacement for *Torchy*, was a pictorial linkage being strategically established between the appearance of the Torchy and Kandy characters? Should we consider Kandy a pointed continuance of the light-skinned

Torchy Brown, a fashionable young woman whose adventures in Harlem and elsewhere began after her relocation from Mississippi? Several scholars, including Tim Jackson, have pointed out that *Kandy* was meant to replace the *Torchy* strip, but it may be useful to consider whether this was truly the case.[41]

Ormes's *Torchy* incorporates the artist's own body, with highly arched, expressive eyes, a pixie haircut, and a light complexion (that often wavered between beige and various shades of brown during the *Carousel* years).[42] In a 2003 interview with Nancy Goldstein after Ormes's death, her sister Delores Towles stated that Ormes drew Torchy and other similar characters as "her perfect self."[43] Indeed, in many of the panels, Torchy functions as an attractive and statuesque pinup, a "Good Girl" adorned in glamorous, form-fitting, and often revealing dress. Typical of Ormes's work during this period, the emphasis is on marking idealized beauty, on fashionable attire, and on Torchy's graceful use of feminized gesture.[44] Ormes, working within the context of African American newspapers of the time, was ever conscious of representation. Her characters documented a rarely seen representation of African American women: independent, stylish, intelligent, questioning, and actively engaged in the social and political events of the day.

Torchy in Heartbeats was a romance/adventure strip that was also markedly political, and this interest in activism revealed itself in several Ormes features. One *Torchy* narrative focused on environmental activism and was set in Southville, a fictional southern U.S. town. Ormes was particularly tuned in to current events and other comic trends, and she researched extensively as part of her ongoing artistic process. For the Southville narrative, she noted, "I had never been to Dixie, but I worked in a newspaper office, and I read everything that was in the paper. It was a whole lot about struggles. Segregation."[45] In the story line, Torchy, having completed training as a nurse's aide, has moved to Southville to join her fiancé, Paul, a doctor. He is working at a rural clinic whose experimental serum later saves the segregated, largely impoverished community by countering the harmful effects of environmental waste produced by a local corporation. Ormes's representation of this heroic, idealized, and pointedly stylish middle-class couple functioned as part of a larger social and political strategy of "acceptable images" for the African American press during this period.

Torchy remained, from its first appearance on September 4, 1937, as *Torchy Brown in "Dixie to Harlem"* through its end as *Torchy in Heartbeats* in 1954, as the only woman-centered and woman-produced strip in the *Courier* comics pages. When *Kandy* arrived in 1954, it also continued as the only female-centered strip in the *Courier* comics pages. Another linkage with *Torchy* may be revealed if we consider feminist or progressive elements in both *Torchy* and *Kandy*. Should we envision the character of Kandy as feminist? She is certainly independent, particularly in the context of other representations of women of her age in mainstream comics.[46] Kandy works for her father yet controls a great deal of the narrative, and she is not engaged in a position that is traditionally associated with mid-twentieth-century women. Kandy is an auto engineer, and in fact, in the first panel, Rod mistakes her for a man when he encounters her while she works on a car, a moment that sets up the romantic tension that follows.

Also, in assessing whether *Kandy* is a continuation of *Torchy*, a linkage may be present between the two strips with regard to genre hybridity. This strategy may have been even more valuable for newspaper comics, in a comics section likely to be read, in its entirety, by all of the family members, as opposed to the specialized nature of comic books. In some respects, Hollingsworth's *Kandy* echoes the narrative and formulaic patterns found commonly in mainstream, mid-twentieth-century U.S. romance and soap opera comics. Yet *Kandy* functions through a form of genre hybridity, a tailored melding of romance, crime, and sports. If the *Kandy* strip was truly meant to replace and maintain some affinity with *Torchy*, did that factor into its resultant genre hybridity, following a similar path forged by *Torchy* and functioning as a romance/adventure hybrid, thus "rounding out" the other strips included in the *Courier* color comics section? In this way, Kandy's genre hybridity, a melding of romance, adventure, crime, and sports, would function as "something for everyone." The strip is fashioned to appeal to anyone from young women who might be interested in the soap-opera-tinged dramas of an attractive couple to sports or auto-racing aficionados to anyone interested in seemingly positive representations of middle-class, African American families to those who are drawn to titillating crime scenes that examine right and wrong, as well as to anyone who appreciates the beauty of an idealized female lead.[47] It also, presumably, addressed the *Courier*'s emphasis on normalcy by adhering to the genres popular in mainstream newspapers and comic books, providing images of Black detectives, sports figures, romantic couples, and others that matched the comic narratives found in King Features and other major syndicates.

Yet, in *Kandy* and in *Torchy*, for all their narrative hybridity, romance is the primary genre. Romance comics or soap opera comics may be exemplified by *Brenda Starr*, a soap opera adventure that was published from 1940 to 2011, and Martha Orr's *Apple Mary*, published from 1932 to 1938 and later continuing as *Mary Worth*, 1938 to the present.[48] Romance comics were formally introduced in 1947 when Jack Kirby and Joe Simon presented *Young Romance* (Crestwood/Prize), fashioning the new genre to attract young women. It included on its front cover an inscription stating that it was "designed for the more adult readers of comics."

The genre declined somewhat after the German American psychiatrist Dr. Fredric Wertham published the infamous *Seduction of the Innocent* (1954), which fueled assertions that horror and adventure/crime comics led to violence and criminality. His efforts led to widespread censorship, the early demise of numerous publishing houses and cartoonists' careers, and the establishment of the restrictive 1954 Comics Code, which hindered progressive and conceptually expressive content.[49] Wertham began critiquing romance titles, which he referred to as "love-confession comics," as vehemently as his earlier judgments on horror comics, assailing them for their "mushiness, the false sentiments, the social hypocrisy, the titillation, the cheapness."[50] Romance-comics publishers then began to censor their content, focusing on traditional, patriarchal narratives that involved courtship, marriage, sexual exploration, and gendered behavioral expectations.[51] *Torchy* and *Kandy*, with their formulaic incorporation of romantic tension and conflict, followed by an eventual resolution, fit squarely into this genre.

Both *Torchy* and *Kandy* may be viewed as romance as well as adventure/crime comics. Crime comics began in 1942 with the publication of *Crime Does Not Pay*, published by Lev Gleason Publications, and the adventure genre was initially popular in the late 1940s and early 1950s. As sales for superhero comic books declined in the years after World War II, other publishers began to emulate the popular format, content, and subject matter of *Crime Does Not Pay*. These textual and pictorial narratives represented an escape of sorts for Depression-era audiences. Examples include Ham Fisher's *Joe Palooka* (1930–1984), Caniff's *Terry and the Pirates* (1934–1973) and *Steve Canyon* (1947–1988), and Eisner's *The Spirit* (1940–1952), as well as comics featuring Flash Gordon, Tarzan, and Dick Tracy. Crime and horror comics in particular, especially those published by EC Comics, were harshly critiqued in the late 1940s and early 1950s for their depiction of crime, criminals, and eroticized Good Girl figures.[52] Adventure comics featured heroes and heroines involved in action-packed, danger-tinged narratives with graphic depictions of violence and criminal activity, often in exotic locales.

With regard to the adventure/crime genre, an emphasis was placed on the moral lessons resulting from the eventual failure of criminal activity. *Torchy*'s narratives focused on several encounters with criminals, including corporate criminality and selfishness in the case of the Southville narrative, while Kandy (and Rod) faced a corrupt businessman and his violent, hired ruffians. In keeping with *Kandy*'s engagement with an adventure/crime formula, it is not surprising that Hollingsworth would produce an image that would appeal to the broad readership of adventure/crime comics, an expansive group that would, regardless of gender, race, or other factors, appreciate an image of an idealized, attractive female character.

Clearly, Hollingsworth's image of Kandy reflected the European-informed beauty standards of Golden Age–era comics as well as an emphasis on colorism that permeated a range of African American media outlets during this period. In alignment with the *Courier*'s respectability-politics-driven initiatives that embraced an African American middle class, *Kandy* was centered on an attractive young woman who coowns a business with her father. In many ways, the strip fit snugly into the *Courier*'s aim of fostering racial acceptance through presenting textual and pictorial content that reflected a nonthreatening, middle-class commonality. To this end, Kandy becomes, like Lena Horne, an alluring and racially ambiguous vision of beauty, one that signified "the perfect woman" for all of the worlds that Hollingsworth navigated in the mid-1950s United States.

Notes

1. See Perry, "Spiral and 'Black Art' in New York City, 1965–1971," in *Life and Art of Felrath Hines*, 62–71.
2. For further details regarding the artist's 1950s through 1970s works, see Hewitt, "Themes of Alvin C. Hollingsworth." Hollingsworth was featured in a 1965 solo exhibition at New York's Terry Dintenfass Gallery and participated in group shows at the Metropolitan Museum of Art, the Whitney Museum of American Art, the Rhode Island School of Design, the Boston Museum of Fine Arts, and the Museum of Modern Art.
3. The Golden Age era, its genres, publishers, and demise (resulting from censorship), are examined in Tilley, "Seducing the Innocent"; and Hadju, *Ten-Cent Plague*.
4. See my entry in *Encyclopedia of Black Comics*, which provides an overview of Hollingsworth's life and career (Beauchamp-Byrd, "Alvin C. Hollingsworth"). Blair Davis's chapter 6 in this volume discusses Hollingsworth's work on comic books in more detail.
5. Hadju, *Ten-Cent Plague*, 166.
6. Ormes's increasing visibility has ensured her consideration as part of an emerging canon of African American cartoonists as well as that of women cartoonists. Burgeoning interest in Ormes may be exemplified by Nancy Goldstein's celebrated text *Jackie Ormes: The First African American Woman Cartoonist*, Ormes's posthumous 2014 induction into the National Association of Black Journalists Hall of Fame, and

the artist's inclusion in *Comix Creatrix: 100 Women Making Comics*, a 2016 exhibition presented at the House of Illustration in London.
7   Ormes's earlier strip was called *Torchy Brown in "Dixie to Harlem."*
8   For additional details regarding pinup girls, see Buszek, "Representing 'Awarishness' "; Meyerowitz, "Women, Cheesecake, and Borderline Material"; and Collins, *For the Boys*.
9   "Good Girl" figures, particularly in the work of the celebrated African American cartoonist Matt Baker, are examined in Pruitt, "It Rhymes with Lust?" Eroticized images of men were known as "beefcake."
10 For a discussion of colorism regarding African American culture, see Hunter, "If You're Light You're Alright"; and Russell-Cole, Wilson, and Hall, *Color Complex*.
11 See Schelly, *Man of Rock*.
12 For a discussion of Gould's uses of physiognomy regarding ethnicity, see Kraus, "Dick Tracy versus the Blank"; and Mooney and Fewell, "Crime in One Long-Lived Comic Strip."
13 B. Walker, *Comics*, 208.
14 B. Walker, 189.
15 B. Walker, 191.
16 Hadju, *Ten-Cent Plague*, 17.
17 For an examination of how Horne's image was employed in *Ebony* and other publications, see M. Williams, "Meet the Real Lena Horne."
18 *Famous Funnies*, published by Eastern Color Printing, was a comics anthology series produced from 1934 to 1955.
19 I am not certain that Hollingsworth, who most often worked as a penciller, provided the colors in *Juke Box* as well.
20 M. Williams, "Meet the Real Lena Horne," 120.
21 Meier, *Negro Thought in America*, 35, quoted in M. Williams, "Crisis Cover Girl," 201.
22 M. Williams, "Crisis Cover Girl," 200.
23 See M. Williams, 207.
24 M. Williams, "Meet the Real Lena Horne," 120.
25 Quoted in M. Williams, 119.
26 M. Williams, 121.
27 "Backstage," 4.
28 "Backstage," 120, 126–127.
29 See Bunie, *Robert L. Vann of the Pittsburgh Courier*.
30 Washburn, *African American Newspaper*, 3.
31 See Hopkins, "You Can Make Them Liars"; and Beito and Beito, "Selling Laissez-Faire Antiracism to the Black Masses."
32 See Hopkins, "You Can Make Them Liars," 1.
33 Wolseley, *Black Press*, 104.
34 For discussion of Harrington's strips in the *Courier*, see chapter 2 of Powell, *Going There*; and Brunner, "This Job Is a Solid Killer."
35 The strip became so popular with its African American audience that in the late 1940s, Ormes was able to design and secure a production deal for a groundbreaking doll based on the Patty Jo character. Ormes retired in the late 1950s and died in Chicago in 1986. As her career evolved and as the nation erupted in the trauma of race-based disturbances and McCarthyist tendencies, Ormes's work became increasingly political. For additional analysis of Ormes's work, see Eli Boonin-Vail's chapter 7 in this volume.

36 Goldstein, "Fashion in the Funny Pages," 96.
37 "New Sections in Pittsburgh Negro Weekly," 46.
38 Published from 1940 to 1952, Eisner's insert was eventually carried by twenty Sunday newspapers, transforming the distribution of newspaper comics.
39 Pfeufer began working as a cartoonist when he joined the *Brooklyn Daily Eagle* in 1935, and he worked as an illustrator for several pulp and other magazines before entering the comics field. At the *Brooklyn Daily Eagle*, he produced a science fiction strip called *Don Dixon and the Hidden Empire*. By 1942, he had begun to work for Marvel, then called Timely Comics, where he worked primarily on the character Namor the Sub-Mariner. Pfeufer then worked for Fawcett Comics, producing illustrations for the popular *Tom Mix*, a western character.
40 Ashe had a lengthy career as an illustrator and also worked as a mural painter. He was active as a comic book artist during the 1940s and worked on the Archie periodicals *Pep Comics* and *Top Notch Comics*.
41 T. Jackson, *Pioneering Cartoonists of Color*, 106–107.
42 Paul Hammond's skin color also fluctuated in the Torchy narratives in the *Courier* color comics section.
43 Goldstein, "Fashion in the Funny Pages," 98.
44 The emphasis on appearance was also reinforced in many *Torchy in Heartbeats* spreads that included a paper-doll section for fans to cut out a statuesque, classicized Torchy and adorn her in a selection of outfits. This additional component of the strip was later called *Torchy's Togs*, part of a larger American interest in pinup girls and fashion, exemplified by the *Katy Keene* strip, a widely popular series featuring a white, fashion-model comic character produced by Bill Woggon in the 1940s and '50s that also featured cutout paper dolls and fashion accessories. *Torchy in Heartbeats*' appearance, along with *Katy Keene* and other series like them, represented newspapers' efforts to provide exotic fantasies and serve as a model for identity formation for women in an environment that was largely becoming subsumed by the influence of television.
45 Quoted in Goldstein, *Jackie Ormes*, 17.
46 Yet Kandy may also reflect the shift in women's occupations during World War II, with the absence of men who were in the service.
47 See Davis, "*All-Negro Comics*."
48 For additional details regarding the romance comics genre, see Barson, *Agonizing Love*; Nolan, *Love on the Racks*; Robbins, *From Girls to Grrrlz*; Gardner, "She Got Her Man"; and Gardner, "True-to-Life."
49 Key sections of the Comics Code included the following text: "Crimes shall never be presented in such a way as to create sympathy for the criminal. . . . Policemen, judges, government officials, and respected institutions shall never be presented in such a way as to create disrespect for established authority. . . . In every instance good shall triumph over evil and the criminal punished for his misdeeds. . . . The word 'crime' shall never appear alone on a cover."
50 Wertham, *Seduction of the Innocent*, 38.
51 Romance comics lost popularity with the approach of the culture surrounding the 1970s sexual revolution.
52 For a comprehensive discussion of EC Comics publications, see Whitted, *EC Comics*.

Part IV

Disrupting Genre, Character, and Convention

● ● ● ● ● ● ● ● ● ● ● ● ● ●

Diabolical Master of Black Magic

• • • • • • • • • • • • •

Examining Agency
through Villainy in
"The Voodoo Man"

PHILLIP LAMARR CUNNINGHAM

In "The Witch Doctor's Revenge" (1941), The Voodoo Man—the titular villain of a series of shorts published in three Fox Feature Syndicate serials—is approached by an elderly Haitian plantation worker.[1] The plantation worker seeks revenge against an unnamed drunken plantation owner who has beaten him and another worker for begging for provisions. The Voodoo Man agrees to assist the elderly victim by constructing a wax figurine of the plantation owner and casting it into a fire. Miles away from The Voodoo Man's lair, the plantation owner dies in agony. After being implored to investigate the plantation owner's death by one of his workers, the American doctor Bob Warren—The Voodoo Man's nemesis—arrives on the plantation with a small group of his compatriots. One of them laments, "[The plantation owner] deserves to die, from what I know of him, but we can't have white men murdered, Bob!"[2] As would be the case in each issue of the Fox serials in which The Voodoo Man appeared, Warren would go on to foil the villain's grander scheme—in this case, capturing Warren's love interest, Lana, in order to sacrifice her to his god, The Bagba. Nonetheless, The Voodoo Man always manages to vex Warren and the other Americans who seek knowledge of "black magic," police the island, or—as is occasionally the case—exploit the Haitian people in a narrative apparently set during the U.S. occupation of Haiti (1915–1934).

In my previous publication "The Absence of Black Supervillains in Mainstream Comics," I highlight the lack of powerful Black supervillains and conclude the essay by indicating that the development of "complex, contemplative, and powerful Black supervillains" would be useful in contesting stereotypes of Black masculinity.[3] Traditionally, Black villains in comics often lack intelligence and agency; indeed, many Black villains rely on brawn or otherwise are incapable of wielding great power simultaneously with great intellect.[4]

"The Voodoo Man" series provides readers with a relatively complex, powerful antagonist whose villainy allows him to navigate a Haiti besieged by white explorers and exploiters. First, this chapter provides an overview of imagined voodoo in popular culture, particularly during the era in which "The Voodoo Man" shorts were published. Next, through narrative analysis, it examines how the series simultaneously evokes and subverts voodoo kitsch conventions through its titular character. Particular emphasis is placed on the ways in which The Voodoo Man undermines the efforts of the apparently virtuous—his nemesis, Bob Warren—and the indisputably devious, such as the white fortune hunters and other ne'er-do-wells who come to Haiti. The chapter concludes by proffering that while "The Voodoo Man" is rife with stereotypes, it nonetheless offers an early example of a complex, contemplative, and powerful Black villain. In this regard, The Voodoo Man is an early exemplar of the transgressive possibilities that villainy affords Black characters.

Imagined Voodoo: Haitian "Black Magic" in the Popular Imagination

Since Haiti's emergence as the first Black republic in the Western Hemisphere, it has remained a site of terror and wonder for the outside world, especially the United States. The enslaved people of what was then French colony Saint-Domingue began revolting against their masters in 1790. Under the leadership of the freedman Toussaint Louverture, the formerly enslaved fought valiantly enough that the French government enacted unilateral emancipation in 1793. Though emancipation momentarily curtailed the insurrection, the success of such a massive revolt resounded throughout not only the Caribbean but also the United States. J. Michael Dash writes of the American reaction, "The fear of slave insurrection ran deep in the white American imagination in the nineteenth century. Reports of carnage in St. Domingue; the arrival in 1793 of the first white refugees fleeing the war-torn 'French Island'; the restlessness among American slaves, when reports about the revolution in St. Domingue began to spread meant that the initial sympathy that existed among some would be swept away by the growing alarm in the United States over the potential for insurrection created by the Haitian example."[5] The early American studies scholar Simon P. Newman also agrees that Louverture's revolt frightened Americans, noting, "American blacks inspired by the Haitians were to be feared above all else. During the 1790s and well into the nineteenth century, white Americans were terrified that black revolutionaries would destroy liberty, property and society itself, bringing race war into the communities of the United States."[6]

Fear of Black revolution was coupled with fear and misunderstandings of Vodou, the religious practices of segments of the Haitian population. Scholars point toward the 1797 writings of the French colonial jurist and historian Médéric Louis Elie Moreau de Saint-Méry as highly influential on the narratives about Vodou that would follow in later years. Moreau de Saint-Méry described Vodou practitioners as veritable cultists and suggested that Vodou robbed its adherents of their senses and was "so strong that whites found spying on the mysteries of this sect and touched by one of the cultists discovering them, have sometimes started to dance and have had to go so far as to pay the Vaudoux Queen to put an end to their torment."[7] He also provided one of the first mentions of the *zonbi*, or a returned soul.[8] Adam McGee suggests that twentieth-century travelogues can be likened to Moreau de Saint-Méry's early musings in that they presented Vodou as "grotesque and carnivalesque" affairs that often involved human sacrifice.[9]

Moreau de Saint-Méry's misrepresentation of Vodou was coupled with the abundance of folklore about powerful sorcerers capable of shape-shifting. Even before the Haitian Revolution began, tales of the renegade François Makandal abounded. Makandal had escaped captivity and initiated a campaign of ravaging and pillaging French plantations. As the tale would have it, Makandal was able to elude capture—at least until his eventual murder by French authorities in 1758—by transforming into a bird or an insect. Similar stories about shape-shifting rebels reemerged during the United States' Haitian occupation in the early twentieth century.[10]

The United States' desire to establish its presence in the Caribbean led to further engagement with Haiti in the latter half of the nineteenth century. This interest came after the United States and other colonial powers spent the better half of the century refusing to acknowledge Haiti's sovereignty and hostilely treating it like a rogue nation. Eventually, as the historian Leon D. Pamphile notes, a trade partnership developed between Haiti and the United States, as did U.S. desire for a naval base in the region.[11] In the early twentieth century, the United States grew more fearful of Germany's increasing political and commercial influence on the island nation and Haiti's indebtedness to France—via reparations to former slaveholders that had been agreed on to stave off French invasion in 1825. Moreover, civil unrest led to the United States sending in Marines to protect U.S. citizens and interests.[12] Under the guise of stabilizing Haiti after the assassination of then-president Jean Vilbrun Guillaume Sam, the United States initiated a nineteen-year occupation in 1915.[13] The occupation not only resulted in the deaths of approximately fifteen thousand Haitian citizens but also opened up Haiti to foreign land ownership and control of its finances.[14]

The occupation of Haiti also inevitably led to increased intrigue regarding Vodou. The Marines stationed in Haiti often recounted tales of ritual human sacrifice and cannibalism. Indeed, the Marines often cast Vodou practices as Satanic rituals and even linked Vodou to an insurgency led by Charlemagne Peralte, a Haitian resistance fighter who led a group of guerrilla fighters known as the Cacos.[15] To contest these tales, Arthur Holly wrote *Les daïmons du culte voudo* (1917), which reconceptualized Vodou as a religion and drew connections between it and Christianity. As the religious scholar Lauren Derby notes, Holly went so far as to classify Vodou as a branch of Judaism and Haitians as a lost tribe of Israel.[16]

Nonetheless, Holly's work did not shape the popular imagination of Vodou nearly as much as texts such as *The Magic Island* (1929), a travel narrative written by the American journalist and occult enthusiast William Beuhler Seabrook. Seabrook's sensationalist ethnography—which some scholars claim is responsible for the term "zombie" entering the U.S. lexicon—heavily influenced imagined voodoo.[17] In an examination of *The Magic Island* in the wake of renewed interest in Seabrook's life (itself a result of the repopularization of zombie narratives), the scholars Margaret

T. McGehee and Emily Taylor highlight how the text reflects the paternalism and sensibilities of a southern white man, particularly in its depiction of zombies.[18] Whereas previous publications depicted zombies as powerful and dangerous, Seabrook portrayed zombies as mindless automatons akin to the faithful enslaved African Americans who appear in postbellum literature.[19] The anthropologist Elizabeth McAlister agrees with McGehee and Taylor, adding, "The horror of the Haitian zombie, for white Americans, was the image of the disfigured body dis-possessed of its soul, will, agency, and hence its interiority and its very humanity. When set against Christian dualisms of body and soul that placed theological priority on the soul, these religious differences were terrifying."[20]

Indeed, the will-less zombie became the subject of a slate of zombie films that emerged in the 1930s. Shortly after the publication of *The Magic Island*, United Artists released *White Zombie* (1932), starring the horror-film stalwart Bela Lugosi as Murder Legendre, a nefarious voodoo practitioner who controls a cadre of zombies on his Haitian sugarcane plantation. The film has all the tropes that would become standard for the genre, including a white man who masters or otherwise resorts to voodoo in order to control the whims of an innocent white woman. *White Zombie* and the slate of zombie films that followed grossly misrepresented Vodou and zonbis.[21]

Other media—including the "shudder pulps" of the 1930s—also took liberties, thus sparking a wave of imagined voodoo that bore little to no resemblance to Vodou. Foremost among these imagined voodoo texts were the "jungle comics" that preceded the modern-day comic book. Newspaper strips such as *Tarzan, Jungle Jim*, and their countless knockoffs were replete with depictions of evil voodoo witchdoctors out to menace the white, ubermasculine protagonist. The "graphic voodoo"—a term devised by the religious scholar Yvonne Chireau—in these jungle comics capitalized on comic readers' desires for escapist content; spurred the jungle comic books that emerged during and after World War II; and appropriated superhero comic conventions, which resulted in the criminalization of the Black voodoo priest.[22] "The Voodoo Man" comics certainly followed suit.

Agency through Villainy

In an extensive overview of Black horror stereotypes, Martin Harris—a contributor to BlackHorrorMovies.com—describes the "voodoo doer" in the following manner: "Somewhere between the primitive and the mystical darkie lies the voodoo doer, who combines the dress and malicious intent of the malignant primitive with the magical powers of the mystical darkie. The voodoo doer is generally more civilised than the primitive, as he may not act unless he feels he's been wronged, and he may actually not speak gibberish! He tends to hail from the Caribbean and often occupies a venerable, if feared, position amongst his people for his ability to be a prick."[23] Ostensibly, Harris's summation rings true, particularly of those cinematic examples he provides (most of which are from the late 1960s to mid-1980s). However, though Anna Fahraeus concedes that Harris is right to interrogate the stereotype, she argues that his description is reductive.[24] Instead, she likens the horror-film voodoo doer to the Renaissance villain of the Moor, such as Aaron of Shakespeare's *Titus Andronicus*, in that he is often motivated by revenge and not just petty thuggery; he is a source of terror, fear, and fascination; and he has little in the way of pretensions in white society.[25] This description also proves to be apt for The Voodoo Man.

Though the argument here is that The Voodoo Man is a more nuanced character than those voodoo doers who preceded him, he nonetheless maintains some of their conventions. In particular, he often was drawn in the same manner as the African witchdoctors who appeared throughout those aforementioned jungle comics. He typically is scantily clad, adorned only in a feathery headdress and grass skirt or loin cloth. His facial features—namely, protruding, bright lips—occasionally are exaggerated, as was typical of Black caricatures of the time.[26] Indeed, the creators of the series seem mostly unaware of Haitian culture or traditions and, as such, present The Voodoo Man as a vaguely African figure. Throughout the series, The Voodoo Man often is referred to as African, and in "Boanga's Zombie Corps" in *Weird Comics* #5, he refers to himself in the third person as "Boanga," a name with Congolese origins.[27]

"The Voodoo Man" shorts chronicle an ongoing battle between the titular character and the white Americans on the island, namely, Bob Warren, an American doctor who, in the first edition of the series, arrives in Haiti to set up a medical practice and to investigate voodoo. Difficulties arise in determining the temporality of the series, which first appears in *Weird Comics* #1 (April 1940); however, given the presence of an American constabulary in several editions, one might assume that the backdrop is early twentieth-century Haiti. As such, the Haiti of "The Voodoo Man" is awash with white Americans pursuing interests that put them into direct conflict with the so-called diabolical master of black magic. While Warren generally is portrayed as a virtuous doctor and most of The Voodoo Man's victims are often seemingly harmless white men and women, the narrative occasionally problematizes the white presence on the island. Indeed, while The Voodoo Man's desires for and his methods of extracting revenge are not wholly justified, he often is positioned as someone who has been mistreated or encroached upon.

For instance, in "Boanga's Zombie Corps," The Voodoo Man—referred to in this edition as "Boanga"—conducts a ritual in the jungle with his followers that disturbs Petro, Warren's loyal servant. Fearful of what is to come, Petro rushes to inform Warren, who serves as a physician on a plantation run by an American named Stanley Hibbert. Moments later, an explosion levels the servant quarters. Warren and Petro rescue a plantation worker from the rubble, and the worker reveals that Hibbert had unjustly fired The Voodoo Man. Meanwhile, The Voodoo Man and his followers steal the intact corpses from the rubble, and The Voodoo Man reanimates them as zombies in his command. The zombies raid the plantation store and return to The Voodoo Man's lair with provisions. Warren trails them, only to be grazed by a bullet fired by The Voodoo Man. Warren flees back to the plantation and tells Hibbert of his experience. Hibbert responds, "I've had enough trouble with this voodoo business! We're going to rout out the known voodoo doctors, and throw them in jail!"[28] Hibbert's declaration suggests that he desires indiscriminate retribution against all the voodoo practitioners on the island. Disguised as a plantation worker, one of The Voodoo Man's followers overhears Hibbert's plan and informs The Voodoo Man. The follower pleads with The Voodoo Man for protection for himself and the others, and The Voodoo Man vows to protect them (figure 12.1).

To ward off Warren and Hibbert, The Voodoo Man entrances Hibbert's daughter, Gloria, and absconds with her into the jungle. He promises his followers, "[I will] kill all whites on the island with my black magic! Boanga

FIGURE 12.1 "The Voodoo Man: Boanga's Zombie Corps," from *Weird Comics* #5 (1940).

will be king, and each of his men a prince, with a zombie for his personal slave!" As the Americans form a posse, a messenger delivers a note from The Voodoo Man that reads, "If you ever enter jungle to try and catch Boanga your daughter will die horrible death!"[29] However, in the end, Warren rescues Gloria Hibbert, and The Voodoo Man apparently is killed in a raging fire—though he obviously returns to combat Warren in later editions.

In a later edition, an American professor's desire for treasure brings him into conflict with The Voodoo Man. In "Captive of the Zombies," the unnamed professor entreats Warren to help his Haitian crewmen, many of whom have died from a mysterious illness while excavating the ruins of a Spanish fortress for treasure. Warren quickly surmises that voodoo is the cause of the illness, but before he can act, The Voodoo Man's zombies capture and imprison him in The Voodoo Man's lair. With an assist from The Voodoo Man's rival Nanti, Warren escapes imprisonment and reunites with his girlfriend, Lana, and the professor at a camp near the fortress. As Warren, Lana, and the professor rest, The Voodoo Man transforms his spirit into a hawk, flies to the camp, and uses his talons to slash the throat of the crew foreman. Warren and the professor rush to the foreman's quarters, where they discover a note from The Voodoo Man warning them to leave the ruins, which are part of The Voodoo Man's domain. Despite the warnings and the crew's trepidations, the professor presses on with the excavation (figure 12.2).

After spending hours without success, Lana uncovers a fountain that has a hidden treasure trove inside. The Voodoo Man instantly appears, and one of the professor's crew moves to attack but is killed instantly when The Voodoo

FIGURE 12.2 "The Voodoo Man: Captive of the Zombies," from *The Flame* #6 (1941).

Man stabs his shadow. The Voodoo Man casts a spell that teleports his foes back into the jungle. As they return to the ruins, they see that The Voodoo Man has turned Lana into a zombie. Nanti agrees to help capture The Voodoo Man, projects his soul as a fierce jaguar, and challenges The Voodoo Man's "death bird" spirit. As they battle, Warren and the professor throw a sack over The Voodoo Man's physical body. The death bird approaches Warren to release his body in exchange for releasing Lana from her zombie state. Defeated, The Voodoo Man disappears in a flaming burst. Warren vows to continue fighting against The Voodoo Man, as the professor takes his stolen gold back to the United States.[30]

In "Villains in Our Mind: A Psychological Approach to Literary and Filmic Villainy," Enrique Cámara Arenas notes that the hallmark of a true villain lies in their ability "to transform the world around by exercising their will."[31] Though The Voodoo Man's quest for revenge and other nefarious schemes are disrupted by Bob Warren (often with the help of others), he nevertheless proves a rather powerful villain who can be defeated but never vanquished completely. Throughout the series, he is a constant source of terror and wonderment who is able to bend the island to his will and shape events. Though he wields great power, he also evidences a keen intellect and proves to be a master of deception. For example, in "The Search for the Cult Temple," The Voodoo Man aligns with an American jewel trader known for his harsh treatment of his Haitian employees in pursuit of hidden jewels hidden inside the temple of a rival voodoo priest. Along their journey, he feigns as if he is simple-minded; however, when the trader betrays him and attempts to shoot him, he reveals that he has cast a spell to make the gun misfire. Nonetheless, after acquiring the jewels, he hands them over to the trader, whom he then stabs in the back.[32]

However, without question, it is The Voodoo Man's great power that allows him to carve out his own space and move about freely in an otherwise besieged Haiti, in which virtually every Haitian is servile. Most of his powers—such as his clairvoyance, his ability to teleport, and his ability to kill someone by stabbing their shadow, for instance—have no origin in Vodou; instead, they are among the powers we see utilized by voodoo doers in popular media texts. As John Bartkowski notes, (imagined) voodoo typically appears as either black magic or superstitious trickery and has the effect of making the genuine article seem foreign and not religious.[33] Indeed, The Voodoo Man is not wholly unlike the Haitian *bokor* of the pulp fiction novels that preceded the Fox Feature Syndicate comics in which he appeared. Roger Luckhurst writes of the pulp fiction *bokor* that the "master of the *zombis*, exercising a demonic hypnotic power over the weak-willed, was fused with a long-established melodramatic narrative about foreign mesmerists and their threat to white women, and therefore to the purity of the race. The Haitian *bokor* . . . was but a new version of the threat represented by Count Dracula or Svengali in the 1890s."[34]

Unlike Count Dracula, Svengali, or the *bokors* (both Black and white) of pulp fiction and cinema, The Voodoo Man expresses no interest whatsoever in amorous relationships with the American women on the island. Whenever he converts a white woman into a zombie, he does so as a means to an end. In "The Voodoo Man Cometh," for example, the reader is first introduced to Lana, the woman who becomes Warren's love interest. It eventually is revealed that she had been a zombie under The Voodoo Man's control, selling jewels that he has acquired in U.S. markets.[35] Throughout the series, The Voodoo Man captures or entrances Lana and other white women, but it usually is in order to enter spaces in which he is not permitted, to raise Warren's ire, or to add to his zombie horde. A few factors may contribute to The Voodoo Man's lack of interest in the white women in the series: first, in "Plague of Jacmel," The Voodoo Man appears to be married or in some form of domestic partnership, as he is joined by a woman with whom he willingly shares power.[36] Also, the Hays Code—the internal policing guidelines that the Hollywood studios established in 1934, which outlawed, among other things, any hint of miscegenation—also had an impact on the comics of that period. Perhaps most importantly, The Voodoo Man held the white people on the island in contempt. He often sought to eradicate them completely (as was the case in "Boanga's Zombie Corps"), undermine their authority, or, at the very least, keep them at bay. In "Havoc in Haiti," for example, The Voodoo Man murders Frank Garland, an American officer who had been tracking him. In an elaborate scheme, The Voodoo Man converts Garland into a zombie and uses him to infiltrate the governor's mansion in a plot to capture the governor's daughter and hold her for ransom. However, Garland fails in his task, and The Voodoo Man openly laments, "I'll do the job myself! Sabunda! Do these foolish whites think that mere bars can prevent my entrance?" (figure 12.3).[37]

Thus far, despite being one of the first shorts centered on a Black antagonist at the advent of the modern comic book, "The Voodoo Man" has received scant mention in scholarship. Yvonne Chireau briefly mentions the series in her examination of Black religions in U.S. comics, situating The Voodoo Man among the litany of voodoo criminals in jungle comics.[38] Her assertions about the ubiquity of voodoo witchdoctors in the comics of that

FIGURE 12.3 "The Voodoo Man: Havoc in Haiti," from *The Flame* #7 (1941).

era are valid; however, what makes The Voodoo Man distinctive is his agency and his positioning as more of a renegade—somewhat like the aforementioned François Makandal—than solely as a criminal.[39] The voodoo criminals to which Chireau refers were mostly one-off antagonists whose sole purpose was to serve as foils for the various white jungle-comic protagonists; however, "The Voodoo Man" chronicles a sustained battle of wills between the titular character and the Americans who operate with both goodwill and bad intentions. Granted, because of the series's loose continuity and its negotiations with genre conventions (both probably a result of different, unattributed writers), The Voodoo Man's raison d'être vacillates. In some instances, his end goal is dominion; in other instances, it is riches. However, while the narrative often presents The Voodoo Man as "evil," he does contest both authority and those who seek to exploit Haiti's wealth. His intentions are not always ignoble, as he evidences a desire to protect sacred ground and to share (to some degree) power with his followers.

Conclusion

"The Voodoo Man" series is not wholly unproblematic; indeed, Allen Spectre—the author to whom the series is attributed—invokes many of the conventions of what McGee has deemed "voodoo kitsch," or the aesthetics of the imagined religion of voodoo that appear in popular culture. McGee distinguishes between "imagined voodoo" and Haitian Vodou and Voodoo, the legitimate religious practices in Haiti and West Africa, respectively, on which the imagined voodoo is derived.[40] Furthermore, the narrative is replete with noble, superstitious, loyal Haitians who are subservient to white interlopers. Nonetheless, "The Voodoo Man," for its time, offers a fairly progressive version of a Haiti where white men either subjugate its people or seek to plunder its wealth, which, in turn, has the effect of making the titular character's schemes somewhat understandable, if not wholly justifiable. The Voodoo Man, as a powerful, contemplative antagonist, not only subverts (at least to some degree) the voodoo witchdoctor tropes of that era but also serves as an early exemplar of the potential that Black villains have for challenging the limits often placed on Black characters in comics.

Notes

1. "The Voodoo Man" shorts appear in Fox Feature Syndicates' *Weird Comics* #1–#7, *The Flame* #4–#8, and *Samson* #3. The shorts all are credited to Allen Spectre, though the artistry and continuity are inconsistent enough to suggest that Spectre was not the only artist or writer behind the series.
2. Spectre, "The Voodoo Man: The Witch Doctor's Revenge," 53.
3. P. Cunningham, "Absence of Black Supervillains," 59.
4. P. Cunningham, 58.
5. Dash, *Haiti and the United States*, 6.
6. Newman, "American Political Culture and the French and Haitian Revolutions," 80.
7. Bartkowski, "Claims-Making and Typifications of Voodoo," 559–560.
8. McAlister, "Slaves, Cannibals, and Infected Hyper-Whites," 459.
9. McGee, "Haitian Vodou and Voodoo," 240.
10. Derby, "Imperial Idols," 394–395.
11. Pamphile, *Contrary Destinies*, 16.
12. Pamphile, 21.
13. Though the United States withdrew armed forces from Haiti in 1934, it retained control over Haitian finances until 1947.
14. Danticat, "Long Legacy of the Occupation in Haiti."
15. Owens, "Beyond Authenticity," 354.
16. Derby, "Imperial Idols," 411. For more on the practice of Vodou, see K. Brown, *Mama Lola*; Ramsey, *Spirits and the Law*; and Michel and Bellegarde-Smith, *Vodou in Haitian Life and Culture*.
17. "Zombie" is a spelling variant of the term *zonbi*. McGee describes the zonbi as "a dead person who has been captured—sometimes in body but more typically as a soul—by a boko (sorcerer), who is then master of the zonbi and can make the poor soul work forever. Zonbi are said to till fields, harvest crops, and do all forms of menial labor formerly relegated to slaves. They are also frequently sent, as spirits, to drive the boko's victims mad" ("Haitian Vodou and Voodoo," 242).

18 McGehee and Taylor, "Mr. Seabrook Goes to Haiti," 58.
19 McGehee and Taylor, 61–62.
20 McAlister, "Slaves, Cannibals, and Infected Hyper-Whites," 472.
21 Platts, "Locating Zombies in the Sociology of Popular Culture," 549.
22 Chireau, "Looking for Black Religions in 20th Century Comics," 405.
23 Harris, "Types of Black Horror Characters."
24 Fahraeus, "Historicising Racialised Objects of Horror," 140.
25 Fahraeus, 139.
26 Allen Spectre—probably a pseudonym—is the only creator credited in "The Voodoo Man" shorts. However, given the inconsistencies in the artistry and scripting, it appears that a handful of different artists and writers were used. The Voodoo Man is often rendered in dramatically different ways throughout "The Voodoo Man" shorts, with the more caricatured drawings of him appearing in the pages of *The Flame* (1941). In "The Voodoo Man" shorts in *Weird Comics* (1940), his facial features are modest. Perhaps most evident of the inconsistencies is the short that appears in *Weird Comics* #4 (July 1940), in which The Voodoo Man inexplicably appears as Mesoamerican before returning as Black in the next issue.
27 No other edition of "The Voodoo Man" mentions the name "Boanga."
28 Spectre, "The Voodoo Man: Boanga's Zombie Corps," 48.
29 Spectre, 50.
30 Spectre, "The Voodoo Man: Captive of the Zombies."
31 Cámara Arenas, "Villains In Our Mind," 7.
32 Spectre, "The Voodoo Man: The Search for the Cult Temple."
33 Bartkowski, "Claims-Making and Typifications of Voodoo," 566.
34 Luckhurst, *Zombies*, 63–64.
35 Spectre, "The Voodoo Man: The Voodoo Man Cometh."
36 Spectre, "The Voodoo Man: The Plague of Jacmel," 46.
37 Spectre, "The Voodoo Man: Havoc in Haiti," 48.
38 Chireau, "Looking for Black Religions," 406.
39 Chireau writes of "The Voodoo Man," "*Weird Comics* (1940) introduced an antagonist called The Voodoo Man, an evil mastermind whose vengeful schemes against government agents, missionary doctors, and other innocents ignited a maelstrom of deceit, fraud, and greed that compounded the collective misfortunes of his African tribesmen" (406). However, one should note that "The Voodoo Man" is set in Haiti, and his foes—particularly in the pages of *The Flame*, published a year after *Weird Comics*—are not always virtuous.
40 McGee, "Haitian Vodou and Voodoo," 240.

13

Love in Color

• • • • • • • • • • • • •

Fawcett's Revolutionary *Negro Romance*

JACQUE NODELL

Negro Romance was a series published by Fawcett Comics in 1950 and devoted to the romantic entanglements of Black characters. While it was groundbreaking, in many ways, the title was no different from any other romance comic title at the time, depicting the thrill of falling in love and the universality of heartbreak. As one of eighteen romance titles published by Fawcett at the time, the stories in *Negro Romance* gave readers a ubiquitous look into romance and ran the gamut from relatable to aspirational. Whether dealing with insecure characters that manifest conflict as selfishness, as in the story "My Heart's Dilemma," or with quirky characters with a knack for charming squirrels, as in "Possessed," these romance stories gave a new audience access to characters that looked like them with just enough romantic fantasy to keep readers coming back. With comic books widely available in candy stores and on newsstands, Black readers were no doubt hungry to get their hands on a comic with identifiable characters. Unfortunately, the series was short-lived.

Today only the Library of Congress holds copies of the complete four-issue set. There are only two other libraries known to have any copies in their holdings. One comic book historian estimates less than fifty surviving copies of each issue in the entire world.[1] With a comic book so rare, it is no surprise that little has been written about it over the years.

I first became aware of the title's details when in 2011, producers of the PBS show *History Detectives* contacted me to be their subject expert on romance comics for an episode featuring *Negro Romance*.[2] I had not ever seen a physical copy of any of the issues until the show's filming. As one of the talking heads on the show, I was tasked with finding out for the owner of the comic book, the professor and author Gerald Early, who created the rare comic and anything else that would prove interesting for the television viewers.

Comics scholarship is generally lacking in the representation of romance comics. Even less has been written about *Negro Romance*. Yet this neglected series was undoubtedly a frontrunner to the comics series that came after it, featuring characters of color, including Jack Kirby's memorable yet unpublished series *Soul Love*. By taking a journey into this little-known series, this chapter seeks to inform readers of what simultaneously was trailblazing and conformed to the conventions typical of romance comics as a genre.

To what do we owe this comic book's rarity? There are a few factors. First of all, comic books have an inherent rarity because of their ephemeral nature. Young people reading the comics at the time of production could never have fathomed the lengths to which people today would go to collect the comics they bought off the newsstands or at the candy store, read while at the breakfast table, passed on to friends, and ultimately discarded when told to clean their rooms. Because of the medium's fleeting nature, we are left with few copies of this particular title. While it is likely that over one hundred thousand copies were printed of each issue, the few that remain are survivors of purged basements, attics, and the eager hands of young readers from years ago.

When World War II ended, the economic status of Black communities was bolstered by troops coming home. While the GI Bill intended to support troops during their transition back to civilian life, the bill was not applied uniformly. Many Black soldiers who had served were short-changed or discriminated against while attempting to use their benefits. However, some economic growth in Black communities meant more disposable income for entertainment such as comic books. While it is hard to believe now because the comic book industry is not the economic powerhouse it once was, comic books were big money and big business. Fawcett had financial incentives to take advantage of this new audience of readers of color. Introducing to the market a comic book aimed at Black readers made financial sense.

Negro Romance came to exist because Fawcett rapidly and extensively published titles to reach various markets. In the 1940s and 1950s, comics were quite profitable, and it only benefitted Fawcett at least to try to reach a diversified audience. It may seem at first glance that *Negro Romance* is groundbreaking. However, when you consider the volume and variance of Fawcett's titles and the fact that it was still a "segregated title," it no longer seems like such an anomaly or quite so bold. After all, it would not be until the 1970s that romance comics were truly integrated and dealt with issues such as race.

What remains a marvel is what this series was not. It was not a series that took stories that had already been published with white characters and then recolored, as was so often the case with later romance comics. Later stories were often recolored to transform white characters into Black characters without changing the story and dialogue or portrayed Black women stereotypically, such as the Mammy character. The overwhelming majority of romance comics from their inception in 1947 to the late 1960s are fraught with romantic love stories experienced by white characters. In the rare instances of nonwhite characters, they were shown in the context of their role as domestic "help" or depicted as exotic or an oddity. One type of illustrated feature that appeared in romance comics showcasing people of color was one-pagers telling readers about "strange" romance and marriage customs from cultures worldwide. Indigenous people were illustrated as "savages," endangering white womanhood (figure 13.1). Before *Negro Romance*, these examples of othering were usually the only place to find people of color in the romance comics.

Negro Romance was not demeaning or stereotypical. It showed that Black men and women pursued the same love and domestic bliss that characterized the pinnacle of American achievement. The characters are fashionably dressed and beautifully coiffed, and the protagonists are "perfect" examples for any midcentury woman to emulate.[3] However, readers of the time would have noticed other qualities besides chicness. The women in *Negro Romance* embody internal traits that would have been considered dignified and becoming: the projection of perfect middle-class womanhood—polite, moral, and pure. While these would have been essential qualities for white characters to possess to be seen as desirable mates, this held a special

FIGURE 13.1 "Romance Oddities," from *Sweethearts* #86 (1950). (Image from Digital Comic Museum.)

significance for Black characters and no doubt additional meaning for Black readers because of the "politics of respectability" pervasive in African American communities of the time.[4]

Negro Romance did not delve into any of the structural inequities that existed in society at the time of the comic's creation. Still, its presentation of Black characters remains admirable. Showing Black characters' comportment on par with white characters demonstrated to young white readers that their Black peers were just as "good" and "pure" as they were and worthy of the same respect and full rights of citizenship. While this may or may not have been the creators' intention, it comes across as quite progressive and subversive compared to other stereotypical popular media of the time.

The actual stories in the series follow the patterns and themes of all the other Fawcett romance comics and are interchangeable in many ways. While the characters were Black, the art, drawn by multiple artists, was in the same approximate style as all other romance comics on the market. This series's entire creative team remains a mystery, but comic book scholars have made some strides over the years in identifying the writers and artists. From these inquiries into the creative team's identity, it appears that this series was, at least in part, created by African Americans, lending a new dimension to the series.

While the title of the series may be awkward to say out loud, due to its outdated reference to people of color, for the time, it would have certainly grabbed the attention of people browsing the newsstands. Most comic book companies were fly-by-night operations and, as such, do not have archives that more corporate publishers have. We know what we know about this title primarily from the actual content of the issues that would have run readers ten cents back in 1950. Topics range from jealousy, choosing the wrong person to love, and even (accidental) forays into crime.

The stories in *Negro Romance* are right at home in the canon of 1950s romance comics. Romance comics were full of domesticity stories, with marriage portrayed as the ultimate goal in a woman's life. *Negro Romance* was no different. Companies that published romance comics often had gimmicks or styles that helped to set their titles apart from other companies. Fawcett's stories tended to straddle the border of sentimental and misogynistic, with apologies and forgiveness at the forefront. All the stories in *Negro Romance* are very similar to other Fawcett stories with white characters. Essentially, the female lead schemes, finds herself wrapped up in a bad situation out of naiveté, or does some devilish deed that makes her lose her lover. Once she regrets her choices and apologizes or begs for forgiveness, she is absolved—though it does not always result in winning her man back. The *Negro Romance* stories are well constructed in both plot and execution, but nothing is dramatically different from their white counterparts published in other Fawcett romances. While many romance comic book stories were reprinted from other stories, and some were even recolored in the 1960s to

FIGURE 13.2 *Negro Romance* #1 cover. (Image from Digital Comic Museum)

portray more diversity, the stories in *Negro Romance* appear to be original, all while consistent in the genre's tropes.

The bimonthly series's debut issue, with a cover date of June 1950, contains three sequential stories and one text story. Immediately noticeable is the cover, with a photograph of two attractive models (figure 13.2).[5] The young woman's hair is tinged slightly red in a curly updo, her makeup on point, and she wears a pair of beautiful earrings and a look of happiness with a hint of longing. The young man's dreamy eyes stare off into the distance, and he wears a wide-lapeled suit. Each issue of the title has a similarly attractive young Black couple on the cover, sweetly embracing or holding hands, with the comic's title boldly displayed above their heads and the names of the stories written in the corners.

Even a casual read of *Negro Romance* reveals a theme that runs throughout almost each and every story: women in need of forgiveness before anyone can love them. One of the main reasons women in these stories need to atone is that they have acted selfishly. Interestingly, this selfishness, whether born of pure malice or merely insecurity, is heavily gendered.

Perhaps no story encapsulates this insecurity-selfishness-atonement triad as well as "My Heart's Dilemma" from issue 1. After Marjorie's parents pass away, she goes to live with her Aunt Lou. Aunt Lou is falling in love with a man named Jim Taylor, but Marjorie does not like it one bit. What accounts for her hostility toward the budding romance? Marjorie does not want any changes or anything to come between her and her aunt, and when she sees an opportunity to attempt to get rid of her potential uncle, she hatches a plan. Though the scheme fails, Jim breaks it off with Aunt Lou because he thinks she is entirely ruled by her selfish niece.

Meanwhile, Marjorie's boyfriend, Ray, cannot believe that she acted so selfishly and dumps her. In the end, Marjorie apologizes to Jim and asks that he see her aunt. Jim does, and Ray takes Marjorie back because she learned her lesson and fixed her mistake. The end of the story has Marjorie reflecting, "My selfishness was gone—but not before it had almost cost me all the finest things in my life. I can only say a prayer of gratitude that I learned my lesson in time."[6]

This error-and-forgiveness cycle is an overarching theme in almost all of the stories of *Negro Romance*. The theme of atonement runs heavily through Fawcett's romance stories in general, perhaps more noticeably than for any other publisher of the time. While most romance comics from other publishers have their leading ladies learning a lesson with a morality-type ending, the Fawcett stories are heavy on blaming the protagonist. *Negro Romance* was not unique when it came to sending a clear message that love is conditional and that women must be redeemed to be loved.

Almost every story in the *Negro Romance* series includes educated and prosperous characters. Characters hold positions as doctors, business owners, attorneys, and other well-respected occupations. In addition to driving the plots with their particular jobs, these characters show readers just how far people of color had come in the United States. They were no longer just "the help" in the scenes' background; they were at the forefront of the show. One of the stories in which a character's occupation is very important is the second story in issue 1, "A Tragic Vow," which follows the childhood friends

Harry and Janet. From the beginning of the story, it is clear that Janet is not on the same page as Harry. Harry is a top medical student, well on his way to having his own practice. When he asks Janet to marry him, she tries every delaying tactic in the book, because frankly, she just is not that into him. After giving Harry the runaround, Janet attempts to buy time by saying that they can get married after Harry completes his internship. As luck would have it, Harry quits interning to appease Janet. She does her best to convince Harry that he is making the wrong decision and that he would be ruining not only his dreams but the goals of his mother and father. Unable to change his mind, she halfheartedly goes along with Harry's marriage plans while continuing to stall and date another guy, Tom. Everything comes to a head when Harry sees Janet with Tom. Next thing Janet knows, Harry's mother visits her and admonishes her for her selfishness. As Harry's mother leaves, Tom walks in, and he too sees that he has made a mistake by trusting Janet's love. He does not want to be led on the way that Harry was. Alone, Janet realizes that she must make things right with Harry. She visits him and convinces him to return to the hospital and finish his internship. In the end, Tom returns to Janet because she did the right thing by convincing Harry to let go of her and pursue his dream. "A Tragic Vow" emphasizes professional achievements and portrays them as an essential part of starting a family. In this story, readers are given the subtle reminder that becoming educated and pursuing one's talents and passions (if you are a man at least) is just as important as marriage.

Another story, in issue 3, titled "The Fateful Decision," features a thriving Black business owner. When secretary Sylvia stays late working for the owner, he lightheartedly admonishes her, saying, "First thing you know, they'll be accusing me of slave labor!" While it is possible that this was a throwaway line, it is also highly likely that this sentence was written playfully and with a wink. Since the stories in *Negro Romance* are overwhelmingly about prosperous middle-class Black characters, especially this one, which tells the story of a successful Black business owner, it is possible that this line was used to show readers how far African Americans had come by playfully acknowledging their past. Again, while we do not know for sure who scripted the stories, it is clear from this line that the writers were adept at using humor to confront and sublimate difficult topics.

One of the more universal themes that run throughout the stories in *Negro Romance* is family. Family bonds are emphasized in many of the stories, pointing to these relationships' importance in the African American community and their utility in promoting respectability. Family is not a

FIGURE 13.3 "The Fateful Decision," from *Negro Romance* #3. (Image courtesy The Library of Congress)

theme that shows up in all romance comics of the time. Stories of these relationships are usually saved for stories that are very focused on a family. Interestingly, these stories of intense family bonds also show up in early romance comic tales of immigrants and characters depicted as first-generation Americans, two groups of people whose assimilation and proper behavior mattered greatly for dispelling stereotypes and prejudice.

In issue 1's "Too Late for Love," the story's bad guy, Hank, a widower and single father, tells his late wife's best friend, Diane, that it was her all along whom he loved. Diane steps in to take care of Hank's neglected baby, Ginny. Though by the end of the story, Diane has broken things off with Hank, she declares that she will beg her ex, Artie, to marry her and vows, "I'm coming back for Ginny. She'll have a new mother and father—the kind she deserves! ... Sob ... Sob ... I promise—!" For Diane, abandoning the child is not an option, and she chooses the baby's safety over a love interest. Readers were undoubtedly cheering Diane on in her family-oriented pursuits.

In *Negro Romance*, family turmoil manifests itself as parents who desire education and prosperity for children above romantic love, as we saw in "A Tragic Vow"; an attachment to extended family turned nuclear, as depicted in "My Heart's Dilemma"; and the difficulty of letting a stepparent into one's life, as is the plot of issue 3's "My Love Betrayed Me!" These stories show that while romance comics were predominantly about romantic love, they were adept at depicting a certain amount of relatability concerning family matters. Whereas white characters are often seen existing alone, characters in *Negro Romance* are heavily engaged with family in nearly every story of the series.

A number of other themes familiar to romance comics in general appear in the pages of *Negro Romance*. The stories "Love's Decoy" and "The Fateful Decision" revolve around crime and almost resemble a pre-Code crime comic more than romance stories. "Forever Yours" uses another plot device loved by romance comic writers, a medical ailment that threatens to come between lovers.

In issue 2's "Love's Decoy," the naïve club dancer Sara longs for her chance in the spotlight and a star on her dressing-room door, so she agrees to plant a letter on her customer and crush Bruce, at the direction of the club's boss, the seasoned criminal Barton. The ruse leads to Bruce's arrest, and Sara gets grazed by a bullet courtesy of Barton's gang. The last issue in the original series of three is much like the first two issues, as love and jealousy abound, but it also contains another story involving the criminal element. "The Fateful Decision" follows Sylvia on her journey from a secretary at a legitimate company to the secretary of a pyramid scheme funded by embezzlement. As if that was not enough, Sylvia's new boss and love interest runs off with her minor sister. These types of romance stories with a criminal element woven in are prevalent in the pre-Code romance comics. Nearly every title had stories that dealt with gangsters, mob bosses, and other ne'er-do-wells.

"Forever Yours," also from issue 2, revolves around a medical ailment. The protagonist, Edith, finds out that she only has two years to live unless she undergoes an experimental treatment. However, she decides to keep it secret from her fiancé in hopes that they can continue with their marriage despite the looming hardship of her failing health. As always in the romance comics, the medical condition miraculously goes away, leaving the couple free to pursue their life as intended. While this story may seem a little trite, stories featuring a character with some sort of unknown and potentially deadly medical ailment made for high drama and dreamy endings and were very common in romance comics.

One story that incorporates many of these themes and is ripe for a more detailed look is "Possessed" from issue 2. In it, Gloria, down on her luck, goes to the park and meets Lloyd Jaimson, a gentle soul who has a knack for charming squirrels. Wanting to help Gloria after she tells him that she has just lost her job, Lloyd takes her to his mother's salon to see if his mother could use any help. Gloria catches on to hairdressing quickly and soon is involved in every aspect of the business. Wanting to ensure that she is indispensable, Gloria becomes entangled in Lloyd and his family's lives, but to everyone's detriment. Eventually, Lloyd has enough of Gloria acting like a martyr, and the two split. Gloria atones for her heavy-handed salon takeover, reinstating Lloyd's mother and sister in the business and then leaving town. After months alone mourning her loss, she comes across Lloyd fighting in a boxing tournament. The two reunite, and Lloyd vows to marry Gloria when he finishes his last semester of college. "Possessed" is a story like many other romance stories of the time. Blinded by love, Gloria drives it away and hurts many people in her wake.

"Possessed" closely revolves around the theme of family; it takes a long, hard look at Gloria's selfishness and finds the theme of atonement, as we examined earlier. It also portrays Gloria and Lloyd's mother as very adept businesswomen. The interesting part of this story is that it is almost more about the relationship between the women than the romance between Gloria and Lloyd. Lloyd leaves the story quite early on while he attends school, and the women are seen acting as a family unit without him. While race, gender, and class are not explicitly discussed in the story, they are issues woven throughout the tale. With Lloyd's father dead and Lloyd away at school, it is clear that the women run the family. While Gloria attempts to make herself vital to the business, she inadvertently brings the salon such good business that she can proclaim to Lloyd's mother, "You go right ahead now, and learn to become a lady of leisure. From now on, there'll be lots of it for you!" The salon is so profitable with Gloria at the helm that she even sends Lloyd money to pay for college. While "Possessed" is at its heart a love story, the relationship between the women sets it apart from most other romance stories.

Nevertheless, what is perhaps noticeable to readers of these three issues is how much they read just like other romance comics of the time. The clothes and hair are fashionable, the cars and clubs fancy, and the characters' dialogue is melodramatic. This is all to say that these three issues of *Negro Romance* are identical to romance comics featuring white characters that most readers would have been accustomed to. The characters are educated and engaging and hold various professional positions. There is only one instance in which an explicit attempt was made to give a nod to Black culture: the nightclub in the story "Love's Decoy" in issue 2 was called "Club Ebonia."[7] There do not seem to be any other indicators that the comic was aimed explicitly at Black readers, as was Jackie Ormes's Torchy Brown character, which appeared in the weekly African American newspaper the *Pittsburgh Courier*, other than the obvious fact that the characters are all people of color.

All three of the Fawcett issues contain advertisements for other romance comics, or "romantic picture-story magazines," as one advertisement called them.[8] These advertisements showcase Fawcett's other titles, including *Sweethearts*, *Exciting Romances*, *True Confessions*, and *Romantic Story*. However, the third issue of *Negro Romance* contains an ad that is not for the publisher's other romance comic books. Instead, the advertisement is for novels—not any novels but books by New American Library's Signet Books, curated to feature "Great Negro Novels," the "best-selling novels on racial themes."[9] Clearly, this ad was aimed at readers of *Negro Romance*.

The fourth issue in the series contains no original material and is a page-by-page reprint of issue 2, albeit by the publisher Charlton. This stand-alone issue was published by Charlton almost five years after the original series because Fawcett sold many of its intellectual properties to Charlton after a legal entanglement with DC Comics over the character Captain Marvel. Fawcett was in a tough spot financially with the lawsuit and declining interest in the medium due to the accusations of comics causing juvenile delinquency.[10] Fawcett responded to these hardships by closing the company's comics arm, and several titles were sold to Charlton, including *Negro Romance*. The cover for issue 4 is the only one of the series that does not have a "happy couple" photo cover and instead is illustrated. It is also the only cover that alludes to a love triangle, with one man sneering while another man woos a woman who appears to be the first man's girlfriend. Inside, the stories are the same as the second Fawcett issue. The only thing that sets the Charlton issue apart besides the cover art is that while the cover says "Negro Romance" in the same font as the other issues, the indicia on the back of the front cover have the title listed as *Negro Romances* (plural). For purposes of collecting, most comic book professionals will use the indicia title as the official title.

In addition to sharing any general information on the comic series, one of the main points of the *History Detectives* episode that I was on was to figure out who the creators of *Negro Romance* were. The search for creators proved difficult for the show back in 2011 and continues to mystify most comic book experts almost a decade later. While we can surmise a few creators from interviews with the editor of the series, Roy Ald, most of the artists are not known. Perhaps someday, as romance comics and artists and their styles are further studied, the other creators will come to light. For now, here is what we do know. Each issue has an editorial staff listed on the splash page. These are some of the first and only concrete clues as to who had a hand in creating the title. These names include Roy Ald (editor), Will Lieberson (executive editor), Al Jetter (art editor), and John Graham (as J. Graham; associate).

Starting with the inception of the title, Roy Ald told the comic book historian Shaun Clancy in an interview in 2011, when the former editor was ninety years old, that he started the romance comics line at Fawcett and that he developed *Negro Romance*. Ald created the concept along with the artist Alvin C. Hollingsworth, and Ald edited the series and wrote most of the stories under a pen name, though none of the stories are signed or credited in the issues.[11]

Hollingsworth was the main artist identified during the *History Detectives* investigation and is still cited today as one of the artists and one of the series's creators. Known for being one of the first African Americans to work in the comic book industry and, later, for his fine art career, Hollingsworth first came to Fawcett to show his work when he was only sixteen years old.[12] There is an image of Hollingsworth's work in the Clancy-Ald interview, possibly from a romance comic. The two women depicted are beautifully rendered and on par with the style of romance comics, making it easy to see how Hollingsworth illustrated at least some of the stories of *Negro Romance*. Born in 1928, Hollingsworth would have only been twenty-two years old while working on the series. There is a maturity in his work that was well beyond his years, probably from the fact that he started in the comic book industry when he was only twelve years old and had his first credited piece published by the tender age of fifteen.[13]

Ald told Clancy that Fawcett did the series because of Hollingsworth. However, Ald mentioned that he was the one who wrote most of the stories: "It may have been created between the two of us, but most likely it was because of my liberal attitude that I initially suggested it. . . . In fact, I'm almost certain of it."[14] Clancy let Ald know during the interview that the series was well written and would appeal to anyone, Black or white. Ald, clearly proud of his creation, said, "I made sure of that myself. I treated African-Americans the same way I treated everyone else."[15]

Interestingly enough, at the time of the interview, Ald said that he remembered there being more than just three *Negro Romance* issues and indicated that there were upward of seven issues.[16] While it is certainly possible that Fawcett commissioned more artwork and stories for the series, they never ended up happening for one reason or another. It is also possible that since Clancy interviewed Ald when Ald was in his nineties, he was misremembering. Though Ald comes across in the interview as overall very sharp, there is, of course, room to infer that he was thinking of some other romance series.

As a publisher, perhaps Fawcett felt it had some atoning to do for its introduction of a character named Steamboat in 1942 into its popular Captain Marvel series. Steamboat was a Black character portrayed incredibly stereotypically and was so offensive that the character was dropped in 1945 when concerned readers protested.[17] The executive editor of the title was Will Lieberson. Having dealt with the Steamboat uproar and being a Jewish man, Lieberson knew full well what it meant to be discriminated against and stereotyped, making him a natural to work on the *Negro Romance* series.[18] Ald did not feel like it was tough to convince the Fawcett family to publish the comic as they only cared if it sold well.[19]

While we do not know who the other artists are, we do have a few clues for the most part. Hopefully, as time goes on, other artists will be identified. Rudy Palais is one other artist identified as having contributed to the series. Palais was not Black, but he did have a long career in the comic book industry.[20] The story "Forever Yours" from issue 2 is credited as being by Rudy Palais by Ald and confirmed by several art spotters.[21]

We do not know who lettered the issues of *Negro Romance*, but it is possible that a woman lettered some of the issues. Al Jetter, the husband of Charlotte Jetter (née Haecker), was an editor and art director at Fawcett. According to another Fawcett artist, Bob Laughlin, Al taught Charlotte to letter.[22] She lettered many comic book stories over the years, including Fawcett stories in the 1950s. Al Jetter is listed in all three Fawcett issues of *Negro Romance* as the art director, so there is a chance that Charlotte lettered at least a portion of *Negro Romance* stories. While Charlotte was not Black, the possibility of a woman lettering the comic adds to the diversity and intrigue of the comic and gives future inquirers about the series another clue as to the roster of creators.

While we do not know who the colorist was on this series, it is noticeable right off the bat (or maybe *not* noticeable) that the coloring is relatively uniform. Comic books featuring characters of color were often colored poorly, for lack of better words. As many devout comic book readers have noticed and as was pointed out by the scholar Zoë Smith in her essay "4 Colorism: The Ashiness of It All," due to the nature of the printing process and lack of better printing technology, many Black characters in comic books were ashy in tone and inconsistent, varying from a grayish color to a green reminiscent of a person unaccustomed to sea travel.[23] No doubt, absorbent newsprint exacerbated this issue. Newsprint dulled colors even further, rendering characters of color even ashier than they had probably been intended to be, especially over time as the paper yellowed with age. *Negro Romance* has characters that are overwhelmingly colored consistently and naturally panel to panel, and it even exhibits a bit of intentional skin-tone variance from one person to another. Though there are some slight inconsistencies, they are not nearly as noticeable as in other comic books. In the copies that I have seen, the coloring has held up well over the years. The attractive coloring gives *Negro Romance* more points on the scale of just how good it was and how much its creators respected all people's love stories, regardless of skin color.

These creator identifications are not universally accepted by all comic book fans/scholars, and some disagree that Hollingsworth had an actual hand in the art. This disagreement seems to be twofold. Some collectors just do not think the work looks like Hollingsworth's.[24] Others believe that it is only his work by proxy, as Hollingsworth had a number of assistants because he had a studio and worked for so many publishers. The artist Tony Tallarico thought that Hollingsworth's assistants drew the *Negro Romance* stories in question.[25] Ald indicated that Hollingsworth had two assistants while working at Fawcett, though he did not say if they necessarily worked on *Negro Romance*. Their names were Al Sargent and Charlie Ferguson, and they were both African American.[26] In totality, it appears likely that Hollingsworth's assistants had a hand in several stories in the series. While Hollingsworth may still have done quite a bit of the art solo, it is possible that some of the issues had multiple pencillers within individual stories due to the quick turnaround required by comic book publishers.

The art of *Negro Romance* is on par with the art of other romance comics of the time. While the artists are not identified concretely because comic book stories often were not signed, it is clear that the series involves several different artists. While Orrin C. Evans, president of the company that published *All-Negro Comics*, touted that his company's comic was illustrated by all African American artists, *Negro Romance* made no such claim. Today, we do not entirely know who is responsible for the art or writing chores. Though we do not know precisely who the artists were, we can tell a great deal just from their visual styles. Hollingsworth's art and characters had a mature sexiness, though not necessarily as "pretty" as other romance artists like Matt Baker. Women drawn by Hollingsworth had heavy, vampy eyes with eyelashes that could kill. His panels are crowded, and empty space is at a premium.

Hollingsworth's distinct art appears throughout the series, though sometimes just in a panel or two. It was not uncommon to have multiple artists work on one story in the comic book industry, especially when working under a time crunch. It was also common practice for artists to emulate a "house style" prescribed by the publisher or use assistants to approximate a lead artist's style. The fact that comics are such a collaborative art form, especially at this time, could very well explain why there are hints of Hollingsworth's style throughout the series in multiple stories.

None of the stories are highly stylized, and all have similar layouts and retain a good balance of art and text—they are neither too busy nor too sparse. Backgrounds on the stories are not distracting and give a glimpse into the overwhelmingly middle-class lives that characters are depicted as having, without taking the emphasis off the characters themselves.

There are no other credited or identified artists, and most creators are still a mystery. However, in the *Negro Romance* entry in the *Overstreet Price Guide*, a name pops out for having art in the first issue: "Evans."[27] It is unclear whether the guide means George J. Evans Jr., the brother of *All-Negro Comics*' creator, Orrin Evans, or George Evans, another cartoonist known for his work at both Fawcett and EC. The story "Too Late for Love" is very likely to have been penciled by George J. Evans Jr., as the art is reminiscent of Evans's work on Lion Man from *All-Negro Comics*. While the titular character is drawn very simplistically, his eyes in "Lion Man" resemble the way the eyes of Diane, the protagonist in "Too Late for Love," are rendered. If the art in "Too Late for Love" were indeed done by George J. Evans Jr., this means that another Black artist worked on *Negro Romance*.

While little exists in the way of evidence to determine how readers felt about *Negro Romance* at the time, another Fawcett publication did earn good reviews from the press: the sequential retelling of Jackie Robinson's career. Fawcett probably felt encouraged to publish *Negro Romance* in part because of the positive reception of its comic book chronicling of Robinson, published in 1949: *Jackie Robinson, Baseball Hero*. An article that appeared in the Black newspaper the *Ohio Daily Express* (Dayton), titled "Fawcett Publications Issues Magazine on Jackie," extolled the virtues of the pioneering comic book:

> We are not supporters of comic magazines by any stretch of the imagination. We feel the deluge of these pointless pulp mags has a dulling effect on the mentallity [sic] not only of our youth, but of the many adults who avidly read them. They help perpetuate the myth of anglo-saxon superiority as well as many other

harmful myths. But there was one sent to us by the Fawcett Publications Inc. some months ago which struck our fancy.... The story was presented with none of the usual condescention [*sic*]. As we remember, the tenor of the story was as if the thing was published by Negroes. There were no excuses, no shabby paternalism or chauvinistic asides.

The article said that the Jackie Robinson comic was a success for the publisher and that the comic would become bimonthly, along with other comics in the same vein. The article's high praise for the comic must have encouraged some readers and parents in Black communities to pick up other comic books from the publisher to read, including *Negro Romance*.

Negro Romance was also mentioned in 1955 on a list of 234 "unobjectionable comic books."[28] Acting as the president for the Organization for the Protection of Children, Ed Bulleit lists *Negro Romance* as one of the approved comics by the Committee on Comic Books appointed by the mayor of Memphis, Tennessee. This list appeared in the *Jackson Sun*, one of the primary newspapers in West Tennessee. While *Negro Romance* is just one of the many comic books listed, its presence indicates an acceptance of the title when many comic books were looked at with suspicion. After the industry had been through the wringer during the U.S. Senate subcommittee's investigation of juvenile delinquency, any sort of endorsement from a children's safety organization would have meant good things for the title and demonstrated its child-friendliness. Despite the positive reactions to the title, *Negro Romance* came to an unceremonious end.

It is difficult to get a whole picture of how many readers had a chance to see *Negro Romance* at the time. If we judge the title on the basis of the fact that there were only three issues published initially, we could conclude that it was not incredibly popular. However, that oversimplification does not explain why Charlton would have reprinted it once it acquired the title. So, why was the series so short-lived? In a sense, *Negro Romance* was the victim of unfortunate timing.

Romance comics were huge after they were introduced in 1947 by Joe Simon and Jack Kirby. Romance comics, funny animals, westerns, and other genres replaced the superhero's popularity after World War II. Former GIs were settling down, and with the baby boom in full swing, romance comics significantly impacted popular culture. In 1949, there was an explosion of romance titles, and by 1950, publishers had oversaturated the market by competing to have the most salacious and dreamy love comics. The comic book historian Michelle Nolan has termed this period the "Love Glut." In her book *Love on the Racks: A History of American Romance Comics*, she cites that a whopping 117 out of 147 titles were canceled or suspended in 1950 alone, and only 33 of those titles ever found their way back to newsstands.[29] *Negro Romance* was only one title out of Fawcett's eighteen romance titles, and sadly, it was one of the thirteen unfortunate victims of the unprecedented culling of romance titles.[30] Though we know about the Love Glut in hindsight, its existence may have escaped comic-book-industry personnel in the trenches, such as *Negro Romance* editor Roy Ald. When asked about the series's end, he could not pinpoint why the comic was discontinued after only three issues. In his words, "It was selling. It was a hot thing at the time."[31]

When I was in Baltimore shooting the episode of *History Detectives*, I was a bit taken aback when the show's host asked me how and when *Negro Romance* "became" a white romance title. When Charlton purchased *Negro Romance* from Fawcett, only one additional issue was published, #4, as *Negro Romances*. Charlton had also purchased the Fawcett title *Romantic Secrets*. Instead of starting the new version over with issue 1, the numbering was continued from *Negro Romance/s*, giving the impression that *Negro Romance* suddenly transformed into a title featuring white characters. This continuation of numbering was done for two likely reasons, neither of which had to do with any uproar over Black characters. The first reason was to save money on obtaining a new second-class postal permit, and the second reason, perhaps more important for sales, was that it made the title seem more established to readers than it would have if it had started at #1.

Negro Romance was ahead of its time. The comic book was published during the Jim Crow era before the civil rights movement gathered full momentum and before the end of government-sanctioned school segregation. This series is significant in comics history because it normalized Black love in a popular-culture medium and gave a voice to the ideology of racial uplift. Revolutionary in many ways and filled with fashionable characters and romance at every turn of the page, this comic also points to the irony of how U.S. society was still heavily segregated. *Negro Romance* is an exception to most comics about nonwhite characters in the genre's early days. *Negro Romance* did not portray African Americans as oddities or as exotic, as they had been in earlier romance comics. *Negro Romance* was unusual in its presentation of exclusively Black characters, but simultaneously, it was the "same" as other romance comics published during this time. While *Negro Romance* did suffer the effects of the Love Glut, it perhaps happened just at the right time. As a pre-Code comic, it had the opportunity to express stories that were far more ahead of its time than later romance comics.

Fawcett had *Negro Romance* on newsstands long before the Kerner Report was published in 1968, advising media outlets to "integrate Negroes and Negro activities into all aspects of coverage and content, including newspaper articles and television programming. The news media must publish newspapers and produce programs that recognize the existence and activities of Negroes as a group within the community and as a part of the larger community."[32] With no official request from the government to have diverse characters, Fawcett, on its own, published this groundbreaking comic.

Unfortunately, romance comics did not suddenly drastically change after the publication of *Negro Romance*. It would have been fantastic if this series had changed things to include more diversity in the romance comic and comics in general, but unfortunately, this series was a one-off. It was not until the late 1960s and early 1970s that African Americans appeared on the pages of romance comics again with some frequency. Even then, many of the stories contained elements of stereotypes. Although Charlton published *Negro Romance* as a reprint, the publisher never made any further effort to publish romance stories with Black characters, whereas DC and Marvel did make attempts. Later in the 1970s, when publishers portrayed Black couples in romance comics, it was usually only on the cover or as secondary characters in the white protagonists' story line. Black characters were an afterthought and not the focus, as they briefly were in *Negro Romance*.

In the 1970s, DC Comics published a series of stories in its romance line recolored to feature African American characters. DC also ran a story line in 1971 called "Black + White = Heartbreak!" featuring the trials and tribulations of an interracial couple.[33] Perhaps the comic with the most similarities as far as featuring exclusively Black characters was Jack Kirby's unpublished *Soul Love*. Not since *Negro Romance* had any romance comic book series featured only characters of color. It is notable that while Kirby meant well, *Soul Love*, created more than twenty years after *Negro Romance*, relied on some linguistic stereotyping that has not aged well. While the entirety of *Negro Romance* was not produced by Black creators, the fact that some of the creators were Black, including Alvin Hollingsworth, makes this a unique comic book, when so few comics were created by people of color. Perhaps most importantly, *Negro Romance* demonstrated that love and romance were for *everyone*.

Notes

1. Tucker, "Love in the Comics."
2. PBS, "Civil War Letters, Aviation Fabric & African American Comic Book."
3. These examples of "perfect" womanhood were based primarily on white womanhood. There is little in the way of natural hair, and there is a lack of diversity in body shape (although feminine body shapes other than hourglass do not appear in the romance comics in general).
4. "Politics of respectability" was a term first described by the historian Evelyn Higginbotham in her book *Righteous Discontent* to explain how Black women of the early twentieth century were expected to behave in order to promote the elevation of Black culture and stave off stereotyping.
5. Unfortunately, cover models were not usually given any credits in the romance comics unless they were big movie or music stars.
6. "My Heart's Dilemma."
7. It is very likely that "Club Ebonia" in the comic is based on the real Club Ebony, which was located in New York City and featured dancers and other entertainment.
8. "True-to-Life Romances."
9. "New American Library."
10. Andrews, "Fawcett," 135–136.
11. Clancy and Ald, "'Is This What I Want to Do . . . ?': Part 2," 79.
12. Clancy and Ald, 79.
13. More information on Hollingsworth's early days as a young comic book artist can be found in Blair Davis's chapter 6 in this volume.
14. Clancy and Ald, "'Is This What I Want to Do . . . ?': Part 2," 79.
15. Clancy and Ald, 80.
16. Clancy and Ald, 78.
17. For a more detailed look at the controversy surrounding Fawcett and the character Steamboat, see Brian Cremins's chapter 10 in this volume.
18. PBS, "Civil War Letters."
19. Clancy and Ald, "'Is This What I Want to Do . . . ?': Part 2," 79.
20. According to the 1940 census, Palais was listed as white. His name is listed on the census as Rudolph Palis, and he is listed as a commercial artist. US Census Bureau, 1940 Census.
21. Clancy and Ald, "'Is This What I Want to Do . . . ?': Part 3," 78.
22. Harper and Laughlin, "I Wanted to Draw Comics," 105.
23. Smith, "4 Colorism."
24. Comic Book Plus, "Index Card/Additional Information for Negro Romance 2."
25. Amash and Tallarico, "You're Going into a Business," 29.
26. Clancy and Ald, "'Is This What I Want to Do . . . ?': Part 2," 79.
27. Overstreet, *Overstreet Comic Book Price Guide*, 833.
28. "Ed Bulleit Offers Comic Book List of Unobjectionables."
29. Nolan, *Love on the Racks*, 62.
30. Nolan, 73.
31. Clancy and Ald, "'Is This What I Want to Do . . . ?': Part 2," 79.
32. Kerner Commission, *Report of the National Advisory Commission on Civil Disorders*, 10.
33. Nodell, "Black + White = Heartbreak!"

An Afrofuturist Legacy

● ● ● ● ● ● ● ● ● ● ● ● ●

Neil Knight and Black Speculative Capital

JULIAN C. CHAMBLISS

> 25 YEARS AGO, JULY 16, 1955: Neil Knight, Black spaceman in the comic strips, uses a spear to kill a sabre tooth tiger on a prehistoric planet that he is stranded on.[1]

These lines from July 19, 1980, edition of the *New Pittsburgh Courier* are one of few cryptic references about Neil Knight that exist in the public record. Knight is arguably one of the first Afrofuturist comic book characters to appear in print, preceding Black Panther by sixteen years. In some ways, this should not be shocking. We have long established that African Americans consumed comic books, and the comics available on the newsstand from the 1940s, as the comic scholar Carol Tilley has noted, included "romance and horror and jungle comics and crime comics and supernatural stories, really just almost anything you could imagine."[2] Those comic books were a direct result of the transformative power of Superman's appearance in 1938. Yet, before that, it was comic strips that shaped our visual culture.

Foundational work on newspaper comics strips points to the racialized caricature that defines the media and calls our attention to the limiting effects of those images of African Americans and white ethnics in the first half of the twentieth century. Ian Gordon argues that comic strips were an "outcome of the process of modernization" and a "humor-based response to the problem of representation faced by a society in transition."[3] As Frances Gateward and John Jennings explain in *The Blacker the Ink: Construction of Black Identity in Comics and Sequential Art*, "comics traffic in stereotypes and fixity," which allows the reader to interact with the cultural messages in the medium all too easily.[4] Thus, the dominant cultural narrative around race is intertwined with the stories, characters, and settings offered in comics. As Rebecca Wanzo highlights, it is no "accident that caricature and scientific racism emerged in roughly the same period."[5] Building on a critical race theory approach that centers racial awareness in the appraisals of institutional inequality, the depiction of African Americans in comics becomes one way to understand how blackness is acted on in U.S. culture.[6] The logic of racial identity in the early twentieth century was unclear, despite the importance of white ethnic immigrants and Black people to visual popular culture. While racism placed Black people at the bottom of the racial hierarchy, most immigrants were not considered white.[7] The impact of the Great Migration brought thousands of African Americans to the urban North and created competition for jobs and housing that by default took on racial attributes. The Black enclaves that sprung up in major urban centers fed a transformation in U.S. culture that brought Black thought and artistry to the mainstream.[8] Despite this, African Americans could find an abundance of portrayals that reinforced the limited perception of Black ability and opportunity in a racist society throughout popular culture. For example, films such as *Gone with the Wind* (1939) romanticized antebellum slavery, and radio programs such as *Amos 'n' Andy* (1928–1943) offered predictable racial stereotypes.[9] In print, Richard Outcault's *Pore Lil Mose* began publication in 1900, providing a vision of a simple and childlike African American character that "lived in some version of an Arcadian paradise and wanted for nothing," affirming post-Reconstruction stereotypes of African Americans.[10] It was not until 1935 with Lothar, the manservant in Lee Falk's *Mandrake the Magician* newspaper strip, that an arguably *heroic* Black comic character appeared. While described as a "slave" and depicted as speaking simple English, he was incredibly powerful and became a central part of the Mandrake mythology. The Black comic book characters that emerged in the 1940s continued to operate within this pattern. Characters such as Ebony White, created by Will Eisner in *The Spirit* (1940), appeared as comedic sidekicks for the white heroes.[11] Within the context of the action and aims of the white characters, these Black figures can support white heroes. Yet the racial subtext of the broader society meant that they were never allowed to be fully realized as human beings.

A consideration of the long civil rights movement clarifies that African Americans understood the damage caused by the regressive images of blackness in popular culture. Qiana Whitted notes that resistance to consideration of race and equality stories in comics by white creators did not stop experimentation that recognized the changing racial landscape in the United States.[12] At the same time, African Americans protested racist caricatures in comic books and created alternative visions. *All-Negro Comics* (1947) demonstrated that Black creators could imagine fuller depictions of the Black experience. Created by Orrin C. Evans, the effort was short-lived but highlighted that African Americans could and did seek to push beyond the limits of what Claudia Rankine has termed the "racial imaginary." While white creators could and continue to work from a place of "transcendence" that frees them to explore, Black writers must "address" the subject experience to access any possible imaginary space.[13] While *All-Negro Comics* lasted one issue, it highlighted the appetite for more fantastic comic imaginary, which newspaper comic strips would achieve in the 1950s.

The 1950s marked a period of seemingly rapid racial transformation for the United States. Yet the reality of African American, women's, Asian American, Native American, and Latinx liberation as a central force working to reshape the American experience stretches back to the country's founding. As Paul Ortiz argues in *An African American and Latinx History of the United States*, "antislavery, anticolonial, pro-freedom and pro-working-class movements" came together in the United States against tremendous odds to advocate for more "democratic ways of living in the Americas."[14] Not surprisingly, he calls attention to the central role of African American newspapers as a tool advocating for freedom throughout the twentieth century. Ian Gordon notes that comics strips "in the United States were the product of a specific set of social relations that ripened in American cities" beginning in the 1890s.[15] Those narratives commodified and amplified white racism. Yet across various fields, Black newspapers were a critical space of counterstorytelling that saw the Black experience in the framework of anticolonialism and global solidarity seeking freedom.[16] Black newspaper cartoonists such as Ollie Harrington offered critical assessments of race paralleling civil rights activism. Harrington's *Dark Laughter*, first published in New York City's *Amsterdam News* in May 1935, chronicles everyday "trials and tribulations" linked to race in the United States.[17] Sheena Howard notes that Black newspaper comic strips "embodied the hopes and dreams of the cartoonists, the editorial heads in the newspapers that featured them, and middle-class African-Americans."[18]

Beyond the impact of political commentary, there can be little doubt that Black newspapers offered an essential space for extending the visual language around blackness and the vision provided to African Americans about their place in the visual culture of the United States. In particular, the *Pittsburgh Courier*, one of the largest Black newspapers, which claimed over a million coast-to-coast readers by the 1940s, was a crucial space for offering an alternative vision of blackness.[19] In particular, *Neil Knight*, which debuted as part of a new color comic section in the *Courier* on August 19, 1950, offered an essential vision of futurity rarely seen by Black readers. Yet placing Neil Knight in a broader context highlights his significance beyond merely being an early Black comic strip character. The *Pittsburgh Courier*'s new comic section, like *All-Negro Comics* before it, offered a counternarrative about blackness by depicting multiple genre stories with characters such as Guy Fortune, a secret agent; Mark Hunt, a private investigator; and The Chisholm Kid, a Black cowboy character. These choices emphasize that the *Courier* sought to normalize the depictions of African Americans in genres that dominated the mainstream marketplace. At the same time, these comics broke from the historical pattern of relying on "multipart stereotype" that justified depicting Black people as humorous and childlike, familiar in white newspaper depictions since the birth of the comic strips.[20] The scripts were published by the Smith-Mann Syndicate for the *Courier*, but their creative origins are obscure. However, Allan Holtz explains that the Smith-Mann *Courier* section is the "only such section ever to be attempted" for a Black newspaper. Smith-Mann was based in New York City and owned by Ben B. Smith and John J. Messmann.[21] *Carousel*, the name for the tabloid-size print insert, was designed to be syndicated to a "general group" of small newspapers as a four-color supplement. Ben B. Smith explained that Smith-Mann aimed to supply color comics to publications that previously could not afford it. The full supplement included eleven comics including "secret agent adventure, historical romance, private eye, fairy tale, jungle adventures, a page of puzzles and game and three 'fact' panels."[22] Both Smith and Messmann had a decade of experience in the comics industry, but Messmann had previously worked with the United Nations.[23] While there is no direct evidence that this shaped the decision to work with Black newspapers, it highlights that the syndicate's leadership had broader cultural experience that shaped their understanding of the potential audience for minority-owned newspapers.

The overall lack of archive consistency means we do not have information to expand on these points about Smith-Mann or access to most of the color supplements it produced.[24] What information we do have credits *Neil Knight* to "Carl and Mac." The Carl is probably Carl Pfeufer. Born in Mexico, Pfeufer grew up in the United States, graduating from Cooper Union High School. He first drew attention in 1935 with his work alongside Bob Moore in the *Brooklyn Daily Eagle*, drawing *Don Dixon and the Hidden Empire* and *Tad of the Tanbark*.[25] The writer for the script is unknown, but we can recognize that *Neil Knight* and the other comics signaled to *Courier* readers a commitment to challenging the systemic antiblackness linked to comic strips in white newspapers. Whether these newspaper comic strips were overtly political satire or escapist fantasy, their existence opened the door to a world not defined by Jim Crow segregation.

Neil Knight arguably speaks to speculative work's centrality as a kind of counterpublic practice. In the cultural critic Mark Dery's definition of Afrofuturism, he calls our attention to the fact that "African-American voices have other stories to tell about culture, technology, and things to come." For us to truly understand Afrofuturism, he stresses that we must seek Afrofuturism in "unlikely places" and "constellated from far-flung points." Ironically, Dery's reading of Afrofuturism relies heavily on a reading of comic books. Indeed, he says that Afrofuturism "percolates" through "black-written, black drawn comics" produced by Milestone Media.[26] We should not ignore Dery's concern for comics as definitional. In the merger of text and image, comics offer a speculative weight that serves as an archive of broader transformation linked to modernity. *Neil Knight* provides an opportunity to understand how a future Black vision was delivered to an African American reading public.[27] In framing *Neil Knight* in this fashion, I recognize that Afrofuturist practice has a greater scope in the Black experience. The theorist Reynaldo Anderson argues that Afrofuturism allows us to explore overlapping "tropes of science fiction, history, trauma, reparation and politic" in the service of transformation and liberation.[28] Moreover, an Afrofuturist framework allows us to see a cultural process that Kodwo Eshun describes as "recovering the histories of counter-futures created in a century hostile to Afrodiasporic projection."[29]

Afrofuturist art, according to Alondra Nelson, is a Black view on modernity that rejects the supposed erasure of race through technology. Instead, Afrofuturist artistic production is a space for the Black imagination to challenge whatever current political condition oppresses Black people and seeks liberation.[30] These ideas provide a robust framework to consider *Neil Knight* through character, story, and theme. The approach mirrors the efforts that Reynaldo Anderson offers in his essay titled "Critical Afrofuturism." In his consideration of visual rhetoric and Black identity in comics, Anderson stresses that Afrofuturism's critical mission "operates from a standpoint that intersects theories of time and space, technology, class, race, gender, and sexuality" and that these issues must be understood in relation to the production of the future.[31] The production process is central to envisioning, managing, and delivering "reliable futures" that contain expectations.[32] Famously, the science fiction vision of the 1950s omitted African Americans, creating a visual narrative in "historical stasis" and offering little positive movement for African Americans. As Adilifu Nama's examination of science fiction film emphasizes, the representation of race in science fiction is "weighed down by history, geography, and social location," emphasizing the limited white imagination about Black futures.[33] Whatever the origins of *Neil Knight*, it offered a vision of the future, projecting blackness into a speculative comic landscape where no one had gone before.

For all the space-faring adventure that characterized *Neil Knight*, the character's adventures were initially much more traditional. Advertisements for the forthcoming color comic section on August 5, 1950, describe Neil Knight as "Dashing Air Ace" on the front page of the *Pittsburgh Courier* (figure 14.1).[34] *Neil Knight* appears alongside nine other titles, including Jackie Ormes's *Torchy Brown* and Wilbert Holloway's *Sunny Boy Sam*. These early adventures were apparently inspired by the exploits of African American military pilots such as the Tuskegee Airmen. Unfortunately, most of these scripts were unavailable for analysis. Nevertheless, the choice to start *Neil Knight* with this focus is meaningful. This choice connected the character to the *Courier*'s wartime Double-V Campaign, which championed defeating fascism abroad and racism at home. Wilbert Holloway created the newspaper's logo for the campaign, establishing a link between Black wartime patriotism and comics that *Neil Knight* could quickly capitalize on.[35]

Scattered archival sources allow us to gain a feel for these earlier adventures. Adventures under the title *Neil Knight of the Air* published before 1954 show the dashing pilot character involved in an action-adventure tale

FIGURE 14.1 Carl and Mac, *Neil Knight of the Air*, August 5, 1950. (Copyright *Pittsburgh Courier*)

set in a post–World War II context. In one story, framed by a criminal called "The Trump," Knight must devise a way to overcome being wrongly accused and capture the drug-smuggling mastermind (figure 14.2). This story line presented Knight as a dashing Black hero, confronting a Black criminal gang. Knight is aided in his quest to clear his name and apprehend the crook by appealing to Rio, The Trump's girlfriend. Knight eventually overcomes the criminals, returning to the United States. While comic strips of this era often provided little space for female characters to have agency, Rio is self-aware and eventually sides with Knight, accepting his appeals to do the right thing. As they return to the United States from The Trump's South American hideout, she worries, "Maybe they won't believe your story! Maybe they'll put you in jail! We could turn back, Neil—land someplace and start

FIGURE 14.2 Carl and Mac, *Neil Knight* #142. (Copyright Museum of Uncut Funk)

a new life—together." Knight reassures Rio, telling her, 'They'll believe me, Rio—The Trump will talk! Turning back would just mean a life of constantly being hunted. And we'll be together you wait and see!"[36]

Knight's belief in the system seems to reject the reality of Jim Crow America. Yet, like many comic characters from this era, he affirmed what Bradford Wright describes as a general turn toward political containment in popular culture that forced even Black newspapers to affirm a pro-U.S. status quo. In the postwar years, comic books dedicated to war and romance highlighted the shifting geopolitics that emphasized the role the United States served as a global policeman. This shift placed Black media in the position of affirming the idea of fairness in the U.S. system, even as they were also critical of discriminatory actions and failure of government action to support Black rights.[37] Comic book publishers were forced to contend with the challenge of real-life racism by offering a vision of racial liberalism. African American newspapers mirrored these efforts. The long legacy of political engagement meant newspapers were invested in narratives that provided a context for Black Americans to orient themselves as citizens. This was no less true in the case of the cartoonists working for these newspapers. Whether overtly politically oriented, such as Ollie Harrington, or providing escapism, potential Black paths were experimented with through the comic page.[38]

Neil Knight's adventure tales were not dissimilar to those of his white counterparts, and that very ordinariness was political. However, the speculative practice on display here emphasizes counterstorytelling that rejected systemic antiblackness. As such, these early tales could be understood as Afrofuturist. While not "futurism" as envisioned by white readers, this take on modernity that affirmed a Black place in society reflects Alondra Nelson's assertion that Afrofuturism is a way to think about Black artistic production.[39]

By 1954, the strip's genre changed. Whether the result of the broader turn toward science fiction or some specific request was made, the postwar setting transformed into a more Buck Rogers–inspired set of adventures. This change offered a stark difference for established representation of African Americans in the era. A decade before the African American actress Nichelle Nichols appeared on *Star Trek* and before Samuel R. Delany, the first African American science writer to be named a Grand Master of the genre, published fiction, Knight offered a clearly science fiction narrative for the general public. It is here that the overt potential offered by an Afrofuturist reading can be best understood.

It is important to recognize that in making the change to this genre, the *Courier* is offering an important counternarrative about race in the future. *Buck Rogers*, created by Philip Francis Nowlan, captured many of the conventions of adventure fiction presented in the pulp genre of the previous decades. As Brooks Hefner writes, "Across various kinds of adventure fiction—domestic, foreign, or supernatural—pulp stories routinely dramatized the interplay between a dangerous non-white sexuality, an imperiled white femininity, and a heroic Anglo-Saxon masculinity."[40] The result was a popular landscape that made racial difference a threat overcome by white male power. *Neil Knight* offers a different fictive reality. If we view the change in genre beyond how it engaged with popular adventure literature, the decision to move *Neil Knight* into a space-themed adventure positioned African American masculinity in the positive light that Reynaldo Anderson associates with the emergence of Milestone Media in the 1990s. Yet *Knight*, appearing much earlier and situated in African American newspapers, was arguably free from the commodification of blackness that Anderson assigns to those comic book images in the 1990s.[41] Instead, *Neil Knight*'s space-age adventures offered a counternarrative that decentered Eurocentric visions of futurism by placing an African American hero in the center of the action. As Qiana Whitted notes in her analysis of EC Comics, graphic narrative could "use the speculative" to undermine racist assumptions and leverage visual media to explore "social identity, technology, and the idealization of progress." Whitted's analysis of the 1953 story "Judgment Day!" in *Weird Fantasy* #18 highlights how that story captured the "fear, anxiety, and hope" linked to the social transformation promised by civil rights activism.[42] *Neil Knight*'s action, the story, and the framework around power and liberation closely align with the progressive ideology associated with the era's civil rights narrative. As such, it offers an important means to understand how the intersection between speculation and liberation that is central to Afrofuturism was expressed through African diasporic people's concerns about oppression, discrimination, and modernity. Thus, while *Neil Knight*'s stories mirror popular space-adventure tropes, the character's agency in these stories speaks directly to Afrofuturist themes.

Knight's adventures center on the peaceful planet of Trinium, led by Kryz. Knight is drawn into Trinium's conflict with Sutanus, the leader of The Umbar. Described as "war-like" and illustrated with slight monstrous features, Sutanus seeks to invade Trinium and has begun setting a "space field" that will allow him to launch an invasion force. Knight aids in Trinium's defense by suggesting to Kryz a daring plan to destroy these staging fields: "One or two men could destroy The Umbars' space field before it really got started, that might be enough to discourage The Umbars from building any others."[43] In the scripts, Knight's interaction with the people of Trinium highlights his heroic persona. He urges them to fight against the aggressive threat presented by The Umbar. The Trinians are portrayed as peaceful and unwise in the ways of war. A sample of color scripts reveals that they were presented in green and brown hues and that the figures were drawn with a mostly human appearance. Kryz is concerned about protecting his people, and after Knight's success in destroying the Umbar base, Kryz meets with Sutanus to discuss peace.[44] Kryz, unaware that Sutanus hopes to capture him and his human ally (Knight) to further his agenda of conquest and striving to avoid conflict, walks into the trap.

While the aliens and potential space battle signal an opportunity for African Americans to see themselves in the 1950s futurescape, *Neil Knight* is linked to futurity in other ways. Afrofuturism emphasizes the intersection of speculative practice and liberation. Those ideas shape this story of a Black space-age hero struggling to protect Trinium from the expansionist/colonial impulse represented by The Umbar. While this idea might seem to align with emerging Cold War narratives emphasizing the United States' security position on a global stage, for Black readers, these stories can be interpreted through other frames. The motivation for the Umbar conquest is never fully understood beyond a desire to control. Yet, by placing a Black hero in the role of defender, the *Courier* gives its audience a dynamic that mirrors expansionist European powers and their aggressive action against indigenous people. Further, the Trinium society is oriented toward learning and peace, giving the African American reading public reason to see the story in the long tradition of a Black newspaper's editorial stance rejecting imperialism globally, reclaiming African American history and culture, and advocating for freedom domestically.

As the story progresses, Knight is further called on to protect Trinium when The Umbar kidnap Kryz's daughter, the princess Zana. Far from a traditional "damsel in distress," Zana is a solid and resourceful character motivated by concern for her people and willing to sacrifice herself to ensure Trinium's safety. Once Zana is captured by Sutanus's forces, Sutanus orders her held on Kranos, "The Scarlett Planet." With a seemingly doomed fate, Zana responds, "I am not afraid! I die knowing that Trinium is still a free planet."[45] Knight embarks on a rescue mission to save Zana, and once he is united with the princess, the two are captured. As prisoners, Knight and Zana work together to free themselves. Here the story is both familiar and surprising. While Knight lacks understanding of this alien world, his observation of the system and ability to think strategically allow him to gain the upper hand. At the same time, Zana's understanding of "common practice" in the alien world means that she is a crucial partner providing insight and information for Knight. Zana's concern with protecting her people and her willingness to resist oppressive forces in partnership with Knight highlight a central trait of Black feminist ideology connected to Afrofuturism.[46] Black women's concern about community places them in the position of promoting and supporting efforts around equity, often taking on the same danger as fathers, husbands, and sons. Throughout Knight's experience on Trinium, he uses an understanding of military tactics to aid the planet. Yet his technical know-how is thin. He is willing to rely on Zana's knowledge of technology and space-faring practice at crucial moments.

While this behavior is similar to adventure stories of the era, in the context of a Black comic character, it was unparalleled. Knight and Zana's experience calls attention to what Isiah Lavender describes as the interconnection between science, technology, and race that he defines as at the core of Afrofuturism's narrative practice addressing the risk and possibilities linked to industrial capitalism.[47] Neil Knight's escapist space adventures also speak to concerns about imperialism and the struggle for freedom as central to the vision of Afrofuturism as Black narrative practice. In comics form, these ideas are given added weight as Knight's humanity and willingness to aid others mark him as an example of the imagined society for African Americans in the post–World War II United States. This story offered a vision of an inclusive citizenship in a future-oriented narrative. Such assumptions took up long-established narratives linked to global freedom struggles. Unspoken but implied in this fictive world is that an inclusive society would, in the future, be the source of liberatory action. Knight continues to aid Trinium, culminating in his devising a plan to stop the Umbar invasion. Relying on his knowledge of military tactics from Earth, he organizes the planet's defense, and the Trinium ships fight off the invading Umbar.[48]

While the defeat of the Umbar marks the end of the dangers for Trinium, Knight's space adventure continues. The story quickly evolves as Kryz takes Knight to the "Astro-Tower" to show him a new planet discovered by Ryd, a Trinium scientist.[49] While Knight does not understand the excitement about the planet, Ryd explains, "This new planet was thrown off by one of the huge suns or stellar constellations and is now undergoing the process to become a living planet!" As a result, Knight sees an opportunity as the planet "would be like Earth many millions of years ago!" Knight, aware of the possibility for scientific advancement, muses, "If I could explore such a planet and take bits of material from it, it could tell scientists back home so much about the beginning of the Earth. It could prove or disprove so many, many theories!"[50] This determination sends Knight on a new adventure exploring this unknown planet, even though Ryd warns Knight that the planet is cooling at an accelerated rate and that it might explode at any moment.

Neil Knight's adventures on the planet he dubs "New Earth" occupy the script from June 5, 1954, to October 1, 1955. Driven by a sense of discovery, Knight explores the "new" planet, marveling at similarities to Earth in its prehistoric age (figure 14.3). However, after Knight struggles to find a place to land his spacecraft on the "unevenly cooling" world, he immediately becomes involved in several altercations that pit his skill and bravery against the danger of a prehistoric planet.[51] His challenges in these adventures include being almost trampled by a brontosaurus and being chased by a tyrannosaurus. In escapist storytelling similar to pulp adventures from previous decades, Knight's motivation to use this planet's primordial state to teach scientists on Earth more about its past is the strongest defining element of these adventures. While that motivation sets Knight on his adventures, it is quickly forgotten as he is faced with more and more creatures to overcome and dangers to avoid. In the course of the experiences on "New Earth," Knight loses his weapon and becomes disoriented and unsure how to get

An Afrofuturist Legacy • 293

FIGURE 14.3   Carl and Mac, *Neil Knight*, June 12, 1954. (Copyright *Pittsburgh Courier*)

back to his spaceship. The challenge of finding a way back to his ship allows for the writer to continue to place Knight in one cliffhanger adventure after another. Eventually, Knight encounters "cavemen" whom he teaches how to "fashion spears and make fire" before finally finding his way back to his ship.[52] Rocketing off on another adventure, Knight leaves "New Earth," only to be caught by magnetic forces on another planet. The last script we have access to shows Knight's ship being approached by an army of small robots. While the next moment of that adventure is not clear, what *Neil Knight* provided to African American readers in the 1950s is easier to understand.

Neil Knight and the other comic strips of the *Pittsburgh Courier* were a clear alternative to the negative depiction of Black people familiar to mainstream white culture in this period. Starring a science fiction adventure character, *Neil Knight* is the earliest example of Afrofuturism in newspaper comic strips. Like other Afrofuturist comics, Knight's adventures offered a space of counterstorytelling about blackness and the future that was impossible for a Black reader to find in other places.

The presence of *Neil Knight* in the pages of the *Pittsburgh Courier* highlights the recovery of what Kodwo Eshun describes as "counter-futures," which serve as tools of intervention that disrupt the assumed narrative of futurity that erases Black people.[53] The counterstorytelling offered by *Neil Knight*, as a newspaper comic strip, disrupted the vision of future whiteness.

It signaled the reality of possible Black futures that were progressive and transformative. The transgressive politics in *Neil Knight* emphasize questions of community, agency, and power that foreshadow the independent voices that would soon change blackness across media in the United States. The legacy of adventure represented by this character emphasizes the potential futures central to African Americans' ability to survive and thrive.

Notes

1. Ransom, "Black History."
2. S. Thomas, "Carol Tilley."
3. Gordon, *Comic Strips and Consumer Culture*, 6.
4. Gateward and Jennings, *Blacker the Ink*, 2.
5. Wanzo, *Content of Our Caricature*, 4.
6. Wanzo, "It's a Hero?," 316.
7. Jacobson, *Whiteness of a Different Color*.
8. Osofsky, *Harlem*.
9. E. Scott, "Regulating 'Nigger'"; M. Scott, "From Blackface to *Beulah*."
10. Gordon, *Comic Strips and Consumer Culture*, 65.
11. Eisner, *Will Eisner's "The Spirit" Archives*, vol. 1.
12. Whitted, *EC Comics*, 7.
13. E. Thomas, "Notes toward a Black Fantastic," 283–284 (quoting Rankine).
14. Ortiz, *African American and Latinx History of the United States*, 1.
15. Gordon, *Comic Strips and Consumer Culture*, 10.
16. S. Nelson, *Black Press*.
17. PBS, "Oliver Wendell Harrington."
18. S. Howard, "Brief History of the Black Comic Strip," 13.
19. Goldstein, "Trouble with Romance in Jackie Ormes's Comics," 24.
20. Gordon, *Comic Strips and Consumer Culture*, 60.
21. "Smith-Mann Syndicate Contribute to EE Campaign," 4.
22. Knoll, "Smith-Mann to Launch Comics Supplement."
23. Knoll.
24. Holtz, "Comics of the Smith-Mann Syndicate."
25. "Something for the Youngsters," 19.
26. Dery, "Black to the Future," 182.
27. Many thanks to Matthew Sanders and Matt Shindell from the Smithsonian National Air and Space Museum for collecting and sharing copies of the *Neil Knight* strips from 1954 to 1955.
28. Anderson, interview by Tiffany Pennamon.
29. Eshun, "Further Considerations of Afrofuturism," 301.
30. Alondra Nelson, "Introduction," 1.
31. Anderson, "Critical Afrofuturism," 183.
32. Eshun, "Further Considerations of Afrofuturism," 289.
33. Nama, "R Is for Race, Not Rocket," 156–157.
34. "In Your New Color Section," 1.

35 Holtz, "Ink-Slinger Profiles"; NAACP, "World War II and the Post War Years."
36 Carl and Mac, "Neil Knight #142," *Pittsburgh Courier*, date unknown (ca. 1950–1955).
37 Wright, *Comic Book Nation*, 109–111.
38 Davenport, "Blowing Flames into the Souls of Black Folk," 118–119.
39 "Afrofuturism Defined by Alondra Nelson."
40 Hefner, "Signifying Genre," 487.
41 Anderson, "Critical Afrofuturism," 174.
42 Whitted, *EC Comics*, 106–107.
43 Carl and Mac, "Neil Knight," *Pittsburgh Courier*, date unknown (ca. 1950–1955).
44 Carl and Mac, "Neil Knight," *Pittsburgh Courier*, date unknown (ca. 1950–1955).
45 Carl and Mac, "Neil Knight," *Pittsburgh Courier*, date unknown (ca. 1950–1955).
46 Morris, "Black Girls Are from the Future," 153–154.
47 Lavender, *Afrofuturism Rising*, 2–3.
48 Carl and Mac, "Neil Knight," *Pittsburgh Courier*, March 20, 1954.
49 Carl and Mac, "Neil Knight," *Pittsburgh Courier*, May 1, 1954.
50 Carl and Mac, "Neil Knight," *Pittsburgh Courier*, May 8, 1954.
51 Carl and Mac, "Neil Knight," *Pittsburgh Courier*, June 5, 1954.
52 Carl and Mac, "Neil Knight," *Pittsburgh Courier*, June 18, 1955.
53 Eshun, "Further Considerations of Afrofuturism."

"For They Were There!"

• • • • • • • • • • • • • •

Dell Comics' *Lobo* and the
Black Cowboy in American
Comic Books

MIKE LEMON

Notwithstanding historical records that indicate the presence of African American cowboys and ranch hands in the western United States, they are largely excluded from the American Western myth. The "Wild West" constitutes a mythic space and geographical location and is largely coded as white, heterosexual, and male. Even when scholars note the multiplicity of Western myths, they must admit, like Mary Lawlor, that these myths "are versions of a will to cultivate non-European space in Euro-American terms."[1] Beginning in the mid-twentieth century to today, history, literary, and cultural scholars have sought to reposition the Black western experience within the American Western myth. Cultural artifacts, such as literature, dime-store novels, minstrel/Western shows, music, television, and film, offer multifaceted and at

297

times paradoxical representations. As Michael K. Johnson has argued, scholars must "reconsider a restricted notion of the literary text and be more open to the discovery of the full richness of the ways the African American West has been experienced, imagined, written, represented, and performed."[2] It is thus important for scholars of the American West to investigate the Black frontier experience and its multifaceted cultural representations. Curiously, though, comic books that depict the Black Western frontier have not received much scholarly attention. However, these cultural artifacts constitute another medium that scholars may analyze to determine how collaborative teams—often composed of writers, artists, colorists, letterers, and editors—imagine, write, and represent the Black Western experience.

Recent graphic novels and comic books have repositioned the Black cowboy into their textual and visual narratives, but arguably Don Arneson and Tony Tallarico's 1965 Dell Comics serial *Lobo* was one of the first. The series follows a former Union soldier who goes out west to become a cowboy. Framed for murder, he deals out justice and protects the innocent. In a brief analysis, Qiana Whitted has argued that *Lobo* demonstrates the variance within cowboy characterizations "that can extend beyond the genre's predilection for clear-cut moral distinctions."[3] For Whitted, this allows readers to perceive Lobo as a heroic Black badman. While this analysis focuses on the moral qualifier in this character, *Lobo* also expands the cowboy archetype to emphasize race. Notwithstanding the series's limited run, it proved revolutionary in portraying a Black male character as participating in the American Western myth, albeit in ways that signal the myth's racial construction. Moreover, Arneson and Tallarico include other Black and Brown characters in supporting roles that challenge Western stereotypes. By analyzing the collaborative team's complicity in and challenges to the Western myth, I argue that while Arneson and Tallarico do not evoke race as a thematic concern within the series, they cannot erase its effects on the comic's textual and visual components or the way it informs Lobo's experiences as a cowboy and Western fugitive.

Dell Comics and *Lobo*'s Place in the 1960s Comics Industry

Before examining the comic's images and texts, I want to provide some background information on *Lobo* and its publisher, Dell Comics. Dell had been a successful publisher in the 1940s and '50s, with licensing agreements to

Walt Disney characters and other series that were marketed as kid and family friendly.[4] Bill Jennings also notes that Dell produced a variety of series across multiple genres.[5] N. F. Ambery observes that "in 1953 Dell was said to have sold 26 million comic books per month," with help from its licensed adaptations of *Get Smart*, *Dark Shadows*, and *Mission Impossible*.[6] Jean-Paul Gabilliet further explains that in 1954, Dell accounted for just under 14 percent of the market; by the end of the decade though, Dell found itself struggling to compete with DC and Marvel.[7] By the 1960s, Dell had lost many, although not all, of its licensed properties; an advertisement page in *Lobo* issue 2 includes comics for *The Beverly Hillbillies*, *Alvin and the Chipmunks*, *Bewitched*, *Mighty Mouse*, and *F-Troop*.[8] Perhaps by not investing too heavily in superhero series, the publisher did not anticipate readers' shifting taste. However, Diana Green has argued that the explosion of spaghetti Western films led to a reinvestment in Western comics series.[9] It is within this context that other Western titles were reintroduced, including Atlas/Timely/Marvel's *The Rawhide Kid* and *Kid Colt*, as well as Dell's licensed publication for *The Lone Ranger*. Lobo as a character and series was created during this time of renewed interested in Western media. Dell published *Lobo* in 1965.

As to the character's creation, there exists the standard controversy of attribution for Silver Age characters: the artist and writer have conflicting perspectives on who originated Lobo and why the series was canceled. The illustrator Tony Tallarico claims that he approached Don Arneson with the character: "[Arneson] brought it in and showed it to [Dell's editor in chief] Helen Meyer."[10] Tallarico's language suggests that the artist created an illustration for the character. Green confirms Tallarico's story, identifying him as the creator.[11] The writer Don "DJ" Arneson disputes this account. In a 2010 interview, he claims that as an editor and writer at Dell, he oversaw new character development. He contends that after reading Philip Durham and Everett L. Jones's *The Negro Cowboy*, he "recognized the potential for a black comic book hero based on historical fact; the Buffalo Soldiers, the name given American Union soldiers in the American Civil War."[12] While he concedes that Tallarico drew up a mock-up, Arneson couples this illustration with the writer's proposal and background information. While there exist multiple origin myths for the character, it proves important to remember that *Lobo* arises from a collaborative effort from Arneson and Tallarico. However, the character and its initial run proved short-lived. Of its initial two hundred thousand print order, only fifteen thousand copies were sold.[13] Arneson has contended that low sales—not Lobo's race—were the primary reason for the series's cancellation; however, he does leave room for the possibility that race could be a factor.[14] Tallarico is a little more forceful in his evocation of race as a motivating factor for *Lobo*'s cancellation. He has called the distributors "prejudiced bastards."[15]

Making Theoretical Space for *Lobo* in the Whitewashed West

Given *Lobo*'s multimodal construction through words and pictures, the following analysis considers how textual and visual components function within a racially encoded white narrative to present the Black Western experience. The graphic novelist and theorist Will Eisner has argued that mid-twentieth-century sequential storytellers often used "certain stereotypical images [to] retain a national character."[16] Cowboys in comic books function as stereotypical national images in this manner; for the American reader, the visual presentation of a man on horseback or a duel on Main Street conjures up the Western myth. For Whitted, the audience's perceptions of cowboys as socially responsible, morally incorruptible, and ruggedly individualistic play into the mid-twentieth century's American values.[17] These images, though, are often coded as white experiences. Literary critics, historians, and media scholars have long noted the metaphysical West's colonial and racialized construction. Nina Silber contends, "In the imagination, and sometimes in the actions, of late-nineteenth-century Americans, the West has become a splendid and mystical place for the development and enhancement of national character."[18] While literature and Hollywood media portrayals of the West include minority characters, including Native Americans, Hispanics, Chinese immigrants, and African Americans, these characters are often reduced to supporting roles. The protagonist is often white and male, reinforcing what Amy Kaplan has argued, that the Western myth "forged the ideology of white masculinity."[19]

The mythic West as a white masculine space can be seen in two comic book contemporaries of *Lobo*: *Kid Colt Outlaw* and *The Rawhide Kid*. *Kid Colt* was first published in August 1948, by Atlas Comics. In the first issue, readers are led to believe that Blaine Colt does not fit into the Western hero type, because he does not carry guns. As a corrupt deputy says, "C'mon ya gunless squirt... start somethin'! Haw, haw! Yore ol' man mus' be proud of his yeller-bellied son, who's skeered to wear shootin' irons like a man!"[20] Failure to enact violence is a mark of shame for white Westerners; Colt's father seconds these sentiments during a conversation with his son. However,

Blaine Colt has an innate knack for firearms but refuses to wear them because of his temper. When he does take possession of his father's revolvers, Kid Colt shows remarkable talents, far exceeding other trained gunmen. Moreover, the issue's editor—most likely Martin Goodman—includes an insert, reminding readers that the six-shooters, with which Colt shares a name, "civilized the West . . . against deadly reptiles, coyotes, cougars and timber wolves as well as wolves in human form."[21] While the last item in the list suggests cattle rustlers, it could also suggest Mexican bandidos and Indigenous tribes. *The Rawhide Kid* also plays into this white masculine Western myth. Although the character first appeared in a 1948 publication by Atlas, Stan Lee and Jack Kirby reintroduced him in August 1960 with an updated backstory. Johnny Bart is a young man who must avenge his adopted father, the ex-Ranger Ben Bart. Like Kid Colt, Johnny shows a knack for firearms, goes by a nickname, and is framed for crimes he has not committed. Furthermore, the Rawhide Kid embodies a code that he, Kid Colt, and other Western heroes seemingly abide by: to use their training to root out corruption and protect the innocent.[22] In these two instances, Kid Colt and Rawhide Kid exemplify the narrative points, talents, and moral code for white Western heroes. They join a large body of characters whose racialized white Western myth has permeated U.S. culture and cultural and literary criticism; this saturation seemingly stands at odds with Johnson's assertion that there exists a "richness of the field of available" literary and historical texts, music, film, and television produced by African American artists.[23]

Comic books, whether published by European American, African American, or transnational collaborative teams, become another avenue for understanding how the Black Western experience complies with or challenges the Western myth. Arneson and Tallarico, in developing their Black cowboy protagonist, must have understood the power of the Western myth and perhaps knowingly created narrative and visual layers that challenge the myth's racial construction. In Arneson's retelling of *Lobo*'s origin, he states, "The comic brought in elements of the American Cowboy archetype. . . . The concept of the black cowboy soldier was enough for me. It had all the elements of adventure that would appeal to a 12-year old."[24] Certainly crafting a Western would attract adolescent readers, but in developing the series around a Black protagonist, the collaborative team must contend with the racialized Western myth in the script and panels. In the United States, racial caricatures also function within national culture, albeit in ways that Marc Singer argues have multiple meanings. Using a Bakhtinian approach, he argues "that comics might heteroglossically incorporate the ideological assumptions of the imagery they draw upon."[25] Because of the medium's multimodal construction, comics can exhibit multiple perspectives. On a textual level, writers and letterists can play with conventional tropes, inviting the reader to see layers within standard tropes. Moreover, artists can include heteroglossic images into their visual narrative; doing so permits readers to reconsider how imagery reinforces or challenges stereotypes.

Taking a heteroglossic approach to the comic's images and text, readers can identify moments when the collaborative team affirms and expands the Western myth to include Lobo. On a visual level, Bryant Keith Alexander has identified similar practices as he analyzes images of Black cowboys. He asserts that these images are composed differently than images of white cowboys, because they are "maybe staged to document the presence of being, the function of engagement, and the documenting of a reality not always represented in the filmic renditions of Westerns and the Old West; working Black cowboys."[26] *Lobo* as a visual-textual document contains comparable documentation patterns. Its first issue provides a visual argument for Arneson's implied claim: that African American cowboys existed and should have their legends told. Presenting the African American cowboy experience in *Lobo* recalls Blake Allmendinger's argument that "'black' Westerns obey the same formulas as traditional Westerns. At the same time, they depart from tradition by introducing racial themes and prominent minority characters."[27] Through *Lobo*'s textual and visual components that invoke conventions within the cowboy myth, Arneson and Tallarico disrupt readers' expectations, starting with the cover and opening splash page.

Complicating the Cowboy Myth

From the cover and opening splash page of *Lobo* #1, the comic exemplifies how Arneson and Tallarico accept and expand the Western myth to include Lobo. Under the title, the main character stands in a dueling stance, his gun drawn. Behind his right arm and shoulder is an enlarged "Wanted" poster, affirming the text: "BRANDED FOR LIFE! An honest man ... blamed for a crime HE DID NOT COMMIT!"[28] Lobo's posture suggests that this new character actively participates in the Western myth. In this, Tallarico seemingly disrupts Alexander's claim that images of Black cowboys often do not engage in standard representations of the Old West. Instead, this enlarged image and two smaller images—Lobo on horseback and engaged in a showdown—insert the main character into the dominant national character.

"For They Were There!" • 303

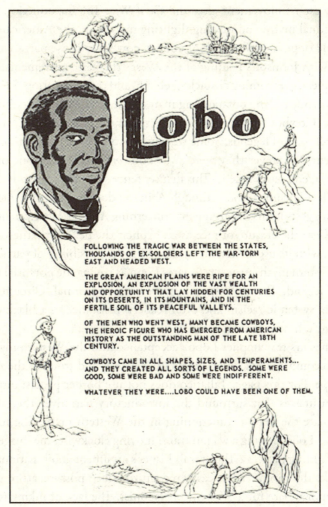

FIGURE 15.1 The opening splash page for *Lobo*. (Arneson and Tallarico, *Lobo* #1, 1)

These smaller insets reaffirm Lobo's position within the myth; however, Tallarico's use of shadow begins to trouble a simplistic reading of the visual narrative. The smaller images obscure the main character's race; readers must identify Lobo through his blue shirt. But the enlarged image firmly establishes Lobo as Black. Doing so arrests readers' attention, because Tallarico has used standard heroic postures for cowboys for Lobo; doing so begins an expanded Western narrative.

The opening splash page further confirms the collaborators' heteroglossic approach to the Western myth (figure 15.1). Arneson positions Lobo within western movement after the Civil War. The introduction follows conventional mythic points, highlighting migration, the American Plains, economic opportunities, and, of course, cowboys. These narrative points overlap with Johnson's reading of the West's thematic movements, including conquest, overcoming obstacles, rebirth, and transformation.[29] Referring to the cowboy as "the outstanding man of the late 18th century," Arneson explains, "Cowboys came in all shapes, sizes, and temperaments . . . and they created all sorts of legends. Some were good, some were bad and some were indifferent. Whatever they were . . . Lobo *could* have been one of them" (*Lobo* #1, 1; emphasis added). This first sentence seemingly expands the cowboy myth to include Lobo, although Arneson does not mention race. Such a move suggests Johnson's argument concerning African American literature of the West: the erasure of race as an explicit theme.[30] Yet Arneson's final thought, with its use of "could," again opens the possibility of participating in the Western myth. Arneson situates Lobo as having the potential to enter cowboy legend. This potential, however, is conditional. Circumstances, including systemic racism and even readers' resistance to a Black cowboy protagonist, hinder his entrance.

If Arneson's text implies Lobo's acceptance into the Western myth, Tallarico's accompanying artwork explicitly expands and troubles the national stereotype. For this page, Tallarico does not use border panels; instead, he has open images that surround the introductory narrative. These illustrations situate the hero as functioning in the Western myth. The top open image has Lobo chasing a wagon train: moving clockwise, the images evoke his gunfighting prowess. They recall Eisner's argument about national influences; like the cover, readers easily recognize Lobo's posture, attire, and setting as appropriate for a Western protagonist. The lack of inking for these images also seemingly obscures Lobo's racial identity. However, the page's most arresting image proves the most challenging to the cowboy myth: the close-up image of Lobo's face. Tallarico positions this image just left of the title, confirming to readers that this Black cowboy is the series's protagonist. Unlike the other images, Tallarico inks the man's face to announce his race when he shades in his brown skin. With this coloration, the image attracts readers' attention; the following pages allow Arneson and Tallarico to position Lobo in the historical and mythic West.

Lobo's journey follows a conventional cowboy narrative that emphasizes the African American presence in the West. Readers follow an unnamed Union soldier as he journeys out west. Arneson includes dialogue that suggests that Lobo was probably never enslaved. After learning of the Civil

War's end, he says, "After four years of being a soldier, I am a free man again! A free man!!" (*Lobo* #1, 2). This information seems oddly ambiguous, especially considering one of the most popular African American Western narratives, *The Life and Adventures of Nat Love*, emphasizes Love's journey from slave to cowboy in ways that erase race as a central theme.[31] Perhaps in this dialogue, Arneson wants to focus the narrative less on the possibility of Lobo's previous enslaved status. Instead, he might be opting to suggest the Western myth's emphasis on freedom and individualism, at the expense of the conventional narrative surrounding mid-nineteenth-century African American men. With the possibility of having never been another man's property, this unnamed Black soldier exemplifies the necessary qualities to become a Western hero.

The next narrative sequence further situates Lobo in a Western myth, while also inserting a trope from slave narratives. While Lobo basks in his newly ensured freedom, a group of Confederates open fire on him and his regiment. With five dead and the protagonist almost killed, Lobo surveys the carnage. In a large panel, Tallarico places Lobo, with his one visualized eye closed, slightly off center to the left; in the middle and background, men lay dead (*Lobo* #1, 3). In the next panel, Tallarico uses a close-up scale to show readers Lobo's opened eyes (*Lobo* #1, 4). Although there is no dialogue, this visual sequence reveals the character's sadness, anger, and resolve. In the following panels, Lobo smashes his rifle, declaring, "No one should have died here today ... not now, not when the war is finished" (*Lobo* #1, 4). In this instance, Lobo does not eschew all violence; like other Western heroes, he signals a strong moral code. He does not glory in excessive violence; however, he will use violence to protect the innocent. Moreover, readers can read Lobo's decision within the trope of the "slave on the road." As summarized by Whitted, this trope allows authors of slave narratives to demonstrate their virtue "by adhering to a higher standard of behavior."[32] While the still unnamed protagonist's Black companions place the violence within the scope of war—they are soldiers—he rejects this rationalization. He reiterates that they are free, and because he is done with fighting, he will leave. Again, this signals Lobo's independence and couples it with his self-control. After leaving his unit, he eventually joins a cattle drive headed to Abilene, Kansas (*Lobo* #1, 9). This places him on the Chisholm Trail, participating in large-scale overland drives from Texas to Kansas.

A four-panel sequence serves as a montage showing Lobo's transformation into a cowboy (figure 15.2). Already an accomplished horseman from his time in the war, he soon becomes adept at lassoing and branding. An

FIGURE 15.2 The former soldier's transformation into a cowboy. (Arneson and Tallarico, *Lobo* #1, 9)

off-panel spectator marvels at his progress, stating, "Never saw anybody catch on so quick" (*Lobo* #1, 9). Like earlier assertions of Lobo's freeman identity, his talents make him a prime candidate for a Western hero. Like his white counterparts, this man acclimates to the work naturally. These panels also encapsulate Lobo's shifting identity in ways that mirror Western narratives. Arneson does not provide his character's name, so others—and even Lobo himself—identify the man by his occupation. At various times, others refer to him as "soldier," "stranger," "cowboy," and finally "Lobo." In refusing to name the protagonist, Arneson and Tallarico emphasize a standard trope in Westerns: the use of nicknames to identify cowboys. Like Owen Wister's *The Virginian*, this unnamed man becomes branded by his actions. Similarly, Lobo's fluid identity affirms a classic narrative convention: rebirth and transformation. Many Western authors, notably European American ones, render the American West as a regenerative space. Jane Tompkins argues that the mythic West becomes "a locale and set of circumstances that expand [men's] meaning, endow them with an overriding purpose, and fill them with excitement."[33] Lobo's lack of name does not diminish him; on the contrary, his new abilities and sense of purpose as a cowboy have rejuvenated him. In a coda to the issue's training sequence, Lobo says to his horse, "Well, Midnight. Maybe you and I have found some peace after all" (*Lobo* #1, 9). The bottom-left panel situates the man within an integrated crew. Tallarico's illustrations again provide images and postures that confirm Lobo's transition into a cowboy. Lobo's inclusion here maintains and redefines the cowboy lore, reclaiming African Americans' active presence on the trail.

Moreover, Arneson and Tallarico include a rival cowboy, Smoker, who is a person of color. While some panels ink him as African American, other panels show a lighter complexion that could signal Smoker's ethnicity as Hispanic or possibly Indigenous.[34] The inconsistency is further complicated with the production team's decision to place Smoker in shadows for most of the issue. This also highlights technological limitations in mid- to late twentieth-century comic book printing; as Zoë Smith has pieced together, poor color fidelity for Brown characters comes down to limited color choices, paper selections, and cheap, letterpress processes. For Brown and Black characters, this means that there was not "any way to consistently produce the color brown."[35]

Notwithstanding inconsistency with color fidelity in this issue, Lobo and Smoker announce the presence of cowboys of color on the cattle-drive crew. By depicting Lobo and Smoker, Arneson can present his readership with his newly acquired knowledge about Black cowboys. Moreover, the collaborative team participates in Quintard Taylor's challenge to "the stereotype of the black westerner as a solitary figure."[36] Scholars have various estimates for how many Black cowboys operated during the mid- to late nineteenth century. Durham and Jones propose five thousand; Kenneth W. Porter claims eight to nine thousand.[37] Taylor disputes these early claims as exaggerations and argues that Black cowboys constituted 2 percent of cowboys, stock raisers, and drovers.[38] Peter A. Howard estimates that "more than seven thousand black or mixed black cowboys worked the thousands of miles of trails stretching from Texas to the Dakotas."[39] Bruce A. Glasrud posits in his introduction to *Black Cowboys in the American West* that "at least five thousand African Americans worked and operated as black cowboys in the years beginning with 1866."[40] While there remain disputes on the number of operating Black cowboys, Porter has argued, after analyzing surviving lists for cattle-drive outfits, that "[African Americans] out-numbered Mexicans by more than two to one—slightly more than 63 percent white, 25 percent [African American], and slightly under 12 percent Mexican."[41] By providing at least two African American characters, Arneson and Tallarico suggest the presence of a larger percentage of Black cowboys.

On the drive, Arneson and Tallarico downplay racial animosity in favor of perceived unity. When the crew makes it to Abilene, Kansas, Tallarico depicts Lobo and Smoker entering a saloon with their white colleagues. There is seemingly no racial prejudice. Arneson reinforces the perception from the saloon owner's perspective. In a panel that places him and a saloon girl in the foreground, the owner looks at the cowboys in shadow. He remarks, "Looks like dry customers, May. Drovers don't stick with their pay very long" (*Lobo* #1, 10). The next panel shows Lobo and his companions drinking at the bar. When it comes to money, the saloon owner makes no racial distinction. Taylor makes a similar claim about Dodge City, Kansas's long history of tolerance, and the influx of money from Black drovers.[42] Allmendinger further contends that until frontier locations became secure, African Americans encountered minimal de facto or de jure racism.[43]

Such readings of the West outwardly suggest that race did not factor in the Black cowboy's experience; however, prejudice persisted on the trails. Notwithstanding Taylor's assertions of forged bonds on the long trail, he also notes the use of racial epithets to distinguish African American drovers on drive rosters.[44] Howard argues that even with the "particular intimacy" that these multiracial crews developed, "there [existed] two certainties regarding a black cowboy's opportunities regarding his role in the crew: he would almost never be appointed trail Boss, and he would likely serve a lengthy 'apprenticeship' as a wrangler."[45] In the narrative of *Lobo* #1, Lobo falls between these two certainties. He does not become the trail boss, but he does not have a long apprenticeship. Returning to the heroic cowboy tropes, Lobo's natural abilities allow him to sidestep some prejudice. However, Lobo's role as the protagonist necessitates moments in which he encounters racism, expanding the traditional Western to include race as a central concern for Lobo's journey to becoming a Western fugitive hero.

The River and the Rope

Notwithstanding the presence and participation of *Lobo*'s African American character in cattle drives, he encounters racial stereotyping that creates tension between the egalitarian mythic "West" and persistent prejudice in the physical American West.[46] The collaborative team introduces this tension through a panel sequence for the character's departure to the West (figure 15.3). The first panel announces to readers Lobo's intentions; as if directly speaking to the audience, he expresses his desire to "ride someplace that doesn't stink of killing" (*Lobo* #1, 5). Tallarico's imagery in the top-right panel shows Lobo mounted on his horse; this posture again suggests this unnamed man's place within the West. The backlighting also obscures the man's race, suggesting the myth's egalitarian conventions. All these visual cues imply that in making the decision to venture out west, Lobo has effectively situated himself within the Western's mythic space.

The bottom-left panel, though, interrupts the Western myth and reinserts Lobo in the United States' racial system. In this panel, Arneson and Tallarico

FIGURE 15.3 Before entering the mythic West, systemic racism forces Lobo to pay in advance. (Arneson and Tallarico, *Lobo* #1, 5)

insist that readers understand that race will impact Lobo's entrance into the physical—and, by extension, the mythic—West. In a panel composed in long scale, a river operator tells the unnamed soldier the cost to ford the river, pausing before demanding the price "in advance" (*Lobo* #1, 5). Arneson's use of an ellipsis is not uncommon; throughout the issue, he uses this device for dramatic effect. Its use here takes on racial significance. Even though Tallarico again obscures Lobo's and the operator's faces with shadow, the operator's inked left hand depicts him as white. The image and visuals seemingly suggest that the man is operating under racial prejudice. The panel's placement also suggests that readers must read how Lobo encounters race before he escapes out west.

This sequence's final panel depicts Lobo backlit by moonlight. Again, Tallarico relies on posturing and landscapes to signal a mythic West. Arneson's borderless caption confirms this move: "An ex-private and a Reb general's horse . . . bought for a sack of flour after a bitter struggle of war and turmoil. Thousands of men headed west. There, on the frontier, a man could start fresh, free from the memories of the past and free to be judged by what he could do . . . and nothing else" (*Lobo* #1, 5). Like the visual narrative, the text returns readers to the egalitarian West, with its promise of freedom and rebirth. Arneson even provides the horse's ironic provenance. On top of a Confederate general's horse, Lobo will seek freedom from prejudice in the mythic West. However, the preceding panel's racially tinged scene and Arneson's final ellipsis demonstrates impending tension. The previous panel's proximity does not give readers room to distance the operator's actions from the next panel's evocation of the West. The two become juxtaposed. The narrative's ellipsis also discomforts. Lobo is "free to be judged by what he could do," which is the promise of the conventional cowboy narrative. However, the pause foreshadows that "nothing else" is not the case.

While overt racial prejudice does not completely disappear from the issue's depictions of the cattle trail, Western conventions and racial violence overlap in complex ways, especially as the Black protagonist moves from cowboy to fugitive. Finding his crew dead and the drive's profits stolen, Lobo is confronted by Smoker and Ace, a white villainous counterpart. Tallarico uses a long-panel format for this scene: Lobo is in the foreground, crouching with his hand close to his gun, while the two villains are in the background. As Lobo protests his innocence, the other cowboys discuss "trail justice," a Western form of extralegal violence (*Lobo* #1, 14). Given Lobo's race, it is difficult not to recognize explicit connections between trail justice and lynching, indicating an uncomfortable truth in Western comics: the disregard for Black, Brown, or Indigenous bodies. This initial confrontation places the villains in shadows and seemingly suggests that Smoker's agency within this violence is limited. After all, Ace tells him to get the rope.

Subsequent panels, however, introduce an uncomfortable realization: Smoker actively desires Lobo's lynching. The protagonist overpowers his would-be assailants—an act that earns him the moniker "Lobo." In this panel, Tallarico reverses the composition. Ace and Smoker are in the foreground, sitting on the ground tied up, and Lobo is walking into the background. From this sitting position, Smoker calls out, "That rope'll find him. No wolf ever run free for long" (*Lobo* #1, 15). This comment is complicated. On one level, it proves Smoker's villainy, firmly rooting him as a black hat within the Western narrative. On another level, it implicates Smoker in inciting racial violence against another Black body. Notwithstanding Lobo's claim to innocence, Smoker would willingly harm him, and when Smoker cannot perform physical violence, he spreads accusations that could lead to Lobo's death. Unfortunately, these rumors are enough to warrant a reward for Lobo's arrest. By being framed, Lobo enters another character archetype shared by Kid Colt and the Rawhide Kid: the wrongly accused noble man who fights for justice outside the law.

But by introducing this trope, *Lobo*'s creative team develop a heteroglossic approach to the cowboy narrative, starting with Lobo's nickname. While creative teams eventually reveal Kid Colt's and Rawhide Kid's real names and origins, readers never learn Lobo's true name. Instead, he is linked to a crime. Moreover, his nickname animalizes the man negatively. Lobos—wolves—were systematically eliminated from the American West. They are even included in the list of predatory animals that Kid Colt's signature guns removed from the West. Lobo accepts this name, while simultaneously recognizing its mark. He tells Smoker and Ace, "If I'm a lobo, it was forced on me" (*Lobo* #1, 15). Here, the man who becomes Lobo acknowledges how this nickname functions like his skin color. His innocence does not matter; his complexion and nickname are enough to brand him guilty. While he works outside the law to prove his innocence, Lobo is the perpetual "slave on the road," meaning that his self-control and high moral code cannot overcome the racial prejudice that marks him.

Issue 1's closing panel again affirms Arneson and Tallarico's complex approach to Lobo's Black Western experience (figure 15.4). In Arneson's concluding remarks, he drives home the story's stakes. Of the thousands

FIGURE 15.4 *Lobo* #1's closing panel. (Arneson and Tallarico, *Lobo* #1, 33)

who ventured to the West, he argues, "many were legends in their own time . . . Many weren't remembered at all . . . But some deserve the recognition they earned. Men like Lobo don't deserve to be forgotten . . . *for they were there*!" (*Lobo* #1, 33). Arneson wants his readers to carve out space within their conceptions of the American West to remember men like Lobo. The emphasis on "for they were there" reveals Arneson's intentions; having read Durham and Jones's book, the writer wants to highlight Black cowboys. Coupled with history and legend, Arneson's closing narrative positions Lobo as a cowboy and noble outlaw. Tallarico's image also supports

Lobo's Western legend. Viewers look up toward the protagonist astride his horse on a rocky bluff, which are drawn from a low angle. Tallarico has the sun behind Lobo, recalling earlier panels in which the character is backlit. Like those previous panels, the hero's posture and Tallarico's angles confirm Lobo's mythic figure. Unlike those earlier images, the use of shadow here reads differently. While preceding visuals had shadows that obscured racial distinctions to promote the West's egalitarian myth, Arneson's text influences the visual reading of this closing image. Instead of obscuring blackness, Tallarico reinforces Lobo's blackness. Not only were Black men and women in the American West, but they deserve a spot in the mythic American West.

Reframing Lobo's Legacy

In analyzing issue 1 of *Lobo*, we cannot ignore the effects that race has on Arneson and Tallarico's textual-visual presentation of the Western narrative, although they seemingly abandoned race as an implied theme by the second issue. Throughout the first issue, the collaborative team evokes and challenges the Western's racial and narrative stereotypes. Arneson and Tallarico situate Lobo and other African American characters in the myth at varying levels of agency. Their doing so reintroduced mid-twentieth-century readers to the multiethnic American West, where African Americans worked alongside Anglo- and Mexican Americans. By the second issue, Arneson and Tallarico downplayed Lobo's race. Published ten months after the first issue, "The King of West" in *Lobo* #2 demonstrates the collaborative team's shift toward conventional Western tropes. Arneson's introductory recap focuses heavily on Lobo's new mission: "to help bring justice to the lawless plains ... ever seeking justice for himself and those like him."[47] Emphasizing justice downplays the character's race, instead making Lobo similar to other (i.e., white) cowboy fugitive heroes. This recalls Whitted's discussion of 1950s Western heroes; the reading public perceives them as moral heroes. Artistic decisions regarding other characters' race also minimize the first issue's discussion of prejudice. Other than Lobo, there is one other character of color in the second issue, a Latina named Maria. Readers will identify Maria's race through Tallarico's use of a darker complexion as well as her exoticized dress. Readers only learn of her past that she is held against her will by the issue's villain, the "King." Maria, then, serves a minor narrative role within the issue; she is a damsel in distress for Lobo to save.

Another narrative point underscores how far the collaborative team distanced the series from discussions of race in issue 2. To discredit Lobo, the "King" orders his men to commit various crimes, so they can frame the falsely accused fugitive. The crimes invoke the West: rob a bank, shoot cattle, steal a saddle. But rather than have a henchman don blackface, the main villain fashions a series of fake Lobo coins, in imitation of a gold coin that Lobo uses to mark his presence. The panel sequences confirm this ploy; for each committed crime, the following panel has a character holding one of the fake coins. These follow-up panels recall the first issue's discussion of implied guilt through rumor. Admittedly, Tallarico includes a white hand in two crime panels, reminding readers that Lobo is not responsible. Perhaps a reader could interpret these panels as suggesting race. However, the emphasis on crimes associated with the Old West and the exclusion of more characters of color lead readers to interpret these scenes through the conventions of the traditional Western. These scenes read as less about race and more about Lobo's status as the heroic fugitive. With only two issues, the first run of *Lobo* leaves readers with mixed textual and visual messages regarding themes of race within Arneson and Tallarico's Western comic that might threaten the series's legacy. While the first issue provides foundations for including inquiries into Black experiences on the trail, the second issue largely abandons those questions in favor of a conventional Western narrative.

Including questions of race within a standard Western comic arguably becomes *Lobo*'s lasting legacy. Ambery observes in his interview with Arneson that Durham and Jones's *The Negro Cowboy* and the 1960s civil rights movement compelled the Dell editor and writer to create *Lobo*.[48] With the series's cancellation, it seems the Silver Age character would not have a legacy. He might be forgotten like those thousands of Black cowboys that Arneson wanted to elevate to cultural memory. Yet *Lobo* still has a presence today. Tallarico received the Pioneer Award from the East Coast Black Age of Comics Convention in 2006.[49] Arneson was recognized by the same organization a few years later.[50] And even though *Lobo*'s copyright elapsed, a new company has released a *Lobo* comic. Starting in 2017, InDELLible Comics has reintroduced the character in several media: three comics anthologies and a collection of novellas. In "Colors," the collaborative team of Dave Noe, Robert Schaupp, Kevin Halter, and Derick Gross Sr. do not elide race from their twenty-first-century reimagining of the character. Instead, prejudice underscores threats of violence, as Lobo contends with two desert robbers. Race becomes a central thematic concern for Lobo;

"For They Were There!" • 315

FIGURE 15.5 Robert Schaupp's redesign for *Lobo* (2017). (Copyright InDELLible Comics)

not surprisingly, Schaupp's character design for Lobo recalls Jaime Foxx's Django from *Django Unchained* (figure 15.5). With increased scholarly attention on Western texts, movies, and music that validate the Black Western experience, it only seems fitting that writers and artists are returning to comics to challenge the Eurocentric Western myth. And fortunately, *Lobo* has returned too.

Notes

1. Lawlor, *Recalling the Wild*, 3.
2. M. Johnson, *Hoo-Doo Cowboys and Bronze Buckaroos*, 5.
3. Whitted, "Blues Tragicomic," 245. Among newspaper comic strips, *The Chisholm Kid* is the first Western comic to feature a Black cowboy as the title character. Created by Carl Pfeufer, the strip was published in the *Pittsburgh Courier* from 1950 to 1956.
4. Andrews, "Dell," 101.
5. B. Jennings, "Dell Comics," 202.
6. Ambery, "Woodbury Man's Comic Book."
7. Gabilliet, *Of Comics and Men*, 45, 55.
8. Arneson and Tallarico, *Lobo* #2, 1.
9. D. Green, "Westerns," 849.
10. Tallarico, quoted in Bias, "Lobo—Black in the Saddle."
11. D. Green, "Westerns," 849.
12. Arneson, quoted in Ambery, "Woodbury Man's Comic Book."
13. D. Green, "Westerns," 849.
14. Arneson, quoted in Ambery, "Woodbury Man's Comic Book."
15. Tallarico, quoted in Coville, "Lobo Creators Interview."
16. Eisner, *Graphic Storytelling and Visual Narrative*, 74.
17. Whitted, "Blues Tragicomic," 244. See also Savage, *Comic Books and America*, 72.
18. Silber, *Romance of Reunion*, 187.
19. Kaplan," Romancing the Empire," 661.
20. Hart, Walsh, and Shores, *Kid Colt Hero of the West*, 3.
21. Hart, Walsh, and Shores, 13.
22. Lee and Kirby, *Rawhide Kid*, 10.
23. M. Johnson, *Hoo-Doo Cowboys and Bronze Buckaroos*, 5.
24. Arneson, quoted in Ambery, "Woodbury Man's Comic Book."
25. Singer, "'Black Skins' and White Masks," 109.
26. Alexander, "Writing/Righting Images of the West," 230.
27. Allmendinger, *Imagining the African American West*, xvii.
28. Arneson and Tallarico, *Lobo* #1, cover. Subsequent references are cited parenthetically in the text.
29. M. Johnson, *Hoo-Doo Cowboys and Bronze Buckaroos*, 10.
30. M. Johnson, 9–10.
31. M. Johnson, 10.
32. Whitted, "Quentin Tarantino's Slave on the Road."
33. Tompkins, *West of Everything*, 12.
34. A panel of *Lobo* #2 that depicts Smoker as African American is on page 15. Panels that depict him with a lighter, caramel complexion are on pages 6 and 7. On page 8, there is another panel that gives Smoker a gray, ashen tone.
35. Smith, " 4 Colorism," 348.
36. Taylor, *In Search of the Racial Frontier*, 22.
37. Durham and Jones, *Negro Cowboys*, 8; Porter, "Black Cowboys in the American West," 112.
38. Taylor, *In Search of the Racial Frontier*, 158. See also 340–341n51.
39. P. Howard, "Black Cowboys," 289.
40. Glasrud, "Don't Leave Out the Cowboys!," 10.
41. Porter, "Black Cowboys in the American West," 112.

42 Taylor, *In Search of the Racial Frontier*, 160.
43 Allmendinger, *Imagining the African American West*, xiii.
44 Taylor, *In Search of the Racial Frontier*, 160.
45 P. Howard, "Black Cowboys," 290.
46 M. Johnson, *Hoo-Doo and Bronze Buckaroos*, 12.
47 Arneson and Tallarico, *Lobo* #2, 2.
48 Ambery, "Woodbury Man's Comic Book."
49 Coville, "Lobo Creators Interview."
50 Ambery, "Woodbury Man's Comic Book."

Acknowledgments

I began writing notes for this book over a decade ago. The research for the five chapters of an earlier monograph resulted in the first of many trips to the archives at the Schomburg Center for Research in Black Culture in Harlem, the Newspaper & Current Periodical Reading Room in the Library of Congress, and the Comic Arts Collection at Virginia Commonwealth University. In a fantastic turn of events, one of the proposed chapters on EC Comics took over and became its own monograph. Other career opportunities (and a second beautiful baby) slowed my progress even further, but I returned in fits and starts, eager to see the original project succeed. Along the way, I also began to meet and talk with other comics studies scholars—at conferences, at invited campus lectures, and through social media—who were doing incredible work in the same archives and deliberating over research questions that complemented my own. I am grateful for those long and enthusiastic conversations for leading me to the realization that this book would work best as a collective effort. I want to express my sincere thanks to the fifteen contributors for agreeing to lend their time and expertise to this book, even in the midst of a global pandemic. I am incredibly proud to be joined by scholars at every rank, including outside the academy, whose critical perspectives reveal important new insights in our understanding of race, popular culture, and comics history. I appreciate their willingness to exchange drafts and share resources and advice and their being patient with me during the process.

Special thanks are due to Brian Cremins, who, along with his brilliant essay, contributed an extra set of eyes and always had time to bounce around ideas. Thanks also to Brannon Costello, Rebecca Wanzo, Julian Chambliss, Andy Kunka, and Jonathan W. Gray for their advice at various stages of the project. I can't express my appreciation enough to Nicole Solano at Rutgers University Press for her guidance and enthusiastic advocacy. I am grateful to the editorial board, design, and marketing teams at Rutgers, to the anonymous peer reviewers, and to Andrew Katz and David Prout for their outstanding work. Thank you to the University of South Carolina's African American Studies and English departments and to the College of Arts and Sciences for generously supporting this research, as well as the librarians and archivists in the Gary Lee Watson Comic Book Collection at the USC Thomas Cooper Library. And as always, my love and thanks to my family: Alex, Naima, and Kenny, who led the way inside the first comic book store that I ever visited in the early '90s and has been by my side ever since.

Bibliography

Adair, Torsten. "We Are Not in a 'Golden Age' of Comics." *The Beat: The Blog of Comics Culture*, October 15, 2019. https://www.comicsbeat.com/we-are-not-in-a-golden-age-of-comics/.

Adoff, Arnold, ed. *Black Out Loud: An Anthology of Modern Poems by Black Americans*. New York: Macmillan, 1970.

"Afrofuturism Defined by Alondra Nelson." YouTube, 2010. https://www.youtube.com/watch?v=IFhEjaal5js&feature=youtu.be.

Aldama, Frederick Luis, ed. *Multicultural Comics: From Zap to Blue Beetle*. Austin: University of Texas Press, 2011.

Alexander, Bryant Keith. "Writing/Righting Images of the West: A Brief Auto/Historiography of the Black Cowboy (Or 'I Want to Be a (Black) Cowboy'... Still)." *Cultural Studies / Critical Methodologies* 14, no. 3 (June 2014): 227–231. https://doi.org/10.1177/1532708614527554.

Allen, Derotha Fields. "The Leisure Time Activities of a Selected Group of Negro Girls." Master's thesis, University of Southern California, 1949.

Allmendinger, Blake. *Imagining the African American West*. Lincoln: University of Nebraska Press, 2005.

Amana, Harry. "The Art of Propaganda: Charles Alstons World War II Editorial Cartoons for the Office of War Information and the Black Press." *American Journalism* 21, no. 2 (April 2004): 79–111. https://doi.org/10.1080/08821127.2004.10677582.

Amash, Jim. "We Considered [Comics] an Art Form." *Alter Ego* 3, no. 91 (January 2010): 3–21.

Amash, Jim, and Tony Tallarico. "You're Going into a Business That Requires People to Be Dressed with Ties." *Alter Ego* 107 (February 2012): 28–44.

Ambery, N. F. "Woodbury Man's Comic Book Has Impact Long after Its Creation." *Litchfield County Times*, October 14, 2016. http://www.countytimes.com/l_c_t_monthly/woodbury-man-s-comic-book-has-impact-long-after-its/article_0eef4972-b77b-5c4a-8ede-d64a80f8f86b.html.

Amirand, Eyal. "George Herriman's Black Sentence: The Legibility of Race in Krazy Kat." *Mosaic* 33, no. 3 (September 2000): 57–79.

Andelman, Bob. *Will Eisner, a Spirited Life*. Milwaukie, OR: M Press, 2005.
Anderson, Reynaldo. "Critical Afrofuturism: A Case Study in Visual Rhetoric, Sequential Art, and Postapocalyptic Black Identity." In *The Blacker the Ink: Constructions of Black Identity in Comics and Sequential Art*, edited by Frances Gateward and John Jennings, 171–192. New Brunswick, NJ: Rutgers University Press, 2015.
———. Interview by Tiffany Pennamon. January 20, 2020. Voice 45455. Voices of the Black Imaginary Collection, G. Robert Vincent Voice Library, MSU Libraries, Michigan State University, East Lansing, MI.
Andrews, Henry. "Dell." In *Comics through Time: A History of Icons, Idols, and Ideas*, edited by M. Keith Booker, 100–101. Santa Barbara, CA: Greenwood, 2014.
———. "Fawcett." In *Comics through Time: A History of Icons, Idols, and Ideas*, edited by M. Keith Booker, 135–136. Santa Barbara, CA: Greenwood, 2014.
"Announcement No. 2." *The Colored American*, April 20, 1901, 8.
Armitage, Shelley. *Kewpies and Beyond: The World of Rose O'Neill*. Jackson: University Press of Mississippi, 1994.
Arneson, Don, and Tony Tallarico. *Lobo* #1 (December 1965).
———. *Lobo* #2 (October 1966).
Arnold, Andrew. "Never Too Late: Interview with Will Eisner." *Time*, September 19, 2003. http://content.time.com/time/arts/article/0,8599,488263,00.html.
"Artists Portray a Black Christ." *Ebony*, April 1971.
Austin, Allan W., and Patrick L. Hamilton, eds. *All New, All Different? A History of Race and the American Superhero*. Austin: University of Texas Press, 2019.
Ayres, Jackson. "When Were Superheroes Grim and Gritty?" *Los Angeles Review of Books*, February 20, 2016. https://lareviewofbooks.org/article/when-were-superheroes-grim-and-gritty/.
"Backstage." *Ebony*, May 1946.
Baetens, Jan. "Revealing Traces: A New Theory of Graphic Enunciation." In *The Language of Comics: Word and Image*, edited by Robin Varnum and Christina T. Gibbons, 145–155. Jackson: University Press of Mississippi, 2001.
Bails, Jerry. "Who's Who of American Comic Books 1928–1999." Jerry Bails's website, October 18, 2006. http://www.bailsprojects.com/whoswho.aspx.
Baker, Matt. *Matt Baker: The Art of Glamour*. Edited by Jim Amash and Eric Nolen-Weathington. Raleigh, NC: TwoMorrows, 2012.
Baraka, Amiri. *The Autobiography of LeRoi Jones*. Chicago: Lawrence Hill Books, 1984.
———. *S O S: Poems, 1961–2013*. New York: Grove, 2016.
Barnett-Aden Collection, The. Washington, DC: Anacostia Neighborhood Museum / Smithsonian.
Barr, Mike W. "Letter to the Editor." In *The Spirit* #6, 5. New York: Warren, 1975.
Barrier, J. Michael. *Funnybooks: The Improbable Glories of the Best American Comic Books*. Oakland: University of California Press, 2015.
Barrow, John. "Here's a Picture of Emmett Till Painted by Those Who Knew Him." *Chicago Defender*, October 1, 1955, National ed.
Barson, Michael. *Agonizing Love: The Golden Era of Romance Comics*. New York: Harper Design, 2011.
Bartkowski, John P. "Claims-Making and Typifications of Voodoo as a Deviant Religion: Hex, Lies, and Videotape." *Journal for the Scientific Study of Religion* 37, no. 4 (December 1998): 559–579. https://doi.org/10.2307/1388141.
Bateman, John A., Francisco O. D. Veloso, and Yan Ling Lau. "On the Track of Visual Style: A Diachronic Study of Page Composition in Comics and Its Functional Motivation."

Visual Communication 20, no. 2 (May 2019): 209–247. https://doi.org/10.1177/1470357219839101.

Bearden, Romare. "Caught in the Tentacles Again." *Baltimore Afro-American*, September 12, 1936.

———. "Lincoln Freed the Slaves in 1863?" *Afro-American*, December 19, 1936.

———. "The Negro Artist and Modern Art." In *The Romare Bearden Reader*, edited by Robert G. O'Meally, 87–90. Durham, NC: Duke University Press, 2019.

———. "The Negro Artist's Dilemma." In *The Romare Bearden Reader*, edited by Robert G. O'Meally, 91–98. Durham, NC: Duke University Press, 2019.

Beaty, Bart. *Comics versus Art*. Toronto: University of Toronto Press, 2012.

Beauchamp-Byrd, Mora. "Alvin C. Hollingsworth." In *Encyclopedia of Black Comics*, edited by Sheena C. Howard, 118–120. Golden, CO: Fulcrum, 2017.

Becattini, Alberto. "Baker of Cheesecake: An Appreciation of Matt Baker, Good Girl Artist Supreme." In *Matt Baker: The Art of Glamour*, edited by Jim Amash and Eric Nolen-Weathington, 36–37. Raleigh, NC: TwoMorrows, 2012.

Becattini, Alberto, and Jim Vadeboncoeur Jr. "The Matt Baker Checklist: An Annotated Index of Matt Baker's Professional Work." In *Matt Baker: The Art of Glamour*, edited by Jim Amash and Eric Nolen-Weathington, 68–93. Raleigh, NC: TwoMorrows, 2012.

Beito, David T., and Linda Royster Beito. "Selling Laissez-Faire Antiracism to the Black Masses: Rose Wilder Lane and the *Pittsburgh Courier*." *Independent Review*, 2010.

Bendis, Brian Michael. Foreword to *Fagin the Jew*, by Will Eisner, 1–2. Milwaukie, OR: Dark Horse Comics, 2013.

Benson, John. "Having Something to Say: Interview with Will Eisner." In *Will Eisner: Conversations*, edited by Will Eisner and M. Thomas Inge, 8–23. Jackson: University Press of Mississippi, 2011.

Berrey, Stephen A. *The Jim Crow Routine: Everyday Performances of Race, Civil Rights, and Segregation in Mississippi*. Chapel Hill: University of North Carolina Press, 2015.

Berry, Daina Ramey. *The Price for Their Pound of Flesh: The Value of the Enslaved from Womb to Grave in the Building of a Nation*. Boston: Beacon, 2017.

Best, Mark. "Domesticity, Homosociality, and Male Power in Superhero Comics of the 1950s." *Iowa Journal of Cultural Studies* 6, no. 1 (2005): 80–99. https://doi.org/10.17077/2168-569X.1126.

Beware #16. New York: Trojan Magazines, July 1953.

Bias, Aaron. "Lobo—Black in the Saddle Again." *Silver Age Gold: The Sheer, Giggly Joy of Silver Age Comics* (blog), February 3, 2010. http://aquamanrules.blogspot.com/2010/02/lobo-black-in-saddle.html.

Bivens, Sarah Lean. "A Comparative Study of the Reading Interests of the Fourth and Fifth Grade Pupils of the Risley Elementary School, Brunswick, Georgia, and the Fourth and Fifth Grade Pupils of Sterling Consolidated School, Glynn County, Sterling, Georgia, 1953–1954." Master's thesis, Atlanta University, 1954.

Blue Beetle #42. New York: Fox Feature Syndicate, July–August 1946.

"Bluford Library Archives: Garrett Whyte '39—Muralist and Civil Rights Cartoonist." North Carolina A&T Alumni in the News, April 26, 2021. https://ncatsualumni.org/bluford-library-archives-garrett-whyte-39-muralist-and-civil-rights-cartoonist/.

Bogle, Donald. *Toms, Coons, Mulattoes, Mammies, and Bucks: An Interpretive History of Blacks in American Films*. Updated and expanded 5th ed. New York: Bloomsbury Academic, 2016.

Bordo, Susan. "It's Not the Same for Women." *Chronicle of Higher Education*, December 13, 2015. www.chronicle.com/article/Its-Not-the-Same-for-Women/234535?cid=cp20.

Boskin, Joseph. *Sambo: The Rise and Demise of an American Jester*. New York: Oxford University Press, 1986.
Brewster, Linda. *Rose O'Neill: The Girl Who Loved to Draw*. Princeton, IL: Boxing Day Books, 2009.
Brooks, Daphne. *Bodies in Dissent: Spectacular Performances of Race and Freedom, 1850–1910*. Durham, NC: Duke University Press, 2006.
Brooks, Kinitra Dechaun. *Searching for Sycorax: Black Women's Hauntings of Contemporary Horror*. New Brunswick, NJ: Rutgers University Press, 2018.
Brown, Jayna. *Babylon Girls: Black Women Performers and the Shaping of the Modern*. Durham, NC: Duke University Press, 2008.
Brown, Jeffrey. *Black Superheroes, Milestone Comics, and Their Fans*. Jackson: University Press of Mississippi, 2001.
Brown, Jim. "Letter to the Editor." In *The Spirit* #5, 5. New York: Warren, 1974.
Brown, Karen McCarthy. *Mama Lola: A Vodou Priestess in Brooklyn*. Berkeley: University of California Press, 2010.
Brunner, Edward. "'Shuh! Ain't Nothin' to It': The Dynamics of Success in Jackie Ormes's Torchy Brown." *MELUS: Multi-Ethnic Literature of the United States* 32, no. 3 (September 1, 2007): 23–49. https://doi.org/10.1093/melus/32.3.23.
———. "'This Job Is a Solid Killer': Oliver Harrington's Jive Gray and the African American Adventure Strip." *Iowa Journal of Cultural Studies* 6, no. 1 (2005): 36–57. https://doi.org/10.17077/2168-569X.1124.
Bukatman, Scott. *Hellboy's World: Comics and Monsters on the Margins*. Oakland: University of California Press, 2016.
Bunie, Andrew. *Robert L. Vann of the "Pittsburgh Courier": Politics and Black Journalism*. Pittsburgh: University of Pittsburgh Press, 1974.
Burgas, Greg. "What Should We Call This Age of Comics?" *Comic Book Resources* (blog), May 5, 2012. https://www.cbr.com/what-should-we-call-this-age-of-comics/.
Burgos, Carl, Bill Everett, Joe Simon, Bill Harr, Maurice Gutwirth, George Kapitan, Jack Kirby, Basil Wolverton, Stan Lee, and Otto O. Binder. *Marvel Firsts: WWII Superheroes*. New York: Marvel Comics, 2013.
Burshtein, Karen. *Walter Dean Myers*. New York: Rosen, 2004.
Buszek, Maria-Elena. "Representing 'Awarishness': Burlesque, Feminist Transgression, and the 19th-Century Pin-Up." *TDR / The Drama Review* 43, no. 4 (December 1999): 141–162. https://doi.org/10.1162/105420499760263606.
Caldwell, H. Zahra. "'I Was Anti-Everything': Cartoonist Jackie Ormes and the Comics as a Site of Progressive Black Journalism." *American Studies* 59, no. 3 (2020): 99–120. https://doi.org/10.1353/ams.2020.0027.
Cámara Arenas, Enrique. "Villains in Our Mind: A Psychological Approach to Literary and Filmic Villainy." In *Villains and Villainy: Embodiments of Evil in Literature, Popular Culture and Media*, edited by Anna Fahraeus and Dikmen Yakah Çamoğlu, 3–28. Amsterdam: Rodopi, 2011.
Campanella, Roy. *It's Good to Be Alive*. Lincoln: University of Nebraska Press, 1995.
Campbell, Eddie. *The Goat Getters: Jack Johnson, the Fight of the Century, and How a Bunch of Raucous Cartoonists Reinvented Comics*. San Diego, CA: IDW, 2018.
Carpenter, Stanford. Introduction to *Invisible Men: Black Artists of the Golden Age of Comics*, by Ken Quattro, 7–8. San Diego, CA: Yoe Books, 2020.
Carpio, Glenda R. *Laughing Fit to Kill: Black Humor in the Fictions of Slavery*. New York: Oxford University Press, 2008.
"Cartoon Feature, The." *Colored American*, April 27, 1901.

Cascone, Charles S. "Letter to the Editor." In *The Spirit* #8, 5. New York: Warren, 1975.
Chireau, Yvonne. "Looking for Black Religions in 20th Century Comics, 1931–1993." *Religions* 10, no. 6 (June 2019): 400–417. https://doi.org/10.3390/rel10060400.
Christopher, Tom. "Orrin C. Evans and the Story of *All-Negro Comics*." *Comics Buyer's Guide*, February 28, 1997. http://www.tomchristopher.com/?op=home%2FComic+History%2FOrrin+C.+Evans+and+The+Story+of+All+Negro+Comics.
Chude-Sokei, Louis Onuorah. *The Last "Darky": Bert Williams, Black-on-Black Minstrelsy, and the African Diaspora*. Durham, NC: Duke University Press, 2006.
Chute, Hillary L. *Disaster Drawn: Visual Witness, Comics, and Documentary Form*. Cambridge, MA: Harvard University Press, 2016.
Clancy, Shaun, and Roy Ald. "'Is This What I Want to Do for the Rest of My Life?': The Roy Ald Interview, Part 2." *Alter Ego* 3, no. 105 (October 2011): 78–80.
———. "'Is This What I Want to Do for the Rest of My Life?': The Roy Ald Interview, Part 3." *Alter Ego* 3, no. 106 (December 2011): 76–80.
Clifton, Lucille. *The Book of Light*. Port Townsend, WA: Copper Canyon, 1993.
Coates, Ta-Nehisi. *Between the World and Me*. New York: Spiegel and Grau, 2015.
Cohn, Neil. *The Visual Language of Comics: Introduction to the Structure and Cognition of Sequential Images*. London: Bloomsbury Academic, 2013.
Collins, Max Allan. *For the Boys: The Racy Pin-Ups of World War II*. Portland, OR: Collectors, 2000.
Comic Book Plus. "Index Card/Additional Information for Negro Romance 2." September 15, 2015. https://comicbookplus.com/?dlid=58739.
Comic-Con International. "Orrin C. Evans." Hall of Fame. Accessed November 12, 2022. https://www.comic-con.org/awards/hall-fame-awards?page=3.
Cooksey, Magnolia. Interview by Stanley Nelson. In *American Experience: The Murder of Emmett Till*, part 2. WGBH Educational Foundation, 2017. https://video.alexanderstreet.com/watch/interview-with-magnolia-cooksey-classmate-2-of-2.
Costello, Brannon, and Qiana Whitted, eds. *Comics and the U.S. South*. Jackson: University Press of Mississippi, 2012.
Couch, N. C. Christopher. "The Human Spirit." In *The Will Eisner Companion: The Pioneering Spirit of the Father of the Graphic Novel*, edited by N. C. Christopher Couch and Stephen Weiner, 19–26. New York: DC Comics, 2004.
Coville, Jamie. "The History of Comic Books." *The Comic Books*, August 15, 1996. http://www.thecomicbooks.com/old/index.html.
———. "Lobo Creators Interview—DJ Arneson & Tony Tallarico." *Jamie Coville* (blog), August 17, 2016. http://jamiecoville.com/blog/blog/2016/08/17/lobo-creators-interview-dj-arneson-tony-tallarico/.
Crane, Walter. *Line and Form*. London: George Bell and Sons, 1900.
Crawford, Phillip. "My Noose around That Pretty's Neck." Accessed June 5, 2021. https://www.philipac.com/my-noose-around-that-prettys-neck.
Cremins, Brian. *Captain Marvel and the Art of Nostalgia*. Jackson: University Press of Mississippi, 2017.
———. "You've Got to Be Yourself! Why You Should Read Fawcett's Jackie Robinson Comics." *Alter Ego* #168 / *Fawcett Collectors of America* #227, March 2021.
Cremins, Brian, and Harlan Ellison. "'Nay, Never Will I Serve Thee, Mr. Mind' or, 'I Think I Was a Fawcett Kid': An Interview with Harlan Ellison." *Alter Ego* #138, March 2016.
Crime Does Not Pay #31. New York: Lev Gleason, January 1944.
Crimes by Women #2. New York: Fox Feature Syndicate, August 1948.
Crimes by Women #5. New York: Fox Feature Syndicate, February 1949.

Crist, Judith. "Horror in the Nursery." *Collier's*, March 27, 1948.
Cunningham, Evelyn. "The Women." *Pittsburgh Courier*, October 8, 1955, City ed.
Cunningham, Phillip Lamarr. "The Absence of Black Supervillains in Mainstream Comics." *Journal of Graphic Novels & Comics* 1, no. 1 (June 10, 2010): 51–62. https://doi.org/10.1080/21504851003798330.
Danticat, Edwidge. "The Long Legacy of the Occupation in Haiti." *New Yorker*, July 28, 2015.
Dark Mysteries #8. New York: Story Comics, August–September, 1952.
Dark Mysteries #10. New York: Story Comics, December 1952–January 1953.
Dark Mysteries #14. New York: Story Comics, October 1953.
Dark Mysteries #16. New York: Story Comics, February 1954.
Dark Mysteries #18. New York: Story Comics, June 1954.
Dash, J. Michael. *Haiti and the United States: National Stereotypes and the Literary Imagination*. 2nd ed. Basingstoke, UK: Palgrave Macmillan, 1998.
Davenport, Christian. "Blowing Flames into the Souls of Black Folk: Ollie Harrington and His Bombs from Berlin to Harlem." In *Black Comics: Politics of Race and Representation*, edited by Sheena C. Howard and Ronald L. Jackson II, 111–132. London: Bloomsbury Academic, 2013.
Davis, Blair. "*All-Negro Comics* and the Birth of Lion Man, the First African American Superhero." *Inks: The Journal of the Comics Studies Society* 3, no. 3 (2019): 273–297. https://doi.org/10.1353/ink.2019.0023.
Deleuze, Gilles. *Masochism: Coldness and Cruelty*. New York and Cambridge, MA: Zone Books, distributed by MIT Press, 1989.
Dempsey, Terrence E. "And the Word Was Made Flesh . . ." *Critic* 43, no. 1 (Fall 1988): 15–39.
Derby, Lauren. "Imperial Idols: French and United States Revenants in Haitian Vodou." *History of Religions* 54, no. 4 (May 2015): 394–422. https://doi.org/10.1086/680175.
Dery, Mark. "Black to the Future: Interviews with Samuel R. Delany, Greg Tate, and Tricia Rose." In *Flame Wars: The Discourse of Cyberculture*, edited by Mark Dery, 179–222. Durham, NC: Duke University Press, 2020.
Dexter, Charles, and Paul Parker. *Roy Campanella, Baseball Hero*. New York: Fawcett, 1950.
Dexter, Charles, and Clem Weisbecker. *Jackie Robinson, Baseball Hero* #1. New York: Fawcett, 1949.
Dolinar, Brian. *The Black Cultural Front: Black Writers and Artists of the Depression Generation*. Jackson: University Press of Mississippi, 2012.
Downey, Kirstin. "1954 Court Case Opened the Door for Urban Renewal." *Washington Post*, May 7, 2005.
Doyle, Dennis. "'A Fine New Child': The Lafargue Mental Hygiene Clinic and Harlem's African American Communities, 1946–1958." *Journal of the History of Medicine and Allied Sciences* 64, no. 2 (October 23, 2008): 173–212. https://doi.org/10.1093/jhmas/jrn064.
———. "'Where the Need Is Greatest': Social Psychiatry and Race-Blind Universalism in Harlem's Lafargue Clinic, 1946–1958." *Bulletin of the History of Medicine* 83, no. 4 (2009): 746–774. https://doi.org/10.1353/bhm.0.0276.
Dozier, Ayanna. "Wayward Travels: Racial Uplift, Black Women, and the Pursuit of Love and Travel in Torchy in Heartbeats by Jackie Ormes." *Feminist Media Histories* 4, no. 3 (July 1, 2018): 12–29. https://doi.org/10.1525/fmh.2018.4.3.12.
Du Bois, W.E.B. "Criteria for Negro Art." *Crisis*, October 1926.
Durham, Philip, and Everett L. Jones. *The Negro Cowboys*. Lincoln: University of Nebraska Press, 1965.

Earle, Monalesia. *Writing Queer Women of Color: Representation and Misdirection in Contemporary Fiction and Graphic Narratives*. Jefferson, NC: McFarland, 2019.
"Ed Bulleit Offers Comic Book List of Unobjectionables." *Jackson Sun*, September 28, 1955.
"Editorial: Negro Heroes." *Los Angeles Sentinel*, June 10, 1948.
Eerie #11. New York: Avon Comics, April 1953.
Eisner, Will. *Fagin the Jew*. Milwaukie, OR: Dark Horse Comics, 2013.
———. *Graphic Storytelling and Visual Narrative: Principles and Practices from the Legendary Cartoonist*. New York: Norton, 2008.
———. *The Spirit* #1. Northampton, MA: Kitchen Sink, January 1973.
———. *Will Eisner's "The Spirit" Archives*. Vol. 1. New York: DC Comics, 2000.
———. *Will Eisner's "The Spirit" Archives*. Vol. 12. New York: DC Comics, 2003.
———. *Will Eisner's "The Spirit" Archives*. Vol. 14. New York: DC Comics, 2004.
Eisner, Will, and M. Thomas Inge, eds. *Will Eisner: Conversations*. Jackson: University Press of Mississippi, 2011.
Eshun, Kodwo. "Further Considerations of Afrofuturism." *CR: The New Centennial Review* 3, no. 2 (2003): 287–302. https://doi.org/10.1353/ncr.2003.0021.
Evans, Orrin C., Leonard Cooper, George J. Evans Jr., William H. Smith, and John H. Terrell. *All-Negro Comics* #1 (June 1947).
Evans, Tammy D. *Silencing of Ruby McCollum: Race, Class, and Gender in the South*. Gainesville: University Press of Florida, 2018.
Fahraeus, Anna. "Historicising Racialised Objects of Horror: From the Black Renaissance Villain to the Voodoo Doer." In *Villains and Villainy: Embodiments of Evil in Literature, Popular Culture and Media*, edited by Anna Fahraeus and Dikmen Yakah Çamoğlu, 135–148. Amsterdam: Rodopi, 2011.
"Fawcett Publications Issues Magazine on Jackie." *Ohio Daily Express* (Dayton), November 29, 1949.
Ferrière, Alexis Artaud de La. "The Voice of the Innocent: Propaganda and Childhood Testimonies of War." *History of Education* 43, no. 1 (January 2, 2014): 105–123. https://doi.org/10.1080/0046760X.2013.816879.
Field, Corinne T., Tammy-Charelle Owens, Marcia Chatelain, Lakisha Simmons, Abosede George, and Rhian Keyse. "The History of Black Girlhood: Recent Innovations and Future Directions." *Journal of the History of Childhood and Youth* 9, no. 3 (2016): 383–401. https://doi.org/10.1353/hcy.2016.0067.
"Forever Yours." In *Negro Romance* 1, no. 2. New York: Fawcett, August 1950.
Foster, William H., III. *Looking for a Face like Mine*. Waterbury, CT: Fine Tooth, 2005.
Foucault, Michel. "A Preface to Transgression." In *Language, Counter-Memory, Practice: Selected Essays and Interviews*, edited by Donald F Bouchard, 29–52. Ithaca, NY: Cornell University Press, 1980.
———. *"Society Must Be Defended": Lectures at the Collège de France, 1975–76*. New York: Picador, 2003.
Frazier, E. Franklin. *Negro Youth at the Crossways: Their Personality Development in the Middle States*. Washington, DC: American Council on Education, 1940.
Fussell, Elizabeth. "Constructing New Orleans, Constructing Race: A Population History of New Orleans." *Journal of American History* 94, no. 3 (December 1, 2007): 846–855. https://doi.org/10.2307/25095147.
Gabilliet, Jean-Paul. *Of Comics and Men: A Cultural History of American Comic Books*. Translated by Bart Beaty and Nick Nguyen. Jackson: University Press of Mississippi, 2010.
Gaines, Alisha. *Black for a Day: White Fantasies of Race and Empathy*. Chapel Hill: University of North Carolina Press, 2017.

Gardner, Jeanne Emerson. "She Got Her Man, but Could She Keep Him? Love and Marriage in American Romance Comics, 1947–1954." *Journal of American Culture* 36, no. 1 (March 2013): 16–24. https://doi.org/10.1111/jacc.12009.

———. "'True-to-Life': Romance Comics and Teen-Age Desire, 1947–1954." *Forum for World Literature Studies* 3, no. 1 (2011): 118–128.

Garland, Hazel. "Things to Talk About." *Pittsburgh Courier*, June 19, 1954, City ed.

———. "Things to Talk About." *New Pittsburgh Courier*, August 31, 1974, City ed.

———. "Things to Talk About." *New Pittsburgh Courier*, August 22, 1981, City ed.

———. "Things to Talk About: About People and Places . . ." *Pittsburgh Courier*, June 23, 1956, City ed.

———. "A Visit with Jackie Ormes." *New Pittsburgh Courier*, September 24, 1977, City ed.

Gates, Henry Louis, Jr. "The 'Blackness of Blackness': A Critique of the Sign and the Signifying Monkey." *Critical Inquiry* 9, no. 4 (June 1983): 685–723. https://doi.org/10.1086/448224.

———. *The Signifying Monkey: A Theory of African American Literary Criticism*. 25th anniversary ed. Oxford: Oxford University Press, 2014.

Gateward, Frances, and John Jennings, eds. *The Blacker the Ink: Constructions of Black Identity in Comics and Sequential Art*. New Brunswick, NJ: Rutgers University Press, 2015.

Gavaler, Chris. *Superhero Comics*. London: Bloomsbury Academic, 2018.

Ghent, Henri. "Interview with Romare Bearden." In *The Romare Bearden Reader*, edited by Robert G. O'Meally, 54–84. Durham, NC: Duke University Press, 2019.

Ghostly Weird Stories #121. New York: Star, December 1953.

Gillespie, Michael Boyce. *Film Blackness: American Cinema and the Idea of Black Film*. Durham, NC: Duke University Press, 2016.

"Girls at the Recorder Picnic [Photograph]." *Indianapolis Recorder*, September 4, 1948. Indianapolis Recorder Collection, Indiana Historical Society. https://cdm16797.contentdm.oclc.org/digital/collection/p0303/id/117.

Giusto, Frank, and Shaun Clancy. "A Great Friendship: An Interview with Friend and Artist Frank Giusto." In *Matt Baker: The Art of Glamour*, edited by Jim Amash and Eric Nolen-Weathington, 122–135. Raleigh, NC: TwoMorrows, 2012.

Glasco, Laurence. "An American Life, an American Story: Charles 'Teenie' Harris and Images of Black Pittsburgh." In *Teenie Harris, Photographer: Image, Memory, History*, edited by Cheryl Finley, Laurence Glasco, and Joe Trotter, 1–22. Pittsburgh: University of Pittsburgh Press, 2011.

Glasrud, Bruce A. "Don't Leave Out the Cowboys!" In *Black Cowboys in the American West: On the Range, on the Stage, behind the Badge*, edited by Bruce A. Glasrud and Michael N. Searles, 3–15. Norman: University of Oklahoma Press, 2016.

Gleason, Mona. "Avoiding the Agency Trap: Caveats for Historians of Children, Youth, and Education." *History of Education* 45, no. 4 (July 3, 2016): 446–459. https://doi.org/10.1080/0046760X.2016.1177121.

Goldstein, Nancy. "Fashion in the Funny Papers: Cartoonist Jackie Ormes's American Look." In *The Blacker the Ink: Constructions of Black Identity in Comics and Sequential Art*, edited by Frances Gateward and John Jennings, 95–116. New Brunswick, NJ: Rutgers University Press, 2015.

———. *Jackie Ormes: The First African American Woman Cartoonist*. Ann Arbor: University of Michigan Press, 2019.

———. "The Trouble with Romance in Jackie Ormes's Comics." In *Black Comics: Politics of Race and Representation*, edited by Sheena C. Howard and Ronald L. Jackson II, 23–43. London: Bloomsbury Academic, 2013.

Gordon, Ian. *Comic Strips and Consumer Culture, 1890–1945*. Washington, DC: Smithsonian Institution Press, 1998.

———. "Rose O'Neill's Kewpies and Early Transmedia Practices." In *Transmedia Practices in the Long Nineteenth Century*, edited by Monika Pietrzak-Franger and Christina Meyer, 79–94. London: Routledge, 2022.

Graham, Richard, and Colin Beineke. "In Love with Magic and Monsters: The Groundbreaking Life and Work of Rose O'Neill." In *Comics Studies Here and Now*, edited by Frederick Luis Aldama, 31–43. New York: Routledge, 2018.

Grantmyre, Laura. "'They Lived Their Life and They Didn't Bother Anybody': African American Female Impersonators and Pittsburgh's Hill District, 1920–1960." *American Quarterly* 63, no. 4 (2011): 983–1011. https://doi.org/10.1353/aq.2011.0053.

Green, Adam. *Selling the Race: Culture, Community, and Black Chicago, 1940–1955*. Chicago: University of Chicago Press, 2007.

Green, Diana. "Westerns." In *Comics through Time: A History of Icons, Idols, and Ideas*, edited by M. Keith Booker, 849–854. Santa Barbara, CA: Greenwood, 2014.

Greenberger, Robert. *Will Eisner*. New York: Rosen, 2005.

Groensteen, Thierry. *The System of Comics*. Translated by Nick Nguyen and Bart Beaty. Jackson: University Press of Mississippi, 2009.

Gubar, Susan. *Racechanges: White Skin, Black Face in American Culture*. New York: Oxford University Press, 1997.

Haag, Ken, and Dean S. Potter. "Captain Billy's Whiz Bang: Captain Billy Fawcett and the Birth of Fawcett Publications." In *Fawcett Companion: The Best of FCA, Fawcett Collectors of America*, edited by P. C. Hamerlinck, 8–9. Raleigh, NC: TwoMorrows, 2001.

Hadju, David. *The Ten-Cent Plague: The Great Comic Book Scare and How It Changed America*. New York: Picador, 2009.

Haley, Sarah. "'Like I Was a Man': Chain Gangs, Gender, and the Domestic Carceral Sphere in Jim Crow Georgia." *Signs: Journal of Women in Culture and Society* 39, no. 1 (September 2013): 53–77. https://doi.org/10.1086/670769.

Hall, Stuart. "Encoding, Decoding." In *The Cultural Studies Reader*, edited by Simon During, 477–487. London: Routledge, 1993.

———. "Race, the Floating Signifier." Transcript of lecture delivered at Goldsmiths College in London. Media Education Foundation, 1997. https://www.mediaed.org/transcripts/Stuart-Hall-Race-the-Floating-Signifier-Transcript.pdf.

Hamerlinck, P. C. *Fawcett Companion: The Best of FCA*. Raleigh, NC: TwoMorrows, 2001.

———. "'The Fawcetts Could Do It as Well, or Better, than Anybody': The Roscoe K. Fawcett Interview." In *Fawcett Companion: The Best of FCA, Fawcett Collectors of America*, edited by P. C. Hamerlinck, 10–13. Raleigh, NC: TwoMorrows, 2001.

———. "Fawcett Writing Rules: The Actual 1942 Writing Guidelines for Various Fawcett Comic Characters." In *Fawcett Companion: The Best of FCA, Fawcett Collectors of America*, edited by P. C. Hamerlinck, 24–27. Raleigh, NC: TwoMorrows, 2001.

———. "Steamboat—Part II: A Portfolio of African-American Characters in Fawcett Comics." *Alter Ego* #145 / *Fawcett Collectors of America* #204, March 2017.

Hamill, Pete. *A Drinking Life: A Memoir*. New York: Back Bay Books, 1994.

Hanchard, Michael. "Afro-Modernity: Temporality, Politics, and the African Diaspora." *Public Culture* 11, no. 1 (January 1, 1999): 245–268. https://doi.org/10.1215/08992363-11-1-245.

Harper, Bill, and Robert Laughlin. "I Wanted to Draw Comics." In *Fawcett Companion: The Best of FCA, Fawcett Collectors of America*, edited by P. C. Hamerlinck, 104–105. Raleigh, NC: TwoMorrows, 2001.

Harper, Phillip Brian. *Abstractionist Aesthetics: Artistic Form and Social Critique in African American Culture*. New York: New York University Press, 2015.

Harris, Pat. "Types of Black Horror Characters." Black Horror Movies. Accessed September 1, 2020. https://www.blackhorrormovies.com/types/4/.

Hart, Ernie, and Bill Walsh. *Kid Colt Hero of the West* 1, no. 1 (August 1948).

Hartman, Saidiya V. *Wayward Lives, Beautiful Experiments: Intimate Histories of Riotous Black Girls, Troublesome Women and Queer Radicals*. London: Serpent's Tail, 2021.

Harvey, Robert C. *Insider Histories of Cartooning: Rediscovering Forgotten Famous Comics and Their Creators*. Jackson: University Press of Mississippi, 2014.

———. *Meanwhile—: A Biography of Milton Caniff, Creator of Terry and the Pirates and Steve Canyon*. Seattle: Fantagraphics Books, 2007.

Hatfield, Charles. *Alternative Comics: An Emerging Literature*. Jackson: University Press of Mississippi, 2005.

Hayton, Christopher J., and David L. Albright. "The Military Vanguard for Desegregation: Civil Rights Era War Comics and Racial Integration." *ImageText* 6, no. 2 (2012). https://imagetextjournal.com/the-military-vanguard-for-desegregation-civil-rights-era-war-comics-and-racial-integration/.

Heer, Jeet. Afterword to *Black Comics: Politics of Race and Representation*, edited by Sheena C. Howard and Ronald L. Jackson II, 251–256. London: Bloomsbury Academic, 2013.

———. "Comics Chronicles: Racism as a Stylistic Choice and Other Notes." *Comics Journal*, March 14, 2011. http://www.tcj.com/racism-as-a-stylistic-choice-and-other-notes.

———. "The Kolors of Krazy." In *Krazy & Ignatz: "A Wild Warmth of Chromatic Gravy": Coalescing the Complete Full-Page Comic Strips, with the Usual Extra Rarities, 1935–36*, edited by Bill Blackbeard, 8–15. Seattle: Fantagraphics Books, 2005.

Hefner, Brooks E. "Signifying Genre: George S. Schuyler and the Vagaries of Black Pulp." *Modernism/Modernity* 26, no. 3 (2019): 483–504.

Hendrix, Leon, and Adam D. Mitchell. *Jimi Hendrix: A Brother's Story*. New York: Thomas Dunne Books, 2012.

Herriman, George. *Krazy Kat*, June 27, 1936. In *Krazy & Ignatz: the Complete Full-Page Comic Strips, 1935–1936*, edited by Bill Blackbeard, 91. Seattle: Fantagraphics Books, 2005.

Hewitt, John H. "The Themes of Alvin C. Hollingsworth." *Black Art—An International Quarterly* 2, no. 1 (Spring 1977): 4–47.

Higginbotham, Evelyn Brooks. *Righteous Discontent: The Women's Movement in the Black Baptist Church, 1880–1920*. Cambridge, MA: Harvard University Press, 1994.

Holbrook, Sabra. *Children Object*. New York: Viking, 1943.

Hollingsworth, Alvin C. *I'd Like the Goo-Gen-Heim*. Chicago: Reilly and Lee Books, 1970.

"Hollingsworth Hosts Series on WNBC." *El Coquí*, November 1976.

Holmes, Linda Janet. *A Joyous Revolt: Toni Cade Bambara, Writer and Activist*. Santa Barbara, CA: Praeger, 2014.

Holtz, Allan. "Comics of the Smith-Mann Syndicate; Part I." *Stripper's Guide* (blog), July 5, 2006. http://strippersguide.blogspot.com/2006/07/comics-of-smith-mann-syndicate-part-i_05.html.

———. "Ink-Slinger Profiles: Wilbert Holloway." *Stripper's Guide* (blog), February 13, 2012. https://strippersguide.blogspot.com/search?q=Sunny+Boy+Sam.

———. "Obscurities of the Day: Four Features from the Chicago Defender." *Stripper's Guide* (blog), November 6, 2008. http://strippersguide.blogspot.com/2008/11/obscurities-of-day-four-features-from.html.

Hooks, bell. "The Oppositional Gaze: Black Female Spectators." In *The Feminism and Visual Culture Reader*, edited by Amelia Jones, 94–104. London: Routledge, 2003.

Hopkins, David. "'You Can Make Them Liars'—The World War Two Funny Pages of the *Pittsburgh Courier*, American's Leading African American Weekly Newspaper." *Journal of Graphic Novels & Comics* 3, no. 1 (June 2012): 1–17. https://doi.org/10.1080/21504857.2011.645246.

Howard, Peter A. "Black Cowboys—In the Shadows of the Trail." In *The Image of the Outsider II in Literature, Media, and Society: Proceedings of 2008 Conference of the Society for the Interdisciplinary Study of Social Imagery*, 289–295. Pueblo: Society for the Interdisciplinary Study of Social Imagery.

Howard, Sheena C. "Brief History of the Black Comic Strip: Past and Present." In *Black Comics: Politics of Race and Representation*, edited by Sheena C. Howard and Ronald L. Jackson II, 1–21. London: Bloomsbury Academic, 2013.

———. *Encyclopedia of Black Comics*. Golden, CO: Fulcrum, 2017.

Howard, Sheena C., and Ronald L. Jackson II, eds. *Black Comics: Politics of Race and Representation*. London: Bloomsbury Academic, 2013.

———. Introduction to *Black Comics: Politics of Race and Representation*, 1–8. London: Bloomsbury Academic, 2013.

Hunter, Margaret L. "'If You're Light You're Alright': Light Skin Color as Social Capital for Women of Color." *Gender & Society* 16, no. 2 (April 2002): 175–193. https://doi.org/10.1177/08912430222104895.

Hurston, Zora Neale. "Mrs. Ruby J. McCollum!" *Pittsburgh Courier*, February 28, 1953, City ed.

———. *Zora Neale Hurston: A Life in Letters*. Edited by Carla Kaplan. New York: Anchor Books, 2003.

Ibrahim, Habiba. *Black Age: Oceanic Lifespans and the Time of Black Life*. New York: New York University Press, 2021.

Inge, M. Thomas, ed. *Dark Laughter: The Satiric Art of Oliver W. Harrington*. Jackson: University Press of Mississippi, 2009.

"In Your New Color Section." *Pittsburgh Courier*, August 5, 1950.

Jackson, Tim. *Pioneering Cartoonists of Color*. Jackson: University Press of Mississippi, 2016.

Jackson, Zelda. "Hello Public." *Pittsburgh Courier*, January 4, 1930, City ed.

———. "Hello Public." *Pittsburgh Courier*, March 1, 1930, City ed.

———. "Hello Public." *Pittsburgh Courier*, May 17, 1930, City ed.

———. "Hello Public." *Pittsburgh Courier*, June 21, 1930, City ed.

———. "Hello Public." *Pittsburgh Courier*, August 2, 1930, City ed.

Jacobson, Matthew Frye. *Whiteness of a Different Color: European Immigrants and the Alchemy of Race*. Cambridge, MA: Harvard University Press, 1998.

Jain, Kajri. "More than Meets the Eye: The Circulation of Images and the Embodiment of Value." *Contributions to Indian Sociology* 36, nos. 1–2 (February 2002): 33–70. https://doi.org/10.1177/006996670203600103.

James, Erica Moiah. "Charles White's *J'Accuse* and the Limits of Universal Blackness." *Archives of American Art Journal* 55, no. 2 (September 2016): 4–25. https://doi.org/10.1086/689713.

Janson, Klaus. *The DC Comics Guide to Inking Comics*. New York: Watson-Guptill, 2003.

———. *The DC Comics Guide to Pencilling Comics*. New York: Watson-Guptill, 2002.

Jennings, Bill. "Dell Comics." In *Icons of the American Comic Book: From Captain America to Wonder Woman*, edited by Randy Duncan and Matthew J. Smith, 193–205. Santa Barbara, CA: Greenwood, 2013.

Jennings, John. "Black One Shot: Lion Man." *ASAP Journal Online*, September 24, 2020. https://asapjournal.com/16-4-lion-man-john-jennings/.

"Joan Bacchus." *Women in Comics Wiki*. Accessed March 26, 2022. https://womenincomics.fandom.com/wiki/Joan_Bacchus.

Johnson, Charles. Foreword to *Black Images in the Comics: A Visual History*, by Fredrik Strömberg, 6–19. Seattle: Fantagraphics, 2003.

Johnson, Michael K. *Hoo-Doo Cowboys and Bronze Buckaroos: Conceptions of the African American West*. Jackson: University Press of Mississippi, 2014.

Johnson, Toki Schalk. "Success Depends on Persistence, Says Jackie . . . : Determination Next Step in Reaching the Top in Any Field, She Counsels." *Pittsburgh Courier*, April 17, 1948, City ed.

———. "Toki Types: About People Here and There Our Christmas Wish for You!" *Pittsburgh Courier*, December 28, 1946, City ed.

———. "Toki Types: Ask for What You Want . . ." *Pittsburgh Courier*, October 18, 1952, City ed.

———. "Toki Types: Resolutions! What . . . Again?" *Pittsburgh Courier*, January 3, 1948, City ed.

Kahn, Michael A., Richard Samuel West, Bill Watterson, and Dean Mullaney, eds. *What Fools These Mortals Be! The Story of "Puck": America's First and Most Influential Magazine of Color Political Cartoons*. San Diego, CA: IDW, 2014.

Kane, Bob, and Bill Finger. *Batman Chronicles*. New York: DC Comics, 2005.

Kaplan, Amy. "Romancing the Empire: The Embodiment of American Masculinity in the Popular Historical Novel of the 1890s." *American Literary History* 2, no. 4 (1990): 659–690. https://doi.org/10.1093/alh/2.4.659.

Kerner Commission. *Report of the National Advisory Commission on Civil Disorders*. Washington, DC: U.S. GPO, 1968.

Kidd, Chip, and Geoff Spear. *Shazam! The Golden Age of the World's Mightiest Mortal*. New York: Abrams Comicarts, 2019.

Kirschke, Amy. "Romare Bearden: The Making of a Black Political Cartoonist." In *Writing History from the Margins: African Americans and the Quest for Freedom*, edited by Claire Parfait, Hélène Le Dantec-Lowry, and Claire Bourhis-Mariotti, 143–158. New York: Routledge, 2017.

Kirtley, Clare, Christopher Murray, Phillip B. Baughan, and Benjamin W. Tatler. "Reading Words and Images: Factors Influencing Eye Movements in Comic Reading." In *Empirical Comics Research: Digital, Multimodal, and Cognitive Methods*, edited by Janina Wildfeuer, Alexander Dunst, and Jochen Laubrock, 264–283. New York: Routledge, 2018.

Knight, Arthur. *Disintegrating the Musical: Black Performance and American Musical Film*. Durham, NC: Duke University Press, 2002.

Knoll, Erwin. "Smith-Mann to Launch Comics Supplement." *Editor and Publisher*, July 21, 1951. https://www.editorandpublisher.com/archives/.

Kraus, Joe. "Dick Tracy versus the Blank: Re-inscribing Ethnicity in Crime." *Centennial Review* 41, no. 3 (1997): 537–546.

Lage, Matt. "'Visual Expression': Will Lieberson–Fawcett Comics Executive Editor." In *Fawcett Companion: The Best of FCA, Fawcett Collectors of America*, edited by P. C. Hamerlinck, 92–97. Raleigh, NC: TwoMorrows, 2001.

———. "'We Were More or Less Inspired,' Otto Binder: An Interview with Captain Marvel's Mightiest Writer." In *Fawcett Companion: The Best of FCA, Fawcett Collectors of America*, edited by P. C. Hamerlinck, 59–64. Raleigh, NC: TwoMorrows, 2001.

Lanctot, Neil. *Campy: The Two Lives of Roy Campanella*. New York: Simon and Schuster, 2011.

Lanning, Michael Lee. *The Court-Martial of Jackie Robinson: The Baseball Legend's Battle for Civil Rights during World War II*. Guilford, CT: Stackpole Books, 2020.

Laubrock, Jochen, Sven Hohenstein, and Matthias Kümmerer. "Attention to Comics: Cognitive Processing during the Reading of Graphic Literature." In *Empirical Comics Research: Digital, Multimodal, and Cognitive Methods*, edited by Janina Wildfeuer, Alexander Dunst, and Jochen Laubrock, 239–263. New York: Routledge, 2018.

Lavender, Isiah. *Afrofuturism Rising: The Literary Prehistory of a Movement*. Columbus: Ohio State University Press, 2019.

Lawlor, Mary. *Recalling the Wild: Naturalism and the Closing of the American West*. New Brunswick, NJ: Rutgers University Press, 2000.

Lee, Stan, and Jack Kirby. *The Rawhide Kid* 1, no. 17 (August 1960).

Leichner, Amber Harris. "'To Bend without Breaking': American Women's Authorship and the New Woman, 1900–1935." PhD diss., University of Nebraska–Lincoln, 2012.

"Let Us Sympathize with Ruby McCollum." *Pittsburgh Courier*, May 2, 1953, City ed.

Little, Vivienne. "What Is Historical Imagination?" *Teaching History* 36 (June 1983): 27–32.

Locke, Alain. "Art or Propaganda? (1928)." In *The New Negro: Readings on Race, Representation, and African American Culture, 1892–1938*, edited by Henry Louis Gates Jr. and Gene Andrew Jarrett, 260–261. Princeton, NJ: Princeton University Press, 2021.

Lorde, Audre. *Zami, a New Spelling of My Name*. Trumansburg, NY: Crossing, 1982.

Lott, Eric. *Love and Theft: Blackface Minstrelsy and the American Working Class*. 20th anniversary ed. New York: Oxford University Press, 2013.

"Love's Decoy." In *Negro Romance* 1, no. 2. New York: Fawcett, August 1950.

Luckhurst, Roger. *Zombies: A Cultural History*. London: Reaktion Books, 2016.

Lupoff, Dick. "The Big Red Cheese." In *All in Color for a Dime*, edited by Dick Lupoff and Don Thompson, 66–95. New Rochelle, NY: Arlington House, 1970.

Lyons, Leonard. "'Pit' Gets Genn; Yeggs Get the 'Carmen Amaya.'" *Washington Post*, July 14, 1947.

Madison, Vernetta Adlee. "A Study of Recreational Opportunities for Negro Children in Norfolk, Virginia." Master's thesis, Atlanta University, 1947.

Maguire, Roberta. "From Fiction to Fact: Zora Neale Hurston and the Ruby McCollum Trial." *Literary Journalism Studies* 7, no. 1 (Spring 2015): 16–34.

"Making of a Master of Sequential Art, The." *Comic Book Creator*, no. 2 (Summer 2013): 40–56.

Maltin, Leonard. *Of Mice and Magic: A History of American Animated Cartoons*. Rev. ed. New York: New American Library, 1987.

Marja, Fern. "Youthbuilders Teach Kids to Use Tools of Democracy." *New York Post*, July 27, 1948.

Markstein, Donald D. "Li'l Eightball." *Toonpedia* (blog), 2010. http://www.toonopedia.com/8ball.htm.

Martin, Charles H. "Communists and Blacks: The ILD and The Angelo Herndon Case." *Journal of Negro History* 64, no. 2 (April 1979): 131–141. https://doi.org/10.2307/2717204.

Martin, Courtney J. "From the Center: The Spiral Group, 1963–1966." *Nka Journal of Contemporary African Art* 2011, no. 29 (November 1, 2011): 86–99. https://doi.org/10.1215/10757163-1496372.

Matthews, Karen. "Evelyn Cunningham: 1916–2010." *Chicago Tribune*, April 29, 2010.

McAlister, Elizabeth. "Slaves, Cannibals, and Infected Hyper-Whites: The Race and Religion of Zombies." *Anthropological Quarterly* 85, no. 2 (2012): 457–486. https://doi.org/10.1353/anq.2012.0021.

McCloud, Scott. *Making Comics: Storytelling Secrets of Comics, Manga and Graphic Novels*. New York: Harper, 2006.

McCrory, Amy. "Sports Cartoons in Context: TAD Dorgan and Multi-genre Cartooning in Early Twentieth-Century Newspapers." *American Periodicals: A Journal of History, Criticism, and Bibliography* 18, no. 1 (2008): 45–68. https://doi.org/10.1353/amp.2008.0001.

McGee, Adam M. "Haitian Vodou and Voodoo: Imagined Religion and Popular Culture." *Studies in Religion/Sciences Religieuses* 41, no. 2 (June 2012): 231–256. https://doi.org/10.1177/0008429812441311.

McGehee, Margaret T., and Emily Taylor. "Mr. Seabrook Goes to Haiti, or Southern (Self-) Mastery in the Magic Island (1929)." *Southern Quarterly* 55, no. 4 (Summer 2018): 53–69.

Means Coleman, Robin R. *Horror Noire: Blacks in American Horror Films from the 1890s to Present*. New York: Routledge, 2011.

Medina, José. "Toward a Foucaultian Epistemology of Resistance: Counter-Memory, Epistemic Friction, and *Guerrilla* Pluralism." *Foucault Studies*, September 12, 2011, 9–35. https://doi.org/10.22439/fs.v0i12.3335.

Mehaffy, Marilyn Maness. "Advertising Race/Raceing Advertising: The Feminine Consumer(-Nation), 1876–1900." *Signs: Journal of Women in Culture and Society* 23, no. 1 (October 1997): 131–174. https://doi.org/10.1086/495238.

Meier, August. *Negro Thought in America, 1880–1915: Racial Ideologies in the Age of Booker T. Washington*. Ann Arbor: University of Michigan Press, 1988.

Mendes, Gabriel. *Under the Strain of Color: Harlem's Lafargue Clinic and the Promise of an Antiracist Psychiatry*. Ithaca, NY: Cornell University Press, 2015.

Mercer, Marilyn. "The Only Real Middle-Class Crimefighter." In *Will Eisner: Conversations*, edited by Will Eisner and M. Thomas Inge, 3–7. Jackson: University Press of Mississippi, 2011.

Meyerowitz, Joanne. "Women, Cheesecake, and Borderline Material: Responses to Girlie Pictures in the Mid-Twentieth-Century U.S." *Journal of Women's History* 8, no. 3 (1996): 9–35. https://doi.org/10.1353/jowh.2010.0424.

Michel, Claudine, and Patrick Bellegarde-Smith, eds. *Vodou in Haitian Life and Culture: Invisible Powers*. New York: St. Martin's, 2006.

Mills, Charles W. *The Racial Contract*. Ithaca, NY: Cornell University Press, 1997.

Mills, Tarpé, and Lorraine Turner. *Miss Fury: Sensational Sundays 1941–1944*. Edited by Trina Robbins. San Diego: IDW, 2013.

Minh-Ha, Trinh T. *When the Moon Waxes Red: Representation, Gender, and Cultural Politics*. New York: Routledge, 1991.

Mooney, Linda A., and Carla-Marie Fewell. "Crime in One Long-Lived Comic Strip: An Evaluation of Chester Gould's Dick Tracy.'" *American Journal of Economics and Sociology* 48, no. 1 (January 1989): 89–100. https://doi.org/10.1111/j.1536-7150.1989.tb02096.x.

Morgan, Stacy I. *Rethinking Social Realism: African American Art and Literature, 1930–1953*. Athens: University of Georgia Press, 2004.

Morris, Susana M. "Black Girls Are from the Future: Afrofuturist Feminism in Octavia E. Butler's *Fledgling*." *WSQ: Women's Studies Quarterly* 40, nos. 3–4 (2012): 146–166. https://doi.org/10.1353/wsq.2013.0034.

Morrison, Grant. *Supergods: What Masked Vigilantes, Miraculous Mutants, and a Sun God from Smallville Can Teach Us about Being Human*. New York: Random House, 2012.

Moylan, Virginia Lynn. *Zora Neale Hurston's Final Decade*. Gainesville: University Press of Florida, 2012.

Mullins, Paul. "Race and the Color Line at the Douglass Park Pool." *African American Suburbia* (blog), March 25, 2016. https://africanamericansuburbia.wordpress.com/2016/03/25/race-and-the-color-line-at-the-douglass-park-pool/.

———. "Romanticizing Racist Landscapes: Segregation and White Memory in Riverside Amusement Park." *Archaeology and Material Culture* (blog), May 6, 2020. https://paulmullins.wordpress.com/2020/05/06/romanticizing-racist-landscapes-segregation-and-white-memory-in-riverside-amusement-park/.

Mulvey, Laura. "Visual Pleasure and Narrative Cinema." In *Film Theory and Criticism: Introductory Readings*, edited by Leo Braudy and Marshall Cohen, 5th ed., 57–68. New York: Oxford University Press, 1999.

Murphy, John P. "Charles White: The Art and Politics of Humanism, 1947–1956." *American Communist History* 17, nos. 3–4 (October 2, 2018): 282–300. https://doi.org/10.1080/14743892.2018.1499263.

Murray, Christopher. *Champions of the Oppressed? Superhero Comics, Popular Culture, and Propaganda in America during World War II*. Cresskill, NJ: Hampton, 2011.

Murray, Derek Conrad. "Mickalene Thomas: Afro-Kitsch and the Queering of Blackness." *American Art* 28, no. 1 (March 2014): 9–15. https://doi.org/10.1086/676624.

Murrell, Denise. "African Influence in Modern Art." Met Museum, April 2008. https://www.metmuseum.org/toah/hd/aima/hd_aima.htm.

"My Heart's Dilemma." In *Negro Romance* 1, no. 1. New York: Fawcett, June 1950.

"My Love Betrayed Me!" In *Negro Romance* 1, no. 3. New York: Fawcett, October 1950.

Myrdal, Gunnar. *An American Dilemma: The Negro Problem and Modern Democracy*. New York: Harper, 1944.

Mysterious Adventures #3. New York: Story Comics, August 1951.

Mysterious Adventures #6. New York: Story Comics, February 1952.

NAACP. "World War II and the Post War Years—NAACP: A Century in the Fight for Freedom | Exhibitions—Library of Congress." Library of Congress—Exhibitions, February 21, 2009.

Nama, Adilifu. *Black Space: Imagining Race in Science Fiction Film*. Austin: University of Texas Press, 2010.

———. "R Is for Race, Not Rocket: Black Representation in American Science Fiction Cinema." *Quarterly Review of Film and Video* 26, no. 2 (March 9, 2009): 155–166. https://doi.org/10.1080/10509200600737812.

———. *Superblack: American Pop Culture and Black Superheroes*. Austin: University of Texas Press, 2011.

"Negro Villain in Comic Book Killed by Youngsters." *Chicago Defender*, May 5, 1945.

Neidich, Warren. "Pierre Molinier and the Phantom Limb." *Journal of Neuroaesthetics* 4 (2005). https://www.artbrain.org/journal-of-neuroaesthetics/journal-neuroaesthetics-4/pierre-molinier-and-the-phantom-limb/.

Nelson, Alondra. "Introduction: Future Texts." *Social Text* 20, no. 2 (June 1, 2002): 1–15.

Nelson, Angela M. "Middle-Class Ideology in African American Postwar Comic Strips." In *From Bourgeois to Boojie: Black Middle-Class Performances*, edited by Vershawn Ashanti Young and Bridget Harris Tsemo, 175–190. Detroit: Wayne State University Press, 2011.

Nelson, Stanley. *The Black Press: Soldiers without Swords*. California Newsreel, 1999.

"New American Library." Advertisement. In *Negro Romance* 1, no. 3. New York: Fawcett, October 1950.

Newman, Simon P. "American Political Culture and the French and Haitian Revolutions: Nathaniel Cutting and the Jeffersonian Republicans." In *The Impact of the Haitian Revolution in the Atlantic World*, edited by David Patrick Geggus, 72–89. Columbia: University of South Carolina Press, 2001.

"New Sections in Pittsburgh Negro Weekly." *Editor & Publisher*, August 26, 1950.

New York City Housing Authority. "Project Statistics July 1947." Accessed June 5, 2021. https://www1.nyc.gov/assets/nycha/downloads/pdf/pdbjuly1947.pdf.

Ngô, Fiona I. B. *Imperial Blues: Geographies of Race and Sex in Jazz Age New York*. Durham, NC: Duke University Press, 2013.

Nodell, Jacque. "Black + White = Heartbreak!" *Sequential Crush* (blog), February 18, 2010. https://www.sequentialcrush.com/blog/2010/02/black-white-heartbreak.

Noe, Dave, Robert Schaupp, Kevin Halter, and Derick Gross Sr. "*Lobo*—Colors." In *All New Popular Comics*, edited by Jim Ludwig, Dave Noe, and Derick Gross Sr., 45–49. N.p.: InDELLible Comics and Amazing Things Press, 2017.

Nolan, Michelle. *Love on the Racks: A History of American Romance Comics*. Jefferson, NC: McFarland, 2018.

Norman Rockwell Museum. "Rose O'Neill: Artist and Suffragette: Special Exhibition Celebrates the 2020 Women's Vote Centennial." August 2020. https://www.nrm.org/2020/08/102388/.

Normanton, Peter. "From the Tomb Presents: Step Into My Parlor." *Alter Ego* 3, no. 165 (September 2020): 49–54.

"Obituary: Louis Dalrymple." *New-York Tribune*, December 29, 1905. https://chroniclingamerica.loc.gov/lccn/sn83030214/1905-12-29/ed-1/seq-16/.

O'Brien, Gail Williams. *The Color of the Law: Race, Violence, and Justice in the Post–World War II South*. Chapel Hill: University of North Carolina Press, 2011.

O'Meally, Robert G. "'Pressing on Life until It Gave Back Something in Kinship': An Introductory Essay." In *The Romare Bearden Reader*, edited by Robert G. O'Meally, 1–30. Durham, NC: Duke University Press, 2019.

O'Neill, Rose, and Miriam Formanek-Brunell. *The Story of Rose O'Neill: An Autobiography*. Columbia: University of Missouri Press, 1997.

Opper, F. "Caricature Country and Its Inhabitants." *Independent*, April 4, 1901.

Ortiz, Paul. *An African American and Latinx History of the United States*. Boston: Beacon, 2018.

Osofsky, Gilbert. *Harlem, the Making of a Ghetto: Negro New York, 1890–1930*. Chicago: Ivan R. Dee, 1996.

Overstreet, Robert M. *The Overstreet Comic Book Price Guide* #50. Baltimore: Gemstone, 2020.

Owens, Imani D. "Beyond Authenticity: The US Occupation of Haiti and the Politics of Folk Culture." *Journal of Haitian Studies* 21, no. 2 (2016): 350–370. https://doi.org/10.1353/jhs.2016.0000.

Pamphile, Leon D. *Contrary Destinies: A Century of American Occupation, Deoccupation, and Reoccupation of Haiti*. Gainesville: University Press of Florida, 2016.

Parker, Elsie S. "Youthbuilders' Experiment." *National Municipal Review* 37, no. 7 (July 1948): 391–392.

Parks, Gordon. *A Hungry Heart: A Memoir*. New York: Washington Square, 2005.

PBS. "Civil War Letters, Aviation Fabric & African American Comic Book." *History Detectives*, season 9, episode 4. Hosted by Gwen Wright. Featuring Gerald Early, William Foster, Jacque Nodell, and Shaun Clancy. Aired July 12, 2011.

———. "Oliver Wendell Harrington (1912–1995)." *The Black Press*. Accessed June 4, 2021. https://www.pbs.org/blackpress/news_bios/harrington.html.

Pederson, Kaitlin, and Neil Cohn. "The Changing Pages of Comics: Page Layouts across Eight Decades of American Superhero Comics." *Studies in Comics* 7, no. 1 (July 1, 2016): 7–28. https://doi.org/10.1386/stic.7.1.7_1.

Peiss, Kathy Lee. *Zoot Suit: The Enigmatic Career of an Extreme Style*. Philadelphia: University of Pennsylvania Press, 2011.

Perry, Rachel Berenson. *The Life and Art of Felrath Hines: From Dark to Light*. Bloomington: Indiana University Press / Indiana Historical Society, 2018.

Pierce, John G. "'One of the Most Real Characters Ever to Appear': An Analysis of Mr. Tawny." In *Fawcett Companion: The Best of FCA, Fawcett Collectors of America*, edited by P. C. Hamerlinck, 31. Raleigh, NC: TwoMorrows, 2001.

Piper, Adrian. "Passing for White, Passing for Black." In *Passing and the Fictions of Identity*, edited by Elaine K. Ginsberg and Donald E. Pease, 234–270. Durham, NC: Duke University Press, 2020.

Pizzino, Christopher. "The Doctor versus the Dagger: Comics Reading and Cultural Memory." *PMLA/Publications of the Modern Language Association of America* 130, no. 3 (May 2015): 631–647. https://doi.org/10.1632/pmla.2015.130.3.631.
Platts, Todd K. "Locating Zombies in the Sociology of Popular Culture." *Sociology Compass* 7, no. 7 (July 2013): 547–560. https://doi.org/10.1111/soc4.12053.
Porter, Kenneth W. "Black Cowboy in the American West, 1866–1900." In *African Americans on the Western Frontier*, edited by Monroe Lee Billington and Roger D. Hardaway, 110–127. Niwot: University Press of Colorado, 1998.
"Possessed." In *Negro Romance* 1, no. 2. New York: Fawcett, August 1950.
Postema, Barbara. *Narrative Structure in Comics: Making Sense of Fragments*. Rochester, NY: RIT Press, 2013.
Powell, Richard J. *Going There: Black Visual Satire*. New Haven, CT: Yale University Press, 2020.
"Power of Cartoons, The." *Colored American*, January 18, 1902.
"Press, The: Ace Harlem to the Rescue." *Time*, July 14, 1947.
Pruitt, Dwain Carlton. "It Rhymes with Lust? Matt Baker and the Ironic Politics of Race, Sex and Gender in the Golden Age." *Journal of Graphic Novels and Comics* 7, no. 2 (April 2, 2016): 197–209. https://doi.org/10.1080/21504857.2015.1135470.
Quattro, Ken. *Invisible Men: Black Artists of the Golden Age of Comics*. San Diego, CA: Yoe Books, 2020.
Qureshi, Sadiah. "Displaying Sara Baartman, the 'Hottentot Venus.'" *History of Science* 42, no. 2 (June 2004): 233–257. https://doi.org/10.1177/007327530404200204.
Ramsey, Kate. *The Spirits and the Law: Vodou and Power in Haiti*. Chicago: University of Chicago Press, 2014.
Ransom, Gerri B. "Black History." *New Pittsburgh Courier*, July 19, 1980, City ed.
Rifas, Leonard. *Korean War Comic Books*. Jefferson, NC: McFarland, 2021.
Ritbergen, Joanna van. "Further Ruminations: An Interview with Matt Baker's Brother Fred Robinson." In *Matt Baker: The Art of Glamour*, edited by Jim Amash and Eric Nolen-Weathington, 118–121. Raleigh, NC: TwoMorrows, 2012.
Robbins, Trina. "C. C. Beck: An Appreciation." Typescript, 1990. Collection of Trina Robbins, San Francisco.
———. *From Girls to Grrrlz: A History of Women's Comics from Teens to Zines*. San Francisco: Chronicle Books, 1999.
———. *Pretty in Ink: North American Women Cartoonists, 1896–2013*. Seattle: Fantagraphics, 2013.
Roosevelt, Eleanor. "My Day." United Features Syndicate, August 1, 1947.
Rowe, Steven. "Fox Feature Syndicate." In *Matt Baker: The Art of Glamour*, edited by Jim Amash and Eric Nolen-Weathington, 46. Raleigh, NC: TwoMorrows, 2012.
Royster, Jacqueline Jones. *Traces of a Stream: Literacy and Social Change among African American Women*. Pittsburgh: University of Pittsburgh Press, 2000.
"Ruby! Good or Bad?" *Pittsburgh Courier*, June 13, 1953, City ed.
———. *Pittsburgh Courier*, June 27, 1953, City ed.
Rulah, Jungle Goddess #18. New York: Fox Feature Syndicate, September 1948.
Russell-Cole, Kathy, Midge Wilson, and Ronald E. Hall. *The Color Complex: The Politics of Skin Color in a New Millennium*. Rev. ed. New York: Anchor Books, 2013.
Russello Ammon, Francesca. "Commemoration amid Criticism: The Mixed Legacy of Urban Renewal in Southwest Washington, D.C." *Journal of Planning History* 8, no. 3 (August 2009): 175–220. https://doi.org/10.1177/1538513209340630.

Sadowski, Greg, ed. *Supermen! The First Wave of Comic Book Heroes, 1936–1941*. Seattle: Fantagraphics Books, 2009.
Saguisag, Lara. *Incorrigibles and Innocents: Constructing Childhood and Citizenship in Progressive Era Comics*. New Brunswick, NJ: Rutgers University Press, 2018.
Sammond, Nicholas. *Birth of an Industry: Blackface Minstrelsy and the Rise of American Animation*. Durham, NC: Duke University Press, 2015.
———. "The Three Lives of Krazy Kat (Part 1)." *animationstudies 2.0*, January 28, 2019. https://blog.animationstudies.org/?p=2868.
Santos, Jorge. *Graphic Memories of the Civil Rights Movement*. Austin: University of Texas Press, 2019.
Savage, William W. *Comic Books and America, 1945–1954*. Norman: University of Oklahoma Press, 1990.
Schelly, William. *American Comic Book Chronicles: The 1950s, 1950–1959*. Raleigh, NC: TwoMorrows, 2013.
———. *The Art of Joe Kubert*. Seattle: Fantagraphics Books, distributed by Norton, 2011.
———. *Man of Rock: A Biography of Joe Kubert*. Seattle: Fantagraphics Books, 2008.
Schimmel, Paul, and Judith E. Stein, eds. *The Figurative Fifties: New York Figurative Expressionism*. Newport Beach, CA: Newport Harbor Art Museum, 1988.
Schreiner, Dave. "Stage Settings." In *The Spirit* #15, by Will Eisner, inside front cover. Northampton, MA: Kitchen Sink, 1986.
———. "Stage Settings." In *The Spirit* #17, by Will Eisner, inside front cover. Northampton, MA: Kitchen Sink, 1986.
———. "Stage Settings." In *The Spirit* #28, by Will Eisner, inside front cover, 16. Northampton, MA: Kitchen Sink, 1987.
Schumacher, Michael. *Will Eisner: A Dreamer's Life in Comics*. New York: Bloomsbury, 2010.
Schuyler, George. "Views and Reviews." *Pittsburgh Courier*, July 26, 1947.
Scott, Ellen. "Regulating 'Nigger': Racial Offense, African American Activists, and the MPPDA, 1928–1961." *Film History* 26, no. 4 (2014): 1–31. https://doi.org/10.2979/filmhistory.26.4.1.
Scott, Mack. "From Blackface to *Beulah*: Subtle Subversion in Early Black Sitcoms." *Journal of Contemporary History* 49, no. 4 (October 2014): 743–769. https://doi.org/10.1177/0022009414538473.
Siegel, Jeanne. "Why Spiral?" *Nka Journal of Contemporary African Art* 2011, no. 29 (November 1, 2011): 78–85. https://doi.org/10.1215/10757163-1496363.
Siegel, Jerry, and Joe Shuster. *Superman Chronicles*. Vol. 1. New York: DC Comics, 2006.
———. *Superman: The Sunday Classics, 1939–1943*. New York: DC Comics, 1998.
Silber, Nina. *The Romance of Reunion: Northerners and the South, 1865–1900*. Chapel Hill: University of North Carolina Press, 1993.
Simmons, LaKisha Michelle. *Crescent City Girls: The Lives of Young Black Women in Segregated New Orleans*. Chapel Hill: University of North Carolina, 2015.
Singer, Marc. "'Black Skins' and White Masks: Comic Books and the Secret of Race." *African American Review* 36, no. 1 (2002): 107–119. https://doi.org/10.2307/2903369.
"600 Newsies Have the Time of Their Lives at Recorder Picnic." *Indianapolis Recorder*, September 4, 1948.
Smith, Zoë. "4 Colorism: The Ashiness of It All." *Inks: The Journal of the Comics Studies Society* 4, no. 3 (2020): 340–356. https://doi.org/10.1353/ink.2020.0025.
"Smith-Mann Syndicate Contribute to EE Campaign." *Pittsburgh Courier*, November 28, 1953.

Solomon, Adina. "The Prolific Illustrator behind Kewpies Used Her Cartoons for Women's Rights." *Smithsonian Magazine*, March 15, 2018. https://www.smithsonianmag.com/history/prolific-illustrator-behind-kewpies-used-her-cartoons-womens-rights-180968497/.
Solórzano, Daniel G., and Tara J. Yosso. "Critical Race Methodology: Counter-Storytelling as an Analytical Framework for Education Research." *Qualitative Inquiry* 8, no. 1 (February 2002): 23–44. https://doi.org/10.1177/107780040200800103.
"Something for the Youngsters." *Brooklyn Daily Eagle*, October 28, 1935.
"South Jamaica Houses: For Whom Were They Built?" *Long Island Daily Press*, June 1, 1940.
Spectre, Allen. "The Voodoo Man: Boanga's Zombie Corps." In *Weird Comics* #5 (August 1940). https://digitalcomicmuseum.com/index.php?dlid=13141.
———. "The Voodoo Man: Captive of the Zombies." In *The Flame* #6 (April 1941). https://digitalcomicmuseum.com/index.php?dlid=19272.
———. "The Voodoo Man: Havoc in Haiti." In *The Flame* #7 (May 1941). https://digitalcomicmuseum.com/index.php?dlid=13586.
———. "Voodoo Man: The Plague of Jacmel." In *Weird Comics* #4 (July 1940). https://digitalcomicmuseum.com/index.php?dlid=4152.
———. "The Voodoo Man: The Search for the Cult Temple." In *The Flame* #5 (March 1941). https://digitalcomicmuseum.com/index.php?dlid=313.
———. "The Voodoo Man: The Voodoo Man Cometh." In *Weird Comics* #1 (April 1940). https://digitalcomicmuseum.com/index.php?dlid=4100.
———. "The Voodoo Man: The Witch Doctor's Revenge." In *Samson* #3 (February–March 1941). https://digitalcomicmuseum.com/index.php?dlid=12154.
Steele, Kyle P. *Making a Mass Institution: Indianapolis and the American High School*. New Brunswick, NJ: Rutgers University Press, 2020.
Steranko, Jim. *The Steranko History of Comics*. Vol. 2. Reading, MA: Supergraphics, 1972.
Stewart, Ronald. "Contextualizing Nankivell." PhD diss., Graduate School of Languages and Cultures, Nagoya University, 2008.
———. "Frank A. Nankivell's Japan: From Means to Marker." In *Unexpected Encounters: Neglected Histories behind the Australia-Japan Relationship*, edited by Michael Ackland and Pam Oliver, 51–72. Clayton, Australia: Monash Asian Institute, Monash University, 2007.
Strasser, Susan. *Satisfaction Guaranteed: The Making of the American Mass Market*. New York: Pantheon, 1989.
Strömberg, Fredrik. *Black Images in the Comics: A Visual History*. Seattle: Fantagraphics, 2003.
Tales of Horror #2. New York: Minoan, September 1952.
Target Comics #11. Philadelphia: Novelty, December 1940.
Taylor, Quintard. *In Search of the Racial Frontier: African Americans in the American West, 1528–1990*. New York: Norton, 1999.
Theriault, Florence. *With Kewpish Love: Memorabilia & Collectibles of Rose O'Neill*. Annapolis, MD: Gold Horse, 2004.
Thomas, Ebony Elizabeth. "Notes toward a Black Fantastic: Black Atlantic Flights beyond Afrofuturism in Young Adult Literature." *Lion and the Unicorn* 43, no. 2 (2019): 282–301. https://doi.org/10.1353/uni.2019.0023.
Thomas, Steve. "Carol Tilley." *Circulating Ideas* (blog), January 28, 2006. https://circulatingideas.com/transcripts/carol-tilley/.
Thompson, Lisa B. *Beyond the Black Lady: Sexuality and the New African American Middle Class*. Urbana: University of Illinois Press, 2009.
Tilley, Carol L. "Comics: A Once-Missed Opportunity." *Journal of Research on Libraries and Young Adults*, March 5, 2014. http://www.yalsa.ala.org/jrlya/2014/05/comics-a-once-missed-opportunity/.

Tilley, Carol L. "Seducing the Innocent: Fredric Wertham and the Falsifications That Helped Condemn Comics." *Information & Culture* 47, no. 4 (November 2012): 383–413. https://doi.org/10.7560/IC47401.

Tisserand, Michael. *Krazy: George Herriman, a Life in Black and White.* New York: HarperCollins, 2016.

Toll, Robert C. *Blacking Up: The Minstrel Show in Nineteenth Century America.* Oxford: Oxford University Press, 1977.

———. "Social Commentary in Late-Nineteenth-Century White Minstrelsy." In *Inside the Minstrel Mask: Readings in Nineteenth-Century Blackface Minstrelsy*, edited by Annemarie Bean, James V. Hatch, and Brooks McNamara, 86–110. Hanover, NH: Wesleyan University Press, 1996.

Tolnay, Stewart, and E. M. Beck. "Lynching." *New Georgia Encyclopedia*, August 12, 2020. https://www.georgiaencyclopedia.org/articles/history-archaeology/lynching/.

Tomkins, Calvin. "Arthur Jafa's Radical Alienation." *New Yorker*, December 21, 2020. https://www.newyorker.com/magazine/2020/12/21/arthur-jafas-radical-alienation.

———. "Putting Something over Something Else." *New Yorker*, November 21, 1977.

Tompkins, Jane P. *West of Everything: The Inner Life of Westerns.* New York: Oxford University Press, 1993.

"Top Talent Featured in 'Stars on Parade' . . . : Leo Weil School to Be Scene of Show." *Pittsburgh Courier*, April 7, 1951, City ed.

Trachtenberg, Alan. *Reading American Photographs: Images as History; Mathew Brady to Walker Evans.* New York: Hill and Wang, 2007.

"Tragic Vow, A." In *Negro Romance* 1, no. 1. New York: Fawcett, June 1950.

"True-to-Life Romances." Promotional ad from the publisher. In *Negro Romance* 1, no. 1. New York: Fawcett, June 1950.

Tucker, Neely. "Love in the Comics: The Star-Crossed Story of 'Negro Romance.'" *Library of Congress Blog*, February 10, 2020. https://blogs.loc.gov/loc/2020/02/love-in-the-comics-the-star-crossed-story-of-negro-romance/.

"Urban League Publishes Comic Book of Heroes." *Chicago Defender*, March 15, 1947.

US Census Bureau. 1940 Census, New York, Queens, New York. Roll m-t0627-02732, page 3A; Enumeration District 41-616. Generated by Jacque Nodell, using Ancestry.com, September 27, 2020. https://www.ancestry.com/search/collections/2442/.

Wald, Gayle. *Crossing the Line: Racial Passing in Twentieth-Century U.S. Literature and Culture.* Durham, NC.: Duke University Press, 2000.

Walker, Alice. "Zora Neale Hurston: A Cautionary Tale and a Partisan View." In *Alice Walker and Zora Neale Hurston: The Common Bond*, edited by Lillie P. Howard, 13–19. Westport, CT: Greenwood, 1993.

Walker, Brian. *The Comics: The Complete Collection.* New York: Abrams Books, 2011.

Wanzo, Rebecca. *The Content of Our Caricature: African American Comic Art and Political Belonging.* New York: New York University Press, 2020.

———. "It's a Hero? Black Comics and Satirizing Subjection." In *The Blacker the Ink*, edited by Frances Gateward and John Jennings, 314–332. New Brunswick, NJ: Rutgers University Press, 2019.

Wardlaw, Alvia J. *Charles Alston.* Vol. 6. San Francisco: Pomegranate, 2007.

Washburn, Patrick Scott. *The African American Newspaper: Voice of Freedom.* Evanston, IL: Northwestern University Press, 2006.

Wertham, Fredric. "Nine Men Speak to You: Jim Crow in the North." *Nation*, June 12, 1954.

———. *Seduction of the Innocent: The Influence of Comic Books on Today's Youth.* New York: Rinehart, 1954.

West, Richard Samuel. *Satire on Stone: The Political Cartoons of Joseph Keppler*. Urbana: University of Illinois Press, 1988.
Whaley, Deborah Elizabeth. *Black Women in Sequence: Re-Inking Comics, Graphic Novels, and Anime*. Seattle: University of Washington Press, 2015.
White, Charles. "Humanist Art." *Masses & Mainstream*, February 1953.
White, Vivian. "The Social Contributions of a Welfare Center for Negro Girls in the City of Los Angeles." Master's thesis, University of Southern California, 1947.
Whitted, Qiana. "The Blues Tragicomic: Constructing the Black Folk Subject in Stagger Lee." In *The Blacker the Ink: Constructions of Black Identity in Comics and Sequential Art*, edited by Frances Gateward and John Jennings, 235–254. New Brunswick, NJ: Rutgers University Press, 2015.
———. "Comics and Emmett Till." In *Picturing Childhood: Youth in Transnational Comics*, edited by Mark Heimermann and Brittany Tullis, 70–91. Austin: University of Texas Press, 2017.
———. *EC Comics: Race, Shock, and Social Protest*. New Brunswick, NJ: Rutgers University Press, 2019.
———. "Quentin Tarantino's Slave on the Road; or, Josiah Henson Unchained." *Qiana J. Whitted* (blog), January 11, 2013. https://www.qianawhitted.com/blog/quentin-tarantinos-slave-on-the-road-or-josiah-henson-unchained.
Whyte, Garrett. "Comic 3—No Title." *Mr. Jim Crow*. *Chicago Defender*, August 27, 1949, 23.
———. "Comic 4—No Title." *Mr. Jim Crow*. *Chicago Defender*, July 9, 1949, 23.
Williams, Gweneira, and Jane Wilson. "They Like It Rough: In Defense of Comics." *Library Journal* 67 (1942): 204–206.
Williams, Megan E. "The Crisis Cover Girl: Lena Horne, the NAACP, and Representations of African American Femininity, 1941–1945." *American Periodicals: A Journal of History, Criticism, and Bibliography* 16, no. 2 (2006): 200–218. https://doi.org/10.1353/amp.2006.0019.
———. "'Meet the Real Lena Horne': Representations of Lena Horne in *Ebony* Magazine, 1945–1949." *Journal of American Studies* 43, no. 1 (April 2009): 117–130. https://doi.org/10.1017/S0021875809006094.
Williams, William. "Letter to the Editor." In *The Spirit* #4, 5. New York: Warren, 1974.
———. "Letter to the Editor." In *The Spirit* #5, 5. New York: Warren, 1974.
Wings Comics #67. New York: Fiction House, March 1946.
Wings Comics #106. New York: Fiction House, June 1949.
Wings Comics #107. New York: Fiction House, July 1949.
Witchcraft #4. New York: Avon Periodicals, September–October 1952.
Witchcraft #6. New York: Avon Periodicals, March 1953.
Witek, Joseph. "The Arrow and the Grid." In *A Comics Studies Reader*, edited by Jeet Heer and Kent Worcester, 149–156. Jackson: University Press of Mississippi, 2009.
Witty, Paul, and Dorothy Moore. "Interest in Reading the Comics among Negro Children." *Journal of Educational Psychology* 36, no. 5 (1945): 303–308.
Wolseley, Roland Edgar. *The Black Press, U.S.A*. Ames: Iowa State University Press, 1971.
Wright, Bradford W. *Comic Book Nation: The Transformation of Youth Culture in America*. Baltimore: Johns Hopkins University Press, 2003.
Yoe, Craig, ed. *Super Weird Heroes: Outrageous but Real!* San Diego, CA: IDW, 2016.
Young, Harvey. *Embodying Black Experience: Stillness, Critical Memory, and the Black Body*. Ann Arbor: University of Michigan Press, 2010.
Young, Kevin. *The Grey Album: On the Blackness of Blackness*. Minneapolis: Graywolf, 2012. https://www.overdrive.com/search?q=B9930218-7888-424D-BD0D-96395F51F904.

yronwode, cat. "The Central City Zeitgeist." In *The Spirit* #2, inside front cover. Northampton, MA: Kitchen Sink, 1983.

———. "Will Eisner Interview." In *Will Eisner: Conversations*, edited by Will Eisner and M. Thomas Inge, 47–78. Jackson: University Press of Mississippi, 2011.

Notes on Contributors

MORA J. BEAUCHAMP-BYRD is a visiting assistant professor of art and design at the University of Tampa. An art historian and curator, she specializes in American art; art of the African diaspora; modZern and contemporary art; museum and curatorial studies; and representations of race, class, and gender in American comics. She has organized numerous exhibitions, including *Transforming the Crown: African, Asian and Caribbean Artists in Britain, 1966–1996* and *Little Nemo's Progress: Animation and Contemporary Art*. She is currently serving as the vice president for publications, an Executive Committee member, of the Board of Directors of the College Art Association (CAA).

ELI BOONIN-VAIL is a PhD candidate in film and media studies at the University of Pittsburgh specializing in film history. His research focuses on American cinemas, Hollywood and non-Hollywood, and their relationship to incarceration, with a particular emphasis on studio infrastructure in its collaboration with penal institutions. He also researches race and American comic books, as well as French film production culture. His work can be found or is forthcoming in *Animation Studies, Inks, Film Criticism, French Screen Studies*, and *Music, Sound, and the Moving Image*.

JULIAN C. CHAMBLISS is a professor of English and the Val Berryman Curator of History at the MSU Museum at Michigan State University. He is faculty lead for the Graphic Possibilities Research Workshop and a core participant in the MSU College of Arts & Letters' Consortium for Critical Diversity in a Digital Age Research (CEDAR). His research interests focus on race, culture, and power in real and imagined spaces. An interdisciplinary scholar, he has designed museum exhibitions, curated art shows, and created digital humanities projects that trace community, ideology, and power in the United States.

BRIAN CREMINS is a professor of English at Harper College in Palatine, Illinois. The author of *Captain Marvel and the Art of Nostalgia*, he is also coeditor with Brannon Costello of *The Other 1980s: Reframing Comics' Crucial Decade*.

PHILLIP LAMARR CUNNINGHAM is an assistant professor of media studies at Wake Forest University. His research primarily focuses on African American representation in popular culture. His scholarly work has appeared in *Journal of Graphic Novels and Comics*, *Journal of Popular Music Studies*, *Journal of Sport and Social Issues*, *Popular Culture Studies Journal*, and various anthologies on comics, film, television, and sports.

BLAIR DAVIS is an associate professor of media and cinema studies in the College of Communication at DePaul University in Chicago. His books include *The Battle for the Bs: 1950s Hollywood and the Rebirth of Low-Budget Cinema*, *Movie Comics: Page to Screen/Screen to Page*, *Comic Book Movies*, and *Comic Book Women: Characters, Creators, and Culture in the Golden Age*. He has written about comics and pop culture for *USA Today*, the *Washington Post*, the *Saturday Evening Post*, and *Ms.* magazine and in numerous anthologies, including *Comics and Pop Culture*, *Working-Class Comic Book Heroes*, and the Eisner Award–winning *The Blacker the Ink*.

MONALESIA EARLE is an independent researcher based in England. She received her PhD from Birkbeck, University of London. Her book *Writing Queer Women of Color: Representation and Misdirection in Contemporary Fiction and Graphic Narratives* received honorable mention for the Charles Hatfield Book Prize and was also a runner-up for the John Leo and Dana Heller Award for Best Single Work in LGBTQ Studies. Her research interests are wide ranging but focus primarily on gender, queer, feminist, and postcolonial studies.

CHRIS GAVALER is an associate professor of English at W&L University, comics editor of *Shenandoah* magazine, and series editor of Bloomsbury Comics

Studies. He has published six books of scholarship on comics and comics-related subjects: *On the Origin of Superheroes*, *Superhero Comics*, *Superhero Thought Experiments* (with Nathaniel Goldberg), *Revising Fiction, Fact, and Faith* (with Nathaniel Goldberg), *Creating Comics* (with Leigh Ann Beavers), and *The Comics Form: The Art of Sequenced Images*. His next project is tentatively titled *The Color of Paper: Reading Race in the Comics Medium*.

IAN GORDON teaches cultural history in Singapore. His most recent works include "Rose O'Neill's Kewpies and Early Transmedia Practices," in *Transmedia Practices in the Long Nineteenth Century*, edited by Christina Meyer and Monika Pietrzak-Franger, and "Bildungsromane and Graphic Narratives," in *A History of the Bildungsroman*, edited by Sarah Graham. His books include *Superman: The Persistence of an American Icon*, *Kid Comic Strips: A Genre across Four Countries*, and *Comic Strips and Consumer Culture*.

ANDREW J. KUNKA is a professor of English at the University of South Carolina–Sumter. He is the author of *Autobiographical Comics* from the Bloomsbury Comics Studies Series and the Eisner Award–nominated *The Life and Comics of Howard Cruse: Taking Risks in the Service of Truth* (also available from Rutgers University Press). He has also published on Will Eisner, Kyle Baker, Jack Katz, crime comics, and Dell Comics, among other topics. He also serves as book review editor for *Inks: The Journal of the Comics Studies Society*, on the board for the International Comic Arts Forum (ICAF), and as the Comics Studies Society Ombuds. He is currently cowriting *The Routledge Introduction to American Comics* with Rachel R. Miller.

MIKE LEMON is a lecturer for the Texas Tech University Graduate School's Interdisciplinary Studies program. Additionally, he works as the instructional development coordinator, helping graduate-student instructors of record feel more confident, engaged, and effective in the classroom. He has taught seminars on race and the immigrant experience in American comic books. He has also been an invited lecturer on gender and comics for college classes and public roundtables. His research includes comic books and fandom, depictions of the African American West in comics, and spatial humanities.

JACQUE NODELL, author of *How to Go Steady: Timeless Dating Advice, Wisdom, and Lessons from Vintage Romance Comics* and curator of the blog and podcast *Sequential Crush*, has a background in museum curation and comics. She has written articles for academic encyclopedias and textbooks, including

Icons of the American Comic Book and *Comics through Time*, as well as forewords and afterwords for Dark Horse and Oni Comics. In 2011, she was featured on the popular PBS show *The History Detectives* for a segment about *Negro Romance*. Nodell lives in Chattanooga, Tennessee, with her husband, daughter, and two mischievous cats.

NICHOLAS SAMMOND is a professor of cinema and media studies and director of the Centre for the Study of the United States at the University of Toronto. He is the author of *Birth of an Industry: Blackface Minstrelsy and the Rise of American Animation* and *Babes in Tomorrowland: Walt Disney and the Making of the American Child, 1930–1960*. His current project, on abjection and resistance, includes the volume *Abjection Incorporated*, edited with Maggie Hennefeld, and the forthcoming monograph *Fluid Resistance*, which explores the practices and performances and of abjection in Cold War vernacular media, including animation and comics/comix. He has published widely, including in *Feminist Media Histories*, *Film History*, *Camera Obscura*, and *WSQ*.

CAROL L. TILLEY is an associate professor in the School of Information Sciences at the University of Illinois. Her comics scholarship focuses on young people's comics readership, especially in the United States during the mid-twentieth century. Her research on Fredric Wertham was featured in the *New York Times* and other media outlets. She is a past president of the Comics Studies Society and has served as a juror for the Eisner, Ringo, and Lynd Ward comics awards.

REBECCA WANZO is a professor in the Department of Women, Gender, and Sexuality Studies at Washington University in St. Louis. She is the author of *The Suffering Will Not Be Televised: African American Women and Sentimental Political Storytelling* and *The Content of Our Caricature: African American Comic Art and Political Belonging*, which was the recipient of the Katherine Singer Kovacs Book Prize from the Society for Cinema and Media Studies, the Charles Hatfield Book Prize from the Comics Studies Society, and the Best Scholarly/Academic Work from the Will Eisner Comic Industry Awards.

QIANA WHITTED is a professor of English and African American studies at the University of South Carolina. She is the author of the Eisner Award–winning book *EC Comics: Race, Shock, and Social Protest* (also available from Rutgers University Press) and *A God of Justice? The Problem of Evil in Twentieth-Century Black Literature*, as well as coeditor of the collection *Comics and the U.S. South*. Her essays have appeared in the *Comics Journal*, *Public Books*, *Journal of Graphic Novels and Comics*, *African American Review*, *Southern Literary Journal*, and Marvel's Penguin Classics Collection on *Black Panther*. She also serves as editor of *Inks: The Journal of the Comics Studies Society* and chair of the International Comic Arts Forum.

Index

Page numbers in italics indicate illustrations.

Abbott and Costello (comedy act), 46–47
Action Comics, 110, 211, 228
Adams, C. LeRoy, 152–153
African American art, 58–59, 79–93, 94n7
African Americans: comics readership among, 163–177, *166*, *169*; print cultures of, 165; in war comics, 5, 18n12
Afrofuturism, 15, 281–294
Albright, David L., 185, 205n42
Ald, Roy, 135, 272–274, 278
Alexander, Bryant Keith, 302
Allard, Al, 211
Allen, Derotha, 170
Allmendinger, Blake, 302, 308
All-Negro Comics, 72, 181–203, 205n54, 275, 283; illustrations from, *182*, *187*, *192*, *193*, *195*, *202*
Alston, Charles, 80, 84, 88–90, 92; "Right between the Eyes," 90, *91*; Spiral art collective and, 227
Amana, Harry, 88–90
Ambery, N. F., 299, 314
American Negro Exposition (Chicago, 1940), 80, 90
American Visuals company, 62
Amirand, Eyal, 51–52, 54, 59
Amos, Emma, 227
Amos 'n' Andy, 64, 68–69, 282

Andelman, Bob, 66
Anderson, Reynaldo, 285, 286, 289
Armitage, Shelly, 25–27
Arneson, Don, 298–313
Arnold, Andrew D., 73
Arthurian romances, 211
Art Students League (NYC), 83
art versus propaganda, 15, 79–81
Ashe, Edd, 238
Asian caricatures, 89, 129
Atlas Comics, 300
Atomic Age of comics, 15, 209
Avon Comics, 130
Azzarello, Brian, 62–63

Baartman, Sara, 25
Bails, Jerry, 225n5
Baily, Bernard, 7
Baker, Matt, 3, 15; *All-Negro Comics* and, 185; Alberto Becattini on, 96, 110–111, 113; Alvin Hollingsworth and, 124, 126, 228; *Phantom Lady*, 95–117, 167; sexuality of, 97, 98, 114–115, 117n16; *Sheena, Queen of the Jungle*, 95; Fredric Wertham on, 95
Bakhtin, Mikhail, 301–302
Baldwin, James, 39, 200, 236
Bambara, Toni Cade, 164
Baraka, Amiri (LeRoi Jones), 163–164, 176

349

Barr, Mike W., 70
Barrier, Michael, 75n16
Bartkowski, John, 255
Bateman, John, 99
Batman, 110, 178n19, 211
Bearden, Romare, 15, 80, 82–85, 88, 92, 227
Beaty, Bart, 80–81
Beauchamp-Byrd, Mora J., 227–242
Becattini, Alberto, 96, 110–111, 113
Beck, C. C., 208–209, 211–212, 216, 225n12
Beineke, Colin, 36
Bendis, Brian Michael, 63
Benson, John, 65
Berelson, Bernard, 5
Berger, Arthur Asa, 51
Berra, Yogi, 208
Berrey, Stephen A., 8
Berry, Daina Ramey, 30
Best, Mark, 225n7
Beware comics, *132*
Biberman, Edward, 85–86
Binder, Otto, 208, 211, 216
Bivins, Sarah Lean, 175
Black Art genealogies, 79–93
Black Arts Movement (BAM), 81, 94n7, 228. *See also* African American art
Black cowboys, 297–315
blackface minstrelsy, 2, 297; Will Eisner and, 62, 64, 66; Krazy Kat and, 40–59; Mickey Mouse and, 37n20; Rose O'Neill and, 27; origins of, 46–48, 58–59; stock characters of, 27, 45–47, 54; vaudeville and, 43, 46–47, 55–59, *58*
Black middle class, 42, 236; Will Eisner on, 70; Gunnar Myrdal on, 171–172; Jacque Nodell on, 263–264; Rose O'Neill on, 23, 35–36; Jackie Ormes on, 143–145, *144*, 152
Black Panther (character), 191, 281
Black Panther Party, 40
bogey man, 27–28
Bogle, Donald, 62
bokor (zombie master), 255–256
Boonin-Vail, Eli, 141–157
Bordo, Susan, 115
Brame, David, 201
Bray, John, 44, 55
Bray, Margaret, 44, 55
Brenda Starr, 240–241
Bronze Man (character), 125, 138n12

Brooks, Kinitra D., 90
Brown, Edmund G. "Pat," 217
Brown, Torchy (character), 228, 237–241, 271–272
Brown v. Board of Education (1954), 10, 92, *93*
Brunner, Edward, 149, 158n24
Buffalo Soldiers, 299
Bukatman, Scott, 126, 132–133
Bulleit, Ed, 277
bullying, 175; Roy Campanella on, 221; Harlan Ellison on, 212
Bunker, Archie (character), 70
Burns and Allen (comedy act), 46–47
Buster Brown comics, 36

Cakewalk dance, 46
Caldwell, H. Zahra, 142, 143
Cámera Arenas, Enrique, 255
Campanella, Roy, 197, *210*, 215–224, *219*, *223*; car accident of, 207–209, *210*; family of, 209–210, 220–224, *221*
Campbell, Eddie, 218
Campbell, E. Simms, 7, 185, 237
Caniff, Milton, 128–129; *Dickie Dare*, 163–164, 176; *Steve Canyon*, 231, 241; *Terry and the Pirates*, 128, 129, 237, 241
Captain Marvel, 217, 222; creation of, 211; Christopher Murray on, 225n12; Steamboat and, 14, 65, 164, 190, 209, 213–214
Carnegie, Andrew, 32
Carpio, Glenda R., 24
Carroll, Lewis, 212
Cascone, Charles S., 71
Cassel, John Harmon, 30
Catlett, Elizabeth, 83
Cat-Man Comics, 123
Chambliss, Julian C., 281–294
Charlton publishing company, 272, 277–279
Chatelain, Marcia, 177
Chesler, Harry "A," 7
Chicago Defender, 7–9, 90, 172–173, 183, 185, 188, 214
Chireau, Yvonne, 251, 259n39
Chisholm Kid, 238, 284, 316n3
Christman, Bert, 72
Christopher, Tom, 196–197
Christy, George, 46
Chute, Hillary, 115

civil rights movement, 6, 23; Orrin Evans and, 197; Alvin Hollingsworth and, 122, 137
Clancy, Shaun, 117n16, 135, 273
Clifton, Lucille, 164, 200
Coates, Ta-Nehisi, 28
Cohn, Neil, 98–113
Cold War, 5, 191, 213
Cole, Jack, 66
Cole, L. B., 7
Cole, Nat King, 207
Coleman, E. Marie, 151
Coleman, Robin Means, 90
"colored," classification of, 41
colorism, 233–236, 274–275; definition of, 229; respectability politics and, 15
Comics Code (1954), 4, 6, 62, 95, 241, 244n49
comics scare, 9–13, *12*, 95, 172–173, 277
Comics Studies Society, 165
Commercial Comics, 188
Continental Features Syndicate, 3
Cooke, Darwyn, 62
Cooper, Leonard, 182–183, 194, 204n29
Costanza, Pete, 208–209, 211, 225n12
Couch, N. C. Christopher, 64
counterstorytelling, 166, 176–177, 181–203, 283–284, 293–294
cowboys. *See* Western comics
Crane, Roy, 14, 75n16
Crane, Walter, 127
Crawford, Janie, 153
Crawford, Phillip, 97
Creech, Sara, 155
Cremins, Brian, 14, 75n16, 207–224
Creoles, 42
crime comics, 121–122, 125, 128–129, 175, 241
Crist, Judith, *12*, 174
"critical fabulation," 97
critical race theory, 282
Crothers, Scatman, 47
Crowley, Wendell, 217
Cubism, 82
Cunningham, Evelyn, 143, 145, 151
Cunningham, Phillip Lamarr, 247–258
Curtis, Constance, 10

Daigh, Ralph, 211
Dalí, Salvador, 131
Dalrymple, Louis, 31

Dando, Michael Norton, 201
Dash, J. Michael, 249
Daumier, Honoré, 81
Davis, Amon, 54
Davis, Blair, 121–138, 183, 191
DC Comics, 62, 75n1; Fawcett and, 272; romance line of, 279
Dee, Ruby, 210
Delany, Samuel R., 289
Dell Comics, 190, 297–315
Dempsey, Terrence E., 126
Derby, Lauren, 250
Dery, Mark, 285
Detective Comics, 110, 178n19, 211
Dew Dillies (characters), 183, *187*, 192–194, *193*, 200, *202*
Dexter, Charles, 209, 217–224, *219*, *221*, *223*, 225n54
Dickens, Charles, 68, 212
Dickie Dare comics, 163–164, 176
Dick Tracy comics, 189, 231
Digital Comic Museum, 5, 18n12
DiMaggio, Joe, 222–224, *223*
Dixon, G. W., 46
Django Unchained, 315
Doby, Larry, 208
domestic abuse, 153
Dorgan, Thomas Aloysius, 218
Douglas, Emory, 40
Doyle, Dennis, 9
Dozier, Ayanna, 147, 151, 154, 157n4
Dracula, 256
Du Bois, W.E.B., 79–81, 221, 235
Dunbar, Paul Laurence, 60n16
Durham, Philip, 299, 307, 314

Earle, Monalesia, 95–117
Early, Gerald, 262
Ebony magazine, 235
EC Comics, 13–15, 90–91, 241; entertaining versus educational aims of, 188; horror artists of, 130; profitability of, 197–198
editorial cartoons, 80, *87*, 89, *91*, *93*
Eisner, Will, 15, 189, 241; on cowboy comics, 300; legacy of, 63; *The Spirit*, 61–74, *67*, *69*, 283; Youthbuilders' petition against, 179n27, 214
Elias, Lee, 128
Ellington, Duke, 125

Ellison, Harlan, 211–212
Ellison, Ralph, 9, 117, 118n59
Emmett, Dan, 46
Eshun, Kodwo, 285
eugenics movement, 282
Evans, George "Geo," Jr., 183, 191, 276
Evans, Orrin C., 15; *All-Negro Comics* and, 182–186, 189–191, 194–202, 275, 283; awards of, 199; civil rights movement and, 197; death threats against, 204n34
Evans, Tammy, 152–153

Fahraeus, Anna, 252
Falk, Lee, 282–283
Fanon, Frantz, 176
Fawcett, Wilford, 211
Fawcett Comics, 72, 197, 208–209; Code of Ethics of, 215; DC Comics and, 272; Alvin Hollingsworth and, 233; *Negro Romance* and, 261–279; Jacque Nodell on, 261–279; Qiana Whitted on, 216
Feiffer, Jules, 67
Felix the Cat, 43, 55
Fiction House, 125, 191
Fine, Lou, 66
Finger, Bill, 211
Fisher, Charles, 65
Fitzgerald, Bertram A., 204n29
Forrest, Nathan Bedford, 86
Foster, Hal, 128, 231
Foucault, Michel, 197, 201, 204n36
Fox Features Syndicate, 191
Foxx, Jaime, 315
Frazier, E. Franklin, 168
Futurism, 82

Gabillier, Jean-Paul, 299
Garland, Hazel, 143, 149–152, 155–157
Gates, Henry Louis, Jr.: on Ralph Ellison, 119n59; on Zora Neale Hurston, 153
Gateward, Frances, 282
Gavaler, Chris, 95–117
Gebhart v. Belton (1952), 9–10
gender dynamics, 289; of Black supervillains, 248, 251; Orrin Evans's comics and, 196; male gaze and, 97, 114–115, 195; nonbinary, 43, 49–51, 54; Rose O'Neill's cartoons and, 33–34; Jackie Ormes's comics and, 141–157, 229; respectability politics and, 142, 149, 151–152, 154, 157n3; of romance comics, 275
genre hybridity, 240
GI Bill, 262
Giusto, Frank, 117n16
Glasrud, Bruce A., 307
Gleason, Lev, 241
Gold Dust Twins, 25
Golden Age of comics, 4–5, 17, 197–198, 218, 228–230
Goldstein, Nancy, 142, 237, 239
Gone with the Wind (film), 282
Goodman, Martin, 301
Gordon, Ian, 23–36, 282
Gould, Chester, 189, 231–232
Gould, Manny, 56
Graham, Billy, 131
Graham, John, 273
Graham, Richard, 36
Green, Diana, 299
Greenberger, Robert, 66
Greene, Sanford, 131
Griffith, D. W., 41–42
Groensteen, Thierry, 81, 112, 188
Gross, Derick, 314–315
Grosz, George, 83
Gubar, Susan, 42

Hadju, David, 228
Haitian Revolution, 42, 249–250
Haitian Vodou, 249–258
Haley, Sarah, 96
Hall, Stuart, 13–14, 97
Halter, Kevin, 314–315
Hamerlinck, P. C., 216–217
Hamill, Pete, 212–213
Hanchard, Michael, 184, 199
Harlem, Ace (character), 181–189, *182*, *187*, 192–196, 200–203
Harlem Renaissance, 80
Harleston, Edwin N., 236
Harper, Phillip Brian, 81
Harrington, Oliver "Ollie," 3, 185, 237, 284; Ayanna Dozier and, 157n4; Jackie Ormes and, 144–145; Rebecca Wanzo on, 92–93
Harris, Charles "Teenie," *16*, 16–17, 203
Harris, Martin, 251–252
Harrison, Ben, 56
Hartman, Saidiya, 41, 97

Harvey, Robert C., 7
Harvey Comics, 62
Hatfield, Charles, 99
Hays Code, 256
Hayton, Christopher J., 185, 205n42
Hearst, William Randolph, 42–45
Hearst-Vitagraph, 44, 55
Heer, Jeet, 2, 18n15; on Roy Crane, 75n16; on Will Eisner's racial caricatures, 73; on George Herriman, 43, 52, 59
Hefner, Brooks, 289
Hellboy comics, 126, 131–133
Hendrix, Jimi, 164
Herdon, Angelo, 85
Herriman, George, 15, 40–59; Matt Baker and, 116; career of, 42–43; education of, 45; genius of, 57; Jeet Heer on, 43, 52, 59; parents of, 42
Herron, France, 212
Higginbotham, Evelyn, 280n4
Himes, Chester, 144
Hogarth, William, 81
Holbrook, Sabra, 213–214, 224
Holiday, Billie, 200
Hollingsworth, Alvin Carl, 15, 121–138; *All-Negro Comics* and, 185; art style of, 125–130; Matt Baker and, 124, 126, 228; Mora J. Beauchamp-Byrd on, 227–242; children's book by, 137; civil rights movement and, 122, 137; fine arts career of, 121–122, 135–137, *136*; floating skulls of, 130, 131; David Hadju on, 228; Joe Kubert and, 123–124, 128; legacy of, 137–138; names of, 227; *Negro Romance* and, 273, 275, 279; Jackie Ormes and, 228; *Trapped*, 228
Holloway, Wilbert L., 183, 185, 236–237, 286
Holly, Arthur, 250
Holtz, Allan, 284
Holyoke Publishing, 123–124
hooks, bell, 115
Hopkins, David, 236
Horne, Lena, 149, 152, 155, *234*, 234–235; *Kandy* and, 229, 242
horror comics, 130, 241; Black aesthetics of, 92; Black stereotypes in, 251–252; of Alvin Hollingsworth, 121–122, *122*, 129–133, *132, 134*, 138
Houston, Bill, 149, 151
Houston, Winifred, 149, 151, 158n25

Howard, Peter A., 307
Howard, Robert E., 212
Howard, Sheena C., 139n37, 197, 284
Huie, William Bradford, 155–156
humanism, 85–86
Hurston, Zora Neale, 155–156; Henry Louis Gates Jr. on, 153; on Ruby McCollum, 152–155; Jackie Ormes and, 142; Richard Wright and, 81, 94n7

Ibrahim, Habiba, 176
"identity hermeneutic," 81
Iger, Jerry, 7, 111
Iger-Roche Studio, 124
InDELLible Comics, 314–315, *315*
Indianapolis Recorder picnic (1948), *169*, 169–172
Indigenous peoples, 46, 301, 307
International Film Service (IFS), 44, 55
Irish stereotypes, 2, 34, 86

Jackson, Ezra, 185
Jackson, Jay, 90, 157n4
Jackson, Ronald L., II, 197
Jackson, Tim, 5, 137, 185, 198, 239
Jackson, Zelda. *See* Ormes, Jackie
Jafa, Arthur, 51
James, Erica Moiah, 86
Janson, Klaus, 127, 129
Japanese stereotypes, 89, 129
jazz music, 125, 137, 200
Jennings, Bill, 299
Jennings, John, 201; *The Blacker the Ink*, 282; *Box of Bones*, 131
Jetter, Al, 217, 273, 274
Jetter, Charlotte Haecker, 274
Jewish stereotypes, 2; in Will Eisner comics, 63, 68–70, 73; in Rose O'Neill cartoons, 34
Jim Crow caricatures, 58–59, *58*; of George Herriman, 42–43; of Garrett Whyte, 7–8, *8*
Jim Crow laws, 24, 57, 188, 213, 288. *See also Plessy v. Ferguson*
Johnson, Charles, 4, 74, 214, 216
Johnson, Fenton, 200
Johnson, Gertrude "Toki" Schalk, 141, 142, 149, 152, 154, 159n48
Johnson, Michael K., 298, 301, 304
Jolson, Al, 56

Jones, Everett L., 299, 307, 314
Jones, LeRoi (Amiri Baraka), 163–164, 176
Juba dance, 46
Jump Jim Crow, 46
jungle comics, 11, 13, 191; of Matt Baker, 95; of Alvin Hollingsworth, 121, 125, 126; voodoo and, 252
Jungle Jim comics, 251
juvenile delinquency, 9–13, *12*, 95, 172–173, 277

Kandy (character), 228–242
Kane, Bob, 110, 211
Kaplan, Amy, 300
Kemble, E. W., 27
Kerner Report, 279
Kewpie dolls, 23–25
Kidd, Chip, 215
Kid Komics, 190
King, Martin Luther, Jr., 122
King Features Syndicate, 7
Kirby, Jack, 262; layouts of, *103*, 104, 106–107, *107*; romance comics of, 241, 277, 279
Kirschke, Amu, 83
Kitchen, Denis, 62
Kitchen Sink Press, 62, 67–68, *69*
Knight, Neil (character), 15, 281, 284–294, *287*, *288*, *293*
Kollwitz, Kathë, 83
Korean War, 5
Krazy Kat, 39–59, *50*, *52*, *55*; film adaptations of, 44, 53–56, *55*; franchises of, 44; predecessors of, 44; speech characteristics of, 41, 48–49, 54
Kubert, Joe, 123–124, 128
Ku Klux Klan (KKK), 7, 53, 153; films about, 41–42; founder of, 86; Charles White on, 86–88, *87*
Kuniyoshi, Yasuo, 230
Kunka, Andrew J., 61–74

Lafargue Mental Hygiene Clinic, 9–11, 173–174
Lage, Matt, 214
Lanctot, Neil, 209
Landon, Michael, 210
Lantz, Walter, 65
Latinx, 283, 307–308, 313
Laughlin, Bob, 274

Lawlor, Mary, 297
Lebeck, Oskar, 14, 75n16
Le Blanc, Andre, 67
Lee, Jae, 122, 126
Leichner, Amber Harris, 159n48
Lemon, Mike, 205n38, 297–315
Levenson, Lewis F., 225n5
Levi, Zachary, 211
Lewis, Joe, 197
Lewis, John, 23
Lewis, Norman, 227
Lieberson, Will, 14, 65, 209, 213–217, 273–274
Li'l Eightball, 14, 190
Lion Man, 183, 186, 191–192, *192*, 196, 200–202, 276
Lobo comics, 205n38, 297–315
Locke, Alain, 79–81
Lorde, Audre, 164
Lothar (character), 282–283
Lounsbury, Chuck, 65
Louverture, Toussaint, 249
Love, Harry, 56
Lovecraft, H. P., 212
Luckhurst, Roger, 255–256
Lugosi, Bela, 251
Lupoff, Richard, 215
Lyles, Aubrey, 54
lynching, 52–53, 96, 145; Rose O'Neill on, 28–30, *29*

Madison, Vernetta Adlee, 171
Maguire, Roberta S., 153
Makandal, François, 249–250, 257
Malcolm X, 122
male gaze, 97, 114–115, 195
Maltin, Leonard, 56
Mammy stereotype, 263
Marion, Phillipe, 115
Marja, Fern, 213
Marshall, Jeremy, 201
Martin, Courtney J., 135
Martin, J., 47
Massey, Cal, 124
Mayhew, Richard, 227
Maynard, Joan Bacchus, 204n29
McAlister, Elizabeth, 251
McCloud, Scott, 98–99, 188
McCollum, Ruby J., 152–155, 159n51
McCrory, Amy, 218

McGee, Adam M., 257–258, 258n17
McGehee, Margaret T., 250–251
McKean, Dave, 138
Medina, José, 204n36
Mercer, Marilyn, 65
Meredith, James, 92
Mesoamericans, 259n26
Messman, John J., 284–285
Mexican American cowboys, 307–308, 313
Meyer, Helen, 299
Meyers, Joseph, 130
Micheaux, Oscar, 41–42
Mickey Mouse, 37n20, 55–56
middle class. *See* Black middle class
Mignola, Mike, 122, 126, 131
Milai, Sam, 89, 237, 238
Milestone Media, 285, 289
Miller, Flournoy, 54
Miller and Lyles (comedy act), 43, 47
Mills, Charles W., 96
Mills, Tarpé, 103–104
Minh-Ha, Trinh T., 96
Minnie Mouse, 56
minstrelsy. *See* blackface minstrelsy
Mintz, Charles, 44, 55
misdirectional gaze, 98–100, 113–117; combined, *109*, 109–110, *112*, *113*. *See also* viewing paths
Miss Fury comics, 103
Moffatt, Laurie Norton, 23
Moore, Bob, 285
Morales, Rags, 62–63
Moreau de Saint-Méry, Médéric Louis Elie, 249
Morgan, Stacy I., 84
Moskowitz, Sam, 212
Mosse, Hilde, 11, 12
Moylan, Virginia Lynn, 153, 155, 156, 159n51
"mulatto," 41–42
Mulvey, Laura, 114, 115
murals, 89
Murray, Christopher, 225n12
Myers, Walter Dean, 164
Myrdal, Gunnar, 171

NAACP, 14, 53; Lena Horne and, 235; Jackie Ormes on, 149
Nama, Adilifu, 18n14, 286
Nancy comics, 170, 178n19

Nankivell, Frank A., 27, 31
Nast, Thomas, 63, 86–87
Negro Heroes comics, 185, 186, 188–190, 197
Negro Romance comics, 122, 135, 197, 217, 261–279
Nelson, Alondra, 286, 289
Nelson, Angela M., 152
Newcombe, Don, 208
Newman, Simon P., 249
Ngô, Fiona I. B., 54
Nichols, Michelle, 289
Nineteenth Amendment of US Constitution, 23, 36
Nodell, Jacque, 125, 230, 261–279
Noe, Dave, 314–315
Nolan, Bill, 44, 55, 56
Nolan, Michelle, 277–278
Normanton, Peter, 130
Nowlan, Philip Francis, 289

O'Meally, Robert, 83
O'Neill, Rose, 15, 23–36, *28*; husbands of, 35, 36; on lynching, 28–30, *29*
Opper, Frederick Burr, 2, 27
Ormes, Earl, 145, 149–150, 158n28
Ormes, Jackie, 15, 116, 141–157, 185; career of, 237, 243n35; childhood influences on, 165; Alvin Hollingsworth and, 228; respectability politics of, 142, 149, 151–152, 154, 157n3; on sexual assault, 146–149, *148*; Torchy Brown character of, 228, 237–241, 271–272
Orr, Martha, 240–241
Ortiz, Paul, 283
Outcault, Richard, 36, 282
Owens, Tammy-Cherelle, 177

Page, Gregory, 114, 115
Palais, Rudy, 274
Pamphile, Leon D., 250
Parents' Magazine Press, 197
Parker, Bill, 211
Parker, Elsie, 215
Parker, Paul, 209, 218–224, *219*, *221*, *223*
Parks, Gordon, 166–168, *167*
passing as white: D. W. Griffith on, 41–42; by George Herriman, 41–44, 51–59, *52*; Oscar Micheaux on, 41–42; Rebecca Wanzo on, 43–44, 54. *See also* African Americans

Patty-Jo 'n' Ginger. See Ormes, Jackie
Pederson, Kaitlin, 98, 107
Peele, Jordan, 90
Peralte, Charlemagne, 250
Pfeufer, Carl, 238, 244n39, 285
Phantom Lady, 95–117, 167
pickaninny caricatures, 25, 192, 194
Pious, Robert Savion, 80, 85, 90–92, *93*
Piper, Adrian, 56–57
Pittsburgh Courier, 141–157, 183–185, 187, 236–238, 284
Pizzino, Christopher, 13
Plastic Man (character), 167–168
Plessy v. Ferguson (1896), 24, 42, 60n10. *See also* Jim Crow laws
Police Comics, 167, 168, 178n11
politics of respectability. *See* respectability politics
Porter, Kenneth W., 307
"post-Black" art, 81
Postema, Barbara, 188–189
Post-Impressionism, 82
Prince Valiant comics, 128
print cultures: African American, 165, 274–275; women's, 141–157
propaganda, 15, 79–81
Pruitt, Dwain C., 117n16
Puck, 2. *See also* O'Neill, Rose
Pulitzer, Joseph, 42
pulp fiction, 255–256

Quality Comics, 167
Quattro, Ken, 5, 7, 117n16, 204n29

Raboy, Mac, 212
race riots, 53, 87–88
racial caricature, 46, 263; Asian, 89, 129; Black masculinity and, 248; Ebony White as, 61–74, *67*, *69*, 283; Will Eisner on, 61–74; Charles Johnson on, 74, 214, 216; in jungle comics, 252; of pickaninnies, 25, 192, 194; as propaganda, 79–81; Steamboat as, 164, 190, 209, 213–214; Stepin Fetchit as, 68–69, 71–72; Uncle Tom as, 28–29, 34, 54, 68, 69; Rebecca Wanzo on, 3, 63, 194, 215–216, 282; in Western comics, 308–309
"Racial Contract," 96
racialized time, 199, 200

Rankine, Claudia, 283
Raymond, Alex, 231
reading path conventions. *See* viewing paths
Reed, Rod, 214
respectability politics, 164, 280n4; art movements and, 94n7, 142; colorism and, 15; gendered notions of, 142, 149, 151–152, 154, 157n3
reversed paths, 105–107, *106*, *107*. *See also* viewing paths
Rice, T. D., 46
Rifas, Leonard, 5
Rivera, Diego, 83
Rizzuto, Phil, 208
Robbins, Trina, 212
Robinson, Chris, 205n54
Robinson, Jackie, 13, 197, 208, 217, 276–277; Charles Dexter on, 209; Clem Weisbecker on, 218
Robinson, Solomon, 201
Roche, Ruth, 116
Rockefeller, Nelson, 151
Rodin, Auguste, 132–133
Rogers, Buck (character) 289
Rogers, Leslie, 185
romance comics, 135, 240–241; of Alvin Hollingsworth, 122, 125; Jacque Nodell on, 261–279
Roosevelt, Eleanor, 183
Royster, Jacqueline, 142

saccades, 99; parallel, 100, *102*, *103*, 104, 106, 110. *See also* viewing paths
Sadowski, Greg, 106–107
Saguisag, Lara, 25n11, 192
Sale, Tim, 126
Salter, Patricia, 5
Sam, Jean Vilbrun Guillaume, 250
Sammond, Nicholas, 37n20, 39–59
Sandberg, David F., 211
Schalk, Gertrude. *See* Johnson, Gertrude "Toki" Schalk
Schaupp, Robert, 314–315, *315*
Schelly, Bill, 124
Schuyler, George S., 183–185, 237; on *All-Negro Comics*, 198; on caricature, 190
Seabrook, William Beuhler, 250–251
segment leaps, 100, 104–105, *105*. *See also* viewing paths

segregation, 170; Gertrude "Toki" Schalk Johnson on, 151–152; Jackie Ormes on, 154, 239; Robert Pious on, 92, *93*. *See also* Jim Crow laws
sexual assault, 146–149, *148*, 164
shadow books, 200–201
Shakespeare, William, 252
shape-shifting, 249–250
Shearer, Ted, 237
"shudder pulps," 251
Shuster, Joe, 110, 211
Siegel, Jerry, 211
Silber, Nina, 300
Silver Age of comics, 4–5, 218, 299, 314
Simmons, LaKisha Michelle, 178n13
Simon, Joe, 241, 277
Singer, Marc, 301–302
slave revolts, 249
slavery, 199
Smith, Ben B., 284–285
Smith, William H., 182–183, 195
Smith, Zoë, 274, 307
Smith-Mann Syndicate, 154, 228, 284
social justice comics ("preachies"), 14–15
social realist art: socialist realism versus, 83–84; Richard Wright on, 94n7
Solomon, Adina, 23
Solórzano, Daniel, 165
Soul Love comics, 262
Spectre, Allen, 257–258, 258n1, 259n26
Spiral art collective, 121, 135, 227
Spirit comics, 61–74, *67*, *69*, 283
sports comics, 13, 197, 208–209, 217–224
Stanton, Lajoyeaux H., 3
Star Trek (TV show), 289
Steamboat (character). *See* Captain Marvel
Stephenson, Gladys, 87–88
Stephenson, James, 87–88
Stepin Fetchit (character), 68–69, 71–72
Steve Canyon comics, 231, 241
Stevenson, Robert Louis, 212
Stoner, Elmer C., 3, 7; *All-Negro Comics* and, 185; Alvin Hollingsworth and, 124
Stripper's Guide blog, 5, 18n12
Strömberg, Fredrik, 4, 64, 74
Superman comics, 110, 282; creators of, 211, 228; family of, 225n7
supervillains, 248, 251, 255
Svengali (character), 256

Swayze, Marc, 212
Swift, Jonathan, 212

Tallarico, Tony, 275, 298–313
Tambo and Bones (minstrel characters), 27, 45–47, 54
tap dance, 46
Target Comics, 176
Tarzan comics, 128, 251
Taylor, Emily, 251
Taylor, Quintard, 307, 308
Terrell, John H., 182–183, 186, 194
Terry and the Pirates, 128, 129, 237, 241
Thompson, Lisa B., 151
Tibbs, Howard A., 156–157
Till, Emmett, 15, 115–116, 143; press coverage of, 157n10, 172–173, *173*; Qiana Whitted on, 176
Tilley, Carol L., 13, 163–177, 281–282
Timely Comics (Marvel), 190, 244n39, 299
Tisserand, Michael, 42, 43, 57, 59
Titus Andronicus (Shakespeare), 252
Tom and Jerry, 55
Tompkins, Jane, 307
Towles, Delores, 239
Trachtenberg, Alan, 165–166
True Comics, 197
True Confessions, 211
True Romances, 168, 178n13
Tulsa riot (Oklahoma, 1921), 53

Uncle Tom caricature, 28–29, 34, 54, 68, 69

Vadeboncoeur, Jim, Jr., 110–111
Vann, Robert L., 157n3
vaudeville, 64; blackface minstrelsy and, 43, 46–47, 55–59, *58*; *Ziegfeld Follies* and, *58*
viewing paths, 97–117; combined misdirectional, *109*, 109–113, *112*, *113*; misdirecting appendages, 100, 107–109, *108*; misdirectional, 98–100, 113–117; mixed, 100–102, *101*, *103*; parallel saccades, 100, *102*, *103*, 104, 106, 110; reversed, 105–107, *106*, *107*; segment leap, 100, 104–105, *105*
visual tropes of blackness, 4–6, 14, 23–36, 61–74
Vodou religion, 249–258
Voodoo Man comics, 247–258, *253*, *254*, *257*
voting rights, 23, 36

Walker, Aida Overton, 46, 59
Walker, Alice, 155
Walker, George, 46, 59
Wamba, Philippe, 200
Wanzo, Rebecca, 26; on Black Art genealogies, 79–93; on Black children, 192, 194; on George Herriman, 40, 43–44, 57; on Krazy Kat's speech, 48–49; on racial caricatures, 3, 63, 194, 215–216, 282; on racialized time, 199; on "real Americanness," 171
war comics, 5, 18n12, 110
Warren Publishing, 62, 70
Waugh, Coulton, 163–164
Weisbecker, Clem, 218
Wellman, Manly Wade, 66
Wertham, Fredric, 9–13, 177, 179nn38–39; Matt Baker and, 95, 114; *Seduction of the Innocent*, 172–174, 241
Western comics, 233, 277, 284; Alvin Hollingsworth and, 125; Mike Lemon and, 205n38, 297–315; Carl Pfeufer and, 238, 244n39
Whaley, Deborah, 144, 158n20
Wheatley, Phillis, 200
White, Ebony (character), 61–74, 67, 69, 283
White, Charles, 40, 80, 85–88, 87, 92
White, Vivian, 171
White, Walter, 53, 235
white middle class, 11, 70, 171–172. *See also* Black middle class
white supremacy, 2, 53, 172; artists' depictions of, 90; James Baldwin on, 39; Romare Bearden on, 84–85; blackface minstrelsy and, 47–48, 58–59; Charles W. Mills on, 96
White Zombie (film), 251
Whitted, Qiana, 1–17, 90–91, 181–203, 216, 283; on Atomic Age of comics, 209; on cowboy comics, 298, 300; on graphic narrative, 289–290; on Emmett Till, 176

Whyte, Garrett, 7–8, *8*
Williams, Bert, 43, 46, *58*, 58–59
Williams, Gweneira, 168
Williams, Kent, 138
Wilson, Jane, 168
Winfield, Paul, 210
Wings Comics, 127–128, 130
Winkler, Margaret, 44, 55
Wister, Owen, 306
"Witch Doctor's Revenge" comics, 247–248
Witek, Joseph, 98–99, 106, 108, 110, 113–114
Woggon, Bill, 244n44
women's rights, 23, 33–34, 36, 137
Wood, Joe, 200
Woodruff, Hale, 84, 227
Woolfolk, William, 66
Works Progress Administration (WPA), 85
Wright, Bradford, 288
Wright, Richard, 9; Ollie Harrington and, 144; Zora Neale Hurston and, 81, 94n7

Yellow Kid (character), 36
Yoe, Craig, 125
Yosso, Tara, 165
Young, Harvey, 56
Young, Kevin, 200
Young Allies, 190
Young Dr. Kildare, 71
Young Romance, 241
Youthbuilders (student group), 14, 65; Brian Cremins on, 75n16; Will Eisner and, 179n27, 214; Will Lieberson and, 209, 213–216
yronwode, cat, 66

Ziegfeld Follies, *58*
zombies, 249–251, 253–256
zoot suits, 181, 189, 190, 204n22